PENGUIN BOOKS

THEM

Francine du Plessix Gray is a regular contributor to *The New Yorker,* and the author of numerous books of fiction and nonfiction including *Simone Weil; At Home with the Marquis de Sade: A Life; Rage and Fire; Lovers and Tyrants;* and *Soviet Women.* She lives in Connecticut.

Praise for *Them: A Memoir of Parents*

"In an arresting new memoir ... (Gray) paints a vivid, often harrowing portrait of her formidable mother and her equally formidable stepfather.... What is so astonishing is ... her ability to wield the cool detachment of a biographer while simultaneously drawing on a daughter's heated reservoirs of memory and emotion.... In these pages she uses all her writerly gifts—her skills of observation, emotional recall, and, yes, detachment—to give the reader an intense and remarkably powerful portrait."

—Michiko Kakutani, *The New York Times*

"A spellbinding, warts-and-all double portrait ... a dazzling account ... With a masterful balance of 'ruthlessness and tenderness,' research and reminiscence, grievance and gratitude, (Gray's) book is a sterling example of the personal memoir exalted to cultural history."
—*Los Angeles Times*

"Francine du Plessix Gray examines in loving but unsentimental detail the lives of her mother ... and stepfather.... Tatiana and Alexander are fascinating characters, but so what? Gray's unapologetically subjective candor and lithe prose are what make their story so lively and so devastating. *Them* is one of the finest memoirs in recent years."
—*Newsday*

"It's a cursed blessing, and a blessed curse, to have strong parents; so novelist and biographer Francine du Plessix Gray makes it appear in *Them*, her beautifully written, often painfully and bravely honest memoir.... She bestows ... the light and warmth of her patient, unflagging attention and the grace and penetration of her words."
—*San Francisco Chronicle*

"Gray's way with words, her insight into the human condition and her almost eerie sense of objectivity about her upbringing have converged to create an enthralling story of the primal bond between a child and her parents. And what parents—the Libermans are two of the most fascinating characters you'll ever encounter in the pages of a memoir, or for that matter, any book."
—*The Seattle Times*

"[An] expansive, compelling book ... This formidable memoir ... is an elegant act of literary commemoration and conciliation.... Here is a daughter's unflinching account of her parents' and her own survival."   —*Chicago Tribune*

"*Them* is blessed with the memoir's equivalent of good bones: epic scope and historic scale.... But the tale is in the telling, and Gray's acumen, honesty, and elegant prose ... are equal to the task of portraying her exceptionally complicated parents, while her exhaustive research and uncluttered perspective allow her to illuminate their relationship to their times in a way most memoirists cannot.... An excellent book."
—*The Boston Globe*

"An exquisite memoir . . . Gray has written that rare memoir never sunk by indulgence. . . . We, as readers, are indeed lucky to devour such a gift."
—*The Philadelphia Inquirer*

"*Them* is the book that Francine du Plessix Gray was born to write. . . . This brilliant and moving memoir [is written with] honesty and rigor . . . a compelling and fascinating book."
—*The New York Sun*

"*Them* is like *Star* magazine for the literary set. Jam-packed with juicy gossip . . . it is guilty pleasure without the guilt . . . probing, sometimes heartbreaking."
—*The Houston Chronicle*

"[A] complex and rewarding family memoir . . . more addictive than any *Vanity Fair* exclusive. Gray is such a fine writer, her family story reads like a novel."
—*Publishers Weekly* (starred review)

"A genre-bending book, part memoir, part biography, part elegy and part lyrical magic . . . Within its sweeping scope are cameos so unforgettable, language so transcendent, that the book achieves the rare feat of offering something for everyone."
—*Milwaukee Journal Sentinel*

"Distinguished journalist, novelist and biographer du Plessix Gray turns her descriptive and analytic powers to the legendary lives of her glamorous, Russian-born mother and stepfather. . . . Famous names and juicy stories, served up with literary elegance."
—*Kirkus Reviews* (starred review)

"Du Plessix Gray [is] a writer of scintillating style and resonant substance . . . An enthralling storyteller and incisive interpreter of the human psyche . . . du Plessix Gray's penetrating and unforgettable memoir of a peerless family reads like a great epic novel."
—*Booklist* (starred review)

"[A] fascinating book."
—*Washington Monthly*

"The story that Francine du Plessix tells in this . . . family history cum biography cum memoir is exceedingly interesting, indeed at times startlingly so."
—*The Washington Post*

"A rich pastry of a book, stuffed with information on the immigrant experience, parent-child relations, social climbing, the fashion, retailing, and publishing industries, and the art world."
—*The Cleveland Plain Dealer*

Them

A Memoir of Parents

Francine du Plessix Gray

PENGUIN BOOKS

PENGUIN BOOKS

Published by the Penguin Group

Penguin Group (USA) Inc., 375 Hudson Street, New York, New York 10014, U.S.A.
Penguin Group (Canada), 90 Eglinton Avenue East, Suite 700, Toronto,
Ontario, Canada M4P 2Y3 (a division of Pearson Penguin Canada Inc.)
Penguin Books Ltd, 80 Strand, London WC2R 0RL, England
Penguin Ireland, 25 St Stephen's Green, Dublin 2, Ireland (a division of Penguin Books Ltd)
Penguin Group (Australia), 250 Camberwell Road, Camberwell,
Victoria 3124, Australia (a division of Pearson Australia Group Pty Ltd)
Penguin Books India Pvt Ltd, 11 Community Centre, Panchsheel Park, New Delhi – 110 017, India
Penguin Group (NZ), cnr Airborne and Rosedale Roads, Albany,
Auckland 1310, New Zealand (a division of Pearson New Zealand Ltd)
Penguin Books (South Africa) (Pty) Ltd, 24 Sturdee Avenue, Rosebank, Johannesburg 2196, South Africa

Penguin Books Ltd, Registered Offices:
80 Strand, London WC2R 0RL, England

First published in the United States of America by The Penguin Press,
a member of Penguin Group (USA) Inc. 2005
Published in Penguin Books 2006

1 3 5 7 9 10 8 6 4 2

Copyright © Francine du Plessix Gray, 2005
All rights reserved

Portions of this book first appeared in different form in *The American Scholar* and *The New Yorker*.
Page 530 constitutes an extension of this copyright page.

THE LIBRARY OF CONGRESS HAS CATALOGED THE HARDCOVER EDITION AS FOLLOWS:
Gray, Francine du Plessix.
Them : a memoir of parents / Francine du Plessix Gray.
p.   cm.
Includes bibliographical references and index.
ISBN 1-59420-049-1 (hc.)
ISBN 0 14 30.3719 6 (pbk.)
1. Iakovleva, Tatiana, 1906–1991.   2. Liberman, Alexander, 1912–1999.
3. Immigrants—New York (State)—New York—Biography.   4. Russians—New York (State)—
New York—Biography.   5. Women fashion designers—New York—Biography.
7. Publishers and publishing—New York (State)—New York—Biography.   8. Sculptors—New York
(State)—New York—Biography.   9. New York (N.Y.)—Biography.   I. Title.
CT275.II5G73 2005
974.7'1004917I'00922—dc22
[B]
2004065944

Printed in the United States of America
Set in Centaur MT
Designed by Claire Naylon Vaccaro

To Them

With love and longing

Contents

PART TWO: THE NEW WORLD

List of Illustrations

Introduction

I have an extremely fertile dream life, and a decade ago, upon the fourth anniversary of my mother's death, I had a powerful dream about her. It went this way:

I am living quietly alone, in a simple country house that is set on a hill overlooking a valley, with a view of another hill of equal height to mine. Suddenly, a message arrives from Mother saying that she wishes me to come immediately to live with her on the opposite hill, which is called "Atlanta." (Oh, clever subconscious! Change the "l" in Atlanta to an "i" and you get the anagram of my mother's name, Tatiana.) Mother's message annoys and riles me, I adamantly resist her command, I send her back the following message: "I'm very happy on my hill, I do not wish to go live with you on your hill, I shall stay where I am!"

Whereupon Mother appears at the threshold of my house, joining me on my own hill. She is the radical opposite of the tall, imperious, flashy mother I knew in real life. She is a very tiny, meek, sweetly smiling old lady dressed in black, wearing a timid little black hat with a dotted veil. And as the dream ends, Mother turns into the happiest old lady I've ever seen, she just stands there by the door of my house, declining to enter but smiling merrily at me and waving and blowing me kisses, and I smile and wave and blow kisses back, and there is an aura of serenity, of mutual approval, of tender understanding between us far greater than any we ever shared in real life.

Upon waking from that dream in 1995, I knew exactly what it was telling me: it was time to have a conversation with my mother, the kind of dialogue that many of us can share with our parents only through the act of writing, the kind of conversation I could never have had with her when she was alive. For my flamboyant Russian-born mother—who was one of the foremost fashion icons of her generation, whose life had to do with the art of putting on a spectacular show and of casting her spell on as many people as possible—was particularly averse to conversation. Tatiana Yakovleva du Plessix Liberman announced rather than discussed, proclaimed rather than communicated, dictated rather than conversed. Moreover, the violent historical upheavals she had survived—the Russian Revolution, World War II—had left psychic wounds that she would never expose to anyone, and that she attempted to cloak in silence. And as I wrote my first nonfiction portrait of her—"Growing Up Fashionable," which was published in *The New Yorker* and is now diffused throughout several passages of this book—I realized why so many writers have turned to the family memoir and seen it as an essential part of their oeuvre: whether we are Colette, Vladimir Nabokov, Maya Angelou, or Harold Nicolson, the process of piercing our parents' silence, of unraveling the webs of deceits that they spun about their true selves, and often ours, is not only a way of bringing our beloved dead back to life: it can also offer us a greater measure of retrospective clarity, of self-knowledge, than any other literary form.

It was obvious to me that those forty pages about Mother as Fashion Icon were the germ of a book I must eventually write. But I knew that I could not narrate her story without also narrating that of my stepfather, her lifelong companion, the legendary publishing wizard Alexander Liberman, who was to outlive her by seven years. To write truthfully about anyone who is still alive is a Utopian task, suspect at best. So I bided my time, looking on a projected family memoir as one of several distant ventures, writing two more biographies of persons as eccentric, in their own ways, as my parents: the marquis de Sade and Simone Weil. And not until 2001, a year after my cherished stepfather's own passing, did I reach a stage in the process of mourning that allowed me to write this book.

While remaining deeply private, these two complex parents of mine, Tatiana and Alex Liberman, were publicity hounds who enjoyed being constantly on show, who splashed their glamorous lives, their nimble wisecracks, their ultrastylish interiors onto the pages of our country's poshest magazines. And in view of the innumerable mementos they hoarded, I suspect that both of them always wished for a biographer. Beyond marriage and death certificates and the many thousands of photographs they squirreled away, my archives are now enriched by documents as diverse as my stepfather's certificate of circumcision, signed in 1912 by the chief rabbi of Kiev; the letters he had written to his parents as a nine-year-old in a British public school; his report cards from his French boarding school; correspondence between his parents that dates back to the 1920s; love letters he had exchanged with my mother in the 1930s; the Nansen passport on which he traveled to America in 1941; his certificate of naturalization as an American citizen; orders he had placed, during his days as a chief executive of the Condé Nast Publications, for my mother's wristwatch bands—a gilt leather model that remained unchanged over the decades and that he ordered by the dozen. Among my mother's papers I found the various passports she held from the 1920s on—Russian, then French, then American; certificates for sick leave, of 1890s vintage, issued to her maternal grandfather, principal director of the Marinsky Imperial Ballet in her native St. Petersburg; a trove of documents concerning her uncle, the distinguished artist and explorer Alexandre Iacovleff, whom I chronicle in the second chapter of this work; love letters from the great Russian poet Vladimir Mayakovsky—he looked on her as one of his two principal muses—which are now integrated into my third and fourth chapters; most every missive I had ever written her from camp, college, or abroad; the *Ausweis* (travel permit) that permitted us to leave Occupied France in the latter half of 1940. In sum, my parents seemed to have deliberately prepared many sets, props, objective data a biographer would need to limn a lavish portrait.

I stress the word "objective." For while living exceedingly public lives, these two émigrés who were one of New York's first "power couples" both remained deeply guarded about their inner emotions; their last decades in particular were laced with a staggering number of deceits and subterfuges. And they had vastly different views of the kinds of biographies they each desired. My stepfather—a man obsessed with controlling all within his reach—wanted it written during his lifetime, by someone other than me. My mother, on the other hand, preferred that it be done after her death, by no one other than her daughter. And if I was able to fulfill her wish and also to discern some truth through the facade of ruses elaborated in late life by both my parents, it was due to my practice of keeping a journal, a habit I have had for over half a century. Because of the illnesses and addictions that growingly plagued them, in the last decades of my mother's and stepfather's lives I felt particularly impelled to record every nuance of their words and their deportment, and this documentation served to flesh out the narrative of those increasingly bizarre years.

But I am the child of three remarkable parents. My earlier writings have several times dealt with my biological father, the heroic Bertrand du Plessix, whose death with the Free French in World War II was the central tragedy of my youth; yet I've often sensed that no portrait of him would be complete until I set him into the context of those two other parents, Tatiana and Alex, in whose lives his destiny played a pivotal role. Not until I finished this book did I ruefully sense that I had finally laid him to rest.

As for my mother, who is this project's original muse, shortly after I'd handed this book to my publishers I had another dream about her, which went this way: I am standing in front of my home, a brand-new house of dark gray stone, when Mother appears again, once more very meek and in every way different from the woman I knew: middle-aged and stockily built, with black hair and a wide, smiling, rather Oriental face. As she comes to my door, she kneels graciously before it, telling me how happy she is to make this visit, what an honor it is to be invited to my home. I in turn kneel before her, telling her how grateful and moved I am to receive her. Once more, there flows between us that great accord and serenity I'd experienced in her earlier appearance a decade ago. The "house" in this most recent

dream, so my instincts tell me, is the edifice of words I have built to commemorate her and the remarkable man who shared her life—a text in
which, like any proper biographer, I strove for a compassionate severity, for
that balance of ruthlessness and tenderness that were at the heart of my
mother's own character and that she might have been the first to respect.

A Note on Transliteration

Transliteration from the Cyrillic alphabet permits a variety of spellings. And the problem is compounded, in my mother's family, by the fact that most every one of its members used a different form of transliteration when the Revolution of 1917 forced them to flee Russia. My great-uncle Alexandre chose to transliterate his name as "Iacovleff"; but both my mother and his sister, Great Aunt Sandra, spelled their names on their French passports and other identity papers as "Yacovlef." To make the issue even more perplexing, the vast body of critical and biographical literature published in the Soviet Union on the issue of my mother's romance with the poet Vladimir Mayakovsky has consistently referred to her as "Tatiana *Yakovleva.*" That is the form of transliteration I have followed, if only because that is the one under which she entered Russian literary history.

It is perhaps fitting that these translations from the Cyrillic have been so anarchically varied. This is a saga about different forms of exile, and the diverse phoneticizations of my Russian family's name strike me as being emblematic of the forging of self-identity undertaken, throughout history, by all émigrés.

Tatiana in her heyday in the mid-1950s, promoting her hats in Chicago. At her side, a Saks Fifth Avenue executive.

PART ONE

The Old World

"We must feel everything, everything we can.
We are here for that."
—HENRY JAMES, *The Tragic Muse*

ONE

Tatiana

My mother enjoyed claiming direct descent from Genghis Khan. Having asserted that one eighth of her blood was Tartar and only seven eighths of it "ordinary Russian," with a panache that no one else could have pulled off she proceeded to drop a few names in the chronology of our lineage: Kublai Khan, Tamerlane, and then the great Mogul monarch Babur, from whose favorite Kirghiz concubine my great-grandmother was descended, and *voilà!*, our ancestry was established.

You couldn't have argued the point with her, for in her quest for dramatic effect Tatiana du Plessix Liberman would have set all of human history on its head. Besides, you mightn't have dared to risk a showdown: in her prime, she was five feet nine and a half inches tall and 140 pounds in weight, and the majesty of her presence, the very nearsighted, chestnut-hued, indeed Asiatic eyes that fixed you with a brutally critical gaze through blue-tinted bifocals, had the psychic impact of a can of Mace. And you may not even have wanted to call my mother's bluff, for a kinship to the great Khan was so symbolically fitting: perennially adorned with large, blazing costume jewelry that recalled instruments of torture or insignias of archaic cults, she strode into a room, shawls spectacularly draped about her shoulders, like a tribal war goddess and moved through life with a speed and fierceness that recalled the howling wind of the steppes. Tatiana was one of the most dazzling self-inventions of her time, a force of nature all right, and those of us who loved her may well remain under her spell until the day we die.

By profession, my mother was a designer of hats—her working name was "Tatiana of Saks"—and according to many authorities she was the finest hat designer of the midcentury. For twenty-three years, she had her own custom-design salon at Saks Fifth Avenue, where over the decades she advised thousands of women how to lure their men, keep their husbands, and enchant their luncheon companions through the proper tilt of a beret or the sly positioning of a black dotted veil. She was hailed by *The New York Times* as "the milliner's milliner," lauded for typifying "the feminine elegance that makes her exclusive creations the crowning glories for discriminating women." She was perhaps best known for her ethereal spring hats—casques of pastel-shaded veiling, leafy pillows of tulle speckled with violets, turbans of frothy gauze swirled beehive-style in shades of lilac, dynamite pinks, and grassy greens, bretons of rose-printed silk surah displaying bundles of silk roses underneath their rolled brims. She never did any preliminary sketching or drawing of her hats but created them by sitting in front of a large mirror, sculpting and draping felt, velours, organza, or satin onto her head, using her own reflected image, eight hours a day, two hundred and fifty days a year. Mirrors were the central metaphor of her life, and I can think of few women whose innate narcissism has been more perfectly fulfilled.

Beyond being a renowned milliner, Tatiana was also one of a small handful of professional women who were looked on as New York City's most commanding fashion presences—others were editor Diana Vreeland, designer Valentina, and Hattie Carnegie's chief stylist, Pauline Potter, later Pauline de Rothschild. Yet Tatiana was by far the least orthodox trendsetter of those three, and no canon of fashion did she transgress more violently than Diana Vreeland's decree "Elegance is Refusal." One might say that Tatiana perfected the art of too-muchness: the great hunks of fake jewelry she flung on herself included eight-inch-wide imitations of pre-Columbian breastplates, four-inch stretches of rhinestone bracelets, candelabras of paste earrings, and—her most famous logo—a massive dome ring of quasi-rubies resembling the top of a bishop's crozier.

If the *tape l'oeil* of Tatiana's style still managed to be renowned as one of New York's most "elegant," it is because elegance is above all a matter of consistency; and her gestures, her speech, her entire manner and presence were absolutely in line with the maximalism of her getup. She was brazen, brusque, intolerant, blatantly elitist, atrociously impatient, prodigally generous, and as categorical in her tastes as a Soviet commissar. She did not converse but proclaimed, and many of her decrees had to do with debunking and deriding conventional symbols of affluence: "Meeeenk is for football," she said. "Diamonds are for suburbs." No arbiter of taste I know of has so militantly proclaimed the gaucheness of displayed wealth, the supremacy of comfort and clean line. She took such pride in the thirty-five-dollar set of Macy's garden furniture with which she equipped our first tiny rooms on Central Park South that it accompanied her wherever she lived for almost fifty years. Upon her death, I had to evaluate the very modest personal holdings she left me, and I discovered that the famous ring of "rubies" with which she had stunned New York for a half century was made exclusively of mediocre garnets and was estimated to be worth some twelve hundred dollars.

The world had to come to Tatiana; she made very few steps toward it, particularly toward the United States. Despite her immense literary culture, in half a century she never bothered to learn more than fragmented English, and at the time of her death in 1991, she was still getting her world news from French periodicals and New York's Russian-language newspaper, *Novoye Russkoye Slovo*. She detested traveling in any part of the Americas and had a 1920-vintage cartoon-strip view of our Midwest: "Butcher!" she shouted at a dentist she disliked after an emergency tooth extraction, "Go back to Cheeecago!" The faux pas she made in the English language were epic: she once went to FAO Schwarz, flanked by my eight- and ten-year-old sons, and announced to the salesman, "I want to buy kike." "*Kite,* Grandma, *kite,*" the children pleaded.

"I want *kike!*" she insisted. Her declarations about whatever she currently thought was The Best—be it in couture, resorts, food, medical doctors, literature—were as flamboyant as her savage jewelry. She had a Nietzschean faith in success ("One does not argue with winners") and fervently believed in snobbism ("Snobs are always right"). Hers was an old-fashioned brand of elitism, in part corny and in part humanistic, indifferent to money and dually geared, like that of many Russians, to pedigree and to public achievement.

An element of Mother's dictatorial largesse was that she wanted to share (some would say impose) every one of her enthusiasms on her friends and loved ones. Her need to control and direct the lives of others extended to the most menial details. Arriving at a beach on the first day of vacation—she was a sun worshipper and a crack swimmer, beaches were her paradise—she would walk very fast ahead of us, her slender arms clanging with tribal gold, and patrol it at length: she critically examined the quality of the sand, the clarity of the water, the status of the population. And then, having found what she judged to be the finest spot on that stretch of seashore, she would holler to her group: *"Venez ici tout de suite, c'est le seul endroit!"* "Come here at once! This is *the* only spot!" And we would all troop along. For we knew that on issues of bodily comfort and of most anything that had to do with the wisdom of life's pleasures she was usually right, and we feared that if we did not follow her orders the arrival of a busload of noisy Swedish nudists would subject us to her derisive "I told you so." It is through this dictatorial spirit that Tatiana characterized not only the art of *savoir vivre* but also the essence of the fashionable mind, which inevitably issues its decrees in the imperative tense—"A *must* for the fall," "The *best* look of the season"—and has to do with spreading, as swiftly as possible, the infection of style.

Yet beneath Tatiana's despotic manner, beneath her exhibitionism and flamboyance, there hid a shy, deeply private, very self-demeaning child-woman whose complexities were forged in the terror of the Russian Revolution.

Tatiana's maternal grandfather, Nikolai Sergeevich Aistov, a dancer and director of the Marinsky Imperial Ballet, late 1870s.

. . .

I have photographs that show my mother in 1912 Russia, age six, an assertive tot with long blond curls dressed in a lavish Paquin frock and seated, Récamier-like, on an ornate velvet couch, already a commanding, shrewdly controlling presence, already fully aware of the effect she is having on her little public. ("Now you know why there was revolution," she often quipped about the photo, pointing at the elaborate Parisian dress.) Born in St. Petersburg, Tatiana Yakovleva came from a family of intelligentsia—architects, lawyers, government officials, and also a great many performing artists—who were suffused with that craving for French culture and luxuries, and also with an adulation of pedigree, from which few upper-class Russians were exempt. She always claimed, for instance, that her maternal grandfather, Nikolai Sergeevich Aistov, one of our most colorful forebears, was "a prominent government official of noble descent." The truth is far more interesting than her elitism would allow. Nikolai Sergeevich, whose father made his living as a singer, was in fact a distinguished dancer and a very successful ballet entrepreneur; one of our best-documented progenitors, he characterizes many of our family traits, most particularly in his affinity for striking poses.

Nikolai Sergeevich Aistov, born in 1853, graduated from the St. Petersburg Theatrical School, where he earned grades of "excellent" for behavior; "good" for math, religion, fencing, history, acting, and singing; and merely "satisfactory" for ballet and ballroom dancing. This did not hinder him, however, from being accepted as a member of the Marinsky Imperial Ballet, where he remained a member of the corps de ballet for over a decade, being ultimately promoted, at the age of forty-two, to the coveted rank of premier danseur. I have a cherished photograph of him, a tall, stately man with features of classical beauty, in full stage regalia. He is, I believe, in the role of the pharaoh in *Pharaoh's Daughter*, one of those early extravaganzas of Marius Petipa, set at the Pyramids, which featured exotic Egyptian dancers, scheming British archaeologists, drug-induced dream states, and awakening mummies.

Perhaps because of his height, Nikolai Sergeevich seemed to have limited potential as an exclusively classical dancer and was better known as a mime-actor and a general ballet *régisseur* than as an agile executor of entrechats and *tours fouéttés*. Apart from the title role in *Pharaoh's Daughter* and *Claude Frollo*, his principal stage personae were those of the Grand Duke in *Giselle* and other characterizations in which he had little to do but swagger imperiously about the stage in ornate regalia, striking a variety of commandeering poses and miming orders to his assembled peons ("Unleash the slaves!" or "Let our warring parties come to peace!"). In sum, Nikolai Sergeevich strikes me as a performer who mostly got by in his chosen vocation—as did a few other members of my family—through his charm and staggering good looks, his imposing presence, and his shrewd capacity for just plain hustling. He may well have been a protégé of Marius Petipa, the French choreographer who for decades was the chief ballet master of the Marinsky, where Nikolai Sergeevich served for a few years as principal director. For they retired from the Marinsky in the same year, 1903, when a new administration took over.

It was on her father's side of the family that Tatiana claimed descendance from Genghis Khan, and this contention, too, might have been based on a minuscule ground of fact. Her paternal grandmother, Sofia Petrovna Iacovleff, née Kuzmin, the cherished babushka who was the great love of my first eight years, was born in the province of Samara, just northeast of the Caspian Sea and due west of Kazakhstan. Having belonged until the sixteenth century to the Genghisid Dynasty, it is an area which still bears such strongly Oriental, un-Russian names as Sagiz, Makat, Chelkar—names that display a powerful influence of the Tartar culture. "Very noble family," "direct descendants of Genghis Khan": That was my mother all over—to desire both the aristocratic pedigree and the freedom to be a barbarian. So, yes, there is a chance in a million that we were descended from the Khan, and my great-grandmother's brother, Piotr Kuzmin, did serve for a few brief years as Marshall of the Nobility in the nearby province of Riazan.

My great-grandmother—Babushka—who seems to have been a powerhouse of a girl, showed great promise in her studies and was given far more latitude in her choice of vocation than most nineteenth-century young women in the eastern Russian provinces. Having displayed a partic-

St. Petersburg, early 1890s, the Iacovleff children with their parents.
Right to left: Alexis, Tatiana's father; Alexandre, the future painter;
Alexandra (Sandra); Vera.

ular aptitude in mathematics, she attended university at St. Petersburg. Family legend has it that she was the first woman in Russia ever to receive a Ph.D. in math and that as she came down from the podium at her graduation ceremony, degree in hand, angry male academics protesting her intrusion into their ranks pelted her with tomatoes. Reserving her mathematical talent for domestic purposes, Sofia Petrovna soon married an architect and engineer named Evgeny Alexeevitch Iacovleff and bore him the following children:

My grandfather, Alexis, who followed in his father's footsteps, also becoming an architect-engineer, and a prizewinning designer of state theaters;

My great-aunt Alexandra (Aunt Sandra), a gifted contralto who made her operatic debut in 1916 singing the role of the Countess in Tchaikovsky's *Queen of Spades* and whose nurturing affection, like Babushka's, was one of the treasures of my early childhood;

My great-uncle Alexandre (Uncle Sasha), a legendary explorer who after the revolution became one of the two or three most eminent artists to emerge in Paris's Russian émigré community and who played a central role in my mother's life;

My great-aunt Vera, the second born, was the only one of the siblings who never accomplished anything of note, having married, at the age of twenty-two, a German fertilizer tycoon whom she had met while vacationing with her parents in the French Alps in 1906.

The four Iacovleff children were all born and brought up in their parents' spacious apartment on Gagarinskaya Embankment, off Nevsky Prospect. And it is precisely there, in her beloved grandmother's living room, that my mother's earliest memory is set. She is about five, and she is—guess what—posing for her portrait. Uncle Sasha is the artist, and she is wearing a flouncy white lace dress of Paquin design. He is telling her to sit still, and she remembers hearing those words while seeing the Neva glimmering through her grandmother's windows.

In her next recollected memory, Mother and her younger sister, Ludmila or "Lila," are in Vologda, 170 kilometers or so east of St. Petersburg, where their father has been sent to supervise the construction of a government theater. She remembers a particular place in her parents' majestic house, a long hall with waxed floors on which she liked to fall down and slide. She also recalls streets covered with snowdrifts, pigeons on the snow, the family driving in their own carriage, the freezing temperatures, the winter coat with matching chinchilla-trimmed muff she was bundled into when taken outside—all the Iacovleff girls' clothes, like their mother's, were sent for from Paris. Tatiana described her mother, Lyubov Nikolaevna, as coquettish, elegant, prodigiously talented in languages and music and particularly in dancing, a gift she'd inherited from her father, Nikolai Sergeevich Aistov. She also recalled her mother, more warily, as being very flirtatious and charming with her admirers but aloof with her own family, and this maternal coolness may well have affected, eventually, Tatiana's relations with me.

Tatiana, center, with her sister, Ludmila, and her father, Alexis Iacovleff, in 1915. Penza, Russia.

Then in 1913, when Mother was seven years old, her father won an architectural competition, and the family—attended, as ever, by a German governess, a maid, a cook, a coachman—made a big move to the town of Penza, some three hundred kilometers southeast of Moscow, where my grandfather was assigned to build another theater. My grandfather seemed to have loved the most up-to-date technology. He was the first person in Penza to own an automobile, and in 1914 he even bought his own airplane, which he named *Mademoiselle.* "He had a pilot's license and flew over meadows, frightening cows," my mother recollected seven decades later. Peasants protested to the local authorities that my grandfather's flights so terrified the cows that they didn't produce any milk. But the governor of the province, who was smitten with my grandmother, settled the incident, and my grandfather continued his flights. "One of these days the Master is going to fall," peasants would say when they saw him flying.

L ife soon grew difficult for Tatiana and her sister. In 1915—they were then nine and seven years old—their parents were divorced. Their father left for America, allegedly because he had invented a new brand of rubber for automobile tires that failed to obtain a patent in Russia but that he was promised in the United States. Soon thereafter, my grandmother married, *en deuxième noces,* a prosperous pharmaceutical entrepreneur, Vassily Kirillovich Bartmer, who lost all his money at the onset of the 1917 revolution. The family was left destitute, and their survival grew all the more precarious in 1921, when the famine affected southeastern Russia with particular savagery and Bartmer died of tuberculosis and malnutrition. Lyubov Nikolaevna tried to eke out a tiny income by opening a dancing school. The family apartment was requisitioned. The three women lived in one room, burning precious books for fuel. My mother remembered spending those days doing the rounds of open-air markets and thrift shops to sell whatever furniture and linens remained to them. Notwithstanding her extremely limited formal education—due to the revolution she had little schooling after the age of twelve—she had developed a very special gift that helped her to survive: she had a phenomenal talent for memorizing poetry, a skill much ex-

Tatiana's mother, Lyubov Nikolaevna Aistova, the year of her marriage to Alexei Iacovleff, 1904.

alted in Russia, the honored status of which the revolution never altered. By the age of fourteen, she could recite literally hundreds of lines of Pushkin, Lermontov, Blok, and Mayakovsky, by heart. And upon the great famine of 1921, she helped her mother and sister survive by standing on street corners to recite poetry for groups of Red Army soldiers, receiving precious hunks of bread from them in return.

The famine took its toll. In 1922, Tatiana contracted tuberculosis, probably caught from her stepfather. Her mother was soon remarried ("She wasn't one to stay unmarried very long," Tatiana commented acerbically) to a kind lawyer named Nikolai Alexandrovich Orlov, whom her daughters seemed to be very fond of and referred to in their letters as *père*. But Tatiana's TB grew worse, and those of her relatives who had already

Tatiana with her grandmother, Babushka, upon her first Christmas in Paris, 1925.

settled in France—her uncle Alexandre, her Aunt Sandra, and Babushka—soon began the negotiations needed to obtain her a visa for France. Uncle Sasha finally obtained the proper papers with the help of the powerful industrialist André Citroën, and Lyubov Nikolaevna accompanied her daughter to Moscow to see her off on the train to Paris. I've often tried to imagine the two women's states of mind upon this departure: brought up since the age of nine by an aloof, narcissistic single mother who twice in recent years had been on the prowl for a new husband, Tatiana does not seem to have been offered much maternal affection. I once asked her what she thought her mother's feelings might have been when she stood at the train station in 1925, sending her daughter on to a new life in France: was it sorrow, I asked? Sorrow mingled with relief at knowing her child would be safe? Shrugging her shoulders, my mother looked at me coolly. "Nothing as complex as that," she said. "Just one less mouth to feed."

So that is how Tatiana came to arrive in Paris, at the age of nineteen, "a gorgeous, unwashed savage," as one of her kin described her when she stepped off the train, voicing her craving for the best clothes, the most brilliant parties and literary salons, and—a particular fixation that marks Russians to this day—a title of nobility. "All the communist garbage and *en plus* she already wanted to be a countess," my great-aunt Sandra would comment when recalling her niece's arrival.

After the frugality of postrevolutionary Soviet Russia, after her years of hunger and deprivation and of living in tiny communal rooms, even her grandmother's modest three-bedroom apartment in Montmartre struck Tatiana as the dernier cri of luxury and comfort. "Babushka is so kind and tender, and fusses over me a great deal," she wrote to her mother in her first ecstatic letter home.

She brings me cocoa in bed, and doesn't let me get up until 11 o'clock. . . . The apartment is wonderful. French doors open onto the balcony. There are silk hangings in all the rooms—orange in my room, coffee-colored in the guest room, and golden, in aunt Sandra's; there are marble fireplaces, and windows to the ceiling; the bathroom has hot water, and there's a telephone. The kitchen has a gas stove, on which everything cooks in half an hour. . . . They had underwear ready for me, as well as linen, silk, and batiste dresses, an overcoat, and a white silk hat. . . . From my balcony I can see the Eiffel tower, which lights up at dusk. There are splendid fireworks, and advertisements spelling out whole phrases. I am very struck by Auntie. She's really very beautiful, she clearly has a splendid voice, I've never heard another like it.

I've recently come to believe that those families that function most richly—those whose members draw most mutual inspiration from one another—are united by the memory of a radiantly benevolent forebear. Our family was blessed to have three such models: The relatives waiting for Tatiana in Paris were extraordinary human beings.

Babushka, the icon of our tribe! Her picture always stood within sight of my mother's bed, as it still stands within sight of mine: firm, square jaw, crown of thick silver hair, eyes as determined as they were gentle. Throughout her life, she emanated an aura of goodness and serene optimism. The happiness of her marriage had been legendary in her St. Petersburg circles—whenever she went out to a dinner party with my great-grandfather, the couple dropped a note to the hostess ahead of time, asking to be seated next to each other. But beneath Babushka's veneer of elegance and genteelness there was a seething energy, a will of iron. Widowed in her thirties—my great-grandfather died young of congestive heart failure, which for several generations has been a family curse—she had assumed the male role in a family of sybaritic men and single-handedly managed the family's foundry business. Benevolence, keen intelligence and deep mysticism blended more harmoniously in her character than in that of any human being I have known. From the age of four on I spent at least one night per week at the flat she shared with her daughter, my great-aunt Sandra, delighting in the flutter of Babushka's silks and mended laces, in the smells of verbena and rose water, dried apricots and steaming kasha, that imbued her rooms. I tyrannized her for hours into games of Durachki, "Little Idiots," the simplistic diversion that is the first card game learned by any Russian child. Released from my governess's tyrannical taboos, I ate *kisel*—the cranberry jelly that is a staple of the Russian diet—by the bowlful, tracing my initials on the gelatinous red surface with dribbles of thick, sweet condensed milk. I was also allowed to read my Jules Verne into the wee hours, relishing the fragrant triple benediction with which Babushka blessed me as she put me to sleep. Over the decades, the memory of her profound goodness and grace was perhaps the strongest bond that united me to my mother: whenever we had an argument, one of us would suddenly look up and exclaim, "What would Babushka say?" and the very recall of our revered mentor led us to fall into each other's arms.

I knew Babushka's daughter, my equally cherished great-aunt Sandra, even better; for whereas my great-grandmother died in 1939, when I was eight, Sandra lived well into the 1970s. At the time Tatiana arrived in Paris, Sandra, a large, handsome woman of angelic disposition then in her early forties, had already had a tragic life. Her first husband, the father of her only daughter, Masha, was killed in action in the

Tatiana's aunt, the opera singer Alexandra (Sandra) Yakovleva, in the late 1920s.

first year of World War I. She remarried a few years later and lost that second husband, also an officer with the czarist troops, during the revolution, when a group of Communist sailors threw him off the fortress of Kronstadt into the sea, feet tied with heavy weights. Shortly thereafter, in 1920, when she sought exile in Constantinople with Babushka and Masha, the latter died of scarlet fever. Having just received their visas for Paris, Babushka and Sandra wound their way alone to Paris via Dessau, Germany, where Sandra's sister, my great-aunt Vera, had settled a few decades before. Their visit there was corroborated for me recently by Vera's daughter, now eighty-seven, who reported that one of her earliest childhood memories concerns Sandra's deep mourning for her daughter, the hours-long, uncontrollable bouts of weeping that overtook her during her stay.

But stoicism runs strong in the family. Upon arriving in Paris in 1922, where she and Babushka initially depended on the financial support of her brother Sasha, Sandra was able to resurrect her singing career. She was eventually offered the role of Aïda, in which she made a very successful debut at the Paris Opera in 1925, a few months before Tatiana's arrival. For the next decade, she appeared in recitals and operas throughout western

Europe and South America. A very partial listing of the thirty-nine leading roles in her repertory: *La Juive, Tosca, Otello, Carmen, Siegfried, Tannhäuser, The Damnation of Faust, Salambo, Cavalleria Rusticana, Ruslan and Ludmila, Eugene Onegin, Aïda, Les Huguenots,* and *Die Walküre,* the last three of which she could sing in five different languages; and of course Tchaikovsky's *Queen of Spades,* in which she had made her debut at the St. Petersburg Opera around 1916 in the role of the aging countess, a demanding contralto part that only a handful of singers in any one generation can handle. Aunt Sandra's years as a young opera star in Russia yielded an anecdote that I bade her repeat innumerable times throughout my childhood: "I'd just sung Aïda in St. Petersburg, it was after a huge snowstorm," she'd tell me, "I dressed in a rush to go to a *grand bal,* and as I waited for my carriage my escort made me laugh so hard that I pee-peed in my pants, the snow underneath me melted, and clouds of steam rose all around me." Aunt Sandra standing in her finery by the banks of the frozen Neva, suddenly swathed like a prophet in a tall column of smoke. Magic.

The Sandra who greeted Mother in Paris in 1925 could not have been very different from the Aunt Sandra whom I cherished during my childhood in 1930s Paris. Her most striking feature was her radiant operatic smile, which she claimed to maintain through the use of a pink dentifrice called Toreador. Majestically tall, like most Iacovleffs, and statuesque, she had dazzlingly milky skin, kind and melancholy brown eyes, and jet-black hair pulled back in a simple bun. Her tastes in music were adorably kitschy. She deemed Rimsky-Korsakov to be the greatest composer who ever lived, and her favorite opera was his *Tale of the Invisible City of Kitej.* She was totally unaffected, generous to a fault, trusting to the point of extreme naïveté, and endlessly affectionate, rechanneling her vast maternal energies toward any emotionally needy person who came along. She was also, like her mother, deeply Puritanical and once exclaimed, when she was told that her brother Sasha was having an affair with the dancer Anna Pavlova, "It can't be true! Who's ever heard of anyone having an affair with a married woman?"

The third member of the closely bonded family that welcomed Tatiana to Paris in 1925 was the intrepid, dashing explorer and artist, Uncle Sasha.

TWO

Uncle Sasha

Ever since I can remember, Uncle Sasha Iacovleff glowed in my mind with the aura of legend. For in my mother's inevitably romanticized accounts he was a superman who had traveled to the most dangerous places on earth, wrestled with wild beasts in distant deserts, explored caves never before entered by any man. Thus the announcement "Uncle Sasha is coming to see you!" was bound to raise intense excitement. What struck me first as he entered my nursery, during the one visit I clearly remember, was his dancelike, feline walk and his exquisitely groomed goatee. There was something disquieting, in fact, about the sleekness of his physical perfection—as I reworked the memory in late adolescence, he reminded me of an inordinately perfect vase or a disturbingly beautiful archaic Greek *kouros*. His beard was so unfleshly and sculptural. His smell, as he bent down to kiss me, was that of an ethereally dry, dry verbena. It was a hot late-spring day, he had taken off his jacket during this informal family call, and as he chatted in Russian with my governess, inquiring about my course of studies, I marveled over the beauty of his lissome, wondrously muscled arms, a flesh more lustrous than any I'd yet seen. Even then, I realized that the attention he lavished on me did not necessarily signal any quality of mine, that his need to cast his spell over any creature he ever encountered was as innate as a lioness's instinct to protect her young. In retrospect, I can't help feeling that there was something dismaying about his impulse to charm others, and the word "Mephisthophelean" comes to mind.

Born in St. Petersburg in 1887, Alexandre Iacovleff, the youngest of my great-grandmother's four children, displayed an eerily precocious gift for drawing and at eighteen entered the Imperial Academy of Art. His skills were noticed early in his career by the most influential Russian painter of his teachers' generation, Aleksandr Benois, who wrote that the young man displayed "a tremendous sensibility to nature. . . . One can not doubt that [his] talent is phenomenal." While in art school, Iacovleff became fascinated with theater and dance; at the age of twenty-three he married a ravishing stage and cabaret performer, Bella Shensheva (also known as Kazarosa), who was particularly noted for her fiery Spanish gypsy dances. I imagine that Uncle Sasha's liaison with Kazarosa was very shocking to Sasha's prim, strong-willed mother. And it is probable that the alliance was stormy from the start, for in 1913, three years into his marriage, Iacovleff's career as a voyaging artist began.

After two years of traveling in Italy and Spain, where he was particularly drawn to the works of Mantegna and El Greco, he returned briefly to St. Petersburg, only to set out again for the Far East on a traveling scholarship from the art academy. He was in Beijing when the Russian Revolution broke out (he was never again to see his native Russia or his wife, Bella, who would die in 1929). In 1918, Uncle Sasha, while in Beijing, devoted himself to the study of Chinese theater and began to sign his portraits in Chinese characters that read "Ya-Ko-Lo-Fu," a pun on "Iaco Le Fou." He ended his first stay in the Orient with a six-month tour of Japan, where he lived for a while among fishermen on the island of Oshima, learning the art of deep-sea diving. A very large, handsome oil of his entitled *The Pearl Divers* hung over the couch of my parents' Paris living room in the prewar years; and there still survive in my archives the underwater photographs he took during that stay in Japan, which he took with one of the first impermeable cameras.

. . .

In 1919, not being able to return to Russia, my great-uncle took a ship to France for the first time and settled in Paris, where a large community of White Russian émigrés was forming. The self-possessed young artist with the light, pealing laugh, the swift, warm eyes, and the faunlike beard quickly conquered enough of Paris to lead a very good life. His popularity could only have been helped by the current rage for all things Russian: the fascination with Diaghilev's ballets and Stravinsky's scores; the notoriety already achieved by *Firebird, Rite of Spring,* and Nijinsky's *Afternoon of a Faun;* the beauty of the hundreds of Russian émigré women who were providing Paris couturiers with their most gorgeous fashion models. Moreover, like many Russian émigrés, Uncle Sasha was a marvel of resourcefulness. Nearly penniless upon arriving in France, he found a seventh-floor walk-up in Montmartre to live and work in and persuaded a nearby restaurant, La Biche, to let him paint frescoes on its walls in exchange for six meals per week. Within two years of his arrival in Paris, Iacovleff had an exhibition of his Chinese and Japanese paintings at a distinguished Paris gallery, and an eminent French art publisher, Lucien Vogel, issued a lavish book on his Asian work.

Iacovleff was now making enough of an income to vacation with a group of fellow artists on the Mediterranean island of Port-Cros. An American artist who summered there with the same circle, the sculptor Malvina Hoffman, remembered him as "a dynamic, imaginative personality around whom an ever widening circle of friends revolved" and tells of his industriousness and his exuberant gift for friendship. He often took breaks from his ten-hour-per-day work schedule to dive for shells and seaweed, plunging to thirty feet below with a clip on his nose and a pair of Japanese sea goggles; his colleagues wondered what purpose his marine booty would serve. One evening, he asked them to go to a certain restaurant for their supper. "We entered a fantastic decor all aglow with mysterious rainbow-like lighting," Malvina Hoffman recalled. "Candles hidden behind iridescent shells were arranged in garlands of patterns around walls; amid these garlands were oval medallions, framed in more shells and seaweed, which held life-size portraits of each member of our group."

Uncle Sasha displaying his muscles in Capri, mid-1920s.

Beyond his affability, his magnetic charm, and his renown as an adventurous traveler, I suspect Paris society also adopted Iacovleff because of his unusually multifaceted talents: He was a prodigious linguist, an eloquent writer, an exceptionally gifted athlete, and an excellent cook; he designed furniture, was skilled at bookbinding and lacquering techniques, and created theater sets and costumes—one of his dramatic projects was a staging of Rossini's opera *Semiramis*. Moreover, there are many accounts of the spell his physical beauty cast over others. "A body, a musculature, made for discus or javelin-throwing," so one description of Iacovleff in 1926 goes, "an extraordinarily long, chiseled face, its traits so precisely drawn that they seem to have emerged from a Persian etching. . . . Vivid, piercing eyes. A warm voice which emits brief, precise statements." I suspect that Uncle Sasha was very aware of his physical appeal and may have been something of a narcissist: In every beachside photo I've seen of him, he is careful to display his muscles in their full glory.

Uncle Sasha was of legendary generosity toward those even needier than he—on many a day he had to put a sign up on the door of his studio that read, "I have no cash today." Yet like most Russians of his milieu, he was somewhat of a snob, enjoyed hobnobbing with European aristocracy, and seems to have delighted in doing the portraits of many preeminent society figures. Among his subjects were the duchess d'Aoste and her son the duc de Pouilles, whose mistress, Princess Marie-José of Piedmont, later became the queen of Italy; the Brazilian millionaire Arturo Lopez-Willshaw; and Louis de Bourbon, brother of the empress of Austria, who was married to the daughter of the king of Italy.

Whatever means Iacovleff used to charm his way into Paris circles, he gained recognition and a measure of financial comfort. In 1922, he arranged for his sister and his mother, both of whom had fled Russia for Constantinople, to join him in Paris, and the three set up house in an apartment in Montmartre where they were eventually joined by Tatiana. But notwithstanding his very close bonds to his family, Uncle Sasha retained a studio a few blocks away where he carried on his numerous love affairs in style. I know of two particularly glamorous mistresses. One was Anna Pavlova, whose superb oil portrait, painted by Iacovleff in Paris in 1924, now hangs in the Tretyakov Gallery in Moscow. The other, a flamboyant theatrical entrepreneur named Henriette Pascar, had a far more fateful impact on my family: She was the mother of a teenage son named Alexandre Liberman who, some twelve years later, would become my mother's lover and eventually my stepfather.

The month Tatiana arrived in Paris, July 1925, Sasha was just ending his most adventurous voyage to date, an expedition across Africa funded by the Citroën automobile empire. It has gone down in ethnographic history as the Croisière Noire. (Citroën's next travel venture, a crossing of Asia, was called the Croisière Jaune; one can imagine the ruckus that such titles would provoke today.) The mastermind of these expeditions, the visionary, notoriously shrewd automobile magnate André Citroën, often referred to as "the Henry Ford of France," had been aware of the civilian potential of the caterpillar tractor since World War I, when it was used in the design of the first military tanks. Eager to patent these novel vehicles before Americans cornered the market, he started manufacturing them in 1920; and in 1922, when he realized that Africana was coming into vogue—the jazz age was dawning, Josephine Baker was soon to start a craze—he decided to sponsor the first automotive crossing of Africa. His Croisière Noire would span eight thousand kilometers of Africa, from Algeria to Madagascar.

Uncle Sasha and Anna Pavlova at the Duchesse de Grammont's estate.

The expedition took more than a year to prepare, for depots storing some eighty tons of foodstuffs and mechanical supplies had to be established along the scheduled route. To be head of the expedition, Citroën chose a vice president of his company, Georges-Marie Haardt, an explorer and art connoisseur who had already traveled extensively in the Sahara. In addition to a formidable team of automotive engineers and mechanics, Citroën's group included a geologist, a zoologist, a medical doctor, two prominent photographers and filmmakers, and an artist, Alexandre Iacovleff, whose role, as Citroën saw it, was to record the people of Africa with an intimacy not readily achieved by the camera.

The convoy of eight caterpillar-treaded vehicles that finally set out in

October of 1924 in Colomb-Béchar, in southern Algeria, would not reach Madagascar until June of the following year. Beyond the immense desert spaces, the expedition also had to tackle vast stretches of virgin forest and swamps in which its vehicles came close to being buried in mud. Rocky passes had to be blasted with dynamite, savanna fires that could have melted the very rubber of the vehicles' treads had to be circumvented. Traveling without any previously prepared map, the members of the Citroën group guided themselves solely by their compasses, as if at sea. Some oases were five hundred miles apart, and precise navigation was needed to avoid running out of water—the Sahara, the travelers soon discovered, was littered with the skeletons of ill-fated earlier voyagers. Throughout the crossing, the expedition also had to watch out for marauding brigands, and at night its camp resembled a war bivouac, with all cars parked into a hollow square and loaded machine guns mounted in defensive positions. Moreover, local chiefs and tribesmen had to be courted, pacified, and befriended all along the way; their festivities had to be patiently attended.

Throughout the crises and complications inevitable to such an expedition, "Iaco," as my great-uncle's colleagues called him, displayed a cheerful calm and industriousness that became legendary among his peers. Always traveling in the same vehicle with Haardt, with whom he formed a deep friendship that was to grow with the years, he filled pages with drawings even when they were racing through the bush and continued working during his comrades' rest periods. Never bored and never idle, he had trained his body to be constantly at work; when there were no models to pose for him, he scavenged for fragments of ancient pottery, piecing them together in an attempt to re-create the

Mother's uncle, artist and explorer Alexandre Iacovleff (Uncle Sasha), during his crossing of the Sahara in the mid-1920s.

Alexandre Iacovleff's portrait of Haile Selassie, 1928.

originals. "Iacovleff, indefatigable, continues to draw notwithstanding the shaking of the vehicle," Haardt wrote in his journal. "A methodical man, never bored with anything except vulgarity, he is the charming companion of often trying hours."

Another task assigned to the suave Iacovleff, who displayed a remarkable ability for acquiring the trust of African tribesmen, was to retain good diplomatic ties with local leaders. Iacovleff was able to finish life-size portraits with astounding speed, in less than an hour, through the use of red Conte crayons ("sanguine" in art parlance), which have the advantage of gliding very smoothly over paper. Sensing that the artist's swift draftsmanship was imbued with magical powers, some nomadic chiefs who had assaulted most earlier travelers allowed the Citroën group to pass unmolested in exchange for a pastel. Iacovleff indeed possessed uncanny insight into the African tribal mind and was even ready to share the most disconcerting local food—in the course of the trip, he often went off on his own to feast with natives on toasted termites or sautéed locusts. The unusual measure of communion he achieved with his African models is recorded in his travel journals.

"Louaho, Chief Waguenia," he jotted in Stanleyville, Congo.

Prototype of the black chief for an ancient edition of Paul et Virginie. Coarse-featured face with bloodshot eyes, but with a kind, childlike expression. He takes great pains to pose conscientiously; drops of sweat appear on his forehead under the hat decorated with multicolored feathers; his necklace of leopard teeth moves perceptibly on his chest, strained by the immobility of his pose. Upon seeing his double on paper, he is struck with wonder. He has a long conversation with his image and ad-

dresses it with great deference, with many salutations and good wishes, before get-ting onto the bicycle that will carry him back to his village.

Nineteen twenty-five—the year *Mein Kampf* was first published and Charlie Chaplin issued *The Gold Rush*—also marked the return of Citroën's Croisière Noire from Africa. The travelers brought back numerous new maps of heretofore uncharted regions; 80,000 feet of filmed footage; some 8,000 photographs; the specimens of 300 mammals, 800 bird species, and 15,000 insect species, many of them up to then unknown to Europeans; and more than 500 paintings and drawings by Iacovleff. The cult of ex-plorers and heroic travelers in the 1920s was somewhat equivalent to the contemporary cult of rock stars and film idols. I have talked to many French citizens, now in their eighties and nineties, whose families had kept vast maps of Africa on their living-room walls and tracked the advances of the Citroën expedition with pushpins as reports of its progress came out in the national press. Iacovleff's fame grew by bounds after the expedition's re-turn. His 1926 exhibit at Paris's prestigious Galerie Charpentier, in which he showed many large oil paintings based on his African sketches, totally sold out. That fall, the Louvre held a massive five-month exhibition of the trea-sures brought back by the Croisière Noire: jewels, arms, zoological spe-cimens, more photographs of the expedition, more Iacovleff drawings. The premiere of the film that documented the trip was attended by the president of the Republic, Gaston Doumergue, and it played at the Marivaux Theater for six consecutive months.

After his return from Africa, Iacovleff became increasingly popular for his portraits of eminent Parisian society figures, predominantly done in san-guine, like his African sketches. Some critics were comparing him to David and to Ingres, and John Singer Sargent was proclaiming that Iacovleff was one of the two greatest draftsmen alive. (We have no record of whom he consid-ered to be the other great draftsman.) The artist who had arrived penniless in Paris less than a decade before could now provide comfortably for his mother and sister, and in the late 1920s bought them a three-room apartment in the sixteenth arrondissement, off the Avenue Foch, where I was to spend some of the happiest days of my early childhood. For in 1929, Iacovleff's niece Tatiana accepted the marriage offer of a young French diplomat, Bertrand du Plessix. It was her Uncle Sasha who bought her trousseau and her beautiful white satin wedding dress, who gave her away in marriage, and whom a year later she chose to be my godfather.

Notwithstanding the increasing celebrity they enjoyed after their return from Africa, Iacovleff and most of his comrade travelers felt a strange emptiness, a restlessness, a spiritual void. "I love traveling, the voluptuous thrill of constant movement, the constant discovery of new wonders," the artist had confessed in an interview shortly after his return. And indeed I doubt if many months spent in the African wilderness can leave anyone indifferent. Such an experience is more likely to affect us like an infection, or a drug. The members of the Croisière Noire expedition seem to have been intoxicated by the sense of limitless freedom that prevails in the desert; by the crystalline silence of nights punctuated only by the jackal's yelp, the hyena's wild laugh, the majestic roar of the lion; above all, by the deep camaraderie bred among men, thrust into situations of dearth and risk, who share a campfire for hundreds of consecutive nights, under Africa's dazzling stars. The travelers had been home for barely two years when they started talking about a new expedition. "Where would our vagabondings lead to next?" Iacovleff wrote in his journals. "This question could be read in the gaze of my traveling companions, grown used to nomadic life. . . . Soon after the exhibitions, films, books were behind us our unquiet spirits took off again in search for new adventures."

André Citroën, too, was inebriated by the glamour brought to his firm by the African trip and wanted more of it. He had recently become interested in the possibility of setting up automobile factories in China, which in the past two decades had begun to admit missionaries and Western traders. What about sponsoring a new expedition, a Croisière Jaune that would send his vehicles on a historic eastward mission across the Asian continent? Although they were aware that Asia presented far vaster dangers and complications than Africa ever had, the adventurous Georges Haardt and his restless friend Iaco cheered the prospect: They were entranced by the notion of following the ancient route on which Arab and Chinese merchants had brought the East's treasures to Europe centuries ago, of crossing the terrain on which, in Iacovleff's own words, "Alexander the Great, Darius, Mohammed, Genghis Khan, and Marco Polo had already left material and spiritual traces." Buoyed by their enthusiasm, in 1928 the two-and-a-half-year preparation for the Croisière Jaune began.

Leaving from Bayreuth, the new expedition was scheduled to cross through Syria, Iraq, and Persia. To avoid the formidable Pamir mountain chain that stretches across Afghanistan and what was then Northwest-India (now Pakistan), the group planned to swerve northward in Persia and enter the Soviet Union south of Samarkand; the travelers would travel across the Russian steppes south of Lake Balkhash, enter northwest China's Sinkiang Province and then pick up the ancient "silk route" to Beijing.

But the entire schedule had to be radically altered three months before the planned departure, in November 1930, when the Soviet Union, which under Joseph Stalin was entering an era of severe isolationism, rescinded its visas for the Croisière Jaune. The route now had to include many treacherous mountain crossings. The travelers divided into two groups: The Pamir group, which included Iacovleff and Haardt, would have to proceed across Afghanistan and tackle the dreaded Pamir Mountains. A smaller group, which was headed by the dashing explorer and naval captain Victor Point and included France's most distinguished paleontologist, the Jesuit scholar Father Pierre Teilhard de Chardin, would travel westward from Beijing. The two teams would meet east of the Pamir Mountains and then return together to Beijing and travel southward into Indochina. The new itinerary was much more complex and perilous

Alexandre Iacovleff's portrait of a Tibetan lama, 1932

than the original one, but men of Haardt's and Iacovleff's mettle seemed to relish such risks: The very difficulties of the trip, Iacovleff wrote, "only strengthen our determination to surmount them."

The expedition headed by Haardt and Iaco proceeded fairly smoothly for the first few months, through Persia, Iraq, and most of Afghanistan. But just as they had feared, the travelers began to encounter great difficulties in the Hindu Kush and the Pamir Mountains. There, Citroën's vehicles had to cross 5,000-meter-high mountains with icy surfaces that, even in summer, could be six meters thick. Weeks were spent breaking up hunks of rock and ice to create passageways for the cars. At any moment, half a mountainside could slide away and stall progress for days. In several instances, the only way to continue was to disassemble the vehicles on one side of a mountain and reassemble them on the other side, forcing the travelers to proceed on foot or atop yaks and mules that were often breast-deep in snow. Footing was never secure. Loose rocks slipped at almost every step. One hundred fifty mule loads were needed for the group's provisions alone—sleeping sacks, toolboxes, tents, food, spare axles, and dismantled car parts—and on the more hazardous passages the expedition could not advance more than four kilometers per day.

There were equally severe difficulties of a political kind. In the last days of August 1931, the two segments of the expedition finally met at their appointed site, in Aksu, China, a few kilometers south of the Soviet border. But several weeks later, as it was crossing the northwestern province of Sinkiang on their way to Beijing, the group was imprisoned by the local governor, Marshal King. The marshal detained them for over a month, until November 1931, releasing them only when Citroën dispatched a dozen of his caterpillar tractors via the trans-Siberian railroad in the way of ransom. The travelers proceeded eastward, but a few weeks later were again arrested, albeit for a shorter time, by Chiang Kai-shek's troops. This series of delays forced the travelers to endure the awesome winter of the Chinese plains just below the Gobi Desert, where temperatures often fall to forty degrees below zero Centigrade, and which they had originally been scheduled to cross in the relatively benign clime of late summer and early fall.

Iacovleff faced his own set of problems on the Asian expedition. Below-zero temperatures presented harrowing material difficulties to his painting. In the ruins of ancient cities just south of the Gobi Desert, where he attempted to make copies of Buddhist frescoes in caves never before entered by European explorers, his colors froze shortly after being squeezed out of their tubes. He finally devised a metal palette that could be set upon a gas burner, but he was still forced to mix them from minute to minute. In China's urban centers, a totally different kind of complication confronted him: It had to do with the veneration of portrait painting in Chinese culture, a culture in which, as Iacovleff himself put it, "the painter incarnates the quintessence of the aristocrat . . . and the portrait painter carries an undisputed title of nobility."

This had become all too evident when the Citroën expedition was being held captive by Marshal King: Scores of local officials clamored to pose for the Citroën group's official artist. In an effort to liberate his comrades, Iacovleff complied with the Chinese officials' wishes and spent exhausting days shuttling from one end of the city to another, doing portraits of mandarin after mandarin in hopes that one of them might persuade Marshal King to release them. He limned a particularly powerful portrait of a local warlord, the former governor of Hami Province. "[General Tchou] posed for me in an immense hall filled with the carousing guests of a wedding banquet," he wrote. "The orchestra's strident sounds accompanied a theatrical production being performed in the open courtyard. Huge vases placed in the corners of the room allowed the joyous guests to alleviate their digestive systems before returning to the frenzied feast. A strong odor of opium (which explained the good general's beatific and soporific countenance) combated that of the local aquavit."

It was an exhausted group of travelers that reached Beijing in February of 1932, after twelve thousand kilometers of travel. Weeks of festivities, organized by Chinese authorities, the French embassy, and numerous other foreign legations, celebrated their heroic journey. But following a year of frugality and solitude, such revelries only disconcerted Iacovleff and accentuated his inexplicable gloom. "Why is the joy of our success tinged by an indefinable melancholy?" he asked himself in his travel notes toward the end of his stay in Beijing. "Is it the renewed contact with civilization?"

Iacovleff's despondency may have been a form of premonition. On the foggy night the expedition members were traveling by ship to Hong Kong, whence they were scheduled to return to Syria via Vietnam and India, his friend Georges-Marie Haardt came into his cabin for a chat. He had been plagued by a bad grippe for the past several weeks and told Iacovleff that he would stop for a few days in Hong Kong to rest, rejoining the group at some later date. "'It's a sinister night, isn't it Iaco,' Haardt said to me at the end of our talk," Iacovleff wrote in his memoir. "I still remember the voice of that rare man, that dear friend, speaking what would be his parting words."

Haardt, who left ship in Hong Kong the morning after that conversation, died ten days later of double pneumonia, shortly before his forty-eighth birthday. The news reached his colleagues in Haiphong. All previous plans for a return through the Near East were canceled. Complying with Citroën's orders, the travelers came back to Hong Kong. Iacovleff, as Haardt's closest friend, was charged with the somber details of the funerary transport to France. In late April 1932, when the group's ship reached Marseille, Citroën was there to greet them. He, too, was in mourning for a cherished collaborator and friend. Haardt, who had remained a bachelor, was buried not far from Edouard Manet's tomb in Passy Cemetery, in a service attended by scores of grieving friends and colleagues.

Notwithstanding their tragic loss, the members of the Croisière Jaune were welcomed back in Paris with the same kind of festivities that had greeted their return from Africa. A few months after their return, a vast exhibition celebrated the achievements of both Citroën expeditions. However, Iacovleff remained despondent, and the grief he had felt upon the loss of Haardt was deepened that very summer by the death of another comrade: In August, Victor Point, the charismatic leader of the Croisière Jaune's China group, committed suicide for the love of a beautiful, unfaithful mistress, the popular actress Alice Cocea.

In the midst of these sorrows, Iacovleff had to think of making a living. His gallery, Charpentier, had scheduled a large show for him in the spring of 1933. He set to work, in Paris and in Capri, to complete a group of paintings based on his travel sketches of Asia, producing 100 paintings and 250 drawings. He wished all of his Croisière Jaune works to be homages to his lost friend, Georges-Marie Haardt: "To interpret, through successive images, the immense trajectory and diverse phases of our nomadic life; to evoke its sense of limitless space . . . such were the directions of my activity, a tribute to the memory of the friend I lost."

The show was a great critical success but perhaps not as remunerative as the artist hoped, for the Great Depression that had struck Wall Street in 1929 was affecting France particularly hard in the summer of 1933. Iacovleff was devoid of any fixed income and had to continue supporting his aging mother and his sister, the latter of whom, then forty-seven, had suffered some setbacks in her singing profession. His devotion and passionate loyalty to the two women, and the financial responsibilities they entailed, were the only plausible explanations for the next, very unexpected phase of Iacovleff's career: In 1934, he accepted an invitation to come to the United States and serve as the director of the School of the Museum of Fine Arts in Boston. Through the scores of Iacovleff drawings reproduced in *National Geographic*—the magazine had dedicated hundreds of pages to the Croisière Jaune—American art connoisseurs had had considerable exposure to Iacovleff's marvelous gifts as a draftsman. And the intensive academic training displayed in his work must have been particularly attractive to a fairly traditional American art school.

Iacovleff, who had never before been to the United States, arrived in Boston in 1934 to assume the post, which he was to hold for three unhappy years. He was now widely known on both continents. Exhibitions of his works were held in Washington, D.C., in Pittsburgh, and in New York's Grand Central Galleries. During his stay in the United States, he occasionally had an chance to visit with his brother, my grandfather Alexis, who had left Russia for the United States in 1915 and whom he had not seen since. Otherwise, Iacovleff—a man who had never been known to complain, who notwithstanding his sunny, affable exterior seldom exposed his innermost feelings, even to close friends—made it clear to all that he was miserable in Boston.

"Boston's atmosphere is not conducive to creation, it is provincial and conservative," he wrote in 1937 to Louis Audouin-Dubreuil, Haardt's second-in-command during both Citroën expeditions. "Though I'm aware of the fact that financial prospects are not brilliant in Europe, I intend to spend the next year there; I'll be able to last one year during which, if I find life too difficult, I might resolve to return to the United States. . . . [T]he Boston school, which sees me leave with great regrets, might well be happy to hire me again; meanwhile it's of vital importance for me to steep myself again in the stimulating atmosphere of ancient, ailing Europe."

Iacovleff's unhappiness in the United States and his longing for "ancient, ailing Europe" were accompanied by a period of great self-doubt as an artist. He seemed to have become indifferent to his peerless gifts as a draftsman. Whenever his Boston students, with whom he was extremely popular, praised his virtuoso technique, he warned them, doubtless in a spirit of self-criticism, that the gift of great draftsmanship might be a peril to some artists. Upon returning to Paris in the spring of 1937, Iacovleff, now striving to make his mark as a painter, set to work in the flat, lusterless tempera medium he had adopted during his travels. He experimented with mythological themes rendered in an expressionist genre—Theseus fighting the Minotaur, odalisques, grotesque sea monsters. These were not his best works, and he was far too intelligent not to realize his shortcomings as an "imaginative" painter.

Uncle Sasha was able to enjoy his freedom for only a year. He was to die in May 1938, of a cancer of the stomach that spread with devastating rapidity. An American art critic ardently devoted to Iacovleff and his work, Martin Birnbaum, has left a vivid depiction of my grand-uncle in the final weeks of his life and of the stoicism with which he cloaked the truth of his illness from even his closest friends.

Birnbaum paid his last visit to Iacovleff's studio on the rue Campagne-Première, in Montmartre, in May 1938. The artist came "bounding rather than walking" down the stairs to accompany the visitor to his fourth-floor studio, and Birnbaum was struck once more by the gaiety and intelligence of his sparkling eyes, his quality of "virile refinement," the ribbon of well-groomed beard "that gave him a resemblance to Pan." The visitor also describes the artist's modest but fastidious surroundings and those details that denoted his intellectual and aesthetic predilections: the collection of rare first editions, bound in red morocco with his initials engraved in gold; the horizontal exercise bar, set in the middle of his studio, on which Iacovleff daily performed a strenuous muscle-building routine; the luxurious set of silver-topped cut-crystal bottles, salvaged from his mother's home in St. Petersburg, that graced his tiny, tidy bedroom.

Upon this visit, Uncle Sasha was packing up his painting materials in preparation for a return to Capri, and he spoke about the important work he would do there that summer, work that he felt would be his "most solid lasting achievement." In the late afternoon, the two men went as planned to a concert at Salle Pleyel, to hear Yehudi Menuhin perform. In the middle of the concert, Iacovleff, suddenly looking uneasy, complained of a pain in his side and confided to Birnbaum that he was scheduled to enter the hospital the next morning for a "slight operation." In a few weeks, he reassured his friend as he drove him home in his little sports car, they'd be visiting together at the Piccola Marina in Capri.

But the operation was one of those in which surgeons open a body, find that the cancer is inoperable and widely spread, and sew the patient up again. Iacovleff died a fortnight or so after that afternoon visit with his admirer, facing his end with the serene gallantry with which he had led his life. I was seven and a half years old and have a vivid memory of his funeral at the Russian Church in Paris's rue Daru. The coffin was totally covered with scarlet peonies, Uncle Sasha's favorite flower. His frail seventy-seven-year-old mother, my beloved Babushka, lay prostrate on the stone floor of the church in an ancient, unleashed gesture of mourning, her arms ahead of her, her tiny feet twisted and helpless a few inches from my own. She suffered from congestive heart failure and survived him by only a year, dying in May 1939 on the very anniversary of her son's death.

Before ending my reflections on the Iacovleff family's most romantic figure, I should mention the various ways in which he influenced our lives. First and foremost, I should emphasize that my mother was his creation, that her evolution into a gifted, polished young woman was in great part his doing.

Under the care of her grandmother and her aunt, the ambitious nineteen-year old waiting to greet Uncle Sasha when he returned from Africa had managed to heal her tuberculosis through a regime of rest and medical treatments. She was now bent on helping her relatives' scant finances through an occupation she had dreamed of during her tough youth in Russia: posing for photographs. She modeled for fur, jewelry, and stockings ads in fashion magazines and worked for a photographer who made Christmas and birthday cards—embarrassingly simpering shots in which her long, beautifully tapered hands are set off in the foreground to maximum display. Immediately sought after by several suitors, Tatiana had to deal with the infatuation of a Prince Menshikov—"handsome and well behaved, a blue stocking"—whom her grandmother enthusiastically approved but whose affection left her rather cold. (Prince Menshikov's mother forced him to call off the romance with Tatiana when she saw postcard photos of her at a newsstand that stood in front of a Marseille brothel.) And throughout these innocent adventures she had retained much of the anarchic extravagance of her Soviet youth: upon entering a restaurant and seeing a group of her friends at the other end of a crowded room, she had simply jumped onto a table and leaped from table to table until she reached her pals, impervious to any disturbance she might cause to the diners on the way.

Alexandre Iacovleff's portrait of his mother, my "Babushka," 1929.

But above all, the beautiful teenager who greeted Sasha upon his return from Africa was getting very restive under the strict supervision imposed on her by her grandmother and aunt, and she was experiencing bitter feelings of loneliness and solitude. Even chaperoned, Tatiana was not allowed out of the house in the evenings, except for a biweekly visit to the movies in her grandmother's company. "It's such a bore," she complained to her mother in a letter to Penza. "I'm not even allowed to go to the movies with anyone without Babushka, she must always come along as chaperone. . . . I'm used to total independence, I found my way alone to Paris, and here they must lead me by the hand!!" So in addition to the phobias and insecurities caused by the turbulence of her adolescence in the Soviet Union, after a few months of Paris life Tatiana was threatening to become unruly.

Alexandre Iacovleff's portrait of his niece, Tatiana, 1929.

Upon his return from Africa, Sasha set to work healing his niece's insecurities and refining his "gorgeous savage," as he called her, into a work of art. He doted on her, and the affection was amply returned. They must have understood each other perfectly: Beneath my mother's flamboyant panache and my great-uncle's suave razzle-dazzle were two intensely private persons who seldom revealed their true emotions. Although he was terrified that his beautiful niece might become a courtesan, Sasha relaxed his mother's chaperoning rules, allowing her to go out in the evenings with a few young men he judged suitable. He also perfected his niece's table manners; dragged her to museums to instruct her in the history of art; took her to Gordes, Carcassonne, Chartres, Mont-St.-Michel to give her a sense of European history and architecture; made her read Stendhal, Balzac, Baudelaire, and other French classics; brought her to friends' couture houses to buy whatever modestly priced models' samples were left in the racks; advised her on how to hold her own at dinner-party conversations. Moreover, can I ever forget that it is Uncle Sasha who introduced Tatiana to the man who would dominate the major part of her life, and become my second father, Alexandre Liberman? Young Alexandre, an aspiring painter, was the son of the woman who was Sasha's mistress from 1924 to 1927, Henriette

Pascar. Alex idolized Sasha and started studying with him in his early teens, and it is in Sasha's studio, as teenagers, that Tatiana and Alex Liberman first met.

In the course of perfecting his niece's education, Sasha, quite sensibly, led her to learn a trade. A year after she arrived in Paris, he had her enter the École de Couture, an institution somewhat analogous to New York City's Fashion Institute of Technology, where she received a degree in less than a year. He then persuaded a former mistress of his, an émigré hat designer with the exotic name of Fat'ma Hanoum, to take Tatiana on as an apprentice. By the time she was twenty-one, she was doing her uncle proud. She had developed hew own private clientele, designing hats often inspired from the paintings he taught her to love. (Cranach and Vermeer would remain particular favorites.) She could now hold her own at a dinner table without more than two or three faux pas a night—some of them retained intentionally, to amuse her audiences. She used her imagination to dress superbly on a minimal income, making beads and a bit of rabbit fur look like a page out of *Vogue*, and was hobnobbing with the crème de la crème of French and Russian émigré circles—Prokofiev, Chagall, Elsa Triolet—and was being courted by some of Paris's most fascinating men.

As the years wore on, as the harrowing, tragic Croisière Jaune succeeded the relatively calm Noire and her beloved uncle met his untimely end, the patterns of Sasha's life sometimes influenced my mother adversely. She developed a repugnance of exotic destinations. She insisted that ancient curses hung over many of those Oriental sites he had crossed, that every member of the expedition who penetrated them came, within seven years, to an eerily premature, mysterious end. She thought it folly for anyone to travel to Africa or Asia or even South America, to any place outside the safe, controllable Western world. "It's sheer folly to go to the Orient! My uncle died of it!" she would say to any friend planning a trip to Turkey or Iran or Egypt. India was a particular target of her disdain. "All that comes from India is dangerous," she declared some thirty years ago, when I told her I was taking up yoga. Yet while bemoaning Uncle Sasha's excessive passion for adventure and risk, she remained awed by his courage and his stoicism, avowed her deep gratitude to him, elaborated on his prodigal generosity, kindness, and elegance, preserved his archives well enough to pass some of them on to me, and missed him deeply for the rest of her days; as, I suspect, every member connected to the Iacovleff clan still does. He has remained our family's most romantic and legendary figure, its principal model of valor and stoicism. He took risks that most of us would never have dared to take on; he lived adventure for us.

Yet notwithstanding her passionate devotion to her uncle, her grandmother, and her aunt, a devotion that would imbue her with a lifelong sense of duty toward her kin, there had been one blight in my mother's life which her relatives had not been able to eradicate: Despite the terrible suffering she had experienced in Soviet Russia, despite the fact that she had barely survived its anarchy and deprivations, throughout her early Paris years she remained, like many of her compatriots, terribly homesick. "Here people take better care of me and I'm eating," she wrote her mother a year after arriving in France, "but all the same, none of it really feels right. Worst of all is the sense of solitude and loneliness. . . . I love love love Russia. Here everything may be wonderful, Paris may be the dream spot of the world, but I'm only a guest, and nothing will ever take the place of my native land, which I so treasure and revere."

In September of 1928, Tatiana's homesickness was allayed by a traveler from Russia—Vladimir Mayakovsky, the revolution's most celebrated poet—who was to be the love of her life.

THREE

Vladimir Vladimirovich Mayakovsky

He was over six feet tall, with a large, square jaw, a thick tousled mane of black hair, the massive-boned body of a boxer or sports trainer. His manner was brusque, brazen, often confrontational. He had a booming street heckler's voice, and in his innumerable public appearances—he was already a celebrity by the age of twenty-two—argued insolently with those who challenged his ideas. Boris Pasternak, who instantly fell under the spell of the brawling young poet, dramatized him as "a handsome youth of gloomy aspect with the bass voice of a deacon and the fists of a pugilist," who "sat in a chair as in the saddle of a motorcycle" and generally reminded him of a "young terrorist conspirator, a composite image of the minor provincial characters in Dostoyevsky's novels."

Mayakovsky was one of the founders of Russian Futurism, which was born in the intellectual ferment that followed the abortive revolution of 1905 and was far more iconoclastic than similar modernist movements in Europe. Beyond finding aesthetic forms appropriate to the machine age, it aimed above all to shock and offend bourgeois sensibility through its sheer impudence and extravagance. Its manifesto, drawn up in 1912 by Mayakovsky and David Burliuk and named "A Slap in the Face of Public Taste," called on all artists to "spit out the past, stuck like a bone in our throats" and to "throw Pushkin, Dostoyevsky, Tolstoy, etc.etc. overboard from the steamship of Modernity." In accord with these Futurist tenets, Mayakovsky's imagery was apocalyptic, deliberately coarse, often violent, as if presaging the cataclysmic changes that would affect Russia in 1917.

In "The Cloud in Trousers" of 1915, words jump into the poet's mind "like a naked prostitute from a burning brothel," the stroke of twelve falls "like a head from a block," the poet's thoughts "mus[e] on a sodden brain / like a bloated lackey on a greasy couch." Perhaps the most radical innovator in the history of Russian poetry, Mayakovsky attacked the hieratic dignity of Russian verse by stripping it of all traditional poetic diction and enriching it with shards of popular ditties, folk sayings, puns, commercial jingles, and irreverent rhyming schemes. Equally revolutionary in his use of prosody, he favored accentual verse over the syllabic-accentual meter of nineteenth-century Russian poetry and often broke up his lines into ladder patterns to indicate where to pause for breath when reading his poems aloud. Here is an example from his "Conversation with a Tax Collector about Poetry," in which he affirms the political power of verse:

> *The line*
> > *Is a fuse.*
> *The line burns to the end*
> > *And explodes.*
> *And the town*
> > *is blown sky-high*
> > > *In a strophe . . .*
> *The working class*
> > *Speaks*
> > > *Through my mouth*
> *and we,*
> > *proletarians,*
> *Are drivers of the pen.*

These innovations, and the poet's penchant for gigantism, created a hortatory art ideally suited to the immense audiences and vast public spaces that characterized Russian cultural gatherings in the revolutionary decades.

However, there were two Mayakovskys. His patriotic odes expressed his rapturous joy in the violent transformation of society and his pride in the new Soviet regime; but the principal themes of his lyric poems—"plaintive . . . majestic . . . infinitely doomed . . . almost calling for help," as Pasternak described them—were those of unrequited love, solitude, and self-destruction: "I am as lonely as the only eye / of a Man who goes to lead the blind"; "The heart yearns for a bullet / the throat craves a razor." This sense of solitude and chronic despair had roots, as it does in most poets, in the hardships of his childhood.

Vladimir Mayakovsky, 1928, photographed by Alexander Rodchenko.

The youngest of three children, Vladimir Vladimirovich Mayakovsky was born in 1893 in western Georgia, in a small village called Bagdati. His father, a member of the impoverished Russian gentry living in Georgia, supported his family by working as a forest ranger. In 1901, the family left for a larger town so that young Vladimir—Volodia to his family—might attend a proper school. Moody, restless, quick-tempered, early absorbed in books, the boy displayed a more than extraordinary precocity for politics. At the age of twelve, in the tumult of the "first" Russian Revolution of 1905, he began to steal his father's shotguns to deliver them to local revolutionary parties. The following year, after his father died of blood poisoning—caused by a pinprick incurred while filing some papers—Volodia moved to Moscow with his mother and two older sisters, Ludmila and Olga. The family lived on the edge of starvation, and it was there, during his first year of high school, that Mayakovsky began to work with the Russian Social Democratic Workers' Party, the radical wing of which was known as the Bolsheviks. By the age of fourteen, he was a full-fledged member of that party, with the nom de guerre "Comrade Konstantine." And at fifteen, having aided in the escape of a group of women prisoners, he spent nearly a year in a Moscow jail, where he read Shakespeare, Byron, Tolstoy, and numerous other classics and wrote his first poems.

By 1915, when he was twenty-two, the flamboyant, garrulous Mayakovsky was fraternizing with Boris Pasternak, Maxim Gorky, and many other prominent writers. (Gorky is said to have been "so deeply touched" by "The Cloud in Trousers" that he wept on the poet's vest.) By that time, Mayakovsky had also fallen desperately in love with the woman who longer than any other would serve as his muse—Lilia (Lili) Yuryevna Brik, née Kagan. The daughter of a prosperous Jewish jurist, the handsome, erotically obsessed, highly cultivated Lili grew up with an overwhelming ambition prevalent among women of the Russian intelligentsia: to be perpetuated in human memory by being the muse of a famous poet. When she was twenty, the vain, red-haired Lili married Osip Brik, the learned son of a wealthy jeweler whose politics, like hers, were ardently Marxist. The two made a pact to love each other "in the Chernyshevsky manner"—a reference to one of nineteenth-century Russia's most famous radical thinkers, who was an early advocate of "open marriages." Living at the heart of an artistic bohemia and receiving the intelligentsia in the salon of his delectable wife, Osip Brik, true to his promise, calmly accepted his wife's infidelities from the start. In fact, upon hearing his wife confess that she had gone to bed with the famous young poet Vladimir Mayakovsky, Brik exclaimed "How could you refuse anything to that man!"

Mayakovsky's sexual relationship with Lili would last only from 1917 to 1923. But his close friendship with Osip, who would become a noted literary scholar and a pioneer of formalist criticism (his books bore titles such as *Rhythm and Syntax in Russian Verse*) created a bond with both Briks that far transcended any sexual attachment. For the rest of his life, "Osia" Brik remained the poet's most trusted adviser, his most fervent proselytizer, and also a cofounder with him of the most dynamic avant-garde journal of the early Soviet era, *Left Front of Art*, which published artists and writers such as Sergei Eisenstein, Aleksandr Rodchenko, and Isaac Babel. In 1918, when Mayakovsky and the Briks became inseparable, he simply moved in with them. Throughout the rest of his life, he made his home at a succession of flats that the Briks occupied. He also had a tiny studio space next to the old Lubianka prison, where he worked and carried on his numerous liaisons with other women. Osip Brik enjoyed his own occasional flings, and the ménage à trois seemed to prosper. The Briks offered Mayakovsky both independence and the stability of a family life, which he had not enjoyed since childhood. In return, the poet, who by 1918 had become a popular idol, became the Briks' principal breadwinner; the substantial publishing royalties and lecture fees the poet earned in Russia and abroad supplemented the meager income the Briks made through literary criticism and occasional work that Lili found in films.

Mayakovsky's liaison with Lili, however, was as tormented as his friendship with Osip Brik was serene. Mutual friends remained amazed, throughout the following years, by the despotic manner in which she treated him and the fearful obsequiousness with which this dynamic, seemingly powerful man catered to his mistress's every wish. ("If I'm a complete rag, use me to dust your staircase," he wrote her in one particularly self-abasing letter.) There was a strong streak of masochism in Mayakovsky, and Lili seemed to have been invented to satisfy it. For years, with her tacit approval, his poems publicly lamented her heartlessness and inconstancy—in "The Backbone Flute," of 1915, he likens her rouged lips to "a monastery hacked from frigid rock." The poet's unrequited passion for Lili even incited him to flirt with death, in 1916, by playing Russian roulette (that first time, he won).

Mayakovsky's self-sacrificing impulses were mirrored in his politics. In October of 1917, he settled into the revolution with greater enthusiasm than any other Russian writer of his stature. "To accept or not to accept? For me . . . this question never arose," he wrote. "It is *my* revolution." No task that exalted the Soviet regime was too menial for Mayakovsky. For some years, repressing the expression of all personal emotions, he celebrated, in rabble-rousing verse purged of Futurist excesses, the building of dams

Vladimir Mayakovsky

and factories, the lyricism of Soviet industrial machinery. "But now's no time for a lover and his lass," he wrote. "All my ringing poetic power I give to you / attacking class." As a member of the People's Commissariat for Education, and as a protégé of Anatoly Lunacharsky, the commissar for education, Mayakovsky was sent to lecture all over Russia to proselytize for the Soviet regime. Covering as many as eighteen cities in one month, this "drum-beater of the Revolution," as he called himself, was particularly adulated by factory workers and younger audiences and could draw thousands to his readings. He is credited with having played an important role in rallying the Russian people to Bolshevism.

Beginning in 1919, during the civil war, he also used his considerable skills as a graphic artist to write and design governmental propaganda posters, sometimes churning out several posters a day. His popular commercial jingles—he wrote hundreds of them in a single year—promoted state-manufactured macaroni products, candies, galoshes, tires, even infant pacifiers: "Clothe the body, feed the stomach, fill the mind / Everything man needs at the Gum [the state-owned department store on Red Square] he will find," and "The best pacifiers ever sold / He'll suck on them till he's very old."

In 1924, Mayakovsky produced a two-thousand-line poem commemorating the passing of Lenin, which was greeted with ovations wherever he read it. ("The genuine / wise / human / tremendous / Lenin . . . Yet wouldn't I / who rarely came close to him / give / my own life / in a stupor of ecstasy, / for one little breath / of his.") Throughout the 1920s, Mayakovsky was also sent to numerous foreign countries to propagandize his nation's achievements, acting as cultural ambassador to Latvia, Germany, Poland, Czechoslovakia, France, and also, in 1925, to Cuba, Mexico, and the United States, where he remained for several months and fathered a daughter by an American woman of Russian descent, Elly Jones. But the frantic pace of the poet's patriotic activities, the tensions between his private and public personae, the suppression of his selfhood for the greater glory of his country took their toll in deepening depressions. Increasingly, he realized that by channeling all his energies into the revolution he was threatening to ruin his monumental talent, that he had stepped "on the throat of my own song." "Only a very great, true love might still save me," he told his close friend Roman Jakobson, who would eventually become one of the twentieth century's most eminent linguists and literary critics. Jakobson looks on 1928, when Mayakovsky met Tatiana Yakovleva in Paris, as a pivotal year in which the poet "broke," when "living alone had become intolerable to him, when he felt the need for an enormous change."

By 1928, Lili Brik's younger sister, Elsa Triolet—a shrewd, winsome émigré who was devoted to her sibling—had been living in Paris and Berlin for eight years. Since Mayakovsky's first trip to France, in 1922, when she served as Parisian guide and interpreter for the poet (who refused to ever learn any foreign language), Elsa had acted as Lili's spy, reporting on each of the poet's romantic escapades. But his foreign affairs did not give the sisters cause for alarm until 1928, when he set off for Nice to see his

American girlfriend Elly Jones. She had brought the daughter she bore him, now two and a half years old, for a first visit with her father. Although Mayakovsky's distaste for children was notorious, and the meeting, from Jones's point of view, was a fiasco, Lili and Elsa were fearful that the poet might be persuaded to follow mother and child to America. To distract him from the American menace, Elsa decided to introduce Volodia to a beautiful, bright young Russian emigré of her acquaintance: my mother, Tatiana Yakovleva. On October 25, the very day of his return from Nice, Elsa took the poet to visit a Paris internist who had close links with the émigré community. She had learned from the doctor's wife that Tatiana Yakovleva had an appointment with him that same morning.

But the sisters' scheming had unexpected results. Volodia kept his appointment at the doctor's, took one look at Tatiana, and fell head over heels in love with her. Upon one of the few occasions my mother mentioned Mayakovsky to me, she said that he insisted on taking her home in a cab, spread his coat over her knees to keep her warm, and upon depositing her at the front door of her grandmother's flat fell on his knees to declare his love. ("Yes, on his knees on the sidewalk," my mother commented when telling the story, "and it wasn't even lunchtime yet.")

The *coup de foudre* seemed to be reciprocal. From October 25, Tatiana Yakovleva and Mayakovsky saw each other every day until December 2, when he had to return to Russia upon the expiration of his visa. Mayakovsky took pride in going about Paris with the tall blond beauty whose dynamism was equal to his, and he even respected her own considerable Puritanism—Tatiana, refusing the bohemian mores of many of her peers, was determined to keep her virginity until marriage. On her part, she was understanding about the enormous complications of Mayakovsky's character. He dreaded solitude and was intensely jealous and demanding about his friends, wanting their undivided attention around the clock, looking on it as treason when a comrade was unable to play chess with him on the evenings he wished. He was in every sense paranoid and had a hypochondriac compulsiveness about physical hygiene, which may have been caused by the circumstances of his father's death—he never touched doorknobs without a handkerchief protecting his hands, always carried a metal soap dish in his pocket, and when in any public place he wiped drinking glasses with his own handkerchief before touching them with his lips.

The relationship was also rife with family difficulties. Severely chaperoned by her prudish and rabidly anticommunist relatives, Tatiana had to do a lot of fibbing to carry on her courtship with the Soviet poet. Lying outrageously to her doting babushka, she enlisted a few loyal friends to say she was going to their houses. "Babushka would have had a heart attack if she'd learned whom I was dining with every night," she recalled fifty years later. "The Bolshevik and her granddaughter, smuggled with great difficulty out of a starving Russia turned into hell by the revolution!"

But Bolshevism didn't seem to pose a problem for the lovers in the nostalgic landscape of Paris's émigré community. Mayakovsky deliberately did not speak of world events to Tatiana, and her own anticommunist scruples were apparently absolved by the great narcissistic pleasure she took in the love of a famous poet. As for Mayakovsky, his infatuation had deepened when he discovered Tatiana's extraordinary knowledge of Russian poetry. Sitting with him at the various cafés they frequented—La Coupole, Le Voltaire, La Rotonde, Le Danton, La Closerie des Lilas—she recited poetry by the hour. How could he not have been seduced when he heard her speak out the whole of his own "The Cloud in Trousers," some seven hundred lines long? He told all his friends that Tatiana had "absolute pitch" for poetry, in the way some musicians have for their medium. She replaced Lili as his confidante. He informed her of his domestic arrangements with the Briks, and notwithstanding her primness she seemed to take his ménage à trois in stride. She even helped him to find a dress for Lili and to purchase the four-cylinder gray Renault Lili had asked him to bring back from Paris.

The poet proposed marriage within the first fortnight, a suggestion Tatiana seems to have received in a mood of cool noncommittalness. Over a lunch at the Grande Chaumière in Montparnasse in November, he presented her with two poems he had composed and dedicated to her. They were written in his neat, slanting hand in a small green notebook, which I now own. One was called "Letter to Comrade Kostrov on the Essence of

Love," the other "Letter to Tatiana Yakovleva." Here are sample lines from
the first one, which recalled their meeting in the office of a Paris doctor:

Picture this:
>   *a beauty*
>   *all framed in furs*
> *and beads,*
>   *enters a drawing room.*
> *I*
>   *seized this beauty*
>   *and said:*
> *—did I speak right*
>   *Or wrong?—*
> *Comrade,*
>   *I come from Russia;*
> *I am famous in my land.*

"Letter to Comrade Kostrov"—the first poem he had ever dedicated to
any woman other than Lili Brik—was the most passionate love lyric
Mayakovsky had written in years, and it intimated that he had found the
"very great, true love" that, as he'd told Roman Jakobson, might yet save him.

To love
>   *means this:*
>   *To run*
> *into the depths of a yard*
>   *and, till the rook-black night,*
> *chop wood*
>   *with a shining axe. . . .*
> *Love,*
>   *for us*
>   *is no paradise of arbors—*
> *to us*

> *love tells us, humming,*
> *that the stalled engine*
> > *of the heart*
> *has started to work*
> > *again.*

"Letter to Tatiana Yakovleva" was even more explicit: it urged her, in no uncertain terms, to return to Moscow with him. (The phrase "I'll take you," in the original Russian, has strong sexual overtones.)

> *Come to the crossroads*
> > *of my big and clumsy arms. . . .*
> *In one way or another*
> > *I'll take you*
> *By yourself*
> > *or along with Paris.*

The couple were both striking in their statuesque beauty, their magnetic, powerful presences. Beyond their passion for poetry, they shared many predilections and character traits, chief among which was their great generosity, their narcissistic streaks, and the exhibitionism with which they each cloaked their shyness and deep insecurities. As Tatiana introduced Mayakovsky to her French and émigré acquaintances, the couple's increasingly public romance was not lost on Lili's sister, Elsa, who lived in the same little Montparnasse hotel as the poet and was beginning an affair with the French communist poet Louis Aragon. (They would subsequently marry and become the star couple of international communism.) Back in Moscow, informed of Paris events by Elsa and perhaps also by the secret police, which already thought of all important Soviet travelers abroad as potential defectors and kept close track of them, Lili Brik fretted: "Who is that woman Volodia is crazy about . . . to whom he's writing poems (!!) . . . and who is said to faint when she hears she word 'merde'?" she wrote her sister.

Lili was to find out soon enough. Mayakovsky's visa expired on December 3, and he had no choice but to go back to Moscow. Although he was scheduled to return to Paris in May, after the first run of his play *The Bedbug*, his separation from Tatiana seems to have been extremely sorrowful. Before leaving Paris, Mayakovsky went to a florist's and ordered that a dozen roses be sent to Tatiana every Sunday until his return; every bouquet was accompanied by his visiting card, each one bearing a different message.

In the first of many letters my mother wrote her mother shortly after Mayakovsky's departure, her grief at her separation from the poet was mitigated by her naïve narcissistic pride in being his new muse.

"He's a remarkable man," Tatiana wrote,

> *totally different from the way I'd imagined him to be. He's wonderful to me, and it was a great drama for him to leave here for at least six months. He telephoned me from Berlin, and it was one shout of pain. A telegram arrives every day, and flowers every week. . . . Our entire house is filled with flowers, it's adorable of him. . . . I felt extremely sad when he left. He's the most talented person I've ever met. . . . I think you'd be interested in hearing the poems "Letter to Tatiana Yakovleva," and "Letter on Love."*

She felt all the more drawn to Mayakovsky because he reminded her so poignantly of Russia.

> *When I was with him I felt I was in Russia, and since he's left I long for Russia all the more. But all of this I write to [you,] my* mamulenka, *and to no-one else. He left me two copies of "my" poems, I'm sending you one. For the time being don't show these [poems] to anyone. They'll be published soon. When he read them here they had a colossal success. They belong to his very best lyrical work.*

A few weeks later, in response to a letter from her mother, she continues to delight in her status as the poet's muse. (She always sends her affectionate wishes to *Père*, as she refers to her second stepfather, Nikolai Alexandrovich Orlov.)

> *However spoiled I am, he was absolutely amazing in his thoughtfulness and concern for me and I long for him terribly. . . . Most of the folk I meet here are "society people" who have no desire to use their brains. . . . M. challenged me. . . . [H]e*

stretched my mind, and, most importantly, he forced me to recollect Russia poignantly. . . . The masses here court him, his poetry captivates even the French with its rhythm and the power of his reading. "My" poems were a great success here. Did Père like them? . . . He evoked in me such a longing for Russia and for all of you. Literally, I almost came back. And now everything seems petty and flat. He's such a colossal figure, both physically and morally, that after him, there is literally a void. He is the first man who has been able to leave his mark on my soul.

Tatiana in Paris in 1929, at the time of her romance with Mayakovsky.

Mayakovsky was writing to Tatiana with equal fervor. It was in his Futurist temperament to prefer telegrams to letters—they got there faster—and he sent her at least one a week. "Write more often got your letter am writing miss you incredibly love you kiss you your Vol," some of his cables of that season read. "Received your letter thank you sent you letter and books miss you love you kiss you Vol." As for letters, they came every few weeks. The first of them was begun on December 24, a few weeks after his return to Moscow.

My own beloved Tanik.

*Letters move so slowly, and I need to know every minute what is on your mind. That's why I send you telegrams. Send me piles of both! I take such joy in each word you write, I received one of your letters just now. I read it until I was saturated with it. . . . I've been writing a new play [*The Bedbug*] twenty hours*

*a day without food or drink. My head swelled so from this labor that my hat ceased
to fit. . . . I work like an ox, my muzzle bent, red-eyed. . . . Even my eyes gave
up. . . . I still have to put cold compresses on them. But never mind . . . it doesn't
matter about my eyes, I won't need them until I see you again, because outside of
you there's no one to look at.*

With a veneer of Soviet patriotism, the closing lines communicate his insistence that she return with him to the Soviet Union; Mayakovsky, however,
seems to be aware that Soviet censors may be perusing his correspondence
with an émigré, and his references to marriage are oblique and often coded.

*Still mountains and vastnesses of work—as soon as I'll finish it I'll rush to you.
If my pen and I collapse from all this business you will come to me. Yes? Yes??
You're not a Parisian, you're a true working girl. In our country all must come
to love you, and everyone is obliged to be happy [when you return]. I'm carrying
your name like a holiday flag on our urban buildings. It is flying and waving
above me and I don't lower it for a millimeter. Your poem ["Letter to Comrade Kostrov"] is being published in* Molodaia Guardiia. *I'll send you the
issue. . . .*

I hug you dearest one, kiss you, and love you. Your Vol.

(This diminutive of Volodia was a play on words. In Russia, *vol* means
"ox," an animal with which the poet particularly identified and in whose
semblance he often caricatured himself in his letters or greeting cards.)

Mayakovsky was usually honest with his women. Upon returning to
Moscow, he had confirmed Lili's suspicions about the beautiful Russian
émigré and read her his "Tatiana poems." "You've deceived me for the first
time!" Lili said, in tears, furious that he had defied her long-held resolve to
be his one and only muse. A short time later, he told her, over dinner at the
flat they shared, that he wished to marry Tatiana and bring her back to Russia. Lili responded by smashing a precious piece of china.

Mayakovsky's second letter to my mother, written on New Year's Eve of
1929, alludes to Lili's jealousy of my mother.

Sweet Tanik, my beloved,

I don't like it without you. Think about it and collect your thoughts (and then your belongings) and adjust your heart to my hope—to take you in my paws and bring you to us, to me in Moscow. Let's think about it and then talk. Let's make our separation a test.

If we love each other, is it good to exhaust heart and time working through the telegraphic poles?

It is the 31st now (at 12 midnight) and . . . I'm totally saturated with melancholy longing. Tender comrade, I clinked glasses and proposed a toast to you, and Lilia Yuryevna chided me, "If you're suffering so why not immediately run to her?" Well, I shall run to you, but for the time being I must press on with my work. I work until my eyes get blurry and my shoulders crack. . . . When I'm totally exhausted I say the word 'Tatiana' and return to my paper. You and the other sun, you will later comfort me. . . .

To work and to wait for you is my <u>only</u> joy.

Love, love me absolutely, please. I hug and love and kiss you.

Vol.

Lili Brik was not the only person worried about the romance. By December of 1928 Stalin had gained absolute power and was greatly tightening government control of the press. "Letter to Comrade Kostrov" came under some critical censure when it was published. The poet had been assigned to write verses about Paris for an official publication of the Communist Party; what kind of bourgeois decadence had he fallen into, celebrating the beauty of an émigré "framed in furs and beads"! Even my grandmother seems to have expressed concern about the romance, for the tone in which Tatiana wrote her a month after Volodia's return to Russia was highly defensive.

I've not at all decided to come back to Russia or, as you say, to "throw myself" at him. And he is not returning to Paris to "pick me up" but to see me. . . . Don't forget that your girl is already 22, and that few women in their whole lives have been as loved as I have been in my short one. (This is something I inherited from you. I have a reputation here of being a "femme fatale.")

The young woman enjoyed flaunting her success to Mom. But she was torn between two conflicting emotions: the pleasure she took in her safe, glamorous Paris life and her budding career; and her temptation to return to suffering Russia and to the loved ones who remained there.

Moreover, on the whole I don't want to get married now: I'm too attached to my freedom and my independence—my hat business, my "orangerie" (my room is always filled with flowers). Various admirers want to take me to various countries, but of course none of them seem like anyone at all compared to M, and I would almost certainly choose him above all others; how wise and learned he is! And the possibility of seeing you again plays a large role in all this; by moments I long for you terribly.

Then there is the first intimation that Tatiana, unbeknownst even to her closest confidante—her own mother—is furtively keeping a few Parisian men on the back burner who might offer her a solid, comfortable high-society marriage. "Furthermore I'm living through all kinds of dramas. . . ." she writes her *mamulenka*. "There are two other suitors, it's a vicious magical circle."

As for Volodia, seemingly unconcerned with the criticism of "Letter to Comrade Kostrov," he rushed back to Tatiana on February 14, three months earlier than he had promised, not even waiting for notices of his play *The Bedbug*. (It was directed by Vsevolod Meyerhold, with a musical score by Dmitri Shostakovich, and received mixed, but some enthusiastic, reviews.) The lovers' reunion seems to have been as idyllic as their first meeting. They again saw each other daily and even traveled a bit together, going to Le Touquet for a weekend. He wrote her more poems, small ones this time, in a style parodic of nineteenth-century verse, which he signed "Marquis VM" (a teasing allusion to her fondness for titles). My mother detected a change in him: "He did not criticize Russia directly," she recollected a half century later, "but he was obviously disillusioned." This impression coincides with the recollections of a Russian friend with whom the poet spent an evening during a brief, financially disastrous gambling trip to Nice, and before whom he broke into sobs, saying, "I've stopped being a poet. . . . Now I'm a . . . state functionary."

In April, Mayakovsky's visa ran out once more, and he was forced to return to Moscow. The suitors decided to meet again in Paris in October, when Tatiana would make up her mind about marrying him. She had given him a Waterman pen as a farewell present. Their farewell lunch, held at the Grande-Chaumière with a group of their mutual friends, had the aura of an engagement party. As they walked toward Mayakovsky's train that evening, hand in hand, at the Gare du Nord, their mutual longing and sorrow were evident to their acquaintances.

The first surviving letter of Mayakovsky's after his return to Russia is dated May 15 and seems to address some pique Tatiana had expressed toward him.

> My dear, my sweet, my beloved Tanik,
>
> Only now has my mind cleared, and I can think and write a little. Please don't scold and yell at me, there have been so many unpleasantnesses, from the very smallest (bug) size to the elephant size—that you mustn't be upset at me. I'll begin in order:
>
> I absolutely and enormously love Tanik.
>
> I'm only beginning to work, I will now with great care write my Bathhouse.

A few lines follow in which he sums up the strikingly generous arrangements he's made for her mother—a prodigality that was not lost on Tatiana—and informs her that he's soon going off on a lecture tour of the Crimea.

The letter continues: "Without your letters I can't go on. . . . I'm longing for you as never before. . . . I love you always and entirely. Very and absolutely—Your Vol."

Another letter came in July. This time, Tatiana seems to have complained that he was sending her more telegrams than letters.

> My dear, my own, sweet and beloved Tanik.
>
> You promised to write every 3 days. I waited waited waited. I crawled under the carpet but the letter was two weeks old and a sad one. Don't get sad, little girl. It can not be that we are not ordained to always be together. . . . You're constantly saying that I don't write you and what are my telegrams, puppy dogs?? . . .

I jump into work, remembering that until October there isn't that much time. . . . My lovely, beloved Tanik don't forget me, I love you so much, and I'm so longing to see you. I kiss all of you, your Vol.

Write *to me!!!!*

By July, both of them are complaining that they're not receiving any letters. And one is led to wonder to what degree Russian security services might have blocked the correspondence between the Soviet Union's poet laureate and his émigré love. One also wonders whether Lili Brik, who had full access to Mayakovsky's studio on Lubiansky Passage, might have intercepted them.

Tatiana's longing, that summer of 1929, seems to have been as deep as the poet's. "Write me and let me know his mood, I yearn for him terribly," she writes in July to her sister Ludmilla, a destitute aspiring actress in Moscow. "Life seems very dull without him. There are very few people of his calibre here." That same month, in a subsequent letter to her mother, she refers to the magnanimous way in which Mayakovsky was continuing to provide for her relatives in Russia: Upon Tatiana's request, he had brought clothes for her sister and sent her some money. He had also organized a trip to the Crimea for her ailing mother, which, to Tatiana's sorrow, her mother had declined, perhaps out of pride.

"I was very sad that you didn't want to go to the Crimea," Tatiana wrote. "I'd so much dreamed about it. V. V. also wrote me a sad letter; he had hoped . . . to arrange this for you. After all, the best thing he can do for me (during such a long absence) is to look after you and Lilochka. . . . And it is this attribute of his that I particularly treasure; a limitless kindness and concern. I await his arrival in the autumn with great joy. There aren't other people of his calibre here. In his relationship to women in general, and to me in particular, he is an absolute gentleman."

"Absolute gentleman" would remain an all-important phrase in my mother's vocabulary until her death in 1991. On the rare occasions she talked about Mayakovsky, she unfailingly stated that he was "a man of irresistible charm and sex appeal," with "a rare sense of humor," a man, moreover, who, as she primly put it, was "extraordinarily careful about my virginity." His "exquisite manners," his "tenderness and concern" for her, his elegance and perfect taste in clothes ("he reminded one more of an English aristocrat than a Bolshevik poet") made him the most "absolute gentleman" my mother had ever met.

But there's no way of knowing whether she would have retained that opinion of the poet if she'd known of the life he led in Moscow after his return from Paris.

FOUR

The Mayakovsky Legacy

T hroughout the thirteen years that Mayakovsky and the Briks had shared a home, Lili, who went through dozens of new men each year, tolerated Volodia's affairs, even approved of them, as long as they remained lighthearted—"let the kid release his energies" seems to have been her attitude. But even though she had not slept with him for several years, any serious emotion he displayed for a woman was a cause for her great concern. There was the issue of family finances: Volodia was the Briks' meal ticket. There was also Lili's determination to remain the unique, unrepeatable love of a great poet's life. So in the spring of 1929, once Tatiana Yakovleva had entered into Mayakovsky's very poetry and inspired his most passionate love lyrics, Lili realized that she was dealing not with another pretty miss but with her most dangerous rival to date. (She could not have been thrilled by the line in "Letter to Comrade Kostrov" that described his emotions for Lili as "the stalled engine of the heart.") Seven months earlier, she had mobilized her sister to counteract the threat of the American girl. This time, she turned to her husband to make the decisive move.

In May 1929, within two weeks of Mayakovsky's return from Paris, a pretty twenty-one-year-old actress at the prestigious Moscow Art Theater received a call from Osip Brik. Veronika ("Nora") Polonskaya, a pert, dim-

pled blonde who was married to a popular older actor of that company and
was just beginning to rise in its lower ranks, was somewhat surprised to hear
from Brik, with whom she had only a brief acquaintance. He was propos-
ing an outing to the horse races with Vladimir Mayakovsky. Would she join
them? She accepted.

Lili had been on target: Volodia began to pursue Nora relentlessly. Although she was initially put off by his brusqueness, upon their first tête-à-
tête the young woman was taken by his "gentle, delicate" manner, by the
beauty of his powerful bass voice, by his commitment to Bolshevik principles. Within a few weeks, "Norochka" was returning the poet's infatuation
and coming to his little studio on Lubiansky Passage every day. That summer, they spent some idyllic time together in the Yalta and Sochi area, where
he had been sent on another extensive lecture tour.

As I read through Nora Polonskaya's memoirs at the archives of
Moscow's Mayakovsky Museum, I was, for the first time, rather confused by
the state of the poet's emotions. After all, this was a man renowned for his
sincerity and forthrightness, a man who had never been dishonest or duplic-
itous with any woman, or, for that matter, with any male comrade. By this
stage of my research, I had grown terribly fond of Vladimir Vladimirovich,
perhaps even a bit enamored of him, and I tended to invent excuses for him
whenever his conduct was questionable. Well, I rationalized on this occasion,
Volodia needed some immediate consolation; he was noted for his highly
developed libido, just think of the frustration he must have experienced
throughout the months of courting my primly chaste mother. . . . But his affair with Polonskaya was made all the more perplexing by the ardor of a letter he wrote to Tatiana on July 16, 1929, just before he left for his lecture
tour of the Crimea, where he planned to meet with the actress.

> Tanik, I've begun to miss you terribly, terribly. You must notice yourself that
> you almost do not write to me. Does it bore you?
>
> My child, write me and promise to visit me if I will need it badly. Give me
> until October (we've both decided), and then I can't imagine being without you.
> From September on I'll begin to make wings to fly to you. Do you still remember
> me? I'm so tall, pigeon-toed and antipathetic. Today I'm also gloomy.

My own beloved Tanik, don't forget that you and I are rodnye *[kin to each other] and that we are each essential to the other.*

I hug, kiss and love you

Your Vol

The phrase I've translated as "we're kin to each other," "*my rodnye,*" is a loaded and deeply tender one. *Rod* means "family, birth, origin"; and when used by lovers "*my rodnye*" implies that the loved one is "one of my own family." These are words that no Russian man would use toward a woman for whom he has an exclusively physical attraction, and they give an added depth of tenderness to Mayakovsky's letters. He uses "*rodnaia*" again as he once more reproaches Tatiana for not writing to him, and he tries to speed her return with yet another salvo of praise for Soviet society.

My own beloved Tanik,

Excuse me for writing so often. You see, I don't pay attention to your silence. Why do you, rodnaia, take so many counts on our exchange of letters?? Detka *[little girl]. . . . We are now better off, in this society, than people have been at any time, in any place. Such a huge communal work has never been known in human history, Tanik! You're a super-capable girl. Become an engineer. You can do it, don't spend yourself entirely on hats. . . . I want this so much, Tan'ka the engineer somewhere in Altai [a mountain chain in central Asia]. Let's do it, right?*

Dear child, write and love. I want to see you sooner.

The notion of my frivolous, luxury-loving mother returning to an increasingly frugal Russia to build socialism as an engineer in central Asia always strikes me as very comical. On the other hand, the last of Mayakovsky's letters to have survived, written on October 5, often brings tears to my eyes.

My own beloved [rodnaia]. I don't have and could never have any other endearments for you. Keep this word in mind for at least 55 years.

Could it be true that you don't write only because "I'm not very generous with words"? This is absurd—Impossible to describe and document all the sorrows that make me even more silent. Or even more likely, could it be that French

poets, or people of more common professions, are now more pleasing to you? . . .
But if that's the case then no one at any time will ever convince me, and you will
not become less beloved to me.

My telegram to you was returned with a message that they could not find you
at that address. Write, write, write, dear child. I still don't believe that you've grown
indifferent to me. Write today. Books are piled up and other news which are making
little screams and begging to go into your paws.

I kiss you, love you
Your Vol

Mayakovsky's reference to "all the sorrows that make me even more
silent" (in earlier letters he had already mentioned "many unpleasant-
nesses") has everything to do with the events of 1929, what Russians call
god velikogo pereloma, "the year of the great turning-point." It was in 1929 that
the relatively relaxed and pluralistic first decade of Soviet culture came to
an end. And to follow the denouement of Mayakovsky's romance with my
mother, one needs to grasp that year's pivotal importance.

The autumn of 1928 had marked the ascendance of Joseph Stalin to
unchallenged power in the Communist Party hierarchy and the beginning of
his violent transformation of Soviet society. This entailed, among other
measures, the forced collectivization of Soviet peasantry; a series of Five-
Year Plans, which called for a quadrupling of the output in heavy industry
and returned the management of all enterprises to the central government;
a resumption of cultural isolation from the West; and—most relevant to
Mayakovsky—the imposition of strict party controls over education and
culture. As steps in the cementing of his dictatorship, in January of 1929
Stalin banished Leon Trotsky from the Soviet Union and soon began to single out cultural organizations and particular writers for opprobrium. By that
autumn, Stalin's regime was making it increasingly difficult to travel abroad.

This "Revolution from Above," as it is called, also enabled the Soviet
Union's most oppressive literary faction, the Russian Association of Proletarian Writers (known as RAPP), to gain ascendance over literature. In December 1929, an editorial in the Communist Party paper *Pravda* demanded
that all Soviet writers join RAPP and adopt its edicts, which required a

strict adherence to proletarian values, and the elimination of all "bourgeois" and "deviationist" writing. This is the context within which Mayakovsky, in the early fall of 1929, was either denied a visa to return to Paris to continue his courtship of my mother or else warned that he should not even risk the political dangers of asking for one.

The autumn of 1929 is also that moment at which any precise rendering of my mother's romance with Mayakovsky becomes extremely difficult and falls prey to conjecture and to aging survivors' capricious memories of the past. But whatever versions are accepted, it is clear that the same historical forces that were about to cleave asunder, for many decades, the two Russias—the increasingly rigid Soviet state and the beloved lost homeland of émigré communities throughout the world—were central to the finality of the lovers' separation.

My mother's version of the denouement goes as follows: Shortly after she received that last October letter from Mayakovsky, she heard from Elsa Triolet that he had been denied a visa. (Although Tatiana's ferocious pride was to keep her from ever admitting it, it is most probable that Triolet, at her sister's suggestion, had also advised Tatiana of his romance with Polonskaya.) Smarting from that revelation, warned by friends of the growing repression in Russia, recalling the poet's repeated hints, in whatever letters had got through to her, about all the great "difficulties" he had been having, she decided, sorrowfully, that their future together was doomed. And she set about making other plans for her life. One of the two persons in the "vicious magical circle" of suitors she had mentioned earlier that year to her mother seems to have been a dashing French diplomat four years her elder, Vicomte Bertrand du Plessix, a specialist in Slavic languages who for the previous year had been posted as an attaché at the French embassy in Warsaw. In mid-October of 1929, when he returned to Paris for one of his rare home leaves, she accepted his offer of marriage.

Unfortunately, between mid-October and late December 1929, the period during which my mother must have first mentioned du Plessix in her letters to Russia and announced her engagement and pending marriage, there is a total gap in her correspondence with her mother: No letters have survived. Documents at the Mayakovsky Museum reveal that in the early

Vladimir Mayakovsky in Moscow, late 1929.

1930s the Soviet secret police made several visits to my grandmother's flat in Penza and absconded with possessions much valued by Stalin's regime: missives from abroad. Whether by coincidence or by design, the visitors seized all letters written by my mother in the last two and a half months of 1929. Her last October communication, posted on the fifteenth of that month, tersely states that "Mayakovsky is not coming this winter." There are no more letters until late December, after her marriage to du Plessix. So for this phase of the romance's denouement, it is instructive to hear out Lili Brik, who decades later recalled in a letter the October evening upon which Mayakovsky first heard of my mother's engagement.

> *We were quietly sitting at the dining room table on Gendrikov Street. Volodia was waiting for his car, he was about to go to Leningrad for several appearances. . . . A letter came from Elsa. As always, I started to read the letter aloud. Along with the various other events that Elsa was sharing with us was the news that Yakovleva, whom Volodia came to know in Paris and with whom, out of sheer inertia, he was still in love, was engaged to marry some French viscount or other, that she was going to marry him in a church, in a white dress and orange blossoms, that she was very concerned that Volodia not learn about this because he might cause a scandal.*

In this transparently disingenuous passage, in which the phrase "out of sheer inertia" gives away Lili's hostility to my mother, Brik then pretends that she would not have read that passage to Mayakovsky if her sister had warned her properly. She continued: "Volodia had grown pale. He stood up and said: 'Well, time to go.' 'Where are you off to?' I asked. 'It's early, the car hasn't come yet.' But he took up his suitcase, gave me a kiss and went out."

Lili's account of the poet's state of mind also includes the recollections of his chauffeur, who related that upon meeting him that night the poet had uttered a curse, then remained totally silent during the ride to the station. "Do excuse me, please do not be angry with me, Comrade Gamazin," he said as they arrived. "Please, my heart is aching." The following day, Lili Brik decided to follow Mayakovsky to Leningrad to boost his morale. As they rode together from one crowded reading to another, Brik reports, Mayakovsky kept making derisive comments about French nobility—whatever his growing dif-

Tatiana and Bertrand du Plessix on their honeymoon in Italy, December 1929.

ficulties with the Soviet regime, he was particularly vexed that he had been up-staged by an aristocrat in the affections of the woman he loved. "'We're not French viscounts, we work hard,' he would say, or 'If I were a baron.'" Even Brik admits that Mayakovsky lived in a state of denial from then on, embittered and refusing to accept the reality of Tatiana's impending marriage.

As for Tatiana's recollections of October 1929, they are excerpted from a series of conversations with the closest friend she had in her last decade of life, the Russian scholar and ballet historian Gennady Smakov. Smakov was planning to write a biography of her, and she spoke more candidly with him about the past than she had with anyone to that time.

"I loved [Mayakovsky], he himself knew it, but . . . my love was not strong enough to go away with him," my mother told Smakov. "And if he'd returned a third time I'm not absolutely sure that I wouldn't have left. . . . I missed him terribly. I might well have left. . . . Fifty-fifty. . . . I got married in order to untie the knot. In the fall of '29 du Plessix came to Paris and started courting me. Since Mayakovsky could not come I was totally free. I thought that he did not want to take on that heavy a responsibility, to be stuck with a young woman. . . . I thought to myself, perhaps he just got scared? How to explain to you? I suddenly felt free . . . [du Plessix] came openly to [my grandmother's] house—we had nothing to hide, he was a Frenchman, a bachelor, it wasn't Mayakovsky, but I married him, and he was amazing towards me."

"Did you love du Plessix?" Smakov asks. A long pause follows. My mother was an honest woman.

"No, I didn't love him," she replies. "It was a flight from Mayakovsky. Clearly, the frontier was closed to him, whereas I wanted to build a normal life, I wanted children, do you understand? Francine was born nine months and two days after the wedding."

My parents were married on December 23, 1929. My mother's letters to my grandmother resume again six days later, during her honeymoon, which was spent in Italy. In the first letter, posted in Naples, she describes her wedding. Her uncle, Alexandre Iacovleff, had given her away. The wedding dress he had purchased for her had been *"kolossal'niy ouspekh,"* "a colossal success." She and Bertrand were about to set forth for Pompeii. He was "enormously caring, a tender husband and a marvelous companion." (Within three years, they were estranged. Perhaps my father sensed that my mother had not loved him. Perhaps he was the first to realize—as I only began to when I finally read these letters—that Mayakovsky was Tatiana's only great love.)

Mayakovsky's last months brought a succession of heartbreaks. His play *The Bathhouse*, a violent attack on the increasingly rigid Soviet bureaucracy, which he felt was betraying the 1917 revolution, was received with what one of his friends described as "murderous coldness." But the public's animosity was becoming far more personal. Even though he seldom used the car he had brought to Lili the previous year and had to get her permission each time he wished to borrow it, he was being censured for owning such a luxurious and foreign-made possession. He was even criticized for the pen of foreign make he always carried on him—the Waterman that had been my mother's parting gift. His exhibition *Twenty Years of Work*, which opened on February 1, 1930—posters, paintings, graphics, diverse editions of his books—was boycotted by all official writers' groups and was visited almost exclusively by students. He paced the empty rooms, with a "sad and austere face, arms folded behind him," as Polonskaya described him. ("Just think, Norochka, not one comrade writer came!" he complained to her.) On a January day, he read his ode to Lenin at the Bolshoi Theater in the presence of Stalin and Vyacheslav Molotov, but this honor did not cheer him. The winter of 1929–1930 appeared to be a year of artistic failures. He felt increasingly isolated, and Polonskaya wrote that with the exception of his poem "At the Top of My Voice," which was to remain unfinished, he was experiencing a true writer's block. The prologue to that poem, in which he describes himself as "a latrine cleaner / and water carrier / by the revolution / mobilized and drafted" and laments that he had been "setting [his] heel on the throat of [his] own song," is as telling a comment as any on his disillusionment. It displays his increasingly painful awareness of the dissonance between communist ideals and their reality, between his personal longings and the stranglehold of the collective, between the oppression of the Soviet state and the freedom essential to any poet's psychic survival.

In the winter months shortly after my mother's marriage, Mayakovsky, according to Nora Polonskaya, began pressing her to leave her husband and marry him. But after the New Year, their affair went through a difficult phase: Nora had been pregnant with his child and had an abortion; afterward, she was sexually indifferent to him. Friends noted that "a mood of helplessness, loneliness, heartache . . . had come over him," and that for the first time in his life he was drinking heavily and regularly.

In February of 1930, in the midst of this emotional disarray, Mayakovsky further alienated his old friends by joining RAPP, the party-led organization that had begun to attack the more independent Soviet intellectuals for their "anarchism" and "Trotskyist deviation." RAPP, which Osip Brik had urged him to join as a way of allaying his isolation, was looked on with horror by the writers Mayakovsky most honored. But even that sinister group reacted disdainfully to Mayakovsky's move: Its officials placed him in a small section of minor and beginning writers and assigned him to the humiliating process of "reeducation." Audiences heckled him increasingly at his readings, and even students—traditionally his most devoted audience—had begun to tell him that his poems were unintelligible. Moreover, the Briks' home on Gendrikov Street had ceased to offer him relief from solitude: Osip and Lili had gone to England at the end of February; it was the first time since they had all lived together that both of them were away. He had no one but Nora to turn to. He insisted she remain with him at every moment of the day. Bitter arguments arose because she wanted to look after her own budding career.

On April 11, for the first time in his life, Mayakovsky failed to appear at a scheduled reading. On April 13, he telephoned several friends to see who was free to dine with him and was pained to hear that they were all busy. "It means that nothing can be done," he muttered to the sister-in-law of one colleague. He ended up by going to the home of his friend Valentin Kataev, who describes the following scene: Volodia and Nora spent the evening writing each other notes on little bits of cardboard torn out of a chocolate box, which Mayakovsky, who drank more than usual that night, tossed across the table to Nora with the gesture of a roulette player. At 3:00 A.M. they went to their respective homes. In the morning, Mayakovsky came by to pick up Nora and take her to his studio. According to Nora's memoirs, they quarreled a great deal—he pressured her to remain with him, while she insisted that she had to go to a rehearsal.

At 10:15 A.M., barely able to free herself from her lover's grip, Nora ran out of his room. A few seconds later, as she was beginning to run down the stairs, she heard a pistol shot. She hastened back into his room. It was still filled with smoke.

Pasternak's description of the mayhem caused in Moscow by the poet's death is now a classic:

> *Between eleven o'clock and twelve the waves were still flowing in circles round the shot. The news made the telephones tremble, covered faces with pallor and urged one towards the Lyubyanskoy passage, across the courtyard into the house, where the staircase was already choked with people from the town and with the tenants of the house, who wept and pressed close to one another, hurled and splashed against walls by the destructive force of the event.*

Pasternak's analysis of Mayakovsky's suicide is particularly lucid: "He killed himself out of pride, because he had condemned something in himself . . . with which his self-respect could not be reconciled."

The poet's suicide was not as sudden as it initially seemed. He left a note, written in pencil in a large, clear hand on three pieces of nine-by-fourteen-inch paper, which he'd apparently started composing two days before his death. "To All [*Vsem*]," it began. "Do not blame anyone for my death, and please, no gossip. The deceased always detested gossip. Mother, sisters, friends, forgive me—this is not the way (I do not recommend it to others) but there is no other way out for me."

The suicide note went on to dictate that all his papers be taken care of by the Briks. Documents at the Mayakovsky Museum indicate that a highly placed official of the secret police (the Cheka or OGPU, as it was also called in those years), whose building was directly adjacent to the poet's studio, was the first of Mayakovsky's acquaintances after Nora to rush into his room. He seized all of Mayakovsky's papers and a few days later handed most of them to the Briks, who, en route back from England, had received the news in Berlin and immediately come home. "I'm rummaging in Volodia's little papers," Lili wrote a friend in May, "and sometimes it seems to me I do what I have to do."

It is widely assumed by Mayakovsky scholars that Lili burned my mother's letters within a few weeks of the poet's death. That is certainly what my mother believed, and she claimed to have proof: "It was outrageous for Lili to burn my letters," my mother said in 1981 in one of her talks with Smakov. "She had no right to do it. . . . I forgave her because she confessed to it in a short note which was delivered to me by a Soviet professor. . . . But I don't understand why she did it. Was it jealousy? Why should she destroy all the traces and tokens of his love for me? If that was her intent, she should have burnt the 'Letter to Tatiana Yakovleva.' . . . Well, that was not in her power."

There was one possible token of Mayakovsky's love for my mother that Lili did not choose to destroy—a poem found, untitled, among recent entries in his notebook, which is now considered one of his greatest love lyrics. This, in fact, was the poem from which he borrowed several lines for his suicide note. (They are in roman type below.)

> *Past one o'clock. You must have gone to bed.*
> *The Milky Way streams silver through the night.*
> *I'm in no hurry; with lightning telegrams*
> *I have no cause to wake or trouble you.*
> As they say, 'The incident is closed.'
> The love boat has smashed against the daily grind.
> Now you and I are quits. Why bother then
> to balance mutual sorrows, pains, and hurts.
> *Behold what quiet settles on the world.*
> *Night wraps the sky in tribute from the stars.*
> *In hours like these, one rises to address*
> *The ages, history, and all creation.*

In using the lines for his last note, Mayakovsky changed only one word of the poem: The line "Now you and I are quits" was altered to "Now life and I are quits."

My mother heard about Mayakovsky's death when she was four months pregnant with me. She was in Warsaw, where she had settled with my father after their honeymoon. Her relatives in Paris had cabled my father, asking him to keep her from reading any Russian newspapers. But in most European cities the news made the front page.

"I was destroyed, utterly destroyed by today's newspapers," she wrote in her first bereaved note to her mother. "It was a terrible shock. . . . You'll understand."

My grandmother seems to have expressed her concern that Tatiana was taking too much of the blame for the poet's death, for two weeks later she wrote:

> Mamulechka moia rodnaia,
>
> *I don't think for a minute that I was the reason, except perhaps obliquely, for the true cause was his psychological crisis. . . . Over here also a lot is written about him, but how little was known about him as a person! Only now are people becoming aware of that, they are saying: "We have overlooked the most important thing—the powerful sources in his soul that led him to such an end."*
>
> *Bertrand kisses you. . . . I kiss you too, endlessly, many times.*
>
> *Your Tania.*
>
> *(The baby is already moving.)*

All three of Mayakovsky's women lived on to a good age, into their mid- or late eighties, and with varying degrees of civility carried on a war of the muses, flaunting the inspiration of this or that poem. Lili Brik, having been named literary executor, could readily claim any creation she wished as one of "her" poems, and for a few decades she managed to expunge all traces of Tatiana Yakovleva from the official Mayakovsky biographies. Along with her sister, Elsa Triolet, she was not above spreading malicious gossip concerning Tatiana, such as the comical legend that she was a courtesan and received men in back of her grandmother's Paris grocery store.

Meanwhile, Nora Polonskaya, short-shrifted because Mayakovsky had never officially dedicated any verses to her, grumbled that Lili had stolen from *her* the poem he excerpted in his suicide note, "Past One O'clock." "There are many phrases there that refer directly to me," she complained in her memoir. "It seems to me that Lilia Yuryevna much underestimated [Mayakovsky's romance with Yakovleva]," Nora also said. "She wished to remain the unique, unrepeatable love of his life."

As for my mother, the only one whose inspirational power was directly recorded in the title of a poem, she pretended to maintain an Olympian aloofness from the muses' fray. Arguing for quality over quantity, however, she coquettishly claimed that "Letter to Comrade Kostrov" and "Letter to Tatiana Yakovleva" were as splendid as any of the numerous poems Mayakovsky had dedicated to Lili: "He wrote her some beautiful lines, but none more beautiful than the ones he wrote to me." (The two women never once met.)

For a few years after his suicide—which was criticized by many as a most unsocialist act—publication of Mayakovsky's work was reduced to a trickle. In the face of the growing Stalinist repression, the Soviet literary establishment was hedging its bets about what stands to take on him. And however one may feel about Lili Brik and her husband, one cannot deny that they were exclusively responsible for reviving a public cult of the poet. In 1935, with the help of her then lover, a very high-ranking army general, Lili got a letter through to Joseph Stalin that asked him to rehabilitate Mayakovsky, reminding him that his verses were "the strongest revolutionary weapon." Stalin replied with complaisant rapidity, writing directly upon the upper left-hand corner of Brik's letter—in red pencil, in his bold, very large, slanting hand—"Comrade Brik is right: Mayakovsky was and remains the most talented poet of our Soviet era. Indifference to his memory and words is a crime." The following day, Stalin's comments appeared as headlines in *Pravda*; from then on, Soviet citizens were ceaselessly reminded, with litanylike repetitions of Mayakovsky's civic virtues, that he was the quintessential "poet of the revolution." For years to come, public squares, schools, subway stations, tractors, minesweepers, tanks, and steamships were named after him. In Pasternak's scornful phrase, Mayakovsky was "propagated compulsorily, like potatoes in the reign of Catherine the Great."

A few decades later, on the main thoroughfare once called Gorky Street and now renamed Tverskaya, at a site one mile up from the Kremlin that is as central to Moscow as Rockefeller Center is to Manhattan, a twelve-foot-tall bronze statue of Mayakovsky was erected. He stands there to this day: His massive torso triumphantly arched, an imaginary wind billowing the folds of his baggy pants, he incarnates Soviet man at his most optimistic and confident, striding toward the greatest future ever devised for humankind.

It is fitting that the only other major landmark on this main artery of the Russian capital is Pushkin Square, for these are the two poets most commonly memorized by Russian schoolchildren born after World War II. Ask most Russian adults which poems of Mayakovsky they had to learn by heart in school, and as surely as they know dozens of lines from Pushkin's "Eugene Onegin," they will spout stanzas from stirring patriotic odes such as Mayakovsky's *"Khorosho"* ("Very Good") or from his "Vladimir Ilyich Lenin" and "Left March." Or if they're under twenty-five and attended high school after the upheavals of 1991, they will have learned Mayakovsky's romantic lyrics, which then began to replace his patriotic poems in school curricula. They might well have memorized love poems such as "Letter to Comrade Kostrov on the Essence of Love," or "Letter to Tatiana Yakovleva."

Because of her secretiveness and her immense powers of seduction, my mother was the kind of woman who inspired a multitude of legends. And the myths that accreted about her have posed some surprising annoyances for me whenever I've returned to Russia. There was a widespread rumor in the 1970s, for instance, that I was Mayakovsky's daughter, a myth in part traceable to a memoir of Mayakovsky written by the poet's oldest friend, David Burliuk, when he was approaching eighty and may have been in his dotage. "In December of 1929 or January, 1930," Burliuk alleges, "Tatiana . . . gave birth to a girl who was Mayakovsky's daughter. . . . Mayakovsky used to refer to her as 'my Froska.'" (I was born in September 1930, and "Froska" was the nickname initiated decades ago by my American husband, who could not pronounce the "Frosinka" diminutive always used by my mother.) The allegation came to haunt me in 1979, when I traveled to the Soviet Union to take part in a Soviet-American literary conference. On a nicotine-reeking night train bound for Tbilisi, Georgia, two of my Soviet colleagues came into my compartment and for some hours tried to convince me that I was the poet's daughter. At the rise of dawn, I confronted them with the date on my passport. "This would have been an elephant's gestation!" I exclaimed. "Someone faked your passport," my Soviet colleagues parried back. So much for postdétente prowestern chic, I mused, which now made it desirable to establish an American progeny for the revolution's most fabled poet.

Fifty years after Mayakovsky's death, upon one of the occasions when her friend Gennady Smakov prodded my mother to speak about Mayakovsky and the impact of his suicide on her life, she had this to say: "If he had come back for the third time in October of 1929 I would have returned to Russia.... I've not been able to reread his letters since his death. Even now I can not.... What I felt was far worse than grief. It was the most dreadful mourning."

Only upon rereading those words in the past few years—"the most dreadful mourning"—did I begin to see why my mother, who loved me deeply, had preferred that I not probe too far into her romance with the kind, doomed poet: Mayakovsky's death, I now understood, had been the central fissure, the principal tragedy, of her life, one to which she never found any closure. And she did not want me to share her "most dreadful mourning" for him, at least not while she was still alive: Perhaps she wished to keep this mourning for herself; perhaps she wished to protect me from it.

And perhaps she was right to do so. Exploring any tormented parental past—a process through which, as if trapped in a maze of distorting mirrors, we often confront our own past sorrows, our own sins and dreadful choices—can be a painful, even dangerous form of seeking information. It is a knowledge for which we all might have to pay a price, which is precisely why many of us keep postponing the task. Probing a personal history as closely linked to the calamities of this century as my mother's and Mayakovsky's, sensing the pain of the separation forced upon them, knowing how close my mother came to returning to Russia and becoming one of the twenty million persons lost in Stalin's purges, has created a state of inner havoc that I'm only beginning to come to terms with. And yet, in the process of researching this segment of family history, I've acquired a new relative. In recent years, Vladimir Vladimirovich Mayakovsky has truly become my *rodnoi*—a beloved lost kinsman whom I think of and grieve for often, but who finally fulfilled his wish to speak to "the ages, history, and all creation." Through him, I may well have come into the most treasured part of my inheritance: my mother's grief.

My mother was not one to continue bearing grudges against any of Mayakovsky's friends. In the mid-1970s, upon hearing that Lili Yuryevna Brik had been ill, my mother wished to send her a sign of conciliation. (Brik, who was crippled with pain after suffering a hip fracture, would commit suicide in 1978, at the age of eighty-six.) One evening in Paris, my mother was dining in her hotel room with a mutual friend of hers and Brik's, Pierre Bergé, who was about to go to Moscow and had asked her whether she wished to send anything to her fellow muse. She went into her bedroom and brought back a small white handkerchief, neatly folded. "Just give this to Lili, and she'll understand," she said.

The messenger flew to Moscow the following day, went to visit Lili Brik upon his first evening there, and handed her the white handkerchief. "Tatiana says you'll understand," he said.

Lili gravely nodded her head. "I understand," she said.

The white flag, in most cultures, is a symbol of peace. For Lili and my mother, a white kerchief seemed to signal a truce of sorts and also became a sign of shared mourning.

My discovery of the letters that enabled me to document my mother's romance with Mayakovsky is a story by itself.

From my adolescence on, I had been aware that my mother was not only one of Mayakovsky's two muses but his last great love and that, somewhere in her possession, there was a cache of the letters he had written her during their romance. But I was equally aware of my mother's profound reluctance to talk about any painful aspect of her private life. And so until her death in 1991 I continued to honor the chill silence she cast over the poet who was a central figure of her youth—in part out of my own dread of confronting the past, in part because like most mothers and daughters we lived in terror of each other.

No one protected my mother's secretiveness more fiercely than my step-father, Alexander Liberman, the artist and publishing wizard who claimed to have been passionately in love with her for fifty years and who had brought me up since I was nine years old, when my own father died in World War II. Alex's career, like my mother's, typified the quintessentially American success story. Starting out, upon our arrival in the United States in 1941, with a menial job in *Vogue* magazine's art department, he had risen within a year and a half to be its art director. Two decades later he had become editorial director of the entire Condé Nast publishing empire, which under his guidance grew to include *Glamour, Mademoiselle, House and Garden, Bride's, GQ, Vanity Fair, Self, Gourmet, Condé Nast Traveler, Details, Woman, Allure, Architectural Digest,* and *Bon Appetit,* as well as the scores of foreign editions—German, French, Korean, Russian, what have you—most of those magazines spawned. Having transformed an elitist little publishing group into a vast press empire whose numerous magazines throbbed with his supple modernist style, my stepfather remained Condé Nast's driving force for nearly forty years. And he was generally looked upon, as the *New York Post* put it in its 1999 obituary, as "the father of modern fashion publishing." "Media World Mourns a Legend," the *New York Post* headline declared upon his death, while the *International Herald Tribune* asserted that in the past century "No man in the West held more power over fashion images."

Born in Russia, like my mother, and educated in Great Britain and in France, Alex was a dark-haired, dapper man of very regal bearing, five-feet-eleven in height, who emanated an aura of steely self-discipline. His most memorable features were his trim mustache, his debonair, enigmatic smile, and the trace of British accent he had acquired in the boarding schools of his early adolescence. Suave, peerlessly trilingual, dressed year-round in vestments of almost priestly monotony—dark gray flannel suit and black or navy-blue hand-knit tie most of the year, beige linen in the summer months—within a few years of arriving in New York he had come to epitomize cosmopolitan elegance and aristocratic "European" manners. For forty years he strode the salons of New York and the corridors of Condé Nast's expanding magazine empire, charming and persuading, carefully honing his inscrutable image, exceptionally skilled at the art of flattery, paying his court to whatever cultural celebrities or society figure could further advance his phenomenal career. Flirtatious but utterly chaste, he became noted for brandishing his adoration of my mother and his unswerving fidelity to her (an exotic aspect of his self-image, which also served, I suspect, to keep the advances of Condé Nast's mostly female staff at bay). At the office, where he had the final say on everything from captions to covers, where he hired and fired at will and clearly relished his power over others, he could be, in turn, extravagantly generous or icily ruthless.

Alex had his acolytes and his enemies. Fans of "the silver fox," as he was often called by his colleagues, were spellbound by the Slavic warmth and charm which he could turn on and off like a faucet; by the authority of his eye; and by his prodigally versatile talents: By 1960, Alex, whose ambition in his youth had been to be a painter, had also become an artist and photographer of note. Notwithstanding his chronically frail health, he had worked tirelessly on weekends and holidays on his own art and had exhibited it in New York's most prestigious galleries and some of the nation's major museums. His mammoth sculptures of welded steel had, by the 1980s, arisen in scores of public sites throughout the United States. And he had produced one particular book, *The Artist in His Studio*, which has remained a classic photographic chronicle of twentieth-century French art.

As for Alex's foes, they could point to his boundless capacity for self-promotion and to the byzantine ruthlessness of his tactics. They knew all too well—sometimes on the basis of bitter experience—that this ambitious polymath's only loyalty was to his employers rather than to his colleagues or underlings; and that the price of disagreeing with him could be a brusque dismissal, a process with which he never sullied his own hands but assigned to his henchmen. But until my mother's death, this malefic, saturnine side of Alex was never once revealed to his family. For a half century Alex held true to his public image as a devoted paterfamilias, serving as a slavishly devoted househusband to my fascinating but deliberately helpless mother, who expected all mountains to come to her and declared

Alex in the 1950s as art director of Vogue *magazine,*
photograph by Irving Penn, 1960.

herself incapable of calling a plumber or rearing her child. Solely attracted, throughout his life, to powerful women, he made it clear that Tatiana was his "goddess" and that his life's goal was to satisfy her every whim. For half a century, "Superman," as my mother and I called Alex, had been an equally affectionate, admirable second father to me. From our first months together in the 1940s, it is Alex who had assumed paternal and maternal roles, who with unfailing patience and tenderness dealt with my teachers and braces and report cards, heard out my heartaches, and imposed curfew hours and taboos on teen behavior. Later, it is he who had given me away in marriage, had soothed my tears as a young bride, and had been the most obsessively doting of grandfathers.

It is this idol of my early youth whom I had to deal with when I began to look for Mayakovsky's letters to my mother.

Even though my mother, when she died in 1991, after a long illness, had willed me all her Mayakovsky letters and documents, the search for them turned out to be extremely difficult. For Alex, who shortly after Tatiana's death and to his friends' total astonishment had married Tatiana's nurse, declined to give them to me for eight consecutive years. "Can't you see I'm too sick to think of such things," he'd say, perpetually falling back on pleas of fatigue or ill health, or "I'm too tired to remember where they are." He was notorious for shying away from confrontations and for being vicious when he was forced into one. So whether from innate tact or Confucian subservience, I continued meekly to accept his account that the famous Mayakovsky letters were in a barely accessible bank vault or had been misplaced among his office files.

My patience wore down in the summer of 1999. It is then that I received a letter from the Mayakovsky Museum in Moscow, informing me that it owned a large archive of letters from my mother to her own mother, Lyubov Nikolaevna Orlova, who had died in 1963, having never left Russia. She had donated them to the museum shortly before her death. Sadly, my grandmother's side of the correspondence had not survived, but my mother's letters—which I had never known existed—described her romance with the poet in the last eighteen months of his life; I had an official invitation from the museum to be their guest while I studied their "Tatiana Yakovleva Archive." But I knew that to make sense of these missives, I must first retrieve and read the Mayakovsky letters my mother had left me in her will. I decided to confront my stepfather one last time and recover a possession that had legally been mine for eight years.

Alex Liberman lay on his bed in his New York apartment on an August afternoon in 1999, eighty-six years old and very ill, so heavily medicated that he seldom remained awake more than a few minutes at a time. He was scheduled to be flown the next day to his other home in Florida, and I asked him one last time: "Alex, dear, could you tell me where the Mayakovsky letters are?" "Oh, somewhere here," his wasted silvery head lolled in various directions, as if scanning the room. "You should have them." With these words his eyes closed, and he fell into another deep sleep. I went home to Connecticut, where I'd lived for some decades. But upon the counsel of my husband and of a close friend who was a lawyer I returned to my stepfather's apartment a few days later and began to look through three-feet-high stacks of envelopes in a corner of his room. After an hour, daunted by the prospect of several days' work, I took a break. Out of some instinct, I walked over to his bedside table and opened the top drawer. There, in an ancient, half-torn envelope marked "Mayakovsky Letters" in my mother's large scrawling script, was the inheritance that had eluded me for years: twenty-seven pages of the poet's letters, twenty-four telegrams, and some original manuscripts of his poems.

Only then, upon reading this correspondence, did I understand why my possessive, jealous stepfather, who had worked hard to create the legend that *he* was the center of Tatiana's universe, was determined to deny the poet's letters to their rightful heir, the adopted daughter he had supposedly cherished. Only then did I know why he was ready literally to defy the law in order to withhold them from the world.

I was to see Alex once more in Florida, two months later, ten days before he died. By then, he was almost beyond speech. As I kissed my stepfather's forehead one last time, thanking him silently amid my tears for having rescued my childhood, I marveled at his capacity for deceit. I kept on marveling at his deviousness a few months later, as I worked in the archives of the Mayakovsky Museum, finally able, thanks to my recovery of the poet's letters, to access the treasure of my mother's past.

It is this Machiavellian man—whose character and early life, like my mother's, were shaped by the mayhem of the Russian Revolution—whom I must begin to chronicle in the next chapters.

FIVE

Alex and His Father

The suave, urbane Alexander Liberman was the grandson of tenant farmers in the Ukraine. His father, Semyon Isaevich, was born in 1881 in a tiny village of that province to which his forebears had moved a few generations earlier. Unlike many Jewish farmers in Russia, the Lieberman family (the first "e" was dropped by Semyon only much later) had preserved its religious traditions. Semyon's maternal grandfather, a lanky, bearded man who wore the long robes traditional to Hebrew scholars, cared far more about studying his Talmud than he did about agrarian issues. He was to have an even greater influence on his grandson than Semyon's practical, bon vivant father, who headed the family's farming enterprise.

Since Jews were not allowed to own land in prerevolutionary times, the Liebermans rented their property, which consisted of some four thousand acres of sugar-beet fields, from a Polish absentee landlord whom they never once met. Living in a mansion that was part of the estate, however, were the landlord's spinster sisters, with whom Semyon's family shared the use of a vast fruit-laden orchard. These ladies liked to stroll by a zigzagging stream lined with weeping willows that adjoined the Liebermans' dwelling, and members of Semyon's family approached them with veneration, kissing their hands and letting them kiss the tops of their heads. The Liebermans, in turn, were treated with loving deference by the two hundred villagers who did the actual toiling on the land and to whom they were closely bonded, remaining attentive to their joys and sorrows and responding to their needs. Semyon speaks of his close links to the Russian peasantry as a determining influence in his life: "This early feeling for the peasants was an important factor in my development. It is my love for them which in time made me a revolutionary."

Semyon Lieberman was the only boy in his generation of children. His mother's family wanted him to follow in the steps of his maternal grandfather and become a full-time scholar. His father wished him to take over his role in supervising the family's farming business. The scholars' faction prevailed, and at the age of seven Semyon, who up to then spoke only Ukrainian and Yiddish, was sent away to a larger village to study. There, he learned Russian as well as classical Hebrew and already displayed considerable intellectual gifts. Semyon also found a protector and mentor in the local Orthodox priest, whose two sons, prominent St. Petersburg government officials who often visited their father, much impressed the young man. Their polished manners and the elegance of their dress led Semyon to daydream of eventually leaving the confines of his province. And at the age of sixteen, with five rubles in his pocket, he ran away to a far larger town, Zhitomir, to live with a distant cousin who was a medical doctor and a liberal Reformed rabbi.

Living on next to nothing in his cousin's home, Semyon studied hard enough to pass the demanding entrance examinations set by the czarist high-school system. Once enrolled, he came under the influence of a particularly beloved teacher who, at the end of each class, silently handed him anticzarist publications printed by underground Marxist groups. Thus the seeds of radicalism were early sown in Semyon's mind. But his "real baptism as a revolutionary," as he put it in a memoir he published decades later, *Building Lenin's Russia,* occurred during one of the many anti-Jewish pogroms staged by local authorities in the Ukraine. During one particular skirmish, a Cossack's saber slashed him near the collarbone and nearly blinded him in the right eye. "The memory of [my] first battle with the Czar's henchmen remained with me forever," he wrote. That evening, coming to in a hospital cot, he pledged to become a full-fledged revolutionary and help topple the czarist system. "I had come out of that Jewish milieu in which the old traditions of romantic mysticism were still alive. . . . What I dreamed of was a kingdom of freedom, equality and social justice."

The Russian university system was as much as closed to Jews. So after finishing high school, Semyon, guided by his egalitarian ideals, set forth for the prestigious University of Vienna, which at the time was a hotbed of social and political radicalism. After earning his way through college by tutoring, he returned to his homeland in 1905, the year massive strikes and nationwide unrest came close to toppling the czarist regime. Once home he immediately joined the Social-Democratic Workers' Party, the major revolutionary group which had recently split into Bolsheviks and Mensheviks: Lenin's Bolsheviks believed in rigid party discipline and looked on the proletariat and the poorest peasantry as potential forces in the next stage of the revolution; the more centrist Mensheviks—with whom Semyon tended to side—sought allies in the liberal anticzarist bourgeoisie and intelligentsia and focused on education and on the formation of labor unions.

Yet while less prone to use violent tactics, Mensheviks in those years could be as aggressive as Bolsheviks. After the abortive revolution of 1905, Semyon returned to his native Ukraine and worked with underground labor unions in Odessa, where a particularly active branch of the Social Democratic Party had formed. He often returned to his native village to evade the authorities that constantly tracked him. But in 1907, after a close shave with the czar's police in his own hometown, he decided to seek the protective anonymity of a large city and moved to Kiev. It was during his years in Kiev that Semyon found his vocation. While continuing his underground activities, he supported himself by working for a timber-exporting firm. And the romantic vastness, the Olympian scale of the Russian woodlands, which contain more than 60 percent of all the forestlands in Europe and Asia, singularly captured his imagination. Timber had traditionally been the nation's most lucrative export item, the very bedrock of its economy. And to Semyon's surprise, the practical aspect of this national treasure—"the commercial side of the sylvan beauty of Russia," in his own words—entranced him as no other field of study ever had. "I plunged into [the study] of timber areas and sawmill capacities . . . as I ate and dreamed, as I dressed and walked and talked, my thoughts were with the woods and their output."

Semyon, who had excelled in mathematics, seems to have had a virtuoso gift for the economics of lumber. While continuing to work with underground socialist groups and acquiring a postgraduate degree from the University of Kiev, he advanced so rapidly in the lumber industry that within a few years he sat on the boards of directors of several major companies. He authored a table of timber calculations that soon came into use throughout the industry, and in 1914 he even became a member of a special commission on timber in the Ministry of Agriculture. By then, romance had come into Semyon's life. Upon one of his near arrests in Kiev a few years back, he had been sheltered by a Jewish tailor with socialist sympathies who, when the police arrived, pretended

Alexander Liberman's father, Semyon Liberman, in Paris in the late 1920s.

that Semyon was his pretty daughter's tutor. Through this family, Semyon soon met his future wife, a young woman who, as he put it, "was also helping the common cause of the revolution."

What we know about the family origins of Semyon's gifted, flamboyant wife, the mother of his son, Aleksandr, can be gleaned from a barely fictionalized memoir, *The Errant Heart*, which she wrote in her later years. Genrieta Mironovna—we don't know her family name, and at some point in her exile she took on the stage name Henriette Pascar—was a voluptuously beautiful aspiring actress who was of part gypsy, part Romanian Jewish origins. (She always preferred to emphasize the gypsy part of her heritage rather than the Jewish one.) The oldest of twenty children, born in 1886 to a wealthy timber heiress in western Romania, she was not given much attention or affection as a child. Her handsome, feckless father—the gypsy—seemed to take great sadistic pleasure in periodically whipping his children. Henriette ran away at the age of seventeen and lived for two years with gypsy cousins in Odessa, where she attended meetings of revolutionary underground organizations, at which, on several occasions, she briefly encountered Semyon Lieberman. After a few years spent in Paris, where she studied French literature at the Sorbonne while supporting herself as a nurse, she returned to Russia in 1911 and lived in Kiev with a married sister, once again taking an active part in revolutionary underground organizations. Like Semyon Lieberman, Henriette was of Menshevik rather than Bolshevik persuasion, and it was through such political activities that she met him again.

When they renewed acquaintance in Kiev in 1911, Henriette, who was then studying acting and stage direction with Vsevolod Meyerhold, found Semyon vastly changed. The innate elegance of this short, fine-featured, bespectacled, courteous young man was now heightened by his penchant for the finest European tailoring, preferably British. As Henriette put it in her memoir, she had remembered "a carelessly dressed Nihilist" and was reintroduced to a highly sophisticated fellow of "distinctly European bearing." She was immediately taken with the thoughtfulness and assuredness of his manner ("a born leader, whose measured words allay all worries"). Although she found him to be "neurotically proud of his Jewish heritage," filled with "a blend of idealism inspired by the Talmud," she was impressed by his strength and integrity of character and recognized in herself "the serene calm that precedes the torment of love." The infatuation seems to have been mutual, and by 1911 the couple settled together in St. Petersburg, another important center of the lumber industry, from which Semyon now ran his growing empire. Their son, Aleksandr Semyonovich Lieberman, was born three months after they were married, on September 4, 1912, in Kiev. His parents were staying there during one of Semyon's extended business trips; his birth was officially registered by the chief rabbi of Kiev before the family started home.

Of St. Petersburg, where the Liebermans lived in a six-room apartment just off the Nevsky Prospect, near St. Isaac Church, little Alex—"Shura"

Alexander Liberman's mother, Henriette Pascar,
in Paris in the mid-1920s.

or "Shurik" to his family—would remember only one prominent detail: His nursery and all its furnishings—bed, bureau, chairs, chest of drawers—were painted white, a great novelty in those years. This had been his mother's decorating idea, and it was to influence him to the end of his days: For the rest of his life, all of Alex's habitations, his offices as well as his homes, were painted a stark, blinding white. He also remembers sitting in his parents' living room and watching his mother reclining on a leopard-skinned divan, having her portrait painted in a gold Fortuny gown. (She encouraged him to squeeze the colors out of the artist's tubes, which entranced him and let him know, then and there, that his mother wanted him to become a painter.) But otherwise he saw little of his parents, for his mother continued to pursue her theater career and engage in numerous love affairs, and his father's business trips were often of many weeks' or months' duration. Along with his administrative duties on various timber boards and commissions, including the czar's, Semyon was managing three large estates, which were scattered from the western end of the Russian empire to Siberia: those of Grand Duke Michael, the czar's brother; Prince Oldenburg, the czar's uncle; and the legendarily wealthy Prince Balashov, a pillar of czarist society, who owned some 2.7 million acres throughout Russia, including much of the timber areas in the Ural Mountains.

It could take an entire month for Semyon to travel across just one of these estates. When no train service was available between two destinations, he frequently had to traverse, by coach, stretches of land in which no human habitation would be found for several days at a time, making it essential to stock up on large reserves of bread, water, hard-boiled eggs, and cheeses. Occasionally, he would seek shelter in some monastery or convent along the way, always havens of peace and hospitality where he conversed for hours with monks and nuns, indulging the mystical streak in his character that had been instilled by his scholarly grandfather and by his friendship with the Christian-Existentialist philosopher Nikolai Berdyaev. "To me these stopovers were romance itself," he wrote, "because of my feeling of being so far away from the main stream of life . . . because of the deep silence of the endless surrounding forest." During his peregrinations, Semyon was also reminded of the harsh exiles being imposed on countless Russians due to their anticzarist activities. His travels often brought him to the town of Perm, a clearing center for revolutionaries being shipped to Siberia. There he sometimes met old friends, both Bolsheviks and Mensheviks, as they were being transported in chains or under heavy police escort to their sites of detention. He tried to help them as much as he could, attending to the convicts' supplies of warm clothing, medicine, and food, frequently lobbying local landowners to arrange for certain groups of prisoners to settle in areas less remote than Siberia. For throughout his journeys across the empire he retained most of the ideals he had held as a radical activist. He was constantly horrified by "the width and depth of the chasm separating the masses of the Russian people from the handful of landlords, bankers, and court officials ruling the country and enjoying all the rights and privileges on earth." And by 1915, he was certain that revolution was inevitable.

There must have been a trace of unease in Semyon's attitude toward the unfortunate revolutionary comrades he encountered during his voyages. For in the years immediately preceding the revolution of 1917, his status as

One-year-old Alex with his father, St. Petersburg, 1913.

Russia's leading authority on lumber allowed him to travel in extremely luxurious conditions, more often than not in his clients' private train cars. Little Shurik, when he reached the age of four, occasionally accompanied his father on these journeys to the estates of the high-born nobility, and these trips were immensely influential on him. In 1916, for instance, while Semyon was inspecting the Caucasian estates of Prince Oldenburg, the prince arranged for him to travel with his son in a seven-car private train. At each railroad station along the way, an imperial officer came to salute the travelers in their compartment, brought them abundant meals, and saw to it that all their desires were satisfied.

It is to these voyages through the vastnesses of Russia, in fact, that Alex attributed the obsession with monumentality that later characterized his art and also his hedonistic taste for opulent living. He often said that his childhood travels throughout Russia were his first experiences of "extravagance and heroic scale." This exposure to the unlimited sumptuousness of the Russian aristocracy led Alex to develop a penchant for luxury that, he readily admitted, became ingrained. He never forgot the rich velvet of these private trains' upholstery, their red damask curtains, the electric candlesticks with little pink fluted shades in their dining cars. And above all, he remembered the lavish service his father received upon these trips. For the rest of his days, Alex Liberman, who inherited more than a measure of his father's magnetic charm—a charm that had to do with a talent for making every passing acquaintance feel important and perfectly remembered—sought the friendship and protection of powerful men who could provide him with what he called "special treatment." Over the years, however straitened Alex's circumstances, he always needed considerable measures of privilege and opulence—be they in trains, hotels, his own homes—to find life tolerable.

In February 1917, five-year-old Alex, leaning out of a window in his parents' flat in Petrograd (the new name given St. Petersburg in 1914), witnessed a scene he remembered vividly throughout his life: "Dark, black masses like black rivers going through the big avenues of St. Petersburg with red flags, chanting revolutionary songs." That very evening, he would recall, he saw a life-size portrait of the czar being burned. "Like any child of five, I suppose I must have sensed my parents' nervousness and terror," he reflected decades later. "As a child brought up in the Revolution . . . [y]ou become prepared for any disruption—upheaval is natural."

The events of 1917 inevitably brought huge changes into the Liebermans' lives. In March, upon the abdication of the czar, Semyon, his socialist beliefs vindicated, wrote letters of resignation to all the companies and landowners that had employed him and offered his services to the Petrograd Soviet. He proved to be invaluable to them; for upon the Bolsheviks' seizure of power in October 1917, the anticommunist army, which was reinforced by a large contingent of foreign troops, had occupied the Caucasus and the Donets Basin, totally cutting off the Bolshevik regime from the coal and oil supplies essential to its railroad system. The fledgling Soviet government became totally dependent on wood fuel for its railroads, and it appointed Semyon Lieberman to head a committee in charge of supplying Russian railroads with the proper amounts of timber.

In March of 1918, five months after the coup d'état which had established Bolshevik rule, the Russian capital was moved from Petrograd to Moscow. Semyon, family in tow, soon followed the government to the new capital. Notified of Lieberman's expertise, Lenin summoned him to the Kremlin in the fall of that year. The two men felt instant trust and sympathy for each other and began a close collaboration that was to end only upon Lenin's death in 1924.

In view of Semyon Lieberman's openly anti-Bolshevik, even anti-Marxist, views, his survival as a high-ranking Soviet government functionary over the following seven years was nothing short of miraculous. This tells us much about the elasticity and open-mindedness of Lenin's first years of rule, and it also speaks to Semyon's own charisma and political agility. Lieberman was one of a handful of noncommunist *spets*—short for "specialist"—whom Lenin retained in his immediate entourage because their expertise was essential to the beleaguered new nation's economic survival. In Lieberman's case, he was made business manager of a five-man Central Timber Council, which oversaw all of the Soviet Union's lumber resources. It is fortunate that many of his Bolshevik superiors, such as Leonid Krasin, who eventually became the Soviet Union's first ambassador to Great Britain, were old buddies he'd worked with decades ago in Odessa or Kiev at meetings of the then illegal Social Democratic Party. In the very first years of the Soviet regime, Lieberman was even tolerated by Felix Dzerzhinsky, "the Torquemada of the Soviets," as he referred to the dreaded Bolshevik director of the secret police, who was shrewd enough to realize the pivotal role of the *spets* in saving the floundering Soviet economy.

Having become an insider, Semyon attended all meetings of Lenin's Supreme Council of Economy, the equivalent of a joint ministry of labor and industry. He was often called to Lenin's office a half hour ahead of such meetings to discuss specific issues of timber supply, met with the leader at least twice per month, and at all times had direct access to Lenin's private phone line at the Kremlin. He seems to have brought his son along on some of these visits, for little Shurik remembered being repeatedly impressed by the great rusted cannons at the Kremlin walls: It is to this vision of aggressive, jutting form that he traces many sculptural motifs that fueled his own artwork a half century later.

Semyon Lieberman's vivid portrait of Vladimir Ilyich Lenin depicts a consummately shrewd, soft-spoken man who knew just how to present himself as utterly cordial and artless; a sorcerer of sorts who pretended to be always putting all his cards on the table; a wondrously charismatic listener who successfully feigned being absorbed in the problems of others. Drawing a vivid contrast between Lenin's warmth and charm and Leon Trotsky's cool arrogance, Semyon Lieberman makes it clear that for some years he was under Lenin's spell. "Our conversations were so pleasant, they so calmed and encouraged me," he wrote of the Soviet leader, "that I looked forward to them . . . with impatience." So it is telling of Lieberman's integrity that however seduced he was by Lenin, he was not enough of an opportunist to join the Communist Party or even to mask his reservations about Marxist theory. Lenin, in fact, seemed to appreciate the probity with which Lieberman remained loyal to his own ideals. Upon one occasion, when Semyon was being criticized for these very failings by the more doctrinaire members of Lenin's entourage, Vladimir Ilyich, having heard out Semyon's problems in a private session, said, "See for yourself, you wouldn't have all these troubles if you were a member of our party!"

"Vladimir Ilyich," Semyon replied, "Bolsheviks, like singers, are born, not made." "Ilyich," as Lenin was also called by his entourage, ended the meeting, as he always did, with a cordial handshake and a warm smile.

Within a year or two of the Liebermans' arrival in Moscow, Alex's mother, Henriette, was also finding good fortune with the new regime. She had immediately been struck by the number of hungry, restless children roaming through the streets of the Soviet capital. Orphaned, homeless, or made vagrant by their parents' lengthy workdays, they were beginning to present a vast social problem. As a way of getting them off the street and channeling their energies, she conceived the idea of a children's theater. The proposal found favor with one of her former lovers, Anatoly Lunacharsky, an enthusiastic supporter of avant-garde art (and of Mayakovsky), who was then serving as Lenin's people's commissar for education. In 1919, Lunacharsky secured funds for Henriette to set up the first government-run children's theater. At first, she merely sat on the theater's advisory board, which included the legendary stage director Konstantin Stanislavsky. But within a year she became the director and sole decision maker of the enterprise. In the following four years, during the heyday of Vsevolod Meyerhold and the Moscow Art Theater, when Europe's most advanced artistic movements thrived in Russia, she commissioned some of the country's most prominent painters and designers to create sets and costumes for her plays, which included adaptations of *The Adventures of Tom Sawyer, Treasure Island*, Kipling's *Jungle Book*, and Hans Christian Andersen tales. Tickets were free. The four-hundred-seat theater was always filled. Henriette persuaded professional actors to volunteer their services and to answer the children's questions after each show. Sandwiches were passed out to the young audience, many of whose members may well have gone hungry for days.

Meanwhile, Shurik, a skinny, anxious, often ailing boy, was more often than not roaming the streets himself, overlooked by his perpetually busy parents. He endeared himself to children his age by giving them food stolen from his parents' kitchen. He joined in young vagrants' often dangerous games, which were held in a rubble-filled lot in back of his family's apartment building. "We played at warfare and threw stones and bits of broken dishes at each other," he remembered decades later. "Many of us were bloodied up. Whoever won the battle would shit in the enemy's trenches." In Henriette's fictionalized memoir, the heroine's young son spends most of his time at his mother's theater, helping to paint sets and handing out sandwiches to the hungry children, often rushing backstage to tell Mama how much he loves her. But in fact, young Shurik spent no more than a few hours per week at the theater, and much of the time he felt as abandoned as the homeless boys he befriended. And although he loved opera and ballet, he was terrified rather than attracted by the experience of being onstage. When he was nine, his mother insisted that he learn to perform publicly and had him coached by a member of the Bolshoi troupe. As he faced his audience at the appointed time, he burst into tears and ran offstage. It is to this episode that Alex traced his lifelong dread of public speaking, a duty he managed to avoid throughout his career.

Shurik had many other severe discipline problems. His parents had different views about his education. His father wanted him to go to a regular school. His mother, who believed that imagination was central to children's education ("fantasy, dreams, and folktales" seemed to be her pedagogical credo), wished him to be tutored at home. At first, his father prevailed. Shurik was enrolled in a school on the opposite side of town and given a sandwich every morning to take along for lunch. But instead of taking the tram, as he was supposed to do, he gave the sandwich to a truck driver in exchange for a ride to school. (The first, nearly fatal ulcer hemorrhage Alex suffered at the age of nineteen might well have been caused by those years of systematic, daily hunger; his disdain for walking—and for all forms of public transportation—never abated.)

Once he got to school, Shurik's behavior grew to be totally anarchic. He lifted girls' skirts, assaulted other boys, insulted his teachers. His instructors found him so unruly that he was expelled and had to be tutored at home, just as his mother had wished him to be. A variety of instructors were hired—and left in dismay after being kicked, punched, and spat upon by the boy, whose favorite trick was to lock his teachers, one after the next, in his parents' closet. Moreover, at the age of nine and perhaps beyond it, Shurik continued to wet his bed at night and occasionally to shit in his pants. Such incontinence led to the only beating he remembers his father ever giving him—a sound thrashing with a leather belt, imposed while his mother, in the next room, shrieked for her husband to desist.

In 1920, the Liebermans, like everyone in Moscow with the exception of the very top-ranking members of government, began to suffer the consequences of the city's enormous recent expansion and of its growing shortage of living quarters. Ordered to share their apartment with two other working-class families, they were reduced to two rooms of their own. Moreover, their coresidents' violent, drunken quarrels made life increasingly intolerable. Little Alex remembered seeing one inebriated tenant beating his wife mercilessly as he chased her all over the apartment, including the Liebermans' rooms; Semyon realized that such behavior presented the worst possible example to his already troubled child. (Even the fairly decorous Liebermans occasionally succumbed to the temptation of alcohol. Alex remembers coming home from one of his street-gang jaunts one evening to find his parents lying on the floor of their bedroom, totally drunk—the turmoil of life in cramped communal quarters had apparently led them to capitulate to a neighbor's offer to share a pail of vodka.)

The only escape from the chaos of communal living available to the Liebermans was a little cottage a few hours by train from Moscow, which they were given access to because its former owners had been exiled or liquidated. There, Alex ran freely through fields and pastures and seemed far calmer and happier. He remembers beautiful etchings of ancestors in gilt frames and a field of wildflowers through which his mother's brother, Naum, rode his horse bareback. Decades later, the phrase "We're going to the country!" was one that my stepfather always spoke with a smile of pleasure and anticipation. From the time I first knew him, in his midtwenties, "the country" was a green place in nature that allowed him to escape from the agitation and responsibilities of the city week and inevitably brought him a measure of serenity and peace.

But in 1920 Moscow, the week inevitably resumed with the tedium of lessons and tutors, and Alex's unruly response to them. His "hysteria," as his parents referred to his fractious behavior, became increasingly problematic, and Semyon began consulting doctors. They all advised him that his son suffered from severe psychological problems. And a few physicians who were old friends of Semyon suggested, confidentially, that he not only get the boy out of their crowded, turbulent flat but out of the Soviet Union altogether. Lieberman began to give that idea serious consideration.

Nineteen twenty was a banner year for the young Soviet Union's economic status: A few European nations began to lift their embargoes, making it possible for the country to resume trade with foreign powers. It was natural that the multilingual Semyon Lieberman, the country's foremost specialist in lumber, would be one of the citizens included in the Soviet Union's first trade mission abroad; it was headed by his close friend Leonid Krasin. The mission was to travel to Great Britain, which was then led by Liberal Party leader David Lloyd George and was the first country to renew commercial relations with Soviet Russia. The delegation, which reached London in the fall of 1920, comprised some twenty experts in various areas of commerce, only five of whom were non-Bolshevik *spets*. These delegates were the first Soviet citizens to be allowed into the country since the revolution, and they were often presented humiliatingly in the British press as "savages who eat with their knives" and "clean their noses with their fists." Mortified by these boorish views of their new society, the Soviet delegates spent a great deal of time replenishing their wardrobes and studying the niceties of British society manners before heading home.

The next country to issue an invitation to Soviet economic specialists was Germany, and this time Lieberman was sent out as a one-man delegation. By then, he had played an important role in shaping Lenin's New Economic Policy, a program to reconstruct the Russian economy through limited reintroduction of capitalistic practices and foreign trade, and Russia's timber industry was more in the limelight than ever. Arriving in Berlin, Lieberman learned, to his delight, that for the first time since the revolution his passion for luxury was being satisfied: A suite had been reserved for him at the city's most sumptuous hotel, the Esplanade. As Semyon moved in, he was startled to learn that some thirty-five rooms in the hotel were occupied by timber importers from all over Europe—Norway, Sweden, Belgium—who had come to negotiate with him. It was clear that he had gained recognition, abroad as well as at home, as the chief spokesman for the Soviet Union's most lucrative industry.

France issued the next invitation a few months later, and Semyon, once more sent out by himself, made his first trip to Paris. The upshot of all these trips is that by the summer of 1921, Semyon could travel in and out of Russia with relative freedom, having proved that he was a trustworthy, loyal ambassador for his country's business interests. However limited they were, the trade agreements he had drawn up with foreign powers had played the role, as he put it in his memoir, "of a political vanguard . . . preparing the ground for better, more normal relations between the Soviet Republic and the rest of Europe." Lieberman's growing prestige had an even greater personal importance: he could now begin the delicate negotiations necessary to get his son out of Russia and settle him in Great Britain for a proper education.

Getting Shurik out of Russia would indeed prove to be a difficult task. For in the early 1920s Soviet authorities looked on all their envoys' families as hostages of sorts, as guarantees that the delegates would return from their foreign missions. Semyon first sounded out his immediate superior, Alexis Rykov, president of the Supreme Council of Economy, and received a pessimistic response. "You should give your son the precious opportunity to grow up not in the bourgeois milieu of England, but with the young Soviet generation," Rykov chided him. Semyon then decided to go straight to Lenin. He gave Vladimir Ilyich a detailed description of his son's medical problems and of the violence attending his family's housing situation, and the leader gave his spoken consent for Alex to leave Russia but told him it also had to be cleared by the Cheka. Here the difficulties began. The chief aide to Dzerzhinsky, the Cheka's dreaded head, categorically refused to allow Shura's departure from Russia. "We have enough good schools in Russia," he told Semyon. "You don't have to look for any in England." Semyon returned to the Kremlin to see Lenin, repeating the bureaucrat's response. "Yes, we know, we know," Ilyich said wearily, as if the Cheka was an all-too-familiar problem. He then picked up a phone and dialed Dzerzhinsky directly. After a brief talk with the Cheka chief, he turned to Semyon and said, "We'll have to discuss [your son's departure] at the next meeting of the Politburo." "Get ready to leave for London," he added as he rose to shake Semyon's hand, "can't waste any time now." Lieberman began to see a glimmer of hope. Indeed, a few days later Semyon received an excerpt from the minutes of the five-member Politburo, the Communist Party's supreme organ, which read thus:

> *Subject of discussion:* Proposal by Rykov and Lenin to grant a passport to Lieberman and his son Alexandr for a trip abroad.
> *Resolution:* To instruct the Cheka to issue the passport.
> *Division of the vote:* Against—Dzerzhinsky and Zinoviev. For—Lenin, Rykov and Kamenev.

The episode was characteristic of Lenin's dealings and is telling of the leader's shrewdness. He could easily have resolved little Alex's visa issue by himself, by issuing an executive decree. But in order not to undermine the party's authority, he habitually made it seem as if nothing was ever his personal decision. He preferred to have all his decrees doled out by the Politburo, knowing that there was always an undecided vote, like the ambitious Kamenev's, which he could swing over to his side.

It was September 1921. Within a few days, Semyon and little Shurik were on a train bound for Germany. The fact that it had taken the Politburo to decide his fate may well have helped to give Alex that sense of self-importance, and the accompanying delusions of grandeur, which were to mark his character.

After the grim poverty of their Moscow flat, the spacious London home of Semyon's old friend Leonid Krasin, who had recently become the Soviet Union's permanent trade delegate in England, made an unforgettable impression on little Shura. Krasin's wife and three daughters had joined him in London that very summer. And after Semyon returned to Moscow, it was at the Krasins' redbrick mansion in Hampstead that Alex made his home for the following three and a half years. Of the three blond, blue-eyed Krasin daughters, Ludmilla, fifteen, was the quietest and most responsible; Katia, the wildest and most beautiful (who a decade later would briefly be a mistress of my own father, Bertrand du Plessix), was then thirteen; Liuba was eleven, two years older than Alex, and, as he described her later, "madly seductive . . . in a flirty yet boyish way." Alex became a kind of stepchild in this spirited family, an adopted younger brother for the girls. They teased him, played tricks on him, sometimes tying him up in his bedsheets, and undressed and bathed casually before him, which by the time he was twelve he found "gorgeously troubling." (Any study of Alex that probes his lifelong preference for imposing, blond older women would indeed have to take the Krasin sisters into account.)

Alex attended three different boarding schools during his three-year stay in England. The first one was close to the Krasins' home, right in Hampstead, and allowed him to return there every weekend; it managed to transform his unruly behavior in a few months, teaching him table manners and the rudiments of the English language. The second institution was the much stricter University School in Hastings, near Brighton, where there were military drills twice a week and brass buttons to be shined. (The rigorous orderliness that was to always prevail in Alex's physical surroundings may well have been inspired by the Hastings experience.) The year he entered his third school, St. Piran's in Maidenhead, he suddenly shot up by several inches; he acquired a great new level of self-confidence and was occasionally censured for excessive arrogance.

At St. Piran's School, Alex acquired two predilections that would have far-reaching results: He developed a passion for Arthurian legend, which with its knightly duties of chastity and obedience, its cult of dominant, unattainable women for whom the knight is ready to perform superhuman feats, had a complex influence on his future love life. And he became engrossed by photography, which he had already fancied as a child, ever since his father had returned from a trip abroad with a vest-pocket Kodak. Despite his mother's obsession that he become a traditional artist, this was the only art form that had interested him thus far. At St. Piran's, he spent a lot of time in the darkroom, developing and printing his own photos. He continued to spend many weekends and all of his vacations with the Krasins, who had quickly adapted to upper-crust English life; they took him horseback riding during their holidays in Cornwall or on weekends in London's Hyde Park. Alex's father made an occasional trip to London but could never stay for more than a few days, being immersed in the carrying out of Lenin's New Economic Policy. And the one letter of Alex's from St. Piran's I have in my family archives intimates that he enjoyed the school but felt rather neglected by his parents. "Dear Mamika," it reads. "How is Papyusa, why doesn't he write to me. Mama . . . please write more often. I am so happy here Mama, please write Major Bryant a letter or he will be annoyed at you. Please [also] write a letter so that Mr. Cracknell will send me some jam, please, and fruits. . . . I feel grand. I kiss you and Papa very hard. Your Shura."

And yet Henriette had begun to embarrass Alex, a feeling that would last throughout his life. She made a brief visit to London in 1922, and Alex, grown accustomed to the Krasins' understated elegance, was mortified to see how dumpy and theatrically overpainted his mother looked. She took him to a hotel in London for the weekend, and he found her so garishly dressed that he told her, point-blank: "I can't have dinner with you looking like that." Henriette had to wipe off much of her makeup and put on a severe black dress before her son would share a meal with her.

In 1922, as Alex was settling in England, Vladimir Ilyich Lenin began to suffer a series of strokes, which would paralyze him and leave him with severe mental handicaps for his last year and a half of life. The Soviet Union began to prepare itself for a transition of rule. The power struggle that occurred during Lenin's last months was marked by the ascendance of a triumvirate—Grigory Zinoviev, Lev Kamenev, and Joseph Stalin—which started systematically persecuting noncommunist members of Lenin's regime. Semyon Lieberman's unsurpassed expertise in the timber industry initially protected him. Henriette, however, immediately felt repercussions in her theater work: In the fall of 1923, she was advised that her theater, whose trademark had been the staging of Western classics, was failing to teach "proper Bolshevik values." She paid no heed to the warning. A few months later, during a rehearsal of Robert Louis Stevenson's *Treasure Island*, right after the cast had shouted "Long live the king!"—a detail never criticized during the relative cultural leniency of the Lenin years—a voice cried out from the audience: "Why not 'Long live the Soviet Socialist Republic'?" Again, Henriette paid no attention, and this time she got her punishment: *Treasure Island* was shut down by governmental order after two performances, and she was dismissed from her post as manager of the children's theater. She could not tolerate the prospect of further oppression. In 1924, she requested and received permission to accompany her husband on his next business trip to London. She never returned to Russia.

On money borrowed from a business acquaintance of her husband—Chatterton Sim, the leading timber importer in London—Henriette set herself up in a comfortable house in Kensington. This now became Alex's headquarters whenever he was not at boarding school. Henriette's marriage with Semyon, by this time, had become a mere formality, and upon each of his

business trips Semyon rented rooms in another part of town. Henriette began
to have affairs with a series of rich British lovers, including a banker who paid
for her couturier clothes and took her to Italy. She installed a private theater in
her Kensington home, in which she hoped to fulfill her new theatrical ambition: pantomimes performed with masks. But she never had a chance to
develop those talents in London. For in the first months of 1925, Semyon
Lieberman, who throughout the early 1920s had gradually spirited most of
his material holdings out of Russia, suffered a temporary financial setback. Being hard-pressed for money, he had to sell Henriette's Kensington house to
Chatterton Sim: Sim's wife, harboring mixed feelings of envy and disdain for
the "Russian savage" who took on a succession of lovers the way other women
change dresses, now wanted the dwelling for herself. Upon learning that she
had to leave her house, Henriette threw a tantrum at her husband and left for
Paris to make her life there, taking Alex with her and leaving Semyon alone, for
a while, in England.

Semyon's definitive fall from power in the Soviet Union occurred, quite
predictably, within two years of Lenin's death in January 1924. In 1925,
there began to be onslaughts upon all kinds of *spets*, who were now looked
on as "borderline elements." Dzerzhinsky's underlings, the leaders of the increasingly repressive Cheka, had long seen Lieberman as a man who "dis-
rupted the Communist front of the people's economy" by failing to toe the
strict Bolshevik line. Moreover, the death of Leonid Krasin, who succumbed
to cancer that year, deprived Semyon of his last support. By the autumn of
1925, the Economic Division of the Cheka had assembled enough of a
dossier on him to appoint a special commission charged with "investigating
specialist Lieberman." When Semyon received a summons to return to
Moscow in November of that year, all his friends implored him not to go.
(Even his wife, notwithstanding the couple's strained relations, beseeched
him not to return to Moscow.) But Semyon, a man of honor through and
through, was determined to face the charges. "I went anyhow," as he explained later, "because it was my duty to my family, to my son, to go back to
the Soviet Union and defend myself against slander. . . . [B]y refusing to return I would only prove . . . that I was really guilty as charged."

Lieberman's stay in Moscow was even more tormenting than he had expected. The Cheka had spread so many rumors about his lack of belief in the Soviet regime that even his old friend and former boss at the Supreme Council of Economy, Rykov, refused to see him. (Rykov, who never left the Soviet Union, was to be executed in the 1930s.) Upon arriving in Moscow, Semyon prepared a 150-page document concerning his years of service to the Soviet state. He sent it to the OGPU, as the Cheka was now known, and then readied himself for suicide, sleeping for nights on end with a razor under his pillow. When he was finally called to the OGPU offices, he withstood several weeks of nightly "talks" with the organization. They took place in a small, poorly lighted room to which he was escorted by an armed guard. "You've spent a lot of your leisure time with so-and-so, haven't you?" a typically trifling question went, or, "Where is your son studying now? Isn't that a very expensive bourgeois school?" He was never dismissed before 4:00 A.M.

Yet suddenly, upon the seventh week of these surreal grillings, on January 2, 1926, as Semyon Lieberman sat dejectedly at his old desk at the Central Timber Council, a Soviet official appeared before him. "Comrade Dzerzhinsky instructs you to leave the Soviet Union within twenty-four hours," he said stiffly. Lieberman first thought he was dreaming, and then realized he was saved. Dzerzhinsky had apparently decided to spare his fellow traveler's life for purely pragmatic reasons: The Soviet trade commission in London was insisting that Lieberman be sent back to western Europe to sign an important trade treaty with Sweden, for the Swedes categorically refused to sign the contract with any other member of the Soviet regime. And so, within twenty-four hours, it was Semyon's turn to leave his homeland for the last time.

After signing the contract with Sweden, Semyon went on to Paris to join Henriette and Alex. For the following months, he remained in a state of emotional turmoil that had all the symptoms of a severe nervous breakdown. And he was eventually committed, for several months of the spring and summer of 1926, to a sanatorium in Switzerland.

Alex Lieberman's youth seems to have been divided into two phases. Until the age of thirteen, he had been more or less in his father's charge, accompanying him on his trips through the Russian steppes, visiting with him in England. But in 1925, upon moving to France, he had come into his mother's jurisdiction.

SIX

Alex and His Mother

Anyone not acquainted with Henriette Pascar's background might classify her erotic behavior—the one-night stands and numerous affairs indulged in every year with dozens of lovers—as a case of simple nymphomania. But her conduct had sources far more complex than the craving of the flesh. It had to do with an astoundingly unleashed ego, and above all with the gypsy provenance that totally dominated her character. For like all gypsies, Henriette had her own codes, her own prerogatives, and above all her own sexual ethos. She came from a race of people who have always prided themselves on being a law unto themselves, who refuse to marry or bond in manners habitual to westerners, who turn caprice, volatility, and shifting allegiances into norms of behavior, who do not accept guilt or regret as valid emotions. You could not censure her for immorality—or even amorality—any more than you could censure a Saudi Arabian sheik or an African tribesman for having five wives. Gypsies are serious business. The manner in which Henriette met the man who was probably her greatest love, my great-uncle Alexandre Iacovleff, is a perfect example of the way she operated.

Henriette first saw Iacovleff in 1925 as she sat across the room from him at one of Paris's gastronomic landmarks, the Restaurant Prunier, near the church of the Madeleine. She was struck by the handsomeness of his physique—the very sharp, fine features that led some friends to compare his beauty to that of "a classical Greek sculpture"; the Mephistophelean cut of his silky, beautifully groomed brown goatee. She wanted him in her life, immediately, and so she scribbled a note and asked a waiter to carry it to him. It said *"Vous me plaisez,"* a phrase that in this context translates more readily into "I want you" than "I like you." Henriette herself, bejeweled and flamboyantly attired in a Poiret dress, was then thirty-six and at the height of her seductive powers. Family legend has it that Uncle Sasha became her lover before the night was over. Henriette was a snob, and Sasha's recent successes were bound to make him all the more attractive to her: his exhibition of Croisière Noire paintings had just sold out, he was the toast of Paris, and he had just ended a long affair with the dancer Anna Pavlova. Sasha was to remain Henriette's lover for three years, longer than any man who thus far had captured her heart.

But despite Henriette's self-indulgence and her feverish amorous life, she was capable of very astute insights into the characters and needs of those she loved. Upon moving with thirteen-year-old Alex to Paris and settling into a studio apartment in Montparnasse, she had to choose a school for him. Notwithstanding her earlier emphasis on "fantasy and imagination" in education, she was determined to get Alex into France's most demanding and elitist school. She set her sights on Les Roches, a Spartan institution set in the rolling hills of Normandy, some forty miles from Paris, which was France's equivalent to Great Britain's Eton and Harrow or our own Phillips Exeter Academy. It was even more rigorous, in its intellectual demands, than most of the government-run lycées he could have attended. And it had the added advantage of being a boarding school. For however obsessively attached Henriette was to her son, since beginning her liaison with Iacovleff she more than ever valued her sexual freedom, which would have been greatly curtailed by the presence of a teenager sleeping in an alcove right over her bedroom.

Moreover, Henriette, like all adventurers, loved challenges. Les Roches was notoriously difficult to get into unless the applicant came from an ancient aristocratic family or from one preeminent in commerce or the sciences. But Henriette, undaunted, pulled some strings with a former suitor whose brother was a deputy in Parliament and managed to get Alex an interview at the school. Although Alex spoke very little French, the headmaster was so impressed by the impeccably mannered youth with melancholy green eyes that he accepted him. Alex began to board at Les Roches at the age of thirteen, in March of 1926. Photos of him at that time show a slender, fine-featured boy with wavy black hair, his mother's full, voluptuous mouth, a large, hawklike nose, and rather prominent ears. Shining through the photograph is already a grace and ease of manner, a polished elegance of stance, that strikes one as precocious and must have greatly added to the charm he exerted over others. Young Aleksandr Lieberman, who had briefly been known as "Alexander" during his stay in England, would now be known to his French classmates as "Alexandre" or Alex. He was said to be the first Jew ever admitted at Les Roches.

Les Roches had no official spiritual affiliations, but it put great emphasis on both Protestant and Catholic students' adherence to their religious practices. Catholic students took Communion daily and did the Stations of the Cross on Fridays. Protestants had prayer meetings every morning and were encouraged to engage in frequent study of Scripture. Henriette was more than cognizant of Les Roches' religious inclination, and upon filling out Alex's application form for the school she had shrewdly written the word "Protestant" on the line asking for her son's religion. So it is natural that within a few days of Alex starting at Les Roches the school's Protestant chaplain, a Swiss Calvinist pastor, took him in charge and started preparing him for his First Communion.

French Protestantism is a reformed brand of Calvinism. It's the austere liturgy and denuded places of worship are considerably chillier than the gilded, incense-swinging High Church Anglicanism that prevailed in Alex's British boarding schools. Commanding a piety among its adherents more fervent than that of most Catholics, it stresses rigorous purity of heart and of morals and extensive daily study of the Bible. There is a proud, dour, defiant aura about the personality of many French Calvinists or Huguenots, as Catholics used to refer to them, which may have to do with the history of persecution that plagued their ancestors. "As a result of all the attempts made to bend them, they retain a great interior stiffness," wrote André Gide, who as a pious Protestant youth carried a Bible on him at all times and immersed himself into an ice-cold bath every morning before beginning a two-hour session of prayer and scriptural study.

Communion, in the French Calvinist rite, is not offered until the aspirant is fourteen or fifteen years old, and it has a dual identity as Communion and Confirmation of Baptism. Alex became very attached to Les Roches' Protestant chaplain, who offered him, as a First Communion present, the copy of the Holy Bible which remained by his bedside for the rest of his life. The pastor had inscribed his gift with a line from the fifth chapter of the Gospel according to St. Matthew: "You are the salt of the earth, and if the salt loses its savor how shall it regain it?" (This passage may well be the quintessence of the French Calvinist sensibility, for it is cited by Gide, in his memoir *Si le grain ne meurt*, as the verse on which the page of his family Bible was always opened.) Throughout his school days, Alex was a devout young man who prayed a great deal and took his religion, particularly its emphasis on sexual purity, very seriously: When the majority of his class trooped to the eminent Parisian brothel Le Sphinx, a rite of passage for well-heeled French adolescents, he was the only boy who abstained from bedding a whore and only pretended to do so, to save face.

The Protestant pastor's instructions had been Alex's first experience of spiritual life; given the milieus in which he was to spend the following many decades, they were perhaps his last. And without ever denying or belittling his Jewish identity, Alex always emphasized that his intellectual heritage, his entire culture, "was exclusively based on a Protestant, Calvinist ethic." For a few decades following his graduation from Les Roches and particularly throughout the war years, references to God and to prayer recur throughout his correspondence. Until the end of his days, he retained great admiration for the very concept of religious commitment, and once he linked his life to my mother's and mine it was he who adamantly insisted that I remain a practicing Catholic and forced me to go to church every Sunday. One might well trace other facets of Alex's personal life—his tendency to sexual abstemiousness, the denuded neatness of his studios and workrooms, the

stark, priestly uniform he wore to his office for over a half century—
to the austerity of the French Calvinist ethos he had taken to heart as an
adolescent.

Although its emphasis on athletics, unusual in the French school system, was based on the British model, Les Roches was characteristically French in its rigorous intellectual demands. Its motto, "Well-Armed
for Life," referred to the formidable intellectual weaponry it provided its
students, such as an ability to memorize and recite hundreds of lines of
Racine or Molière. As the school's headmaster had guessed, Alex was intensely motivated and a very quick study. He learned French in a matter of
weeks and soon began to excel in several subjects. Already displaying that
mercurial adaptability which would distinguish his entire career, he was also
extremely popular with his teachers and his fellow students. One of his two
closest friends at Les Roches was Jean-Pierre Fourneau, now a retired
chemist and a very lucid ninety-one when I recently spent time with him.
He has these memories of Alex and of his family setting: "He was a mid-
dling to good student, with amazing facility for every branch of learning.
We were always surprised to see how well
he could do with a minimum of work.
He was graciousness exemplified and
spent a lot of his time networking, culti-
vating friendships with his fellow students. . . . He was terribly spoiled by his
mother, she saw to it he was always
equipped with the very latest technologi-
cal gadget. My first memory of Alex
involves the luxurious new three-speed
bicycle he arrived with at Les Roches, it
was the first bike any of us had ever seen
which was equipped with gear shifts."

In addition to being popular, while at
Les Roches Alex proved to be a superior

Alexandre Lieberman in
Paris, age nineteen.

athlete and became a star rugby player and hundred-meter dash runner. This impulse to excel in all fields may well have been heightened by the anti-Semitic slurs that occasionally confronted him outside of his immediate school milieu: He once overheard a conversation between members of a visiting track team in which one boy said to another, "I didn't know they had Jews here." And shortly before graduating, as he was renewing his Nansen passport alongside his father, a clerk looked up at the two Liebermans and said, "*Alors vous n'êtes que deux youpins,*" "So you're just two kikes," leading Alex to feel that he would be forever ostracized from French society. But within Les Roches' liberal, sheltered aura, Alex's social life remained dazzlingly successful. In his last years, he was elected prefect, head boy, of his house. His two closest friends, with whom he often spent weekends, came from extremely eminent families. François Latham, whose stepfather was the popular right-wing writer Jean de la Varende, lived in a grand seventeenth-century château near the school. Jean-Pierre Fourneau, whose father was himself a prominent chemist, spent his summers in an equally expansive family domain in the Basque country. Alex's own home in Paris was no less privileged: By 1926, when Semyon definitively left Russia and settled in Paris, the Libermans themselves enjoyed fairly luxurious quarters in a brand-new building on avenue Frédéric Le Play, near the École Militaire.

Yet notwithstanding his parents' privileged life, there was one aspect of Alex's family life that caused him to suffer considerable social unease while at Les Roches: the flagrant disparity between his school's exalted elegance and the hoydenish aura of his brazen mother, who remained, as Fourneau put it, "*une gitane jusqu'au bout des doigts,*" "a gypsy through and through." This incongruity could never have been easy to live with. It came to a head on one particular weekend in his second-to-last year at Les Roches, when his friend François Latham, a sexually precocious boy who had lost his virginity in his early teens, ended up in Henriette's bed. Although Alex always dismissed the impact of this dalliance, saying it had no emotional effect on him, it may well have contributed to the severe physical breakdown he suffered a year later.

Considering the psychological complications she created for her son, it was just as well that Henriette farmed Alex out to tutors or to friends for the major parts of his summers. One such mentor was a Russian émigré who taught biology at Les Roches, Monsieur Imchenetsky, of whom Alex was very fond. He was engaged in summer to reinstruct Alex in his native Russian, which Alex had in great part forgotten while learning English and French. Their first summer vacation was spent in a pension in Brittany, the second one in Cannes. Imchenetsky, a bookish, deeply religious bachelor, made Alex read reams of Russian poetry and fiction and managed to rekindle in him a passion for the Russian language, which Alex was to retain for the rest of his life. He assigned him to read the Russian classics—Tolstoy, Turgenev, Dostoevsky, Pushkin; and he taught him a very pure, aristocratic form of Russian, untainted by Semyon Lieberman's Jewish-Ukrainian intonations, which would long be admired in émigré circles for its prerevolutionary elegance.

Other summers were emotionally more complex. On one vacation, Alex was packed off to St. Jean de Luz in the care of Ludmila Krasin, the oldest and most responsible of the Russian diplomat's three daughters—she was six years older than Alex, and he developed a crush on her. Another summer, he went to Italy with his mother and Alexandre Iacovleff, who greatly encouraged Alex's nascent artistic ambitions. When they returned to Paris, Iacovleff invited Alex to his studio to give him lessons in drawing and painting and, eventually, to do Alex's portrait. (During these visits, the youngster was very taken with his teacher's art library, a collection of books opulently bound in red leather, which had an important impact on Alex's life.) In addition, the painter always looked in on Alex when he came to visit Henriette, carefully observed whatever drawing he was working on, and commented, "Go deeper!" Alex, in fact, so revered Iacovleff that once he started painting seriously, he spent a good decade trying to imitate his virtuosic style; and like Iacovleff, he would particularly excel at hyperrealist portraits.

It is during a visit to his mentor's studio in Montmartre, when he was fourteen, that Alex briefly met the painter's niece, a beautiful twenty-year-old named Tatiana who had recently arrived from Russia. One of the interesting aspects of this encounter is that although Alex always described it with much relish, my mother preferred to avoid any mention of it, since it emphasized the six-year difference in their ages. All we know of the episode is that although the gawky youth barely out of knee pants stared with admiration at the adult belle, Tatiana, who had been swept up into the highest circles of Paris and émigré society, could not have been more bored by the boy. In those "Années Folles," when the French lived in euphoric delusions of perennial prosperity and peace, "Tata," as she was called by many of her acquaintances, was attending Josephine Baker's appearances at the Café de Paris and hobnobbing with a glamorous set that included steel magnates, prominent artist friends of Iacovleff, and the beautiful, promiscuous Krasin girls.

Shortly before meeting Iacovleff, Alex had attended an event that would greatly influence his choice of vocation: the Exposition des Arts Décoratifs held in Paris in 1925, which promoted that era of modernism to a wider audience than any other event of the decade. Alex was particularly impressed by the graphic arts in the Soviet pavilion designed by Konstantin Melnikov, where Constructivist experiments in typography, architecture, and poster design were prominently featured. The exhibition was "one of the most important events" in his life, he later said to his earliest biographer, Barbara Rose, "its futuristic forms, structures and shapes made an incredible impression on me." This 1925 Art Deco show, his mother's pressure for him to be a painter, the example set by his treasured friend Iacovleff, and the further encouragement of Alex's art teacher at Les Roches were the principal influences which, in his midteens, were drawing him to art. In his last years at Les Roches, he particularly excelled at industrial drafting, displaying a great ability for working with severe geometric forms, a predilection that would be amply displayed a quarter of a century later, in his first exhibitions of hard-edge paintings in New York.

By the fall of 1926, Simon Liberman (he westernized "Semyon" and dropped the first "e" in his surname at about this time) had recovered from the nervous breakdown he suffered after his last trip to Russia. He had resettled into his new Paris apartment, on avenue Frédéric Le Play, and his family was finally reunited. It was the first time they had lived together since 1921, when Alex was nine years old, and certainly the first time since the Russian Revolution that they had lived in great comfort. In this new home,

Henriette entertained the crème de la crème of émigré society and of the Paris art world—beyond Iacovleff, her intimates included Jean Cocteau, the painters Fernand Léger and Natalia Goncharova, the ballet luminaries Sergei Diaghilev and Bronislava Nijinska. But glamour did not necessarily mean harmony. Romances were never the issue of disagreement—Simon and Henriette had long accepted each other's dalliances. (Many of Simon's liaisons, which were considerably more discreet than his wife's, were with opera singers, including a brief one with my cherished great-aunt Sandra, Iacovleff's sister.) A far more pressing incentive for quarrel was money: *Mamasha*, as Henriette was referred to by her husband and son, always wanted more cash for her extravagant wardrobes, and even her affair with Iacovleff collapsed when she sent him a bill for a very expensive set of Vuitton luggage.

Equally troublesome was Henriette's tortured relationship with Alex, which, she was the first to admit, was rooted in her violent, uncurbed love for him. Her fictionalized memoir is revealing on this issue, exposing with unabashed candor her hysterical, para-incestuous infatuation. She admits that "all that comes from [my son] enchants me," that "this love absorbs, possesses and torments me," that "what I feel for him I have never experienced for any other being on earth." Beyond the delirious maternal love which she displayed in her book, Henriette also had an innate need for violent psychodrama; throughout Alex's teenage years, she created scenes in the most exploitative manner. He recalled her saying dreadful things about his father, swearing that she was about to leave him forever, tearing off her clothes and threatening to throw herself off the balcony. When he was thirteen or fourteen, he came home from Les Roches and found her sobbing. He stood his ground, not showing any emotion, and she slapped his face repeatedly for not showing her more sympathy. He smiled and said, "Do you feel better?" "That was my British training, never to show emotion," he recollected decades later. "This, of course, drove her mad. . . . I was sorry for her, but I'd seen her cry like that too often."

As for Simon Liberman's company, it offered Alex little solace. For however close they had been throughout his childhood, Alex found it difficult, from his adolescence on, to communicate with his father, whom his classmates remember as being silent, even taciturn, during family visits. Notwith-standing their separate lives, Simon doted on *Mamasha*, and he was intensely jealous of her consuming passion for Alex. "I'm not like Mother, I don't spoil you," he would say when reprimanding Alex about anything. Moreover, Simon was as stingy about his son's spending allowance as he was lavish with Henriette's; for decades, he played a wickedly sadomasochistic game with Alex on the issue of money, forcing him to beg hard for every franc or dol-lar, enjoying his son's abject pleas for financial aid and his tormenting filial dependence. The silences and the lack of warmth between the two men made Alex all the more vulnerable to Henriette's manipulations.

However, none of these family tensions affected Alex more deeply than the enormous embarrassment he experienced whenever his mother per-formed on the stage. For her theatrical ambitions had grown with the years. From the time the family had moved to the apartment on Frédéric Le Play, she frequently staged dramatic numbers in her salon for a small group of invited guests—performances derived in part from Isadora Duncan's cho-reography, in part from the French mime tradition. But in time, her ambi-tions required a larger stage, a wider audience. And in the spring of 1929, Simon agreed to finance a performance at the popular Théâtre des Champs-Elysées; Henriette's friend Marc Chagall designed her body-revealing cos-tumes for the show as well as its decor; her friend Darius Milhaud wrote the music. In Alex's view, it was this event that set off the health crisis which, at the age of eighteen, nearly killed him.

Nineteen twenty-nine—his senior year at Les Roches—was the year Alex was preparing to take the most difficult examination the French gov-ernment has to offer, a double baccalaureate: In addition to the examina-tions every French schoolboy has to take to pass his *bachot*, Alex had opted also to take a special exam in mathematics and philosophy, the *matelem*. These grueling tests required many additional hours of study. Moreover, an entirely new complication had arisen as Alex dealt with a sexual problem: Still a virgin, he had spent months trying to seduce the pretty twenty-four-year-old French girl, Louise, who served as his mother's maid. Louise, too, was a virgin. When the moment came, both young people proved to be to-tally incapable, and the episode, as Alex put it, was "a complete disaster."

(From the way he spoke about his subsequent sexual failures, by "disaster" Alex seems to have meant that he did not even manage the act of penetration.)

This fiasco, which, curiously, strengthened his friendship with Louise, occurred in the very weeks when Alex had been preparing his exams and shortly before Henriette's spectacle at the Champs-Elysées. He had helped Iacovleff to design the posters for the event, which had been successfully advertised throughout Paris for weeks in advance. The only problem was the performance itself. Henriette had insisted on going through with it notwithstanding a recently broken knee, incurred while skiing, which left her with a limp. The stocky, garishly dressed forty-three-year-old woman slowly, awkwardly walked around the stage striking pretentious attitudes, and Alex, who already suffered from a tortured blend of affection and revulsion for his mother, found it to be the most embarrassing vision he had ever seen.

The very next afternoon, shortly after returning to Les Roches, Alex started vomiting blood. The nurse at the school infirmary told him that "nobody vomits blood" and that he'd probably eaten too much currant jelly. But he continued to feel very ill and took the two-hour train ride back to Paris. The Libermans' family doctor was called and dismissed the episode as indigestion, telling Alex not to eat any more game. But that night, after his parents had gone out to dinner and Alex had gone to bed, he started having a truly serious hemorrhage, with blood issuing from both ends. Not having the strength to get to the phone, he managed to throw a shoe up to the ceiling, which indicated to Louise, whose room was directly above his, that she was needed. She rushed downstairs and took care of him until his parents came home. Failing, perhaps providentially, to reach their family practitioner, who had left for the weekend, the Libermans called in a local doctor who finally made a correct diagnosis of bleeding ulcers. Alex had lost so much blood that for a few days his life was in danger. He spent the following month in bed, taken care of by the excellent local doctor and by his cherished Louise. And one is tempted to think that Louise's role in saving his life made him all the more vulnerable, a half century later, to the charms of another affectionate nurse.

Numerous tensions had contributed to the outbreak of Alex's nearly fatal illness: the anxiety caused by assimilating as swiftly as he had into French society; the pressure to excel in every possible way in his academic and social life; the unease he felt as a Jew in an overwhelmingly Christian society; his particular anguish about his double baccalaureate; his botched attempt at reaching sexual manhood. But over and above all these causes, Alex always singled out the intolerable dismay of seeing Henriette in her first public performance in Paris, a sight that nearly embarrassed him to death.

Having spent more than a month in bed, Alex accompanied his mother to Aix-les-Bains, where he studied for the easier portion of the *bachot* he had missed, having decided that he must take its two sections a year apart. He passed the exam in Paris in late July, receiving a *mention bien*, the equivalent of a B or B+. In the autumn, he returned to Les Roches to study for the philosophical section of the exam, or *philo*; and the following spring—May 1930—he again passed with the same fine grade. His good showing in these government exams qualified him to apply to one of the distinguished graduate schools—École Normale Supérieure, École des Sciences Politiques, Hautes Études Commerciales—that train young men for careers in government, industry, or the teaching profession. This is what his father greatly wished for him. But his mother was pressing him more than ever to be an artist, and since his apprenticeship with Iacovleff that notion had increasingly attracted him. While still studying for his second *bachot*, he had joined a class at the studio of André Lhote, an irascible, authoritarian second-rank Cubist who expected students to ape his own style. On one occasion, upon looking at a bright-hued painting of Alex's, Lhote scrubbed away at the wet pigment, blending it into a mud hue, and drew some Cubist apples over it. (Fifteen years later, my own husband-to-be, who had enrolled in Lhote's class as a GI, had precisely the same experience with the painter.) After that incident, Alex, appalled, left Lhote's studio.

Trying another branch of art, Alex successfully passed the École des Beaux-Arts' demanding examination for its school of architecture, and equally excelled at this discipline, achieving the distinction, in his first year, of being named *"chef cochon,"* head student. But he soon grew weary of the complex mathematical and scientific knowledge demanded by architecture. And he was happy instead to arouse the interest of the famous Russian-born designer Adolphe Cassandre—yet another fellow smitten with Henriette—whose posters and advertising strategies were transforming commercial art as radically as Picasso had transformed painting. (Cassandre's most famed achievement was the renowned logo *"Du, Dubon, Dubonnet."*) Alex started to work as a part-time assistant for the designer in 1931, going to his studio in the afternoons, after his morning architecture classes. It was, in turn, through Cassandre that he attracted the attention of France's most famous magazine publisher, Lucien Vogel, a close friend of both Iacovleff and Cassandre who happened to be Henriette's *current* lover. Vogel was a very tall, blond, blue-eyed Anglophile dandy, renowned for his amorous exploits, who dressed in flamboyant pale-yellow waistcoats and high, starched collars with bow ties. He was always on the alert for fresh new talent, and in 1932, upon beginning an affair with Henriette, he started insisting that her gifted son leave Cassandre's studio to work for the art department of his magazine, *Vu.* The Great Depression had begun to ravage the French economy in the fall of that year, three years after it had struck the United States. All Vogel had to offer Alex in the way of a salary was fifty francs a week, the equivalent of some ten dollars. Alex accepted and became the assistant art editor of France's most illustrious publication when he was still nineteen. He had no qualms about quitting architecture school and putting an end to his formal education. And many decades later, he came close to ruining several careers by counseling his young protégés to follow his shining example, leave college, and "learn through experience" by working for him at Condé Nast.

In the past decade, Vogel had published some of the country's most distinctive luxury art editions—among them the drawings of Chinese and Japanese theater sets Iacovleff had made during his very first trips to the Far East and, later, the special editions of Iacovleff sketches for the Citroën expeditions. *Vu,* however, was his most innovative publication to date, a pioneering magazine with a stated purpose to "bring France a new formula—illustrated reporting on world news." Its distinctly left-wing

Alex's cover design for Vu: *March 1934, "Colonization."*

views were inciting it to document the rise of fascism in Italy and Germany in groundbreaking special issues. It had also become a showcase for the decade's most important photographers: André Kertész; Man Ray; Henri Cartier-Bresson; Robert Capa, who would cover the Spanish civil war for the magazine; and Brassaï, chronicler of Paris nightlife. A true modernist, Vogel was always looking for innovations. And the first photomontage covers Alex made for *Vu*, which were based on those very Constructivist principles that had enthralled him at the Exposition des Arts Décoratifs when he was thirteen, delighted his boss. Alex, in turn, loved the quick decision making and capriciousness involved in the creation of a weekly news magazine. He shared the office with Irène Lidova, a Russian émigré six years his elder who taught him the basic elements of layout. He often remained in the darkroom until the dawn hours, sleeping on a narrow cot in his office, perfecting photomontage technique through endless experiments of cropping and juxtaposing images. Within a few months, he was given exclusive responsibility for all of the magazine's covers, which he signed with the name "Alexandre."

Always living grandly and needing cash, Alex plumped up his tiny salary by taking on numerous freelance jobs—window displays, department-store catalogs, and even some notably kitschy commercial advertisements: one of his creations, showing Santa's sleigh being pulled by six Peugeot sedans, embarrassed Alex greatly when it was published as a double-page spread in *Vu*. A great fan of light, corny Depression-era Hollywood comedies, Alex also wrote film reviews for the magazine, which he signed with the pen name "Jean Orbay." And although his political leanings, like those of most Russian émigrés, were distinctly conservative, throughout his years with Vogel he carefully concealed his distaste for his boss's left-wing opinions. (He remained equally apolitical for most of his public life, usually pretending to hold the views of whatever mogul currently employed him.)

So as we might say in contemporary parlance, Alex was quite a package. What with his sleek good looks (a blend of Melvyn Douglas and John Gilbert, friends would say), his seductive cosmopolitan manners, his athletic skills, his considerable artistic and literary culture, his total mastery of three languages, his important job at France's most illustrious news mag-

Alex's cover design for Vu: *April 1934, "Hitler Arms."*

azine, and the bylines he was already getting, age twenty-one, for his covers and film reviews, he had attributes—status and glamour—far more impressive to women than money. And he could well have bedded Paris's most entrancing girls. Yet how far could he get, sexually, with all his attributes and charm? That was a different matter.

SEVEN

Alex and His Women

M y day-to-day recollections of Alex's physique—which go back to
my eleventh year, when my mother and I fled to America together
after the fall of France and finally settled in Manhattan—have to
do with his poor health, his rigid ulcer diet, and most particularly his glaringly white, many-mirrored bathroom. This was the exclusive site for his
grooming rituals, for my mother's took place in their bedroom, at a dressing table set a bit beyond, but symmetrically between, the two double
beds—one at either end of the room—that constituted their sleeping
arrangement. And my recollections of Alex's cosmetic habits focus almost
exclusively on the array of metal objects—tweezers, nail files, and an amazing variety of scissors and clippers, each with a slightly different curve to
them—that were set in parallel order, with surgical precision, on the top
shelf of the mirrored surface that surmounted his sink. From the time—
1942—we moved into the brownstone on East Seventieth Street that our
family was to occupy for forty-nine years, my mother and I were under
orders not to touch these implements, for Alex looked on his grooming
routine, which was carried on behind closed doors, with a particular insistence on privacy, as a significant ritual. Once or twice each year, when
Mother or I needed one of these tools for a cosmetic purpose of our own,

we'd whisper to each other, *"J'ai emprunté ses ciseaux pour une seconde,"* and in-deed spirit them back as fast as we could. Every few years it would happen: He would notice one of his tools missing, and then he would roar out twice, once into the master bedroom, once into mine, *"Qui a emprunté mes ciseaux?"* And if we brought them back with a contrite enough air, he would wag his finger with mock severity, threatening punishment for our next transgression.

These metal objects (serious metal, metal deeply etched into his per-sonality, metal that decades later would come to symbolize the surgical meanness with which he excised my family out of his life after my mother's death) were central to Alex's toilette, for they had to do with the heart of his personal cosmetic concerns: his mustache and the hair that grew abun-dantly in his ears and in his large, slightly beaked nose. Like many men de-termined to combat racial stereotypes, he was obsessed with controlling facial hair. And several times a year, as my mother opened the bathroom door to fetch herself a towel or some other object she needed, I saw him standing in front of his sink, his head bent way back as he cut delicately up-ward, with a special set of slender, curved scissors, inside his nostrils; or, his neck craned sharply sideways, he'd be cutting with still another kind of dainty implement the wayward hairs growing out of his ears; or else he'd be staring straight forward to lightly trim his thick, wavy eyebrows, which arched handsomely over his large, extraordinarily beautiful green eyes and were the only of his physical features to which he permitted a certain mea-sure of lyrical disarray—an aesthetically wise decision without which he might have looked distressingly sleek.

It was the mustache ritual that was most secretive and that I somehow failed, year after year, to observe. Since, for a half century, he kept his hair cut at the same medium length, wore the same self-invented Calvinist uni-form year after year—the same dark suit and knit ties, the same model of black rubber-soled loafers—Alex's mustache was the only physical feature to which he allowed himself to apply some degree of choice or fantasy. Over the years, as I look back on it, Alex's mustache took on distinct nu-ances and timbres of self-identity. As I see it in photographs taken in the 1930s and a few years beyond our arrival in the United States, it is a tad too thin and waiterlike, verging on the ridiculous. In my teens—the 1940s, when he became an increasingly active paterfamilias—it grew a bit in width and bushiness, in self-assertion. By the late 1950s and sixties, when I was a young wife and mother and Alex was an uncommonly engaged, adoring grandfather and had also grown famous in New York circles, it had begun to gray and become a distinctive social trademark. It intruded, in fact, into most every public description of him, leading to an abundance of phrases such as "the dapper, mustached art director of *Vogue*," or later, when he took on the editorial direction of the entire company, "Condé Nast's mustached, aristocratic director."

But the mustache, beyond being a public token of Alex's sophistication and cosmopolitanism, had a wealth of private meanings for us, his family. It was both a barometer and a concealing mask for his state of mind, for whatever he had of genuine emotions or opinions. "Alex's mustache twitched" and, later, after my children had begun to analyze his moods, "Grandpa's mustache twitched" became family passwords for those moments in which we were trying to decode Alex's all-too-frequent refuges in inscrutability. "Grandpa's mustache twitched" denoted his disposition upon the many occasions when he disapproved of something we'd done or said or felt ambivalent toward it but did not want his displeasure or even his equivocation to be on record. The mustache, in sum, was both a semiotic banner and a barrier between the public and utterly private Alex, a banner/barrier that, when it seemed in the least bit ruffled or transgressed, often helped us to chart our next course of action—which was usually to circumvent him. And I'm sure it had different meanings for each of us: Because of its touch of slightly ridiculous, groom-on-the-wedding-cake slickness and also because of its potential for masking his true feelings, Alex's mustache became, to me, a dual token of his asexuality and his often byzantine slyness.

I return to Alex's bathroom. It was a small, rather plain bathroom, with a floor of small, rough white tiles common to New York brownstones built in the 1920s and 1930s; the color of its towels, for a half century, remained light blue; since he shared it with my mother, its walls were lined with an unusual number of mirrors, and it was lit with very high-wattage bulbs. This space exuded an odor of plain cleanliness that, as a Catholic child, I somehow associated with Alex's Protestantism; it was occasionally enhanced by the Yardley's Lavender Soap, which he kept on his sink. The most immaculately scrubbed being I have ever known, Alex never took any baths or even showers, both of which he detested, but stood in front of the sink far longer than most men, meticulously sponging every inch of his body, barely splashing any water on the floor in the process. (Only in his last years, when I discovered the Jekyll and Hyde aspect of Alex's character and realized the extent to which he had inherited his mother's gypsy character traits—her deviousness, pushiness, inconstancy—did I start to read up on gypsies, learning that they loathe to be immersed in water and clean themselves in just the same way.)

In Alex's closet at the right of the sink—the top half of it consisted of open shelves, the lower part of pull-out drawers—were arrayed several dozen identical white shirts, a tall pile of white cotton handkerchiefs, and a row of gray wool socks, all stacked with equal neatness by Mabel Moses, the housekeeper who remained with the family for more than forty years. ("He always needs socks and handkerchiefs," my mother would answer, perennially stymied by the frugal limitations of Alex's wardrobe, when I asked her what he wanted for Christmas.) Finally, there was a cabinet on the wall opposite the sink in which Alex kept his medications—he was forced to take a great many but did not ever want to be seen taking them and was covert about even having them in evidence. In sum, Alex's bathroom was a cool, impersonal, ascetic space that I associated with his chronically frail health and in which I never observed any object in the least associated with sexuality or sexual enticement—except just once, when I was in my late teens and saw, pathetically curled up in a neat heap, a little yellowish condom, clearly unused, an observation that led me to reflect that my mother might once more have pleaded a headache or that he might have had another of the heartburn attacks caused by his ulcers.

Since 1940, when Tatiana and I started living with him full-time, I had always been aware of Alex's fragile health. The strict diet he had adhered to since the age of eighteen, when he had that first, nearly fatal hemorrhage, consisted of broiled meats, fish, and poultry (preferably breast of chicken) and steamed or boiled vegetables; he was encouraged to splurge on mashed potatoes, rice, and Cream of Wheat. He was forbidden all raw vegetables or salads, all onions, spices, and garlic, and alcohol had never so much as passed his lips. The chronic seriousness of his condition was confirmed when he suffered his second grave hemorrhage in 1945 and another serious one some seventeen years later, for which there was finally surgery as a cure.

What these rambling glimpses of our early home life—and particularly of those illnesses of Alex's that plagued it—add up to is that I never associated Alex with any sexual smell, gesture, or emanation. The chastely unused condom has remained symbolic to me: He was the most sexually *neutral* man I have ever known. Perhaps, as a teenager, I was disembodying him as a way of positing a barrier, of avoiding any possible attraction between us—he was, after all, only eighteen years older than I. But as I began to question Alex's oldest friends a half century later, eliciting impressions and recollections of him, their memories were utterly consistent with the sexual void I had perceived as a child, a teenager, a grown woman. "He had the aura of a flirtatious eunuch," said Zozo de Ravenel, who had known him since the 1940s. (She reported that upon being asked whether Alex was homosexual, Nicolas de Gunzburg, a *Vogue* colleague and equally old friend of Alex, replied, "He wouldn't dare.") "He was a man with a terribly limited libido," said François Catroux, who had known him since the early 1950s. "He made a great spectacle of his adoration of Tatiana, but that was in part a useful image with which to promote his career." "He was too fundamentally glacial to be capable of any great surge of sexual emotion," said Bernard d'Anglejan, also a friend for a half century. So whereas other children speculate about their father's philandering or alcoholism or irascibility, I speculated, with far greater serenity than I would have concerning any of those failings, about Alex's curious lack of sexual presence.

But one can not sum up Alex's curious libido, which was already curtailed by the Puritanism of his schooling and by his potentially fatal illnesses, without emphasizing the torturous blend of affection and revulsion he felt for his mother. For whatever limited erotic proclivities Alex developed were a form of rebellion against his mother's highly charged sexuality. Whereas Henriette's sensuality had a distinctly Oriental aura, until a few years before his death Alex usually went for blond, Nordic women—he uses the euphemism "an aureole of blondness" when describing many of his infatuations. Whereas Henriette, a shameless exhibitionist, had brandished her grossest appetites, picking up her men in cafés, at bullfights, in the Bois de Boulogne, Alex, an early devotee of Arthurian legend, tended to impose chivalric ideals on whatever women he courted, idealizing them into spiritual nymphs barely tainted by physicality. Whereas Henriette had paraded her lovers before the world, Alex flaunted his chastity and his capacity for marital fidelity, attributes that eventually became judicious, highly original tactics in his rise to power. Whereas Henriette's femaleness was of the most heavy-handed kind, abounding with lacy lingerie, extravagant makeup, and all the hip swaying and eyelash batting that can compound feminine kitsch, Alex was drawn toward tomboyish women who cultivated a streamlined, athletic look.

I can now turn to whatever Alex had of a love life in the early 1930s.

Alex always said that his "first serious love affair," as he called it, was with Irène Lidova, the Russian émigré with whom he shared the art direction of *Vu*. The affair was complicated by the fact that Alex was clearly supplanting Lidova as the boss of *Vu's* art department; by the fact that she was married to a rather jealous ballet photographer; and by her great dread of getting pregnant. And it is a striking indication of Alex's sexual hang-ups that the physical particulars of this "first serious love affair," which he carried on between the ages of twenty-one and twenty-three in a social and professional milieu noted for its promiscuity, consisted of very heavy petting.

His romance with another of his "lovers," his boss's brilliant, beautiful, politically radical daughter Marie-Claude Vogel, was equally chaste. He admired her as he had admired few women in his life and might well have married her if her politics had not been so left-wing. (Soon after her brief romance with Alex she married a prominent French communist, Paul Vaillant-Couturier, and became a standard-bearer of the party.) Chaperoned by Marie-Claude's maternal uncle Jean de Brunhoff, of Babar fame, Alex and Marie-Claude went skiing in Megève together in the winter of 1935–1936, when his liaison with Lidova was waning. They eluded her uncle's supervision to snuggle in Alex's hotel bed, kissing and hugging. Again, for reasons that are not clear (sexual morals in France's left-wing circles were notoriously relaxed), their erotic activities did not extend beyond the heavy-petting stage. Alex returned to Megève alone the following month, having decided that skiing was an excellent way to meet pretty girls. It was then that he met the beauty who was to become his first wife, a fashion model and star skier of German provenance named Hildergarde ("Hilda") Sturm, whose "aureole of blondness," as he put it once more, immediately seduced him.

Like Lidova, Marie-Claude, and most every woman in his life, Hilda, at twenty-five, was older than Alex, albeit by only two years. She made no secret of her numerous former liaisons—at the time she met Alex, she had just finished a romance with a wealthy newspaper publisher and was involved with an American sports promoter, Charles Michaelis. These affiliations did not seem to bother Alex, who proposed to her three months after they met, defying his parents' violent opposition to the match. They were married in August 1936, in a civil ceremony in Paris, with no friends or relatives present. Hilda, a good-hearted and totally unpretentious young woman, was the daughter of a Bonn schoolteacher, and one suspects that her prim family background made the respectability of marriage seem all the more appealing. She also appeared determined, to Alex's great embarrassment, to "make a man" out of him and whip him up to a very sophisticated level of sexual performance—she stripped the bed free of all sheets and blankets every night, turning it, as Alex put it, into "a sports arena." During their honeymoon in Annecy, he took numerous nude photographs of Hilda, photos of a sentimental artiness that later would make him blush, but this did not seem to increase his libido. And although one may assume that she was the first woman who enabled the twenty-four-year-old to achieve the principal stages of sexual success he was clearly humiliated by his failure to advance to greater levels of refinement. A few months after their wedding trip, when he had resumed his job at *Vu*, he came home to find Hilda playing with a white poodle. It was a present from the American sports promoter, and from then on he was plagued by suspicions that she had renewed her affair with "the poodle man."

The autumn of 1936 was a difficult period for all of France. The political events of the past three years—Hitler's rise to power in 1933 and the subsequent beginning of Germany's rearmament program—had already caused considerable alarm. The massive strikes staged in the spring of 1936, throughout the first months of Léon Blum's tenure as premier, had greatly weakened the nation's economy, cutting France's productivity by half and causing widespread unemployment. By the fall of the year, support for Blum's Popular Front had much waned. The Spanish civil war had become of increasing concern when Germany's and Italy's fascist governments started sending men and supplies to support Generalissimo Franco. Germany's reoccupation of the Rhineland that year and the signing of the Hitler-Mussolini pact made French centrists wary of forming closer ties with the Soviet Union and led the right to campaign for "peace at any price" and for pacification with Germany.

These political crises were bound to have their repercussions on a periodical like *Vu*. Its conservative Swiss backers had been made increasingly edgy by Vogel's openhearted support of Blum's Popular Front and by the magazine's forthright attacks on Nazism. This concern came to a head when, in the September 16, 1936 issue, Vogel decided to publish a political document of unprecedented boldness: a map of Germany marking the first concentration camps established by the Nazi regime. Headlined *Répartition des camps de concentration, maisons de correction et prisons en Allemagne,"* this map located several of the fatal sites, including Dachau, in which some twenty million persons, in the following decade, went to their deaths.

Within two weeks of publishing this document, Vogel received notice that *Vu* had been sold to a right-wing businessman (he later turned out to be a close friend of Pierre Laval, the future architect of collaborationist policies under the Vichy government). Vogel saved his honor by resigning, and the new owners promoted Alex to the rank of managing editor. Alex, short of cash, eager to advance his career, and little concerned with political leanings, stayed on for a few months. He continued to design covers, to streamline the magazine's typography, and to sign movie reviews. To

Alex's photograph of Hilda with her poodle, Sainte Maxime, 1937

appease his mother, who continually pestered him to publicize the new children's theater she had started, he even wrote a tongue-in-cheek review of one of her shows, heaping praise on "the ravishing costumes and sets designed by Alexandre." But in the beginning of 1937, with his ulcers growing worse and the magazine's political orientation moving—even for him—uncomfortably to the right, he too resigned from *Vu.* He hoped that he could persuade his father to offer him some means of financial support and that he might finally devote himself full-time to painting.

That same winter, Alex went to Kitzbühel with Hilda, hoping to recapture the bliss of that February a year earlier when he had met and courted her, but the vacation was disappointing: She paid little attention to her husband, being constantly surrounded by handsome, deeply bronzed ski instructors who whizzed down slopes far faster than Alex. When they returned to Paris, Alex, devoid of a job, spent a few months making a film—on the theme of women in French art. He redecorated a larger, handsomer apartment for Hilda in Villa Montmorency. On weekends, the couple went to the country house Alex's parents had recently bought in a suburb of Paris, Chatou. This increased Henriette's opportunities to sabotage her son's marriage: She hired detectives to follow Hilda, and they reported that Hilda was indeed seeing "the poodle man" again.

Alex's portrait of Hilda painted that same month.

Alex's ulcers, and his anxiety about his marriage, grew worse, and in the fall of 1937 he suffered a total physical and nervous breakdown, as his father had a decade earlier. He spent three months at a sanatorium in Switzerland, sleeping and reading Tolstoy, Balzac, and *Gone with the Wind*. Hilda came to join him at the end of December, and, trying to get their marriage off to a new start, they traveled together to Simon Liberman's seaside villa in Sainte Maxime, near St. Tropez. While convalescing in Switzerland, Alex's determination to be a full-time painter had grown even firmer. This decision was enthusiastically approved by his mother; and his father, though his finances were still being drained by the whims of the omnivorous Henriette, gave Alex a small allowance to this end.

Alex had hardly painted at all for five years, since he had gone to work at *Vu*. He had surprisingly little contact with the avant-garde art of the past decades—Picasso, Braque, and Matisse were still ciphers to him. He took his palette and easel out of doors for several weeks and did some plein air landscapes of the countryside near St. Tropez, trying to emulate the only "modern" artist he truly loved, Cézanne. He was still hampered by the sense of inferiority imbued in him by Iacovleff's virtuoso draftsmanship, and he

Alexander Liberman, self-portrait, 1938

despaired of ever equaling it. After a few weeks, he sensed Hilda's restlessness, and to keep her busy he asked her to pose for a portrait with her poodle. The painting was slickly realistic and terribly stiff, direly failing to depict the charms of the blond goddess who had so staggered him two years previously; as he finished it, he despaired of what he could do to keep Hilda from being bored. She loved jigsaw puzzles, and in the past weeks he had already kept her supplied with the largest puzzles available in the south of France. So in desperation he called Brentano's in Paris to have the largest puzzle they had in stock shipped to Sainte Maxime—composed of several thousand pieces, it took up a good part of the villa's living-room floor.

As Alex used to tell it, Hilda disappeared the morning after she had finished the largest puzzle in France. She rose before dawn, packed her dog and her belongings into her Peugeot, and drove off without so much as leaving a note. She never made any demands, then or later, and in many ways Alex was relieved by her departure. Although their divorce was not legalized until the summer of 1940, they never saw each other again. Shortly after her divorce papers came through, Hilda married the poodle-loving sports promoter, had a son with him, and enjoyed a very long and happy life.

That spring of 1938, Alex supervised the renovation of the gardener's cottage that stood below his father's villa in Sainte Maxime, so as to have a house and studio to himself. He also traveled to London to begin making a film on British art and there reencountered one of his childhood friends, Liuba Krasin, the youngest of the diplomat's three daughters. A peppy, high-spirited young woman with "a wonderful animal grace and extraordinary lavender eyes," as Alex described her, she had recently divorced Gaston Bergery, a left-wing deputy in the French parliament. To be close to her widowed mother, she had moved to London with her son, eight-year-old Lalo, and was working as a fashion model at Schiaparelli. Alex, who had entertained romantic fantasies about all three of the Krasin girls, had had a particular crush on Liuba since he had been nine and she was eleven, when she had bossed him around and tied him up in his bedsheets. "Just wait until I get older!" he had told her then. And fifteen years later, in 1938, the provocative, quasi-erotic teasing game they had indulged in as children resumed. For years, she had failed to take him seriously, calling him with the childish diminutive Shurik, but now she seemed ready to be seduced by him.

So without becoming lovers, Liuba and Alex started living together in the same apartment. Alex, once more, was terrified to take the initiative sexually. When they traveled to Paris for a few days on their way to the south of France, he slept in his own apartment, while she stayed at a hotel. He learned that during this brief time she found occasions to entertain former lovers in her room, and this revelation seems to have paralyzed him sexually even more. Then they got to the south of France, where the situation grew to be even more complicated.

Alex's villa in Sainte Maxime was barely furnished. And upon going antique-shopping with Liuba, soon after arriving, he saw a pair of arm-

Alex's photograph of his childhood friend Liuba Krasin, 1938.

chairs that he decided he must have. But the *antiquaire* said he couldn't sell them because they were reserved for Vicomtesse du Plessix, who was just moving into a new apartment in Paris. "That's Tata!" Liuba exclaimed. "We must call her!" Alex remembered having met Tatiana at Iacovleff's studio when he was a youngster and having subsequently glimpsed her—tall, blond, imperious, a model of Parisian elegance—at a few of his mother's cocktail parties, he was equally pleased to see her again. Liuba and Alex inquired further and found out that Tatiana was staying near Sainte Maxime in the company of a Russian-born American plastic surgeon, Eugene de Sawitch. Liuba and Alex contacted them, and the very next evening Tatiana and Dr. de Sawitch came to dinner with them.

De Sawitch had come into Tatiana's life two years earlier, in the south of France, when she was riding in a friend's convertible on the way to a lunch at Aldous Huxley's. The driver, who had lost a leg in World War I, took a turn too fast, the car overturned, and Tatiana's larynx was pinned under a seat. Her life was saved by the fact that the driver's artificial limb, which had been torn off and lodged near her neck, was thick enough to protect her larynx from being crushed. She was blue in the face from lack of oxygen, however, and the inept local police, upon arriving at the scene, decided she was dead and took her to the morgue at Hyères. My father, who was then in Paris, was contacted immediately. He hired a plane and within two hours arrived in the company of de Sawitch, a friend of his. They felt her pulse and had her transferred to the Toulon hospital. De Sawitch immediately performed the first of many operations that would save Tatiana's arm, which had been severely burned by acid that had dripped onto it from the battery of the car. He continued his work two weeks later when she was transferred to the American Hospital in Paris; in the course of the following year, he rebuilt her limb through a series of eighteen grafting operations, falling in love with her in the process.

So there was Tatiana, back in Liuba's and Alex's lives. She had emerged from her ordeals with a hoarse voice, a crippled right hand, which she kept swathed in a silk scarf, and an acute case of claustrophobia that was to last her entire life. But her joie de vivre and ebullience were undiminished. She had successfully resumed her career as a hat designer and continued to enjoy a friendly relationship with her husband, Bertrand du Plessix. Tatiana had grown enormously fond of de Sawitch (their friendship remained undiminished until his death two decades later) but had made it clear that she was not in the least drawn to him romantically. The four new companions—Liuba, Alex, de Sawitch, Tatiana—saw one another frequently during the next two weeks, sharing trips to the beach, trying out new restaurants and nightclubs. Tatiana was attracted by Alex's cosmopolitanism, elegance, and, as she put it later, "upper-class good manners." Alex may have been all the more captivated by the bold, statuesque blond beauty because of her kinship to Iacovleff, the recently deceased hero of his youth. One night, when they were returning from a restaurant, the two were sitting by each other in the backseat. Alex touched Tatiana's arm and said, "You have wonderful skin." She may have responded with a smile; that is when he felt the first surge of desire for her.

August 1938 came to an end. Tatiana went home to her atelier and her social life in Paris; de Sawitch returned to the United States; Liuba went back to her London home, her son, Lalo, and her job at Schiaparelli. Alex also returned to London to live with Liuba and Lalo. He spent the following weeks painting, as usual; one of his projects was to finish a portrait of eight-year-old Lalo, who had grown very fond of him. Liuba seems to have decided that Alex was going to marry her, but two circumstances got in the way. One was a warning issued to Alex by Liuba's mother, Madame Krasin, who had been devoted to him since he was nine years old and was all too aware of her daughter's instability. She cautioned him that Liuba might well hurt him if he became any more deeply involved with her. "Just leave, Shurik," she told him. "It would be better for you."

There was an even more important reason for the breakup of Alex and Liuba's romance: A letter from Tatiana arrived in London, asking Alex whether he was interested in purchasing any books from the library of her uncle, Alexandre Iacovleff, who had died in the spring. Tatiana was the executor of his will; it was normal that she would think of Alex, who had adored her uncle Sasha, as a potential buyer.

Tatiana's letter, written in early October of 1938, a few weeks after

Edouard Daladier, Neville Chamberlain, and Adolf Hitler had set the stage for World War II by signing the Munich accords, was like a flare, a signal for Alex. He decided to decamp immediately for Paris. He left Liuba and Lalo as abruptly as Hilda had left him, slinking out of the house early one morning with all his possessions, without saying a word or leaving a note. A few hours after arriving in Paris, he went to see Tatiana and bought most of her uncle Sasha's books—many volumes of art history, a ten-volume edition of J. H. Fabre's *Souvenirs entomologiques,* a fine morocco-bound set of Buffon's *Histoire naturelle*—a small, handsome collection that stands on my shelves to this day. They started to see each other every evening. After a few tête-à-tête dinners, they returned to Alex's studio at Villa Montmorency. He found her as fearful of sex, as anxious about it, as filled with *pudeur*—a barely translatable word that denotes a Puritanical chasteness of mind and body—as he had been all his life. "I was both afraid and triumphant," Alex told one of his biographers. "I think she was wearing a black or green satin gown . . . and a Cossack hat on her blond hair. . . . It was . . . the most extraordinary experience of my life. After we slept together for the first time, I knew that my life had changed forever."

It was a month or so later that I had my first glimpse of Alex. On an autumn Thursday of that year, when I was staying with my great-grandmother at her flat near the avenue Foch—a weekly visit, which occurred on my governess's day off—I had fallen ill and started running a fever. On this particular afternoon, Mother had come to pick me up at Babushka's. It must have been at least October, for she had swathed me in her fur coat before lifting me up in her arms. The occasion was notable because there were quite a few instances when I had fallen ill at Babushka's, and this was the very first time that Mother had stepped into the nitty-gritty of child care.

Now that I recall it, I marvel at her wondrous sense of theater: This would be the first time that she was allowing the two opposite poles of her life to meet—the first time Alex, her new lover, was to see her child—and she was staging the performance with utmost care, putting on the "Look at how good a mother I can be!" show. This is how she choreographed it: Blond, fragrant Mother carried me toward an affectionately smiling man whose thin mustache, almost slick in its neatness and brevity, accentuated

Tatiana at Alex's house in the south of France in 1938,
at the beginning of their lifelong romance.

the prominence of his generously arched nose. His graceful, photogenic gestures bordered, like my mother's, on the theatrical. This was one of the great photo ops of their lives, and he posed for it as expertly as she did, leaning on top of his white convertible, his right elbow supported by his left arm, right hand supporting his chin, right index finger thrusting up a bit on his right cheek. As I came closer to him, I noted his exceptionally well-groomed dark hair, the kindness of his smile. His most distinctive expression—the expression that most instantly struck me as he eased me gently into his car—is best described by the French word *attendrissement,* that blend of compassion, pity, and tenderness that tells a child that the adult has been truly *moved and affected* by her, that she has begun to make him malleable to her every desire; which is the way Alex was to remain with Tatiana and me for many decades to come.

He drove us to the doorstep of our family flat on the rue de Longchamp, and as I said good-bye to him I remember thinking that he was the nicest man I'd ever met.

A few weeks before Alex and Tatiana began their courtship, Nazi forces had invaded Czechoslovakia's Sudetenland. The French government was terrified by recent reports of Germany's air strength and was doubtful that its own army, weakened by years of pacifist policies, could strike effectively at Hitler's troops without suffering dire consequences. It eagerly approved Neville Chamberlain's suggestion to sign the Munich accords, which, by sacrificing a good portion of Czechoslovakia, France's ally, seemed to postpone the grim prospect of another war with Germany. The French left and pessimists of various political stripes (my father among them) looked on Chamberlain's accords as the most cowardly of capitulations: They feared that Hitler's capture of Czechoslovakia's great Skoda arms complex and the collapse of the Czech defense line would free the Wehrmacht to deploy its full weight against France. But the majority of the nation greeted the Munich accords with rejoicing, and the delusionary aura of the Années Folles was sustained.

Many merry new songs became popular that fall and winter. At fashionable nightclubs such as Le Boeuf sur le Toit and Grand Écart, Alex and Tatiana held hands as the waiflike twenty-one-year-old Edith Piaf sang "Mon Légionnaire"("*Il était blond il était beau / il sentait bon le sable chaud*") and Jean Sablon crooned "*Vous qui passez sans me voir / Sans même me dire bonsoir.*" They attended the popular six-day bicycle races at the Vel' d'Hiver, the huge stadium where, four years later, some 13,000 French Jews would be incarcerated in subhuman conditions by the collaborationist French police. They went to see Jean Gabin in that fall's hit movie, Marcel Carné's *Quai des brumes*. They wept over Jean Renoir's *La grande illusion*, which contradicted all cinematic precedent by presenting a wealthy young Jew as an exemplary French soldier. They also went to poetry readings, concerts, and many plays. Such cultural pursuits were more suited to my mother's tastes. But just as he would always adapt to any compromise beneficial to the advancement of his career, until the end of his days Alex would instantly adopt the proclivities of whatever woman he was in love with. With Hilda, he had whizzed down ski slopes; with Irène Lidova he had attended exhibitions of typography at the Musée des Arts Decoratifs; with Marie-Claude, he had attended left-of-center political discussions; with Liuba, he had Charlestoned in nightclubs; with Tatiana, he went to hear Robert Casadesus play Mozart. The first year of their love was sweet, so sweet in that last year of Europe's peace.

It was also during those weeks that the first phase of Alex and Tatiana's correspondence began.

Her letters are loving but breezy, chatty. On December 26, 1938, she's getting ready to go skiing in St. Moritz with her suitor of the past few years, a tall, courtly millionaire, twenty years older than she, named André Wormser. After dismissing Wormser, whom she's attempting, as gently as possible, to ease out of her life, she plans to meet on the ski slopes with Alex, who is currently in the south of France.

"My love," she writes from Paris as she's packing up for her trip. "I can't go away without telling you that I love you so much and I'm so happy to be with you. I'm leaving with a hope of returning quickly to your gentle arms."

"Don't forget . . . Bach and Mozart records [and] your ski things," she writes the following day from the resort.

"I'm being very careful," she reports on December 29 about skiing conditions, "because the streets are full of the one-legged and one-armed. It's considered an elegant notion, but I'll do my best to avoid it. I have a dire need to get to you in one piece. W. [Wormser] caught a strep throat and stays in bed the whole day till 6 pm, when I come down to play Lexicon with him. It suits me well and I feel pity for him. How we're going to ski!! How I adore you! How happy our life will be. This is only the beginning."

"I've just woken up and I love you and miss you frightfully," she writes him the following day. "The [ski] lesson lasts until 12:30, then we go downhill to St. Moritz for lunch, and resume the lesson at two until 4:30. At 5 I have some pastries with fellow sufferers, at 6 I meet some friends at the bar, or I play cards with W. Dinner is at eight followed by a long hot bath and bed, at which time I fall asleep immediately. . . . While falling asleep I keep thinking about you and your gentle hands and about everything that is so dear to us. I love you."

For the year 1938–1939, only one letter from Alex to Tatiana has survived—he was more fastidious about preserving their correspondence than she was. But that one surviving letter is the real thing.

"How spoiled we have been by this rare love which only offers its gifts to those who know how to truly love," he wrote her in November 1938. "You know how to love me as no woman has ever loved me, and thanks to you a man was born. . . . To love you has become a prayer, a benediction sent by heaven. . . . I only know life through our glances, our bodies, our thoughts, I have loved you I love you and shall continue to love you until the day when death will part us."

After skiing together in St. Moritz in January 1939, the lovers went to spend time together at Alex's new house at Sainte Maxime. The week they spent together there was, in Alex's words, "the greatest moment of my life." "The feeling was indescribably strong. I knew, and I'm sure Tatiana knew, that this was for life."

Decades later, one of Alex's closest friends, the editing wizard Tina Brown, had this to say about Alex and Tatiana's relationship: "She seemed to have had the same impact on him as Wallis Simpson had on the Prince of Wales. . . . [W]atch that phrase which always recurs in his conversation: 'Tatiana made a man out of me.'"

EIGHT

Tatiana and Bertrand

To all appearances, Tatiana's marriage to Bertrand du Plessix, which was celebrated in Paris on December 23, 1929, had gotten off to a marvelous start. The couple went to Naples for their honeymoon— a first trip to Italy for both of them—and Tatiana's letters to her mother glow with the serenity unique to young brides. "Bertrand is enormously caring, a tender husband and a marvelous companion," she wrote from Pompeii. I seem to have been conceived within a fortnight of my parents' marriage—my birth date is September 25, 1930, and my mother used to joke that I had "saved her honor by two days." Directly after her honeymoon, she settled in Warsaw, where my father, a linguistic whiz who spoke flawless Polish, had been serving as commercial attaché at the French embassy; initially Tatiana seemed happy with her new home. The first surviving letter she wrote her mother from the Polish capital is dated March 30, and she seems to have already informed her of her pregnancy: "They do an analysis every three weeks, so far so good. There's no nausea, I take a lot of strengthening medications. I spend a lot of time in the fresh air, drive to the tennis court to see Bertrand play, and almost every day go to the races, where we have a box, to cheer the French horses." They plan to take their summer vacation, she reports, on the seashore at the Gulf of

Finland. She also tells her mother about a recent Prokofiev concert at which the composer himself conducted the orchestra and played the piano; it was such a "colossal success" that the march from *The Love for Three Oranges* had to be performed twice as an encore. Their social schedule was hectic, she adds, because the many French and Italian businessmen passing through Warsaw have to be feted, and she constantly entertains guests at lunch. The postscript to that missive, written in Bertrand's hand, reads "*Je vous embrasse, chère mère.*"

This euphoria of young wedlock was broken, of course, by the news of Mayakovsky's suicide, which Tatiana received less than three weeks after that March letter. Bertrand seems to have handled her emotions with enormous understanding and tenderness. "He's a real friend, and it seems

Tatiana and Bertrand du Plessix at an "all white" ball at the French Embassy in Warsaw in 1930.

most unlikely that we could ever live without each other," Tatiana wrote her mother in the first days of May. Less than two weeks after the tragedy, Bertrand arranged a trip to a spring fair in the western city of Poznan to cheer her up. On the road, "everything was flowering and green," and Tatiana's spirits temporarily brightened. She continued to love their apartment, which was also surrounded by greenery—"there's a sea of green outside the widows and no sense of being in a city, Warsaw is a big village, not at all like Paris." The night before they had heard Feodor Chaliapin as

Mefistofele, who was still marvelous "despite his age," and he too had had a "colossal success." As for her pregnancy, it was going as well as ever; her only complaint was that she was eating for three and growing fat.

Two months later, she exults in the news that Bertrand has arranged for her to go with him to Paris, where she could see her grandmother, her sister, and all her relatives and friends. She would travel four days ahead of him by steamer, and he would fly. It was 35 degrees Centigrade in the shade in Warsaw, and she greatly looked forward to the sea voyage. Yet under this veneer of cheer, one senses that Tatiana was still obsessed by the Mayakovsky tragedy. She asked her mother to send her any other newspaper clippings she came across concerning the poet and reassured her once more that she was not blaming herself exclusively for the catastrophe. "There was . . . a combination of many reasons, plus his psychic illness."

What about Bertrand du Plessix, who was trying to bring happiness to a young woman still tormented by the century's bloodiest revolution and the suicide of her great first love? One of the several traits my parents shared is that they were both seeking refuge from their pasts. Tatiana had been fleeing from the desolation of postrevolutionary Russia. Bertrand had been fleeing a family wrecked by generations of poverty and pride. When I think of what my father fled from, I recall the genteel crumbling château in a flat plain of the Vendée, a few miles from Nantes, where five earlier generations of du Plessix were born and where his oldest brother, Joseph, lived until his death in the 1950s. I see it in a mist of small, raw rain, for it is a dank, bleak place, ransacked by indigence and prejudice and piety. I see crucifixes on the peeling walls of every room; windows closed in highest heat against the dreaded *courants d'air*; and aunts with sad eyes and deep body odor burdened by the ignorant penny-pinching hygiene of French provincial life, by many pregnancies, and by infant deaths. I hear the language of church festivals cited to denote every event of the year: we cut our first hay at Pentecost; at Assumption we went to see Aunt Marie in Brest. I smell the dust of sadistic Confirmation cards preserved in the pages of ancient missals, depicting young humans who writhe in the fires of hell. I recall images of ancestors in military costume being honored like Confucian shrines: your great-grand-uncle de Laromicière, who completed France's conquest of Algeria! Your uncle de Montmorencie, a hero of the battle of the Marne! I think of the pamphlets scattered about the house proselytizing for ultraright-wing groups—Action Française, Croix de Feu—that preached cults of Joan of Arc and Nostradamus and a return to a heroic medieval France purged of Semitic and foreign blood. I think of a cousin who until recently composed, in Alexandrine couplets, attacks on legalized abortion for the Catholic press. I think of other cousins who still go into mourning clothes and celebrate a funerary Mass every January 21, to observe the anniversary of the beheading of Louis XVI. I think of narrowness and resignation and a desperate refuge in the swamp honor of a past.

All that is what my father fled from; I am the child of two ambitious refugees. Like my mother dreaming of glory in her own dismal Russian province, he had longed for the brio and glamour of the siren Paris. His parents had died of diphtheria when he was fourteen, and as the youngest of five children he was left in the care of older brothers and sisters. He was extraordinarily handsome—tall for a Frenchman, with dark hair and hints of Valentino in his soft-cheeked, doe-eyed face—and he had his unruly side, but he was obsessively studious. He fled the dim province of his birth by passing the entrance exams to two of France's most prestigious graduate schools, Hautes Études Commerciales and École des Langues Orientales. He had linguistic gifts equaled by few of his contemporaries, mastering fluent English, German, and Polish by the time he was twenty-five, earning an appointment at the French embassy in Warsaw at twenty-six. But there was an eccentric, Dionysiac side to Bertrand du Plessix's character that may have come from the Celtic Brittany blood and has affinities with the Slavic temperament. While making a career in the social sciences, he had become an accomplished musician; a passionate lover of poetry; a licensed pilot; an expert in Chinese sculpture, Pompeian glass, and many other branches of the visual arts. There was also a melancholy, depressive streak in his character for which romance seemed to be the principal palliative—he was definitely a Don Juan and had a taste for beautiful, elegant women. The same adventurous, reckless side that enticed him to all those proclivities led him to fall in love, in the late 1920s, with a dazzling Russian girl who was being ardently sought by a very famous poet—in retrospect, the thrill of the

Bertrand du Plessix at right, greeting officials at Warsaw airport, 1930.

competition must have all the more fired "Vicomte" du Plessix's ardor for
Tatiana.

I set off that title because it has to do with another trait my parents
shared: My father's snobbism, albeit of a different sort, was quite equal to
my mother's. Our family tree traces our ancestry to a "Sieur" Jochaud du
Plessix who lived in the region of Nantes in the sixteenth century. Although the family might be called "noble" in the very widest sense, none of
my father's brothers or uncles used the title "vicomte." Notwithstanding
the fact that it had not been used for generations, some elitist impulse
prompted my father to engrave the title on his own calling cards when he

took his first diplomatic post. (Neutral observers have told me that it was not uncommon for young diplomats of vaguely noble lineage to similarly embellish their credentials abroad—besides, Poles were notoriously receptive to titles.) However he came to it, the word "vicomte" could not have failed to impress my mother when they were introduced by mutual friends, in late 1928, in the lobby of the Ballets Russes de Monte Carlo, during one of his home leaves.

Here is the way I understand my parents' courtship in the context of Tatiana's Mayakovsky romance: Bertrand and Tatiana meet in the last weeks of 1928, after the poet's return to Moscow. They make a strong impression on each other, see each other often, and when Bertrand returns to Warsaw they start a correspondence of growing ardor. When Mayakovsky arrives in mid-February 1929 for eight weeks, Tatiana keeps du Plessix on the back burner; but one particular sentence from a letter to her mother, written just before the poet's return to Paris, indicates that the Frenchman is already pressing his suit: "Various admirers want to take me to various countries," she writes, "none of them seem like anyone at all compared to M." It's clear that du Plessix paid court to her more fervently than ever when he returned in late spring, after Mayakovsky's final departure. Tatiana must have spent an anxious summer, torn between the eminent poet who offered to fulfill one of her principal ambitions—fame as a great artist's muse—and the elegant Frenchman who offered her, in however ersatz a form, the aristocratic credentials she'd craved much of her life. The rest of the denouement is clear: Bertrand returns in October, when Tatiana has realized that Mayakovsky is destined not to return, and she accepts his offer of marriage.

There is no need to dwell on Tatiana's reaction to Bertrand's family when, shortly before their wedding, he brought her to the du Plessix' genteel, shabby family estate in the Vendée for the obligatory introductions: "*Tout a fait brave*," she would describe her future in-laws to her friends, "but they haven't bathed since the Middle Ages." As for his relatives' astonished reaction to Tatiana, he had strayed much too far from their ways to pay attention to it. On the bride's side of the family, her status-conscious Russian relatives were overjoyed by their girl's fiancé: His polish, his elegance, his gift for Slavic languages charmed them at first sight, and the affection they bore him was always amply returned. His title particularly satisfied Uncle Sasha's elitism: One can imagine his elation when he was able to order, as a wedding gift for his beloved niece, a twelve-piece silver toiletry set embroidered with viscountal crests.

A year and a half into her marriage, in June 1931, Tatiana writes her mother to tell her that yours truly, then nine months of age, has just been weaned. "The little girl is growing," Tatiana relates at the end of a long letter which also describes the success being enjoyed in Paris by her sister Lila, who with Uncle Sasha's help had been able to emigrate from the Soviet Union earlier that year. (Lila had just won a beauty contest in Paris.) "I've just stopped nursing the child," Tatiana resumes,

> and therefore I'm driving to Vilna tomorrow to a friend's house for the Trinity holiday, it'll be the very first time I shall have left her. Luckily there's a phone, and one can telephone every hour, day and night. . . . The child is growing prettier, and to the great envy of Bertrand already says "Mama" and "Nyanya". She weighs 10 kilos: a truly fantastic weight. Write me what you want me to send you in the next parcel! No doubt your lilacs are blooming and beautiful. Loving kisses to you and Père.

That letter of June 1931 is the last one of Tatiana's missives from Warsaw to have survived. In the following months, some somber turn of events dispatched the du Plessix home to France. For by the next letter, dated spring 1932, Tatiana is back in Paris, living with Bertrand and me at Square Henri Pathé, near the Tour Eiffel, and her new hat business is already flourishing.

> I write you now from a village where we're spending Easter with friends, we'll return in three days. Babushka is looking after the little one, and is sleeping in our apartment. I've been absolutely exhausted, these past weeks, by the Easter hats. I've made an unbelievable quantity of them, so much work! Moreover Bertrand most inconveniently came down with grippe: I've had to look after him more carefully. Here I'm already well rested: it's a true 18th century country house with no conveniences,

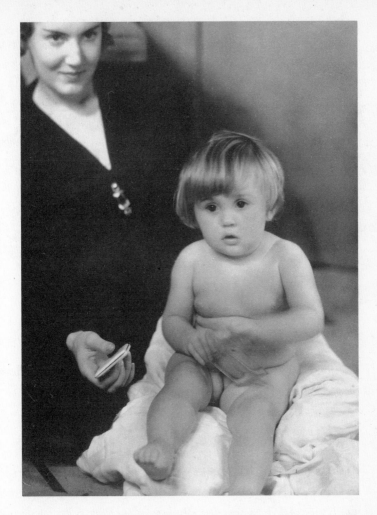

Tatiana and eight-month-old Francine, Warsaw, 1931.

but extremely sympathetic. And, most important, one doesn't have to think of any-thing. In the mornings—instead of hats, I collect salad. Uncle Sasha will be coming back in a month from Asia. His expedition has ended very sadly. His boss [Georges-Marie Haardt] died of pneumonia, and Babushka will worry frantically about Un-cle Sasha until she gets definite word that he's left that dreadful place. It's all terribly sad. . . . The little one grows at an unbelievable rate, and when nurses in the park are told that she's only 1½ they're very chagrined, because she looks at least 2½ years old.

Tatiana sunbathing by the Mediterranean in the early 1930s.

The following letter, dated a few months later, shows the du Plessix still prospering on a summer vacation in the south of France.

Beloved Mamulenka,

We've already had two weeks at the sea shore, where we've rented a dacha from one of our friends. Francine has been swimming for the first time: she really loves it, and cries when she has to leave the water. She's very sunburned. . . . I'm sending you a shot of the family, and of Froska naked. She's very appetizing, in a month she'll be two years old, and I think to myself "Well, just look at what I produced!" I feel as if I've just given birth to her. . . . Babushka is at her brother's at Arcachon, and Tyotya [Aunt Sandra] is at a spa healing her legs. Later she'll come to us, so write her at this address.

But two years later, in September of 1934, my father seems to be out of a job again, Mother's hat business appears to be the mainstay of the du Plessix' finances, and the family has not been able to afford even a summer vacation.

Beloved Mamulenka,

I congratulate you on your name day—today we celebrated Francine's fourth birthday. She received lots of presents. We've had a big change. I've dismissed her nyanya, who had to return to Poland. But everything's fine, Froska gets along very well with her new governess, who by the way is far more suitable than the old nurse. I've again been so submerged in work that I didn't take any vacation. But I feel well because I didn't stop the gymnastics, I did them every day all summer. Bertrand for the time being is working at home. Sasha went to Boston for a year, where he's going to lecture on portrait painting and reorganize the museum. It's a wonderful uncle we have.

There are several versions of why the du Plessix left Warsaw, apparently in a precipitate way, in 1931. According to my mother's face-saving account, the decision to leave was taken of my father's own free will, because he wanted to go to work for the Agence Havas, France's leading news agency, which had offered him a job as correspondent. But everyone else I have talked to, including those friends and relatives who loved my mother, put the blame squarely on her. According to their reports, after a few months the provincial constraints of a less-than-glamorous diplomatic post—the rigid protocol, the dinners for the Papal Nunzio, the entertaining of commercial attachés from Oslo and Addis Ababa—made her restive for Paris and led her to commit some serious faux pas. One might have sympathy for her. She had fled the barbaric East, crying out, "To Paris! To Paris!" as desperately as Chekhov's protagonists cry out "To Moscow!" And rather than enjoy the glamorous cosmopolitan life she'd coveted, she'd been brought to a dinky Polish city nine tenths of the way back to the Soviet nightmare she'd fled—in retrospect, it doesn't seem quite fair.

The kinder rendering of the particular transgression that led to the du Plessix' dismissal from Warsaw is that my mother had loudly announced, at an official dinner, *"Je déteste les Polonais."* The more serious allegation is that the penniless couple was undone by my mother's proclivity for high living and her inability to limit herself to the modest diplomat's salary, which was their only source of income. According to this variant, she put great pressure on my father to furnish her with the luxuries she had always dreamed of—good clothes and furs—and my father, who himself loved to put on a show, complied. He appears to have sold diplomatic favors to shady commercial interests, to have gotten caught, and to have been asked to resign. This is the account I received from both my great-aunt Sandra, who adored my mother but was mindlessly candid, and my aunt Lila, who disliked her sister and was savagely shrewd. The hysterical denials issued by my mother when she learned that I'd been given this version of the story only corroborate the veracity of my aunts' reports.

At first, the du Plessix' Paris life seemed to hold to the same fashionable pattern it had had in Warsaw: They continued to be one of the handsomest couples in town, to win waltzing prizes at balls. They retained close ties with the diplomats whom they had met in Warsaw—among them were William Bullitt; George Kennan; John Wiley, my godfather, who had been second in command at the American embassy in Warsaw and had become their closest friend there; and an entrancing chargé d'affaires at the German embassy, Hans Gunther von Dincklage, also known as "Spatz," who was later transferred to Paris and was to reenter my mother's life in a curious way during World War II.

My mother rented a little atelier a few blocks from home where, with the help of an assistant, she designed and sold her hats. As my father worked in various businesses—I suspect he never found his proper niche after being eased out of the diplomatic corps and resented my mother bitterly for having ruined his career—they cultivated moneyed acquaintances who might make up the clientele for Tatiana's business. To upgrade her standing in the Paris *monde*, Tatiana struck a deal with one of Paris's most prominent couturiers, Robert Piguet (of Fracas and Bandit perfume fame), whereby he dressed her for free on the condition that she wear only his clothes.

Then, within a few years of their return from Warsaw—probably in early 1935—another event darkened my parents' lives. One afternoon, Tatiana came home earlier than expected from her atelier—perhaps she had a migraine, to which she was prone—and found her husband in bed with her friend Katia Krasin, one of the three sisters whose erotic appetites seem to have affected my family's destiny. This is an episode which, in later years, my mother related with that matter-of-factness which is often the readiest mask for deep pain. With generous leniency toward my father, she put all the blame on the Krasin woman—a vampish dark-haired beauty married to an alcoholic Polish aristocrat—for whose charms many a Parisian husband had strayed. "Listen, how could Bertrand help it?" my mother commented a half century later. "He was so seductive, he had such charm that every woman in Paris was ready to open her legs for him; *plus* [she often used that word for emphasis, pronouncing it in the Russian way, "plious"] *"plious* Katia was drugged much of the time, and very beautiful, and a famous nymphomaniac, she threw herself at him. . . . It wasn't his fault at all," she concluded, shrugging her shoulders. Tellingly, Tatiana's next missive to her mother, a breezy note dated 1935, is the first of her letters that makes no mention whatever of Bertrand. It is also the first of her missives to reflect the stranglehold of censorship during Stalin's terror: Any letter that gave a negative impression of Soviet Russia now risked being intercepted and destroyed, and many Russian citizens had begun to be imprisoned or sent to labor camps on the mere ground that they had received compromising letters from abroad. Tatiana seems shrewdly cognizant of these dangers and even knows to include comments flattering to the Soviet regime.

Mamulenka,

I write you from the country, where I'm resting for 24 hours. Notwithstanding my great love of reading, in Paris I'm so occupied with work and social life that for months on end I don't open a book. I only have time for newspapers. I saw here at the cinema the sports parade in Moscow, it's truly remarkable. The health and beauty of the youth and of the sports give the nation great honor. Sports are practiced here also, but only in privileged circles. . . . I'm dreaming of tearing myself away in the fall for winter sports, which I've already not done for three years. Francine now looks wonderful. She goes to kindergarten, and is learning to read and write. She's huge and very noisy and quick—but on the whole an absolute treasure.

PS. For heaven's sake don't give anyone anything about Mayakovsky— anything. It would be unpleasant for me if anything were said about that.

Seeing that her social milieu in Paris is predominantly conservative and that tensions between the Soviet Union and Western democracies are growing by the day, it is understandable that Tatiana now wants to conceal her romance with the Soviets' national hero. What is far more opaque, in these years of her life, is her true attitude toward my father's tryst with Katia Krasin. Tatiana could afford to be lenient about that episode fifty years later, but at the time she must have been deeply hurt, deeply shocked. She was, after all, the daughter of decorous, Puritanical Russian gentry; she had been a virgin when she married my father; her most beloved female mentors were her gentle, very devout Babushka and Aunt Sandra; her notoriously scrupulous sensibility had early been derided by Elsa Triolet, who reported that Tatiana "fainted at the sound of the word *merde*." And it must have been agonizing to come home one afternoon and see her husband and her old friend wrangling on her bed. (When I try to imagine the episode, I see it in tones of glaring white—Katia's pale skin and amber hair, the sunlight on the white sheets—and even I, to this day, am offended.) My very first memory of my father and mother together, in fact, concerns a dreadful quarrel in their bedroom at Square Henri Pathé, and I have often wondered whether it was related to the Krasin incident.

In this first memory of my parents, I am in their bedroom, standing by my father on the window side of the bed, and a large object flies high above us, thrown by my mother toward my father to the sound of violent imprecations. As the missile thuds behind us, missing us by a few inches, I turn around to look at it. It is a squat, yellow tome, a telephone book. Standing across the room, by the door of her closet, my mother continues to shout, waving her arms. My father stands very still, looking at her with a faint smile, attempting to look bemused. After a few more stormy imprecations, she looks at herself briskly in the mirror that faces the closet, smooths her hair, and leaves the flat, slamming a door behind her. If the altercation concerned a sexual transgression, it probably related to my father's fling with beautiful, drugged Katia, for none of his later affairs would have evoked a tantrum—from that day on, my mother slept in a different room.

And from that time on, my memories of family life are totally fragmented, as if stored in drawers of memory that never connect—moments alone with my father, alone with my mother, alone with my beloved

Babushka and great-aunt Sandra. Although my parents continued to live in the same apartment until the fall of Paris in June 1940, I can remember very few occasions I shared with both of them, and this sense of their great apartness gave me a feeling of superfluity, of unworthiness, that was to last for many years. I have only two other recollections of seeing my parents together before 1939: In one, we are standing side by side at Babushka's deathbed, clutching one another's hands, each of us weeping profusely as she rasps her last breaths. In another, we are sitting at the dining-room table of our apartment, I bite lustily into an apple, and in a rare moment of shared contentment my parents' eyes meet somewhere over my head to offer me that most precious treasure—approval of the fact that I exist at all.

But these are exceptional moments, for they lead quite separate lives. I am left with one particularly vivid memory of my father announcing that he's taking me to see a friend, whisking me into his car. Hurray! We drive at reckless speed through the Paris streets; he is one of those impatient, foolhardy drivers who enjoy scaring others with the risks they take. And Father is particularly eager to scare me because I'm a sissy, because my reclusive governess is turning me into an invalid, and it is all the fault of the Russian women—my mother and the governess she insists on keeping. Wouldn't I like to change governesses for a young, pretty one who would take me horseback riding, teach me tennis? I am appalled by this notion. No, no, I shout, but the shout is also a cry of alarm for the dangerous swerve Father takes around the quai de Passy, burning a red light, narrowly avoiding a collision as he passes a Peugeot that had the right of way. I am not unused to this: His scaring me, my shouting back is part of a familiar game. He often drives like this during our summer trips together. See how fast we can go! The speedometer reading 150, 160 kilometers per hour as we catapult down a country road, Father relishing my yells, accelerating to make me cry out all the louder. As he drives, he talks to me constantly; he seldom stops talking, and in his monologues the word "intelligence" and the word "Jews" often recur—anti-Semitism is one regrettable element of Vieille France ideology he never shed. "All those Jewish friends of your mother's!" "Jews are intelligent but detestable." "Léon Blum! Another Jew ruining France." I strive hard to retain neutrality throughout his monologues—I sense there's something very wrong about saying a whole people are detestable, and I'm concentrating so on remaining neutral that as we cross the Seine to the Left Bank I don't even ask whom we're going to see. The car comes to a halt a few blocks from the river, and I read the street sign, rue des Saints Pères. "This is going to be a lovely visit," Father repeats, "an invitation to tea!" We get out of the car and cross a pretty courtyard. I still think we might be dropping in on yet another of his monocled former colleagues from the diplomatic corps who will give me lemonade and go on raving about the influx of foreigners polluting France, the threat of war. So the surprise is all the greater.

We enter a small hall and see a woman in red standing above us at the head of a red-carpeted stairway, and the walls on either side are red, all about her is drenched in red. She is laughing with pleasure, her white teeth and pale skin and dark hair seem to be the only substances that are not red. She wears a floor-length tea gown of that color, she sparkles with rubies, she holds out her red-tipped hands to me, saying, "At last I see her! What a darling!" I go slowly up the stairs, startled, pleased that I am pleasing; Father also seems to be delaying the trip upward, prolonging his pleasure in her approval of me; the woman is beautiful and inviting, and I go toward her with great avidity, with the same delight I take in anyone who pays as keen attention to me as she does. I go toward her like a puppy, smelling a new perfume, sniffing her great redness. She takes us into a drawing room, and I make conversation with father's friend, showing off my knowledge of world capitals, multiplication tables, kings of France, feeling suddenly grown-up and adequate. And what is most glorious is that the lady finds me amusing, finds me fascinating. She hangs on my every word and asks many questions, her velvet slippers daintily crossed as she pours tea. She laughs a great deal, she asks me more questions, the fire burns hot, there are red stones on her wrist, she speaks French with a faint foreign accent that is unlike my mother's. And I shall not see her again for some years because she is American, in a few months' time World War II will be declared, and she will have gone home. During one of father's army leaves, I shall ask to see her again, and he will ruefully say, "I'm so glad you liked her, darling. She had to go back when the war began." Her name, I realized much, much later, was Bettina Ballard, and she had been, in those years, head of the Paris bureau of *Vogue* magazine, an institution that, not unlike the Krasin sisters, would continue to intrude upon my family's destiny.

Or else—one more memory of him—Father takes me stunt flying at Le Bourget. Whoopee! It is a Sunday, and we are in a tiny two-seater plane he has rented for the afternoon, this is the happiest Sunday of the year. He is talking about the principles of stunt flying and shows me how the plane can fly on its side, wings perpendicular to ground, how it can somersault and cut zigzags like a fancy diver plunging into a pool, *and all that without falling to your death.* There is a strap of khaki webbing about my waist, while feeling faintly nauseous, I yell with joy at every swoop and swerve, crying out, More! More! "Good little soldier!" he shouts back, and he tries it again, more dangerously this time; at a flick of his wrist, the plane can do a triple somersault, can twist and turn like a piece of spaghetti in boiling water. . . . Father is all the more brave and smart because he obtained his piloting license *against the law.* He is color-blind, and it is illegal to obtain a piloting license if you have faulty vision. As many of his friends put it, he is all the more brave because he fooled, tricked, outwitted the dunces who make those stupid laws about who should fly or not!

He was a loyal patriot of the world's most anarchic people. An idealist and a fighter through and through, he was ever ready to take on the enemy and risk his life in an honorable war. He belonged to that small, maverick sector of the French right wing which although anti-Semitic was ardently Anglophile; which began to see the threat of Nazism from the very beginning of the movement; which deplored France's lack of military preparedness, its fatal reluctance to rearm in the face of the Nazi threat. Like General de Gaulle, whose Free French movement he joined in the first days of its existence, Father early perceived the moral corruption that pervaded the French government, the delusions and cynicism that suffused its General Staff, the tragic ineptitude of a High Command that was to allow Germany to overrun France in a mere five weeks. Lieutenant Bertrand du Plessix died over the Mediterranean in the summer of 1940, his plane shot down by fascist artillery, and became one of the first four Frenchmen to be honored with the Croix de la Libération, de Gaulle's highest award. The paragraph dedicated to him in the *Mémorial des Compagnons*, available to this day in Paris at the Compagnons de la Libération headquarters on avenue de la Tour-Maubourg, reads thus:

Lieutenant du Plessix, refined, distinguished, cultivated, was posted at the French Embassy in Warsaw before the war. When mobilized, he served as liaison officer to the Polish Army during the Polish campaign. Today [June 18, 1940], *he does not hesitate to follow the call of his conscience.*

M y prewar memories of my mother are far gentler, fewer, and more discreet. The most haunting one concerns a morning vision of her at her dressing table. I am seven years old, and we have settled into a new apartment, many steps up the hierarchy of chic, moving from the Tour Eiffel area to the rue de Longchamp, two steps from the Place d'Iéna. Mother has designed a bathroom in which every accessory is *le dernier cri*. Particularly magical details—the floor, covered in a new brand of linoleum, electric-blue in color and wondrous in its cushiness, and the mirrored dressing table, on top of which is displayed the sterling-silver toiletry set engraved with my father's alleged viscountal crest and my mother's initials: T. I. P. I watch her smooth her marcelled golden hair with the silver brushes. I study her from a corner of her bathroom, terrified that any movement of mine might trigger her to annoyance and dismissal. Every one of her gestures to me has always been utterly gentle, yet there is a certain harshness about the silence she maintains with me, all the more so because with the rest of the world she is notoriously loquacious, exuberant. After I come in for my almost daily crouch (arms about my legs, head on my knees to make myself as unobtrusive as possible), every few minutes she blows me a kiss with her fingers and then returns full attention to the image in the mirror, to the buffing and polishing of that marvelous face. Not a word is exchanged. The silence of that bathroom is a kind of chastisement to which I return almost every day. (And yet, perhaps it was much finer, this silence, than the hapless babble with which other fashionable women insult their children—"how are you, baby doll, hootsie-koo." As I look back on it, the silence was pure and principled, it had no pretense; it may have been a lesser violence. I'd learn later that she was deeply shy, that much of her garrulousness and bravado were masks for her great timidity; that she had not evolved a language to communicate with a child often set against her by a father who excelled at verbiage; that perhaps she had not dared to compete with him.)

Whatever blown kisses and sparse words she offers me, I follow her like a puppy as she gets up from her dressing table, ready to start work, and goes to a small atelier right off her bedroom where she crafts her hats with the aid of her assistant, a melancholy, round-faced fellow emigré with the difficult name of Nadezhda Romanovna Preobrazhenskaia. Nadezhda Romanovna, yet another member of the proper Russian gentry whose husband now helps support his family as a taxi driver, often kisses and hugs me during her bouts of émigré tears, her sobbingly whispered recitatives—Ah, *dushenka,* the beloved country we left behind, the dachas and the meadows and our own staff of servants, and now reduced to this! Often weeping, Nadezhda Romanovna sits at one end of the table, which is heaped high with rolls of felt, with reams of tulle and veiling and lamé, with gorgeous spools of grosgrain, with velvet and satin ribbons, with bouquets of aigrette and peacock feathers and lavish pink cloth roses, the whole lovely heap surmounted by the large round steam press that will force felt and straw to take on their ultimate shape of bretons, boaters, casques, berets. And at the head of the table mother sits, again, in front of a large oval mirror, sculpting velours, draping organza or satin onto her head, using her own reflected face as the medium of creation.

Upon my eccentric father's wishes, I do not go to a regular school. I am instructed at home by my possessive, hypochondriacal Russian governess, Maria Nikolaevna Chimanskaia, under the supervision of a tutoring establishment, Cours Hattemer, which I attend one day a week. Throughout the day, in between my lessons, I take every opportunity to continue spying on my idol, Mother. I peek through the keyhole of her bedroom–fitting room, where, standing at yet another mirrored dressing table, she holds a bunch of globe-domed pins in her mouth as she adjusts jerseys and moirés to the head of Madame de Rosières, the comtesse Dessoffy, the duchesse de Gramont. And in the evenings, after she has exited for yet another client-hunting trek in the haut monde, I continue to seek out Mother in her closets, studying and caressing her cashmeres and velvet and silks. I recall feeling an especially exquisite sensation—as closely akin as I remember to childhood masturbation—from stroking a particular evening dress of brilliant, electric-blue satin, inevitably of Piguet design, and scented with his dry, terse Bandit. Fondling it at length, I felt a powerful sensual consolation from its texture, as if the cloth that had lain against Mother's skin was the only replacement I had for her longed-for embrace, her longed-for nuzzling, for the lost breast of my infancy.

I never realized the measure of my idolization of Tatiana or the magnitude of the spell which her sorcerous, silent presence wielded over me until decades later, when I found, in a school notebook of the 1930s, the very first artifacts I ever made. They were not, to my dismay, poems or prose pieces or any other signs of an emerging literary talent. They were, quite the contrary, fashion designs, drawings of imaginary day dresses and evening gowns and at-home peignoirs, all worn by blond ladies bearing a strong resemblance—as close a resemblance as an eight-year-old draftsman could achieve—to Mother. And it is evident that they were created with one single purpose in mind: finally to glean her love by saying, "I'm joining you, I'll do what *you* do when I grow up! *Now* will you pay attention to me?"

So how treasurable, how cherished those rare occasions—governess's day off, father traveling, Babushka ill—when Mother and I go out together on the town. How shyly yet tenderly she takes my hand, with a fond look, as we step out of the apartment. We often go to visit the exotic friend from whom she had learned her trade a decade ago, Fat'ma Hanoum Samoilenko. ("The widow of a very *noble* Ukrainian," Mother explains the picturesque name.) Fat'ma, who is still a popular Paris hatmaker, tells terrific jokes and has a large brown beauty mark on her left cheek and chain-smokes pungent Black Sobranies and offers me a Turkish sweet, *rahat loukoum,* the rose-scented variety of which I'd still walk miles to get my hands on. Sometimes Fat'ma, Mother, and I hire a cab for a few hours and go on a tour of wholesale stores to stock up on the materials from which their exquisite creations are made—specialty shops that offer one hundred hues of grosgrain ribbon or dozens of varieties of aigrettes, or scores of

*Tatiana in her Paris apartment in 1940, a few weeks
before the German invasion of France.*

variously textured *voilettes*, the flirtatious kind with little dots all over it or
the opaque kind used for the chapeaus of widows or the sequined variety
set upon a velvet skullcap for evening wear.

Mother is loyal about visiting old friends. We go with equal frequency—certainly once per month—to the music store of one Monsieur

Graff, on avenue Victor Hugo, to listen to recordings of the classics. He is
a lively, dapper Jewish gentleman (destined to die at Auschwitz) who puts
me into a listening booth with a new disk of the Brandenburg Concertos,
and I'm out of the adults' way for hours, in a trance, while Monsieur Graff
and Mother exchange the mundanities of their trade: the duchesse de Gramont came in yesterday to buy the new recording of *Parsifal*, Madame de
Rosières was in last week to order a cocktail hat of tulle and aigrettes. Or
else we go out to the Bois with a young American doctor, Justin Greene,
who is studying medicine in Paris and has a big crush on Mother and
particularly loves playing with children; he bounces me in the air and
catches me or gives me a strenuous calisthenic routine. (He eventually became one of New York's eminent child psychiatrists.) Or else on yet other
afternoons—these moments are particularly mysterious and entrancing—
Mother and I post ourselves at the entrance to our building to wait for a
very special friend of hers, Monsieur Wormser.

Monsieur Wormser is very rich and has a long, black, gleaming car and
a liveried chauffeur. Monsieur Wormser is tall, silver haired, and, like all men
to whom my mother would condescend to give the time of day, exquisitely
mannered. I think of Monsieur Wormser as the bestower of a great many
luxuries in my early life: my first pair of white kid gloves, unctuously soft, offered when I was five or six and kept in a special drawer long after they'd
ceased to fit me, until our hasty flight from Nazi troops a few years later.
My first outing to the circus, during which Monsieur Wormser called the
clown over to our ringside seats to shake hands with me and I, a very formal
child, burst into tears, saying, "We haven't been introduced!" My first taste
of ice cream, a delicacy which my governess forbade and which Monsieur
Wormser and my mother watched me savor, at Savarin's on the Champs
Elysées, with that same conspiratorial glance of shared contentment I'd noticed in my parents' eyes when I ate an apple. I do believe that André
Wormser ("a very distinguished banker," my mother explained later) was the
only lover my mother had until she reencountered Alex Liberman. I know
from the one cousin still alive who knew my mother well and loved her,
Claude de Laromiguière, now eighty-six, that Monsieur Wormser offered
Tatiana superb vacations and sumptuous presents—no more than two or

three pieces of jewelry, but very fine. I sense that she must have kept him at arm's length, resorting to all kinds of subterfuges, pretenses of illness to indulge as little as possible in the carnal act. And I suspect that his elegance, kindness, delicacy, and thoughtfulness were balms in my mother's hard-working life, which, until the Alex era, was assuaged solely by the keen pleasure she took in her own beauty, her marvelous capacity for friendship, and, to a lesser extent, by her deep, timid love for me.

But by the autumn of 1938 I sensed, with that shrewd sixth sense unique to estranged children, that Monsieur Wormser was being replaced as the center of my mother's attention. In the new flat on the rue de Longchamps that we had moved into that fall, my room adjoined my mother's, and my bed was separated from hers by one thin wall. (As is habitual among families in which the parents lead totally separate lives, my father's quarters were at the other end of the apartment.) Every morning, at about 8:00 A.M., I heard Mother pick up the phone and talk to someone in Russian in tender, confidential tones—in a loving tone of voice I'd never heard her assume with anyone. It was during that very span of months—in October or so of 1938, so I would piece it together later—that Mother started an affair with Alex Liberman. I also sensed that there was a trait mutual to Monsieur Graff, Monsieur Wormser, and the mustached friend in the white convertible—Alex Liberman—to whose studio I would go with my governess with enormous pleasure, throughout the winter of 1938–1939, to pose for my portrait: All three were *Jewish*. And because most of Mother's close friends seemed to be Jewish, I instinctively took exception, with an uneasy sense of disloyalty, to my father's singling out of Jews as "detestable."

I do not want to make it sound as if there was constant, audible warfare between my parents, Tatiana and Bertrand. Far from it: There was a fresh, cool friendship between them, a highly structured separateness, rather than a series of upheavals. There was even considerable mutual devotion, exemplified by the swift, dedicated way in which my father saved Tatiana's life right after her car accident, an act of characteristic decisiveness she always spoke of with lavish gratitude and praise. There were to be those taxing wartime days in the spring of 1940 when he lay for a month in a military hospital with a terrible case of jaundice and she went to his bedside daily with magazines, books, his mail, a freshly cooked meal. And for years before that, there were the evening outings with a few friends and relatives for whom they both had special affection.

The Monestiers were such a couple. Simone Monestier was a second cousin of my father, an expansive, sophisticated woman of considerable wit and erudition who had studied music with Vincent d'Indy. As a young bride, she and her husband, André, a genial graduate of Polytechnique who ran a chain of prosperous paper factories in Picardy, had given my father a second home when he was a graduate student in Paris; cosmopolitan and multilingual, far closer to him in their tastes and intellectual formation than his own provincial siblings, the Monestiers had immediately adored, and charmed, Tatiana. They were close friends and confidants of both my parents and had again saved the day in the 1930s, a few years after the du Plessix' return from Warsaw, when Uncle André offered my father a job running his Paris office, a position my father retained until World War II. My mother and Simone had forged particularly close bonds. Simone would inevitably protect my mother's interests throughout my father's dalliances, warning or reassuring her: "Don't worry about this one, she won't last a month," or "Watch out for the redhead, she's seriously trying to get her claws on him."

The Monestiers were both adventurous, romantic, fearless. They enjoyed skiing in the Carpathians and trekking mountains in Tibet. Deeply religious but always reaching out to whatever was most progressive in Catholicism, as early as the 1930s they had taken part in ecumenical seminars in Indian ashrams and crossed stretches of the African desert in the company of missionaries. And throughout thirty years they had remained deeply in love, constantly bickering about domestic details but concurring on all major issues, so used to each other's presence that they seized each other for an embrace when they had been apart for a few hours. "Ah there you are, my darling," Uncle André would cry out, "how I've missed you!" "But where were you all morning, my treasure?" she would reply.

Simone was an indefatigable redhead with a violent need to shelter,

nurture, and share—a variety of atypical French impulses caused by her unfulfilled yearning for ten children of her own. Part of these impulses were
redirected to me and to the tending of her two country houses—a manor in
Picardy she had inherited from her family and an eccentrically secluded estate in the Gorges du Tarn—where I spent most school breaks and vacations
throughout the year. I was a sickly child, often underweight, prone to bronchitis and chronic anemia. Aunt Simone, who had earned a degree in nursing during World War I, believed that my feeble health was due to the archaic
ministrations of my hypochondriacal governess, and that only her own
methods would restore me to health. And, indeed, I always thrived in her
care. When the Monestiers' boundless hospitality ran riot while I was staying with them, I was put to sleep on a cot at the foot of their bed. I listened
with wonder to their whispered endearments—how much I love you, my
life, my treasure—the first intimations ever offered me that violence between
men and women could be avoided, that love could endure even what seemed
an infinity of thirty years. Seeing the circumstances of my own parents' marriage, the Monestiers brought me far more than joy and physical health.
They were the only reassurance, throughout my childhood, that a man and a
woman could love each other serenely throughout a lifetime.

The Monestiers' only child, Claude de Laromiguière, mentioned above,
as dear a relative as I have left in the world, was eighteen in 1936, and remembers that the du Plessix would go out with her parents at least once a
month. They frequently attended the theater or concerts together and then
would go to their favorite restaurant, the downstairs room of the Rond
Point des Champs Elysées. "Tatiana would come down the stairs, *éclatante
d'élegance et de beauté*, always dressed by Piguet," Claude recalls, "and Bertrand
would be very proud to see all eyes turned toward her—he would carefully
observe the different persons who directed their attention to her. And then
a few minutes into the evening she'd say something that exasperated him,
and so it went, an evening punctuated by his alternation of pride and exas-
peration . . . but on the better evenings they acted like the greatest, most devoted of friends."

The Monestiers were one of two couples my parents saw together. The
other was Jacques and Hélène Dessoffy, who will also reenter my narrative

later. The comte and comtesse Dessoffy were one of those well-to-do French twosomes of the prewar era who had enough money never to need to work, and they channeled most of their energies into buying and redecorating houses. Hélène was the daughter of a high-ranking naval officer, a horsy, long-legged, chain-smoking woman with a lean, boyish body, brown hair worn in a plain bun, and a wry, swift wit that delighted both my parents. Even at the age of thirty-eight or so, when my memories of her begin, she was suntanned to the point of leatheriness, and her voice, which was of naturally low, mannish register, was made even hoarser, deeper by her four daily packs of Gauloises. Although my parents never touched a mind-altering substance stronger than a glass of wine, like several of their friends both Dessoffys were considerably addicted to drink and drugs. Jacques Dessoffy, a spectacled, very cosmopolitan fellow from the minor gentry who had befriended my father at the École des Langues Orientales, spent much of his time in North Africa, where he could get the best opium swiftly from the growers themselves.

As for Hélène, her dependence on whiskey had increased since the end of her one serious love affair: She had had a liaison since the mid-1930s with an immensely handsome, charming German former diplomat, Hans von Dincklage, also known as "Spatz" (sparrow), who pretended to have been forced out of the diplomatic corps in 1934 because he was married to a Jew. My father, who had befriended Spatz in Warsaw, had helped him get a job as a journalist in Paris and had introduced him to Hélène. A torrid affair ensued, which in turn had to be terminated in the autumn of 1938, at the time of Munich, when my father advised all his friends to cut off relations with Spatz and any German nationals living in France. Hélène had followed his counsel. But her separation from Spatz and her growing awareness that he had all along been a spy—a suspicion initiated by my father and soon acknowledged by all her friends—had made her very mournful. It became clear that Spatz had used Hélène's home near Toulon, an important naval base, as a center for his espionage activities. She was just beginning to get over her melancholy and her rage at her former lover (who throughout the Occupation years—the fellow had taste—would be the lover of Coco Chanel).

Tatiana's closest friend, Hélène Dessoffy, and her lover Hans ("Spatz") von Dincklage, who turned out to be the head of the Third Reich's espionage network in France.

There was a very pleasant, benign, sunny absence to both Dessoffys: Wreathed in clouds of smoke and surrounded by their beloved schnauzers, they seemed to move in an euphoric world, somewhat beyond the domain of sexual contact, into which they seemed ever ready to welcome you, as long as you did not disturb their insouciant bliss. If they have enough money never to encroach on you, I learned through them, opium smokers can be most pleasant companions. The Dessoffys' lovely villas in the south of France (they lived rather separate lives and usually inhabited separate houses) were comfortable in a modern, functional way—large chalk-white rooms with spacious sofas sensibly upholstered in linen and cotton. I remember air, lightness, joking, prancing happy dogs, perpetual sunniness around Hélène, and the mild, enduring smell of the best Scotch. My father had such brotherly devotion to her that in the spring of 1939 he bought a ramshackle old farmhouse a few minutes from her villa—in Sanary-sur-Mer, near Toulon—which he planned to remodel "as soon as the political situation permits."

Another unusual trait about the Dessoffys was that they were rich enough and spaced-out enough to remain in a constantly partying mood and to welcome anyone who amused and interested them into their lives. In the early 1930s, they had formed deep bonds of friendship with both of the ever-so-amusing du Plessix; and they seemed to take to Alex with equal affection when he entered my mother's life. So God only knows who was testing whom during the following episode, which occurred in the spring of 1939, when my father and I were staying with Hélène at her newest house in Sanary.

In this memory, we are in Hélène's kitchen. It is shortly after Hitler has occupied the remains of Czechoslovakia, in flagrant breach of the Munich accords signed the previous fall. My father is giving one of his characteristically pessimistic monologues about the threats presented by Hitler and the French government's incompetence in dealing with them, a diatribe that Hélène, in her state of habitual nirvana, nods at with absentminded approval. Why hadn't France taken on Germany in 1936, Father is asking, when the Nazis had marched into the Rhineland? Germany was then only beginning to rearm, the French Army could have made mincemeat of them! That idiotic old general Gamelin is at fault, a coward if there ever was one. Not to speak of Léon Blum and all his Jewish pacifist friends, and the labor unions constantly striking and slowing up our rearmament! *Le résultat?* Munich, a debacle over which every Frenchman should hang his head in shame! Since then, the Germans have developed umpteen Panzer divisions, Messerschmitts speedier than any plane anyone has ever seen! And now they've just devoured the remains of our old ally, Czechoslovakia, without us even lifting a finger! What are those fools at the Elysée waiting for?

In his more turbulent moods, my father, especially when he's staying in the country with friends, often calms himself by cooking a good meal, which he here sets out to do as he finishes his invective. An accomplished gourmet chef (another maverick trait highly unusual to Frenchmen of the prewar era), he has recently taught me to make chocolate truffles; and while Father is at the stove, stirring a *boeuf bourguignon* he's concocting for dinner, I am studiously rolling unctuous little balls of chocolate paste around a dish of cocoa powder to coat them evenly. This is an odd context for the conversation that follows: "*Tu connais les Libermans?*" Hélène asks my father. "*Sales petits Juifs,*" my father answers impassively, stirring his stew. "*Oh, ils sont bien gentils, surtout le fils,*" Hélène says. "*Oui, le père est bien pire,*" my father responds, and then repeats: "*Sales petits Juifs.*"

The words stung. For the first time, I almost hated my father. I had grown very fond of Alex. During my visits to his studio, he had utterly won me over with his unique blend of charm, thoughtfulness, and warmth. And I was also old enough to muse over the following questions, which I ponder to this day: Did Hélène set up this conversation to find out how aware my father was of Tatiana's new affair? Or was she asking him the question in front of me in order to test *my* awareness of the situation? Hélène had no children to practice on—a deliberate choice, I suspect, for one could not imagine her being responsible for any creature more demanding than a schnauzer—but this was a very odd bit of child psychology testing indeed.

That was the last spring vacation I spent with my father. It was the last spring of a peace which the majority of the French, for the past two decades, had deemed to be eternal.

A half century after that episode in Hélène Dessoffy's kitchen, I had the good fortune to come across the following passage from the novelist Maurice Sachs, which expresses with eerie succinctness the delusions the French nation had been steeped in throughout the Entre Deux Guerres era—delusions that my father, to his credit, was ever ready to battle.

> Neither 18 Brumaire, nor the Empire, nor Waterloo . . . nor the Second Republic, nor the Second Empire, nor [the defeat of France at] Sedan, nor the Commune, nor the birth of the Third

Republic shook France as profoundly, to the depths of its entrails, as the war of 1914 and the peace that followed. . . . [T]he peace of 1919 announced an eternal peace. . . . [T]he French, charmed by delicious illusions, were the first to think that this peace (which . . . differed from others only by the demented hopes it created) once more marked the Fatherland for a unique destiny. . . . Crowned as they were by the charming attributes of victory, this state of mind . . . authorized all excesses, all licenses, all follies.

NINE

1939–1940

Notwithstanding the grave threats posed that year by Adolf Hitler, in 1939 French citizens of all walks of life took their habitual summer vacations. Prime Minister Edouard Daladier sailed on a friend's yacht off the Côte d'Azur in the company of his mistress, the marquise de Crussol. The president of the Republic, Albert Lebrun, vacationed in his home village in Lorraine, Mercy-le-Haut. Minister of Justice Paul Marchand spent twelve days at Evian, doing a liver cure. Finance Minister Paul Reynaud rested at Le Touquet on the English Channel before joining his longtime companion, the comtesse de Portes, at Arcachon on the Atlantic coast. The minister for the colonies, Georges Mandel, who had long urged his government to forcibly resist Germany's increasing belligerence, was clearly more concerned than most others and took only three days off at Deauville.

As for the du Plessix family, we spent most of August 1939 at the estate in the Gorges du Tarn that my uncle André Monestier had bought a few summers back, La Croze. A secluded complex of rustic, gray stone buildings on the banks of the rushing river, it still remains a microcosm of romantic perfection for anyone attracted to untamed nature. For all practical purposes, it can be reached only by boat, for it perches on that steep, rocky side of the Tarn canyon on which there is no road for twenty kilometers, and no one in the family has ever attempted to cross the densely forested mountain to reach that road. On the bank opposite La Croze, the nearest village, La Malène, is five kilometers away. Other than the boat crossing, the only possible approach to civilization, occasionally undertaken by the adventurous and fit, is to walk upstream on a rough, steep forester's path, toward La Malène, where the Tarn can be crossed by foot-bridge. La Croze is in keeping with the traditions of its region, the Lozère, where the legendary Boy of the Aveyron is said to have been raised by wolves, and which remains one of France's most rustic areas. And it is a most beautiful site. (I am using the present tense for the estate, barely altered, still remains in the family.) Wildflowers grow in rich profusion here, the swift river below glimmers like a ribbon of platinum between rows of silvery poplars, the air is of a purity found in few places in Europe.

The postal system at La Croze—and the delivery of groceries—is characteristically eccentric: Mail, food supplies, and day-late *Le Figaro*s arrive in a large wooden crate, strung on cables, which is hauled over the river by cranking on a large cable wheel. Most communication with the other side of the river is done through a lot of shouting. "Monsieur Legrand," one bellows to the grocer, "could you be kind enough to find us a good *gigot* for the weekend?" And in the days when there was no phone, unexpected guests from all parts of France hollered across the river to announce their arrival: Cousins drove up, parked at the other side of the river, and yelled: "We're the du Plessix (the la Laurencies, the d'Argenteuils) from Perpignan (Nantes, Angoulême), can we come for lunch?" "Of course" was the inevitable reply. Throughout the decades, Aunt Simone and, later, my cousin Claude, both brilliant cooks, have overseen a sizable staff of village girls in the kitchen. To this day, the region is poor, domestic helpers are happy to work for pittances, and rare are the meals at which there are fewer than twenty at the table. La Croze has always aspired to be a refuge from the humdrum world, a private kingdom of sorts. And with the exception of the weekly trip to La Malène for Sunday Mass (there are some joyous Sundays when a priest is a guest at La Croze and can say Mass at home), an expedition to the village is looked on as a capitulation.

The same adventurous streak of character that had incited the Monestiers to buy La Croze had led them to form close friendships with my mother's relatives. They had revered Babushka. They had much admired Sasha Iacovleff and collected his works. They equally loved my gentle, melancholy great-aunt Sandra, who was now trying to make ends meet as an opera coach. So it was natural that in 1939, the summer after Babushka's death, they invited Aunt Sandra to come with us to La Croze for a month, wishing to console her in her deep mourning.

It was with this happy group of loved ones that I spent most of that month of August, in the last summer of the long armistice that had lasted since 1919. My parents' overlapping schedules at La Croze were as complex as ever. Having dismissed my governess for the month in hopes that I would fare better in my aunt's care, my father had driven Aunt Sandra and me to La Croze on August 1. He had stayed for two weeks, gone off in midmonth to "see some friends" (the lady in red, I suspect), and was scheduled to drive us back to Paris toward the end of the month. My mother had arrived on the thirteenth, the day before he left, with the intention of staying a week before returning to the south of France (and surely to Alex). La Croze and Mother were hardly a perfect match. However much she adored the Monestiers, she loathed oil lamps, the dearth of bathtubs, and the general rusticity of the place. She kept rowing across the river and getting into her car—which terrified us; since she'd gotten her driving license only the previous spring—under the pretext of finding special foods for me, especially a powder called Banania, intended for underweight children. But she was obviously also looking for nearby villages in which she could peacefully write and send her postcards to Alex.

"It's so wild and beautiful here, Auntie says it reminds her of the Darial Gorge in the Caucasus," she wrote Alex on August 17.

> *There is a total lack of comfort, neither electricity nor roads. If you were here with me it might be very charming, but without you it is very desolate. I'm finding my solace in Francine and the serenity of the place. . . . I love you so tenderly and endlessly and guard you inside me like my own life. Write to me and I will meet the mail myself, hauling it in on the rope.*

"It is so sad that you haven't written," she complained on the nineteenth in one of four postcards she wrote him that day alone.

> We have a lot of thunderstorms here but I still go for swims and walks in order not to lose my sanity without you. Auntie is so nice, and I exploit her completely. Unfortunately Froska doesn't look too well, no better than in Paris, and the children's games tire her out very much.

"At last, I received your letter," she exulted the same evening in yet another card,

> and Aptimtim [a code name Mother and Alex had developed for each other] it was such a nice delicious letter. . . . My life, in two days I will be with you. . . . [O]ur love is a happiness so undeserved that we have to guard it as the world's greatest treasure.

I have only a few precise memories of that last summer of the peace, when I was not quite nine. I remember the general bliss of being surrounded with the five people I most deeply loved: my mother and father, Uncle André and Aunt Simone, Aunt Sandra. I remember waking to the sound of my uncle's voice crying out his welcome to the postman. "Bonjour, Monsieur Lefèvre! I'll haul it over!" I remember sitting at the long oak table at breakfast, watching my mother, who was hopeless in a kitchen, struggling to make me a cup of Banania and softly saying "Merde" as she spilled a quart of milk. I had not yet learned to swim, my governess having looked on that skill as too perilous; and I recall wading knee-deep in the river with Sandra, looking up at her face and being dazzled—heaven knows why at that particular moment, since it was one of the dearest sights of my childhood—by the blazing operatic whiteness of her teeth, the sheen of which she maintained with a delectably scented pink dentifrice called Toreador. I also recall the endless conversations between my father and my uncle concerning the threat of war—France and Great Britain's urgent need to sign a pact of nonaggression with the Soviet Union, the negotiations undertaken for that purpose since March of that year, Daladier's incompetence and foot-dragging. And I recall my parents, on the one day they were both at La Croze, sitting on the banks of the poplar-lined, glimmering river, my mother regaling the Monestiers with details of the July social season in Paris. It had been of unsurpassed, whirlwind brilliance, she said; the most glamorous party of all had been the yearly ball held at the Polish embassy—Madame de Portes, mistress of minister of finances Paul Reynaud, had looked a tad less ugly than usual in a superb Patou gown of violet silk; the ravishing French wife of Otto Abetz, chargé d'affaires at the German embassy, was in an almond-hued *peau de soie;* the grounds were lit with thousands of fairylike lights; at 3:00 A.M., the ambassador had bidden all his guests to take off their shoes, and the entire crowd had danced a polonaise all across the embassy lawns. . . . "The feast before the famine," my father quietly interrupted her, looking morose and brooding, as he did whenever any issue associated with Poland—an urgent political issue that summer—was brought up.

But what I recall most vividly, perhaps because it was a rite of passage for me, was taking the legendary five-kilometer hike from La Croze to the bridge at La Malène, a walk that only "grown-ups" usually ventured on. It was the day after my mother—who tended to coddle me, like my governess—had left for the south. My father had as much as dared me to take the walk, and after three weeks in Aunt Simone's care I felt strong enough to accept the challenge. We moved at a brisk clip through the dense forest of evergeens, guiding ourselves by the ribbon of river gleaming below us, sliding often on thick beds of fragrant pine needles. It was a cool, sunny day, and my excitement was such that I never felt much fatigue. After two hours of walking, upon glimpsing the first village houses across the river, I even felt a kind of void—I'd met the challenge and felt the need for another. As we sat down to rest under a tree before crossing the bridge, my father praised me as he seldom had before, lauding my strength, my speed, my courage. Inhaling the smell of the spruce and fir trees that surrounded us, I thrilled to his compliments—I was his good little soldier, he said with pride; think of all the walks we could do together now, in the Morvan, on the Brittany coast!

It was the very following day—August 23—that the summer's electrifying event occurred: The Soviets, after five months of fruitless negotiations with Great Britain and France, announced that they had signed a nonaggres-

Bertrand and Francine hiking in the Gorges du Tarn, August 1939, a few weeks before the outbreak of World War II.

sion pact with Germany. The mailman had shouted the news across the river to my uncle, even before we held our daily noontime session over the wireless radio. "That's it, there'll be war any time now," was my father's grim response. Our summer vacation was abruptly cut short. It was decided that everyone should vacate La Croze within twenty-four hours and return to Paris. My next memory is of driving back to the city, seated between my father and Aunt Sandra, my head on her lap. It is night. In a calm, resigned tone this time, my father is lecturing Sandra on the imminence of World War II. God only knows how much he hates the communists, he is saying, but the way the French and English dragged their feet throughout their negotiations, what did you expect the Russians to do? Marshall Voroshilov was ready to put in thousands of ar-

mored divisions into the fray; the British and French had only a couple of hundred to offer! Tanks, tanks are what the French should have concentrated on, instead of that inane Maginot Line. . . . My pacific, deeply apolitical aunt begins to nod over his words, her head now slumping toward my prone body. "And now our only ally in the east is the dear, antiquated Polish cavalry," my father continues. "Their idea of warfare is so archaic they still look on horses as the crucial components of any army." "Are you leaving for the war soon?" I ask him as my aunt's head thuds against my shoulder. "Yes, my rabbit, very soon," he

Tatiana and Bertrand at St. Moritz, mid-1930s.

180

Bertrand du Plessix on military duty in the Mediterranean in the last months of 1939.

says, stroking my head. "Aunt Simone and Uncle André and Maman and Aunt Sandra will take good care of you."

He was mobilized the day after we returned to Paris. A day or two later, the Monestiers took me to spend the week at their other country house, in Picardy. My father was expected for a brief visit that Saturday, on his way to join his unit. I recall the canine patience with which I waited for him on the steps of the house, staring at the green, lush little circular driveway, bordered by my aunt's roses, which faced the front steps. He was due to arrive at three, but the traffic—many Parisians were fleeing the capital in expectation of imminent war—delayed his arrival by six hours.

I kept on sitting on the steps of the porch, surging with excitement each time I heard the sound of a car approaching the Monestiers' estate, impervious to the adults' call for me to come out of the chill, weeping and screaming when they tried to cajole me into the house. I wanted to see Papa in his new uniform! I wanted to catch sight of him the very second he came out of his car!! They let me have my way. Finally, the familiar burgundy Peugeot appeared in the driveway and he came out of the car, the gold braid gleaming on his officer's uniform. He swept me up into his arms, and we went in to dinner. Soon after the meal, I began to doze off—it was way past my bedtime—but I grasped the sense of the conversation: My father had brought a copy of his last will and testament. In case "something happened" to him, he wished Uncle André Monestier (who, like all men over forty, was not to be mobilized until some months later) to be my legal guardian until I was twenty-one.

G ermany attacked Poland on September 1. War was declared by Great Britain at dawn on September 3 and by the reluctant French eight hours later. By August 29 my father had already left for the Polish front. As a specialist in Polish affairs, he had been assigned to be liaison officer to Air Force General Jules Armengaud, who headed the unit sent by the French government to offer standby assistance to Poland even before the war officially began. "For the third time in seventy years"—I remember words to that effect creating a headline of *Le Figaro* in early September—"the Venus de Milo has left the Louvre for safekeeping in a secret location in the provinces." During those first weeks of the war, it was de rigueur to carry one's gas mask in a canister, hung over the shoulder, a habit I found very glamorous and soldierly. Throughout the early days of September, air-raid alarms shrieked repeatedly through the night. My mother, my governess, and I rushed to the assigned shelter, in the cellar of the neighboring house, which was filled with hysterical women in bathrobes and curlers. Declaring that "the next time it might be the real thing," my mother, after a few weeks, decided that my governess and I should seek refuge in the country. She felt that the Monestiers' Picardy estate might be too close to the action—my father had always warned that when Germany attacked France it would be across the Ardennes and the Belgian border. My governess and I were to go instead to a little house in the Gironde that had belonged to Babushka's brother, Great-granduncle Alexandr Petrovich Kuzmin, which he had left me in his will the previous winter.

A lthough far more modest, Uncle Kuzmin's house, in a village near Arcachon called Gujan-Mestras, was as familiar to me as La Croze, as the Monestiers' house in the Picardy, as any treasured site of my childhood. Situated in a stretch of flat, monotonous swamp marsh, it was a claustrophobic three-room wooden cottage, devoid of running water or electricity, in which Uncle had sought refuge after suffering the central tragedy of his life: Upon fleeing Russia and settling in Germany, he had fallen deeply in love with and married a circus acrobat. Soon after their marriage, he had spent his life savings buying her a riding academy of her own, but she had fled with a trapezist. Left penniless and heartbroken, he had settled in Gujan-Mestras to while away his time playing solitaire and rereading the Russian classics. By the time I knew him, "Le Monsieur Russe," as he was referred to by the villagers, was a benign, doddering pensioner with a senile habit, which embarrassed me deeply, of letting his tongue protrude from his perpetually smiling mouth. He vaguely kept up with world news through Russian-language newspapers but otherwise seemed to have sunk, in his advancing age, into Oblomovian lethargy. And he clearly lived for the six summer weeks when Babushka, Sandra, my governess, and I descended on him from Paris.

We crammed into the tiny house, Babushka and Sandra sharing one of the bedrooms, my governess and I another, Uncle Kuzmin happily making his bed on the living-room couch. There was nothing much to do during our vacations at Gujan-Mestras beyond reading, shopping in the village for the daily victuals, carting water from the rusty pump at the end of the dirt road, and helping Babushka to prepare our frugal Russian meals. And yet I deeply loved those summer nights when we sat around the green glass oil lamp set on the living-room table, under the melancholy stare of the beautiful icon, hung in a corner of the room, that my great-granduncle had preserved during his exodus from Russia. In the tiny room suffused by the smell of steaming kasha, Uncle Kuzmin would be absorbed in his perpetual solitaire, my governess would read or repair some garment, and Babushka would have been badgered into a game of cards or checkers with me. Aunt Sandra played operatic recordings on a crank-up Victrola. Occasionally, while following an aria from *Tristan and Isolde* or *Le Coq d'or* in her voluminous, cracking mezzo, her eyes filled with tears at the memory of her glory days at the St. Petersburg opera, and her trembling voice dissolved into a medley of sobs punctuated by a few heroic tremolo notes. Uncle Kuzmin stopped his solitaire, his tongue darting nervously in and out of his mouth. My great-grandmother rushed to Sandra's chair and rocked her large, sobbing daughter in her arms. "My soul, my treasure," she whispered, "you've had a splendid career, none of us can go on forever." Upon which the entire family, filled with nostalgia for the lost Russia of decades past, burst into tears, and I readily followed suit.

But my stay at Gujan-Mestras in September 1939 was deprived of those beloved relatives. In the past year, Uncle Kuzmin and Babushka had both died; Sandra had joined the war effort by working full-time for the Paris Red Cross; and I painfully felt the desolation and void created by Babushka's death. It was the beginning of the school year, and my governess and I set upon the same bleak schedule we'd followed in Paris for years. We took my temperature upon waking. If it was over 37.5 centigrade, I was confined to bed for the rest of the day, which suited me just fine, since I could pursue my project of reading all of Jules Verne's novels—*Le Rayon vert* was my favorite of that season. If the mercury stood well below that mark, we started on our lessons: French dictation, Russian dictation, history, math. The tutoring establishment I'd attended in Paris never failed to send us the assignments, week by week. Every few days, we went to the post office to put in a phone call to my mother, who had sought refuge from the anticipated bombings of Paris with friends just outside the city. (It became clear to me only later that she was staying with Alex at his parents' weekend house in Chatou.) Our only distraction was the daily walk to the village grocer, on the way to which we would pass the house of Gujan-Mestras's mayor, a portly communist, perennially attired in a red shirt, who every Sunday sat on his porch, playing recordings of the "Internationale" on a Victrola. And there were occasional visits with a village girl named Colette who'd been a summer playmate for years and who this year began vaguely to initiate me into the mysteries of procreation: Behind the pipi hole, she said, pulling down her pants, was another hole into which men stuck *their* whaddya-call-it. We couldn't imagine how guys could stuff that limp little thing, which we'd seen once or twice on dirty old men in public places, into anything whatsoever; and we dismissed the entire report as a rumor.

Our exile at Gujan-Mestras seems to have lasted from about September 10 to the early days of November. Meanwhile, in Paris, those who had relatives abroad were busy reassuring their loved ones that they were safe. On

September 13, Alex wrote a long letter to his father telling him that he was with Tatiana at Chatou (cannily predicting that Jews would be wiser to move out of Europe for the next few years, Simon Liberman had recently settled in New York City). It was clearly a difficult time for Alex, who was feeling considerable guilt—and a certain macho loss of face—because his health had led him to be classified as unfit for military service. Moreover, his hyperpossessive *mamasha* was doing all in her power to break up his passionate liaison with Tatiana; Alex, in turn, was doing all he could to talk his mother into joining his father in the United States.

"My beloved," Alex's letter to his father reads,

Above all don't worry about mamasha *and me. I'm so glad that you're not here, and I'm sure you can be much more useful to France over there than here. We're living in Chatou now,* mamasha, *Tania and me. Unfortunately* mamasha *is very nervous and jealous and it's hard to be around her—what with her health and nerves, she shouldn't be here. It would be wonderful if you could find a way to get her to America.*

With Pollyanna idealism, Alex goes on to praise the delusionary confidence of the French's wartime spirit. "The atmosphere is amazing. Such calmness, courage and decisiveness that one's spirits are lifted and one is proud to be French . . . and there's absolute faith in victory!!" He continues with a passionate statement about the strength Tatiana has offered him, emphasizing, once more, *mamasha's* hysterical jealousy.

I used to be afraid of war, not because of any physical fear, but because I had not experienced happiness yet. . . . But everything has changed. This last year I've experienced such love. It's made a man out of me and allowed me to create. I've found my way, my creativity, my truth in everything. . . . Tania is always next to me, we're inseparable. . . . Everything is so much simpler when you're with the one you love. . . . I'm sorry for mamasha. *She suffers and makes others suffer. The most painful thing of all is to observe her egoism precisely at the moments when egoism has to be overcome with one's entire being, when we all have to rise above pettiness and live for something so important beyond us. Now she certainly feels more lonely*

than ever. . . . Her jealousy is a torture and there's nothing I can do about it. . . .
I want to tell you only one thing. I can only tell it to you. I have never been hap-
pier in my life than I am now with Tatiana. And I have never loved so, and have
never been so loved. Remember this, moi rodnoi—*whatever happens, my soul is*
relieved that I told this to you, to my real friend.

I kiss you tenderly, Shura.

In those same weeks, Tatiana was writing to the Soviet Union, responding to a worried letter from her mother and reassuring her that her family was faring fine in wartime. It was the first time since 1935, when the Soviet terror began to hit its peak, that the two women had exchanged letters, and it is startling that this exchange was even allowed: Lyubov Nikolaevna took a considerable risk by urging her daughter to write her back, and Tatiana once more maintained the cryptic, guarded tone essential to protecting loved ones from persecution.

My unseen Mamulichka,

I was made endlessly happy by your letter. If you didn't write for so long, you
yourself know why, it doesn't mean you didn't think of me. For heaven's sake don't
worry about us. Here all is in order and we all feel terrific. Of course our husbands
are not home, but that's the general condition. Francine's in the country with her gov-
erness, where she's faring wonderfully. Lila also is in her country house. I work hard
in Paris, so does Auntie Sandra.

She goes on to mention all the deaths that have affected the family in the past few years: Sasha in May of 1938 ("awful . . . his unexpectedly premature death terrified everyone here"); Great-uncle Kuzmin in October of the same year; Babushka in the following May ("for us all that was a dreadful loss, and she so adored the little one"). She informs her mother that her hat business has grown greatly, and that Bertrand and Albert Darse, the Parisian hotel owner Lila had married three years earlier, are faring well at the front. "I kiss you and *père* tenderly," she ends, "don't imagine things here to be any worse than they are in reality."

The last thing in the world my mother could have mentioned, in a letter to the Soviet Union, was her husband's difficult mission on the Polish front. The Soviets, in collaboration with Hitler, had just occupied a good hunk of eastern Poland, and my father had barely escaped with his life. His assignment with General Armengaud had kept him on the Polish front throughout that disastrous campaign, which, in great part due to the dazzling superiority of the German Luftwaffe, lasted only for some three weeks. On September 27, when Poland capitulated, whatever Allied troops were still there had to flee for their skins. Armengaud and his retinue found some way to get to Romania, still a relatively neutral country, and then fled on to Albania, whence they took ship to Beirut, and then traveled to Syria. Syria, at the time, was still a French colony and an extremely important military base—the future prime minister Pierre Mendès-France and a considerable number of other prominent French officers were currently posted there. Though most of his unit remained in Syria, Armengaud, one of those *frondeur* officers who had kept warning the French High Command for years that it was direly misconstruing the pivotal importance of long-range bombers in contemporary warfare, soon returned to Paris. Upon settling in the capital, he wrote a scathing memo to the Ministry of War concerning the French troops' technical backwardness. But his warning fell, as ever, on deaf ears: the French High Command was headed by the seventy-two-year-old General Gamelin, who was still mired in the trench-based tactics of World War I. And Armengaud was actually demoted to an administrative post at the Ministry of War in punishment for his "progressive" views.

In early November, we were reassured that my father had safely reached Beirut. My mother called me back to Paris that month, when droves of other Parisians were returning to the city, realizing that a German attack was not imminent. By this time, Paris life seems to have returned to the heedless gaiety of the Années Folles, and my memories of that season are almost exclusively auditory: When I recall those early months of the *"drôle de guerre,"* I think of brazenly cheerful songs by Maurice Chevalier: "Prosper, yop la boum"; "Ah si vous connaissiez ma poule"; "Ça sent si bon la France"; "Amusez vous" (*"La vie, entre nous, est si brève / Amusez vous comme des fous"*). I also recall popular 1939 ditties by Charles Trenet: "Y'a d'la joie" (*"Y'a d'la joie, bonjour bonjour les hirondelles, Y'a d'la joie . . . Y'a d'la joie partout"*) and "J'attendrais, j'attendrai toujours," which beyond its tone of personal longing also expressed the helplessness and boredom of the soldiers waiting in their trenches, experiencing no action beyond desultory patrol duties, for the first eight months of the war.

But there are two songs that prevail over all others as symbols of the illusions and escapism of that particular year: One is called "Tout va trés bien, Madame La Marquise," a ditty mocking the fecklessness of the upper classes, which is narrated by a butler reciting to his employer the misfortunes that have befallen her country estate while she has been away. The news gets worse and worse as the song goes along: Her favorite gray mare has died, the loss was caused by a fire in the stables, which in turn was started when the entire château burned down, which occurred when the marquis committed suicide, igniting some candles in the process—but each calamity is counterposed with the reassuring refrain, *"Mais à part ça, Madame La Marquise, tout va trés bien, tout va trés bien!"* And above all there was "Nous allons pendre notre linge sur la Ligne Siegfried," also sung in Great Britain as "We're gonna hang out the washing on the Siegfried Line," which my little class at the tutoring establishment sang and danced to weekly at recreation time, our hands clasped to one another's in a circle. It deserves to be quoted to grasp the tragic, inane optimism the French nation was plunged into throughout the first months of the war:

> *We're gonna hang out the washing on the Siegfried Line*
> *'Cause the washing day is here. . . .*
> *We're gonna hang out the washing on the Siegfried Line*
> *If the Siegfried Line's still there.*

My other sensory memories—sights, sounds, smells—pick up again in February or so of 1940, when my father, who had fallen very ill in Syria, was flown back to Paris and placed at the military hospital, Val de Grâce. He had contracted a bad case of typhoid complicated by jaundice. My governess and I visited him every few days, trying to take turns with my mother, who brought him meals, magazines, and books and generally attempted to cheer him. Pitifully thin and wasted, with a truly yellowish tinge to his skin, my father lay flat, his head on a white pillow, smiling weakly, devouring me with his large brown eyes whenever I went to see him. "My rabbit, my treasure," he said each time, "I'll be back soon." But he did not come home for at least two months, and I can still remember the names of the Metro stations between our stop at the rue de Longchamp (Metro Iéna) and the hospital—take the Montreuil line to Strasbourg St-Denis, then the Porte d'Orléans line to Châtelet–Les Halles, travel three stops on the Montrouge line to Port-Royal.

In March, it was my turn, and my governess's, to be sick. I came down with hepatitis, possibly contracted during my visits to the hospital. My governess fell ill with a bad bronchitis. While trying to keep her hat workshop going, my mother now turned to full-time nursing, putting me to bed in a corner of her own room, behind a large gold-and-black Chinese screen Uncle Sasha had brought her from the Far East. In fear that I would also contract one of my recurring attacks of bronchitis, she forbade my governess any visits and tended to both of us by herself. Aunt Sandra and Aunt Simone Monestier took turns coming for a few hours of the day so that Mother could continue bringing food and cheer to my father. (Unbeknownst to me, she was being ferried to the hospital almost daily by Alex, who read patiently in the car while she visited with her husband.) I have a cherished memory of those days spent behind Uncle Sasha's screen, dozing, reading, and being comforted by the three women I most loved. And I believe that this was the first time that I sensed my mother's potential for heroism and for great tenderness, the first time she truly awed me, the first time I began to give her my trust.

At the end of April, just as I had recuperated enough to resume some activities without my governess, who was still in her sickbed, my father came home from the hospital. Moody and wasted, he was on a month's convalescence leave from the Ministry of War. Barely two weeks after his return, the *"drôle de guerre"* ended, and World War II began in earnest. On Friday, May 10, at 4:31 A.M. French time, German Panzer divisions headed by General Heinz Guderian, who had pioneered the very technique of the Panzer attack, crashed through the frontier of Luxembourg. In the following forty-eight hours, they moved so swiftly across Belgium and Holland that by Monday they had pierced the rugged Ardennes region and crossed the Meuse river, terrains that France's tragically incompetent High Command had thought impregnable to the Germans' mighty tanks.

Throughout the weekend, my gaunt, solemn father sat at his desk, pretending to work, answering my questions monosyllabically, keeping his radio blaring late into the night. Early on Monday the thirteenth—by this time Holland was two days away from capitulation—I went into his room and was surprised to see him in full military uniform. "But Papa," I exclaimed, "you're still on convalescence leave!" "I must go to the ministry," he said. "I'll let you know what happens." He returned that afternoon, more somber than ever. His hands trembled terribly. My mother was out, delivering hats, and I followed him into his study. He locked the door behind us and slumped into an armchair. He bent over double, his face on his knees, and burst into tears. I ran to him, enfolding him in my arms. "They've turned me down!" he sobbed. "They say I'm too sick to fight, too sick to fly!" He fell to the ground and now began to sob uncontrollably, like a two- or three-year-old having a tantrum. I knelt on the floor next to him. I stroked his head, weeping also, whispering, "Papa, you'll get stronger soon, you can fly again by next month." My governess started pounding at the door, begging to be let in. "Leave us alone, Maria Nikolaevna!" he howled. He was now my own child, the little boy I'd always wanted. I held him in my arms, caressing his head, his cheek, sobbing with him. His familiar litany of insults resumed, admixed with his personal griefs: General Gamelin, General Weygand, a bunch of doddering idiots, fighting the Panzer units with their archaic World War I tactics. He'd been assigned to a seedy old desk at the Ministry of War, they wouldn't let him go back to his squadron, just when his country needed him the most they wouldn't let him fight.

I kept looking at the sunny street outside, rue de Longchamps, thinking of the safe, beloved landmarks of my childhood: Just to the left, a few buildings away, was the Musée Guimet, where Father often took me to look at beautiful Tang vases and his favorite Sung Dynasty landscapes; a few blocks to the right, down the avenue d'Iéna, the Trocadero, with its sweeping view of the Tour Eiffel. . . . "The idiots won't let me fight," my father

continued to howl. "They won't allow me to fight on!" "Papa, you're getting stronger by the day, maybe by next week you can fly." I took my role as
protector and nurturer with gravity and pride, and yet I was desperate for
another adult to be there, to comfort him alongside me, to help.

Finally, I heard the key turn in the outside door, my mother's hurried
steps toward my father's study, her brief whispered conversation in Russian
with my governess. It was she, this time, knocking at the door. "*Ouvres,
Bertrand,*" she pleaded. "*Bertrand, chéri, ouvres la porte!*" Still sobbing, he half
stumbled, half crawled to the door. Still sobbing, he fell into her arms.
"*Mon chéri,*" she whispered, "*mon pauvre chéri.*" "Dial Jasmin 34-10, Frosinka,"
she told me, "tell her to come right away." It was Aunt Sandra's number—
I, too, knew it by heart. She was in, and I hardly needed to explain—she
would be over as fast as possible. I returned to my parents. The three of us
remained in one another's arms, weeping together, weeping, I suppose,
about the shambles of the world as we had known it, and through my haze
of tears I felt a sudden rush of gratitude for the fact that the three of us
were, after all, a family.

Then my mother began to be practical. She made my father lie down
on his bed, took off his shoes, loosened his collar. Sandra arrived. The two
women briefly huddled by the window—it was clear, they agreed, that he
was "on the verge of a breakdown." My father sobbed on uncontrollably, lying on his side now, his head buried in his hands. Sandra dialed the phone.
Within twenty minutes, our beloved Dr. Simon, the family doctor who had
taken care of all of us since my infancy, was by my father's side, giving him
an injection.

My father is sedated now, lying flat on his back. Dr. Simon, an Alsatian
Jew of angelically even temper much teased in the family for his boundless
optimism, has joined us and sits at his bedside, quietly talking to his friend.
"Your job at the War Ministry is just as important as any you could have at
the front, *mon vieux,*" he is saying. "You're in an elite unit of Air Force Intelligence, you can help them as few people can." "They've crossed the
Meuse, and they're heading towards Sedan," my father moans. "Do you
know what that means? The game is over." "Bertrand, dear Bertrand, don't
always be so pessimistic," Dr. Simon whispers. "We'll reconstitute a new

front any time now." "Their Panzers will go through Belgium in three days, and then they'll start marching on Picardy," my father insists, now beginning to stifle some yawns. My mother and my aunt still stand at the window, whispering. "Depressions: extremely common after jaundice," my aunt says assertively.

My father was right, as he usually was in the realm of political issues. In the fortnight following that family reunion, as my father grew resigned, accepted medication, and slowly resumed his desk work at the Ministry of War, German forces made short shrift of Belgium, forcing its capitulation within a fortnight of Holland's. Having bolted across France's Département du Nord, they had necessitated the heroic evacuation, at Dunkirk, of more than 330,000 Allied troops. At the end of May, German forces obliged the French Army to reconstitute its front at the Somme River, a two hours' drive north of Paris. And on June 6 they broke through that last defense line, causing such panic among French troops that generals, their originally scheduled maneuvers made impossible by the tide of civilians clogging the country's roads, ceased to accept commands from the General Staff, and hundreds of thousands of soldiers of all ranks abandoned their regiments to seek refuge in their homes throughout France. By June 8, as German forces speedily approached the capital, having overwhelmed what was recently considered to be continental Europe's most powerful army, it was clear that the French High Command had been taken ignominiously by surprise; that it had totally misjudged both the extent of the Panzer divisions' effectiveness and the angle of the Germans' approach; that the word "*débâcle*," which came into historic usage that summer, was carrying its full weight of associations—of national shame, of communal failure, of widespread social disintegration.

On the evening of Sunday, June 9, my father came home from the Ministry of War, where he had been working around the clock, to tell my mother that she and I must get on the road to Tours as early as possible the following morning. The government was being evacuated to Tours at dawn; he was going to sleep on a cot at his office. At 8:00 P.M., he stood at the door of our flat, his little suitcase in hand. "*Á très bientôt, mon trésor,*" he said as he embraced me. "*Occupes toi bien d'elle,*" he whispered to my mother as he embraced her tenderly in turn, "Take good care of her." His eyes were filling with tears. Hers were, too. He fled down the stairs, taking them two at a time.

Early the following morning, Aunt Sandra arrived to see us off, tearful, sentimental, but efficient. "*Bozhe moi,* dear God," she knew all too much about exiles, she said with many sighs. Two decades ago, she'd lost her beloved daughter, lost her husband, lost all she possessed during her long exodus out of Russia. However much she loved us, she couldn't face another exile. She helped my mother finish packing, sent me to the charcuterie to get some cold food for our trip—it was the first time I was allowed to go out of the house and do an errand by myself, without an adult. My governess, barely recovering from her bronchitis, still coughing and running fevers at night, sat glumly in an armchair, agreeing with Aunt Sandra's feelings about exile: No, she, too, couldn't face one again. It was time to leave. The concierge's husband came up to carry our luggage. How tenderly, lovingly my mother held my hand as we slowly descended the staircase, waving, blowing kisses to the two forlorn women above us who, along with Aunt Simone and Babushka, had been my principal mentors since infancy.

TEN

The Debacle

As my mother and I left Paris on the gloriously sunny morning of June 10, 1940, we became part of a panic-stricken caravan, the surreal mayhem of which haunts me to this day. The road to Tours, the destination of most Parisians, was clogged with every possible invention that could move on wheels. Amid a cacophonous din of bleating horns, fire trucks, ambulances, ice-cream vendors' vehicles, funeral carriages, municipal street-sweeping trucks, tourist buses racily labeled "Paris La Nuit," even wheelbarrows and prams mingled with the chic limousines, sports cars, family sedans all heading south toward the Loire, where, so deluded gossip had it, French troops might still "reconstitute a front." Barely moving at the pace of a human stride—it was taking three days to travel a distance usually covered in three hours—these vehicles, crammed with children, women of all ages, old men, and boys under eighteen, were surmounted by an astounding variety of hastily assembled personal possessions. Tied onto their roofs amid mounds of sheets, blankets, and mattresses were birdcages, bicycles, cradles, sewing machines, saucepans and various other cooking utensils, collapsible tents, cuckoo clocks. Swarming amid the vehicles, at times totally stopping their advance, large bands of haggard, desperate-eyed soldiers searching for their retreating units stumbled alongside hordes of pedestrian refugees who carried their possessions on their backs: They were part of the million and a half citizens who had taken to the roads in the past four weeks, in the wake of one of the most catastrophic defeats in military history.

This torrent of humanity registered no ill will and little rage, simply a shared despair and benumbed stupor. For few members of that exodus knew where their loved ones were. It was as if a monstrous explosion had blown hundreds of thousands of families into fragments, scattering them all over the landscape, causing the ones left behind to phone every possible hostelry in the country and to send ads to the papers such as "Jules Monnet, your loving parents are in Auxerre." As our tiny Peugeot wheezed southward in the bumper-to-bumper traffic, we knew that throughout France hundreds of thousands of our compatriots were searching for loved ones and wondering about their survival, with an anxiety equal to ours.

My mother's anxiety was threefold: By the end of the first afternoon, she knew that given the pace of the Germans' advance, there was little chance that we would reach Tours in less than three days; she was realistic enough to realize that my father's ministry—which had left at 4:00 A.M. in a special government caravan, plowing its way through the traffic with horns blaring—might already have left Tours by the time we reached the city and gone on to yet another southward destination. She was equally anxious about Alex's whereabouts—he had left Paris on the eighth, *Mamasha* in tow, with the intention of winding his way to the south of France; but as a Russian Jew with a Nansen passport, he was particularly vulnerable to persecution by the notoriously anti-Semitic French police. Moreover, as we sputtered toward Tours at the rate of five kilometers an hour amid the horrendous traffic, our engine constantly stalling, I was aware that notwithstanding the kisses she kept blowing me to boost my spirits, Mother was very worried about whether we could even make it to Tours ahead of the Nazis. So to cheer her up, I kept humming my favorite ditty of the season, "We're gonna hang our linen on the Siegfried line . . . if the Siegfried Line's still there."

For three days, we slept in the car, living on the reserves of bread, water, and hardboiled eggs we had brought from Paris, scrounging occasional scraps of fruit in local cafés. Our destination was Villandry, a Renaissance château a few miles from Tours that is graced with one of France's loveliest gardens. It belonged to a friend of my mother, Isabelle Carvallo de la Bouillerie, a woman of considerable mettle and generosity who had recently worked alongside my mother at the Auxiliaire Social, an organization in Paris that sheltered refugee children. Villandry, originally built by François I's minister of finances, who had served as French ambassador to Rome, has long been looked on as the ideal prototype of the Renaissance château. It has been owned by only two families since the sixteenth century and at the turn of the twentieth century was bought by a wealthy Spanish-born eye doctor, Joachim Carvallo, who saved it from destruction and designed its famous boxwood plantings, drawing inspiration from Renaissance gardens. In May 1940, when the German Blitzkrieg began, his daughter Isabelle had opened a center for refugee children on the Villandry grounds. In recent weeks she had also begun to share her château with various Parisian acquaintances who were fleeing, and we had the luck of being included in this group.

It was upon arriving at Villandry that my mother received the first of several desperate letters Alex was to write her there throughout June, before he was even sure that she was there. He had had his own share of troubles during his exodus from Paris with his mother. Having left Paris two days earlier than we had, with several canisters of gasoline in his trunk, he managed to travel southwestward on the smallest back roads, having been ordered off the main thoroughfares early on by a French officer who put a revolver to his head. Alex and Henriette had finally reached Royan, on the Atlantic coast, where my mother's sister, Lila, whose marriage was happy enough but who had always had a crush on Alex, had also fled. Under his mask of suave courtesy and charm, Alex was a very controlling man, all too given to violent jealousy; and this first letter, written on June 11, already reflects a certain rancor, which would color our family relations for a long time to come: Heedless of the political crisis, he resented the fact that my mother's devotion to me and her dutifulness toward my father's decisions had led her to act independently of him.

My beloved,

You of course are so preoccupied that you scarcely have time to think of me. Lila is just as sharp-witted as you are, and thanks to her we found two rooms in a very agreeable villa—I am constantly gripped by the terrible sense that I've lost you. I think of you ceaselessly, and it seems that you were indifferent to our separation, and I suffer from that idea. Perhaps I'm mistaken, and my feelings are the result of solitude and loneliness. Beloved, write me as soon as you can that you love me passionately and will love me whatever happens. This is all a lesson for me: I'm learning that I need you more than you need me.

Quickly write me to tell me I'm wrong. . . . To spend 24 hours a day with mamasha is very hard. With Lila it's just as difficult because she's looking for something other than what I can give her—but she is very sweet. I roam from café to café like all the other refugees and think of you, everyone finds me sad—and I am—because . . . I was already outside of your life—and your plans for a while had been made without me. My love I adore you write to me quickly before I despair—

I kiss you and kiss you and adore you.

He wrote her again the following day, June 12, two days before the fall of Paris, mostly worrying about the paintings he had left behind in his studio.

I wait every moment for a word from you. What are you doing? Are you planning to stay put, or are you taking Francine to the Gorges du Tarn? I suffer a lot from having left all the paintings behind—they've surely perished! However I'll make more, if God wills it.

It's atrocious, it's difficult to be separated from you, especially in times like these—Here crowds of refugees are arriving all the time, I live from one radio to the other—there are no newspapers, no more news. Mother is calming down a bit. Write soon you're the only window open on a world still filled with sun.

I hug the whole the whole of you.

She wrote him the day she received his first letter, on the thirteenth, the day after we'd arrived at Villandry. "How can you be in doubt, I love you more than life and am only thinking of our future life together," she reassured him amid a rush of news about the displaced children in her charge and her struggle to get enough gas coupons to drive anywhere. "I can't live without you. You're indeed vital to me. I'm totally unhappy and lost without you."

During that particular week of the debacle, the French postal system seems still to have been functioning normally. Alex received her letter of the thirteenth within two days and wrote her on the sixteenth, two days after Paris fell, warning her that she mustn't wait too long before leaving Villandry.

I've just received your first letter. You can't imagine my joy. Tears welled up in my eyes. I beg you, please forgive me my first letters. I was in such a terrible state without you, with Mother acting up all the time etc. And all of a sudden I felt your passionate love again. I adore you so endlessly, I think only about you day and night. . . . I am so happy that you are working and helping out. I love you endlessly for everything you do. It's hard for me to live without you. . . . [A]ll hotels here are requisitioned. My heart stops at the thought that I might see you soon. . . . There was an air raid last night and radio Stuttgart announced that we were about to be bombed. . . . I beg you not to stay in Tours until the last minute, for if a new front is established you won't be able to leave any more. . . . My only true love. My life, my everything, write and come. *I can come to fetch you. . . . Command and I shall obey,* je t'aime.

Throughout that week, the Villandry community had kept up with events on the château's one wireless, some twenty of us gathering every afternoon in the living room to hear the calamitous news. On June 16, Premier Paul Reynaud resigned after his cabinet voted down Churchill's extraordinary offer temporarily to fuse the British and French nations into one union. Marshal Pétain was named head of state in his stead. And on the seventeenth—it was the day before the Germans arrived in Tours and we were bidden to gather in the living room earlier than usual, at noon—we heard the eighty-four-year-old Pétain announce the end of the war in his quivering, curiously high-pitched voice: "I make to France the gift of my person to allay its misery. . . . It is with a heavy heart that I tell you today to cease all combat."

Our room at Villandry was at the end of one of the two main wings of the U-shaped château, and it looked out, on the left, on its celebrated boxwood gardens. Straight ahead, we looked onto the little country road that linked the village of Villandry to Tours. The day after Pétain's speech, June 18—it was a very sunny morning; I remember that entire tragic month as being drenched in sunlight—we woke before seven to the sound of powerful young voices singing. My mother leaped out of bed, exclaiming *"Les Boches sont arrivés!"* ("The Germans have arrived!") She grabbed my hand as she ran to the window, and we looked down upon a German regiment's first parade on their newly conquered terrain: goose-stepping smartly, four abreast, a few hundred yards from our window, the Nazis, fresh faced, very young, very glaring, their heads held high toward us, their helmets and bayonets blazing in the sun. If my memory serves me right, their marching song that day was "Lili Marlene":

Vor der Kaserne, vor dem grossen Tor
stand eine Laterne, und steht sie noch davor. . . .

As children, I suspect, we are all born collaborationists; we do everything in our power to enchant and charm the enemy, to save our skins, to survive. With an enjoyment I knew to be infamous, I thrilled to the radiance of the young Germans' stern faces. I wanted to kill them, yet I felt the thrill of a child admiring anything that is sleek, streamlined, powerful. My crass little soul delighted in the pomp of uniforms, in all appurtenances of rank and might. I thought back with pity and rage to the haggard, desperate French soldiers we had seen on the road out of Paris. I stared hard at the young Germans, trying to summon up hatred, feeling disloyal to my father (who might at any moment, wherever he was, be killed by one of them) for admiring their beauty, their futurity. I know my mother felt no such ambivalence. She stood at the window in a defiant posture, her hands on her hips, as if confronting someone in a brawl, and quietly whispered, loathing in her voice, *"Quelle merde."*

General de Gaulle's appeal, which was broadcast at 8:00 P.M. that very day, June 18, was heard by only a very small minority of French citizens. Reports of it only reached us in the following days, along with the story of his daredevil escape from France, the bravado of which has not received proper attention. General Edward Spears, who had gallantly led the British Expeditionary Force throughout the fall of France, was ordered to leave Bordeaux on the evening of the seventeenth, a few hours after Pétain's announcement of the armistice. Through a plan arranged that afternoon by the two generals, who were close friends, de Gaulle assigned himself the task of seeing off Spears at the Bordeaux airport. In full sight of the French officials who would later become eminent members of the Vichy government, de Gaulle stood by Spears's tiny four-seater plane, briefcase in hand, saying good-bye to his British colleague. At the very last minute, after the engines had started up, Spears reached out a hand to his comrade and yanked de Gaulle into his plane. To the consternation of the bystanders, off the two generals went, reaching London an hour later. On the evening of the following day, de Gaulle, after a considerable amount of maneuvering with the British cabinet and with the dauntless support of Spears and Foreign Secretary Anthony Eden, went on the BBC to tell his compatriots that "we have lost a battle, but we have not lost a war."

I recall our hostess, Madame de la Bouillerie, rushing into our room the day after the "Appel du 18 Juin" to give us the news: De Gaulle was calling on all French to join him in London and continue the struggle against Germany! Upon hearing this, my mother grew very quiet. She waited until we were alone and everyone was out of earshot, then took my hand and whispered excitedly, "I suspect that your father will at any moment join him, join de Gaulle!" She was absolutely right.

A few days after we heard about de Gaulle, on June 22, Pétain agreed to the ignominious terms of the 1940 armistice and signed it into law. France was divided into two zones, the Occupied Zone (which included our temporary refuge, Tours) and the so-called Vichy Zone, headed by Pétain's Collaborationist government. Royan was scheduled to be occupied by the Germans, and by defying a series of border guards at the frontier between the two zones Alex managed to get to the little town of Ascain, a few miles above St. Jean-de-Luz; there, he had sought temporary refuge, his mother still in tow, with his friend Jean-Pierre Fourneau. Since mid-June,

Alex and my mother had not received any letters from each other, and due to new censorship rules they were to remain incommunicado until well into July. Although he still was not yet technically a French citizen, upon the armistice Alex keenly felt the depth of the French tragedy and seemed to have sought solace in the Protestant faith of his youth.

June 23rd

    My life, my everything,

    I am writing to you on this dreadful day. I don't know where you are, what's happening to you. I don't know if you'll ever receive this letter, but I believe that God will have mercy to such great and true a love. I suffered so much, I worried so much about you and Francine. . . . My soul aches for our country, and I feel so helpless. Everything is happening on such a world scale, that personal sufferings, worries, desires seem trifling. . . .

    Whatever happens now, I am grateful to you for my happiness, and in all the sufferings that probably await me I will think about you and it will help me to endure everything. Always remember how much I love you and how much we need each other. My love, wherever I may be, I will only wait for a moment when I see you. Since we parted, I have an image of you before my eyes, and at every turn of the road, of the street, it seems to me that I will find you. I believe I will find you.

    I pray to God for France, for you, for us. Believe in me the way I believe in you. Don't leave me, the way I don't leave you.

    Yours For ever and completely,

    A.

My mother, too, was anguished by the dearth of news about Alex's whereabouts. On July 6, she wrote him four separate letters, addressing them to four possible destinations.

"My love," she wrote him in the version she sent to Sainte Maxime, "I am sending out four copies of this letter. What if not a single one will reach you?! I'm going crazy from missing you and desiring you. On Monday I am going to Vichy to organize the trip to the South with Francine. . . . I adore you and love you more than ever. I hope you will manage to get in touch with me in Villandry as soon as you can."

"My love," he wrote her that same week, suggesting that he intended this missive to serve as his last will and testament,

> *I write you a word again, and I don't know if you will ever receive it. . . . My life, we are trying to reach our house in the South, and there we shall wait for events. Where are you? What is happening to you? My life stopped since we parted. If anything happens to me, everything I own—paintings, books, furniture, means of support, I give to you in the name of the happiness you gave me.*
>
> *I pray to God for you, for us. Yours for ever. Alexander Liberman.*

The lovers' communication finally resumed in mid-July: On the four-teenth of the month, Tatiana responded to a telegram she had just received from Alex, who had safely reached his house in Sainte Maxime. But by this time, a guarded tone had to be maintained in any correspondence between the two zones. All of Tatiana's subsequent correspondence from the Occu-pied Zone bears the stamp *"Ouvert par l'autorité militaire."*

"My Dear Life," she wrote him.

> *Finally I received your telegram with the address. I was feeling so completely lost without you. My Love: I miss you SO MUCH!*
>
> *Here we have our personal dramas. 40 children left for Villandry yesterday in an ambulance and still haven't arrived. . . . We haven't found any lodging for the kids, so Isabelle is taking them in. Can you imagine this hovel? Yesterday we went four(!!) times to Tours for beds, etc.*
>
> *I am waiting anxiously for your letter and I wonder how you are coping there without my pragmatic counsel. Francine is enjoying the life here and the gar-den is a great background for her type of beauty!*
>
> *What to do to see you? I kiss you tenderly, as much as I love you.*
>
> *PS My love to Mamasha.*

In the second week of July, my mother and I had our first face-to-face encounter with the Nazi regime. We had driven in our tiny Peugeot to Tours to get flour for Villandry's refugee children. A few blocks from the prefecture, where the Germans had established their *Kommandantur,* our tiny car was crashed into by a huge Mercedes filled with German officers, three times the size and weight of our vehicle. The windshield shattered and glass struck our foreheads, hitting particularly hard on the passenger side, and my memories of the next few minutes are drenched in blood. Although my mother's terrible driving might have been at fault, she bounded out of the car, seething with rage, and in her very limited German accused the officers of irresponsible driving. The officers may have been taken aback by her vehemence—these were the days when docility was counseled upon any encounter with the occupying forces—but she was gorgeous and distinguished looking enough to keep them temporarily at bay, and they limited themselves to asking her for our identity papers. She whipped them out, along with her visiting card. Seeing the title "vicomtesse" engraved on the card, the officers, apparently sensitive to issues of social hierarchy, offered to take us to the hospital. "Not at all," my mother demanded, "I want to see the Kommandant." Startled but bowing, they acceded. Our Peugeot was still drivable, and we followed the Germans' Mercedes amid a blaze of klaxons to the *Kommandantur*.

M y mother was a shrewd and cunning woman; and I suspect that for the past few weeks she had been wondering about how to eventually obtain an *Ausweis*, a permit, to get us to the Vichy Zone and on to Alex's house in the south of France. What luck! she had immediately thought upon the occurrence of the accident. She might meet the Kommandant of Tours! As our car reached our destination, she lovingly commended me for my calm as she wiped off some blood from my face and combed my hair for our important visit. We were ushered into the main office, where a French *préfet* had reigned until a few weeks earlier. The Kommandant was a tall, courtly, scholarly-looking man in his late thirties with horn-rimmed glasses and a handsome mustache. Upon ushering us in, the officers handed him our identity papers. "Is your husband by any chance descended from the cardinal de Richelieu?" the Kommandant asked in accent-free French, after perusing them. "Anyone in their right mind," my mother answered snappily, "would rather be descended from la Dame aux Camélias."

The Kommandant gave a broad, enchanted smile and called his orderlies to come and dress my wounds. As I was being tended to, he held a lively discussion with my mother concerning the relative merits of Dumas *père* and Dumas *fils*. We learned that Kommandant Hebert was a professor of French literature at the University of Heidelberg. A box of chocolates was offered us, a car was called for to take us home to Villandry. "*Schön kleine Kontessen*," he whispered as he kissed my hand in parting. I'll never forget the graze of his mustache on my wrist, the very great kindness—an almost pleading kindness—of his eyes, my deepening confusion as to whether it was permissible to think of him as a nice man, to like a highly placed member of the armed forces that were my father's enemy.

In mid-July, a few days after our first meeting with the Kommandant, my mother received a letter and an *Ausweis*, asking her to drive to the Ministry of War at Vichy. The letter notified her that it had information about my father and stipulated that she must leave me behind at Villandry as a hostage of sorts. She left me in the care of a fellow exile, Gitta Sereny, a precocious seventeen-year-old Hungarian girl whom she had befriended in Paris in the weeks before the debacle, when they had worked together at a refugee center. It is in Vichy that a minor official of the Ministry of War gave Mother the news, briskly and coldly, about my father: That very month the Vichy government would impose a death sentence on de Gaulle on grounds of treason, and like all of de Gaulle's recruits my father was being listed by Vichy as a defector. Mother also learned that Lieutenant du Plessix had left Bordeaux shortly after June 18 and flown to Casablanca, where he had organized a squadron of Free French aviators. He had been shot down over the Mediterranean in early July, on his way to joining de Gaulle in London, and until further knowledge he would be listed as missing in action. (Throughout the following year, not daring to break the news to me, my mother led me to believe that my father was "on a secret mission.")

My mother seems to have informed Alex of our family tragedy the very day she was notified of it, through some form of coded telegram: In view of the censorship, it obviously would not have been safe to inform him openly of Lieutenant du Plessix's heroic actions with de Gaulle. The shockingly buoyant, casual letter she writes Alex the day after she received the news concerning my father expresses no grief, no sense of loss, little more than her overriding obsession to assemble enough gas coupons to drive to the Vichy Zone and join Alex.

"My Life, my Life, my Life," she writes to Alex in her letters of July 15 and 16, during her twenty-four-hour stay in the Vichy Zone.

It was hard to get out of the Germans' hands, but the path is clear now and the next time will be easy. I got to the Parc-Hotel [where all the Vichy France ministries had their offices] and sent you the telegram right away. I'm trying to procure some gas to go to the South, but I still need 50 more liters. I do have 40 liters at Villandry, that could get us to Vichy, but I need more gas for the rest of the road. On Friday I'm going back to Villandry, where Francine is staying. I'm dreaming about getting to you at the beginning of next week. I wish I could remain in the South till the end of this whole nightmare. Write to Villandry at once. I would like to leave after getting your letter. I kiss you as much as I love you.

But in those very days of mid-July, several issues got in the way of our going south to stay with Alex. Mother could find no more gasoline. ("The ministries that passed through Tours have requisitioned everything.") A few of the refugee children fell very ill, and Mother did not want to leave Villandry until she had found someone responsible for them. She herself came down with severe bronchitis and a high fever. Moreover, her sense of prudishness and propriety came to the fore—what would people think, she might have asked herself, when they heard that she had brought her child to live with her lover?

But even more important, my father's wishes concerning my future, which were stated in a series of letters he had written to her and to the Dessoffys in the weeks before his death, started to gnaw at her conscience. Notwithstanding his own record of infidelities, he seemed to have been more profoundly jealous and resentful of Alex than he had been of any of her earlier lovers. And now that I was exclusively in my mother's charge, what alternatives had he had if he had wished to see me safely refuged in the Vichy Zone yet kept out of Alex's sight? His options had been very narrow. Everyone who had helped him take care of me throughout my childhood—my governess, Aunt Sandra, and the Monestiers, the last of whom had already started working with resistance movements—had decided to remain in the Occupied Zone. Apart from those trusted relatives, all of my parents' close friends had been partying hard throughout the previous decade, and come the debacle they seemed reluctant to rearrange their lives for a nine-year-old. This entire correspondence—which thank heavens I did not get to read until a few years ago—reminds me of some lost-parcel episode. Help, everyone is calling out! Lost child here, misaddressed, needs to be re-expedited! How to re-expedite this burdensome child?

According to my mother, the last letters my father wrote her in late June—they did not get to her until after he was reported missing in action—insisted that she call for my governess, Maria Nikolaevna, to come down from Paris. She should then install the two of us in his primitive little farmhouse in Sanary. "I've been forwarded a letter from Bertrand asking me to send Francine to his house in [Sanary]—to this farm that doesn't even have any beds," my mother had written Alex while she was still ill in the third week of July. "In his view she could live there on stuff sent from the city, waiting for the end of the war, which he thought would come soon." "Yesterday my temperature was better—39.5—and I hope to get out of bed soon," she reports the following day, still seeming torn about whether to join Alex. "Francine has taken wonderful care of me."

Meanwhile, Alex, safe in his house in Sainte Maxime, was chafing at the notion that my father would not have allowed me to stay with him. My father's wishes were related to him by the nonchalant Dessoffys, who lived forty-five minutes away in Sanary and were visiting him frequently. They reported that my father had indeed asked them to take charge of me there. In his letters to Mother, Alex seems keenly aware of the Dessoffys' fecklessness, their fairly chronic state of druggedness, and their general unsuitability as guardians—they appear to have vanished the second they were asked to take charge of me. Moreover, Alex pleads, the farmhouse did not even have any furniture or running water. (My father's totally absurd edicts had indeed reflected the general mood of irrationality that seized French citizens upon the debacle.) Alex, the only one making sense throughout that month, offers to finance and oversee the completion of the house, but thinks that the whole notion is absurd. The only solution, he pleads, is for my mother to get another *Ausweis* and come straight down with me to his house.

"I sense that you have a new problem—your daughter!" he writes my mother in the third week of July, before he's received her letter from Vichy.

> *How can it be that in a difficult moment like this B[ertrand] couldn't understand that for Francine's sake it would be better for her to be here! Three weeks ago B. wrote to Hélène to keep an eye on Francine, but she can't do it now and Jacques doesn't know what to do. He has a letter from B. addressed to you, it is "recent." Maybe it advises you to do something altogether different? What will Francine and Maria Nikolaevna do without a car, in the middle of nowhere? Don't worry about money. As long as I have money, you and Francine have it too. I can not stand it without you—as soon as I hear a car on the road, I think it's you and my heart stops. We've already bought the bicycle for Francine! Decide everything here when you've arrived, after you've read B's last letter. What a terrible, difficult life! Come!!!*
>
> *P.P.S. Jacques just called again . . . he opened B.'s last letter to you. It instructs you to do what you wish, but 'not to expose Francine to Sainte Maxime.' And he asks Hélène to take care of Francine.*
>
> *Are there no relatives? No other friends? We might also rent a hotel room for the two of you while you wait for Maria Nikolaevna.*

It is at this point that the Kommandant of Tours, Herr Professor Hebert, reentered our lives. His kindness was revealed to us once more in an episode that I did not witness but heard my mother relate many times in later years. In the last days of July, just as she was recovering from bronchitis and was wondering how she might go about getting an *Ausweis* for both of us, she received a message from Kommandant Hebert asking her to visit him in his office, alone. The way she recounted it, he sat her down courteously in an armchair and said words to this effect: "I hear from our intelligence reports that your husband joined the Free French and is missing in action. There may be problems for you. It might be safer for you and your daughter to travel to the Free Zone." And he offered her an *Ausweis*. They parted again on the warmest of terms, and for the following decades my mother, a shame-

First photograph taken by Alex of Francine after her arrival in the south of France in September 1940.

less boaster, would announce to the world that Kommandant Hebert had been passionately enamored of her.

A week or so later, in mid-August 1940, we were back in our little Peugeot, sputtering and stalling every few minutes—my mother never would learn to work a clutch properly—toward the Vichy Zone and the south of France. Heedless of my parents' sacrifices and suffering, I remember little else than my constant joy and excitement, throughout those dreadful months, at the sense of finally being the center of my mother's affection. I took great pride in my father's "secret mission," the possible routes of which I painstakingly traced every few days on the atlas I had brought from Paris. Upon learning that we were finally going to the south of France, I felt keen pleasure at the prospect of seeing the nice man with the little mustache again and of sitting in his seaside studio while he painted another portrait of me.

I believe our car broke down in Montélimar, for my mother kept consoling me with boxes of that city's famous nougat candy. Within a few hours, Alex had sent a car and chauffeur to fetch us there and bring us to Sainte Maxime, a gesture characteristic of his resourcefulness and prodigality—who else but Alex Liberman could have found a car and chauffeur in the middle of the oil shortage and general mayhem of the 1940 debacle? That same night, we arrived at his house, Va-et-Vient, and saw Alex leap out of a thicket of bushes like a faun, his face and hands trembling with excitement.

I recall waking up the following morning in the blessed heat of the south and wandering through the house, lonely and hungry. Food has gotten scarce, but suddenly Alex comes bursting out of his kitchen with a precious breakfast ferreted out on the black market that dawn: cornflakes topped with a fried egg topped with ketchup. As I devour my meal he watches me with his great green eyes and asks, in Russian, "Is it good, Frosinka?" "Oh, so good," I say, thinking, This man will provide for me. He then presents me with a possession my governess had never allowed me to have, a gleaming turquoise-blue bicycle, which he teaches me to ride in a matter of hours; by the end of the week, he has taught me to swim like a fish.

Another banal tale of survival, another instance of destiny being kind. I was a tough, resilient, endlessly optimistic child who already adored to travel and welcomed the challenge of constantly adapting to new situations, new protectors, new exiles, new friends. My mother, or God, or my beloved Babushka's genes, seemed to have granted me a great inclination to happiness. For although the delusions and deceptions attending the events of 1940 would have awesome repercussions for me in later years, I recall those tragic summer months as some of the most blissful ones of my life.

ELEVEN

Leaving All Behind

For the following few months, we were crammed into Alex's sun-drenched little house, a coquettish pink stucco villa a hundred yards from the beach, with terraces that looked out upon the Gulf of St. Tropez. Designed to house four persons at the most, it now overflowed with a motley crew of rotating houseguests—Parisian refugees, like ourselves, seeking shelter in the south before deciding what to do for the rest of the war. Irena Lidova, Alex's former colleague and lover, was there for a few weeks with her pleasant husband, a dance photographer. At times, our crowded circumstances led to outbursts of temper. Being swift of tongue, on occasion I may have been impertinent, and at some point I must have made a brash comment to Lidova, for one afternoon as we were walking down the corridor that led to my room she roundly slapped my face. My parents had not believed in corporal punishment; no one had ever so much as rapped my hand. Mother, who was walking ahead of us, wheeled around and shouted fiercely at Lidova, "No one slaps my daughter's face! Is that clear? No one!" And she slapped Lidova's face in return. Poor Lidova! It must have been difficult for her to live in the same house with the woman who, she most probably realized, was Alex's great love.

Mother and I had gotten to the south just in time: by September, passage from the Occupied Zone to Vichy France had become almost impossible—few if any travel permits were being issued. Food was getting scarce, and the bass Alex caught spearfishing in the Gulf of St. Tropez every day became our principal source of protein. As he stalked his prey, I swam alongside him with a mask, elated by my first marine experiences. I helped carry his catch to the kitchen and watched Maria, the young local woman who served as his housekeeper, bake it with mounds of fennel for lunch, which we ate on the sunny terrace, still dressed in our bathing suits.

I remember those months of the late summer and early fall as being suffused with sun and joy. On days when food was particularly scarce, we entertained one another by thinking up the most dreadful combinations of food imaginable. Whoever thought up the most disgusting blend won, and I scored highest by coming up with sardines topped with chocolate sauce. During our first weeks together, I also discovered that Alex could make me laugh as no one before had. He had a brilliant gift of mimicry, which he exhibited to small, select audiences; his repertory included one particular pantomime that we referred to as "a man gone wild," which I would beg him to perform again and again until I was well into my teens. He would start jumping up and down and every which way, taking huge leaps and emitting weird, piercing noises, like an ape leaping in the jungle from tree to tree, his limbs wildly loosened and eerily elastic, as if barely attached to his body. I don't know whether he invented the impersonation for me or for some earlier young fan. The wildness suddenly released by this tender but rigorously self-controlled man came from some deep inner source— perhaps from his own mother's gift for pantomime—and would last a minute or two, sending me into bouts of uncontrollable laughter.

My mother sunbathed, read, and hugged me wordlessly more than ever. There was constant talk of American relatives and acquaintances who were helping us to obtain the proper papers to emigrate to the United States. John Wiley, a high-placed American foreign-service official who had befriended my parents in the 1930s and whose wife, Irena, was Mother's close friend, was helping to prepare our immigration visas. Another diplomat—William

Bullitt, the American ambassador to France, who had recently been called back to Washington—was writing letters on our behalf, as was my mother's father, whom she had not seen since she was exactly my age. Meanwhile, Simon Liberman, who had been living in New York since 1939, was helping to get an immigration visa for Alex.

I did not yet know the meanings of the words "mistress" or "lover." Alex was simply presented as a dear childhood friend of my mother of whom she was very fond, a relative of sorts who would protect and take care of us until my father returned. Yet I sensed—with that sixth sense particularly strong among children from troubled families—that Alex was to my mother what the lady in red had been to my father. And in our new life with Alex, I stopped asking questions about my father's whereabouts. For I was somehow made to understand that Alex and Mother would rather not hear such questions, and I restructured my life around the crucial goal of obtaining and preserving their love.

And so I cloaked my worries about my father with a mask of silence. Now that we were with Alex, it felt nicer, more proper, to lock my father into some quiet inner space. My silence was a vault into which the deepest part of me—the part that wished to know about my father—was hidden. The outer husk encircling this crypt remained bright and cheerful. My twinkling surface gaiety made my inner chasm all the more secret, all the more my own, like a cave that only I could enter. So I smiled, curtsied, danced, made charming dinner conversation, twinkle, twinkle, little star, praises whirled and sparkled like a rainbow about me, my mother glowed with pride. Meanwhile, there lay inside me a private chamber in which I'd carefully buried my fears, a chamber that no one else could enter—oh, curses and banishment on anyone who tried to break into it.

For my secrecy was also like a cloud, a veil, that shielded and protected my father from all possible harm—I believed that only silence, secrecy would help to keep him alive. And as Mother and Alex were painstakingly preparing our move to the United States, it is in this inner crypt of my imagination that I nurtured fantasies about my absent, silent father: He was in Syria, acting out clandestine missions for the Free French, helping to plan an Allied invasion of France; or he was shuttling back and forth between the French and British coasts, carrying such crucial messages that an interception by the Nazis could cause many deaths on the Allied side; or he was carrying out similarly hazardous secret missions in Bangkok, in Dakar, in all the distant exotic places depicted in those paintings by Uncle Sasha that had surrounded my childhood.

I nurtured these muffled, private thoughts throughout those joyously sunny last months in the south of France. There was only one nighttime experience I remember from that entire autumn. It was also a kind of mission—a mission given me by Alex for the sake of his health, which I could accomplish only in the late afternoon and evening, as it was getting dark.

A lex's ulcer diet stipulated a quart of milk per day. But by the fall of 1940, most victuals had grown scarce, transportation was very limited, and we lived on whatever goods were produced in our immediate locale. Milk was particularly hard to find. Whatever there was of it had to be gotten from local farmers who kept cows—in the south of France they were few and far-between, and they sold milk only to children. So a few weeks after our arrival, I was sent out almost every night to a farm, five miles inland from our seaside home, to get Alex's milk. By this time, I was whizzing through all kinds of terrain on my gleaming blue bicycle, and my mission filled me with pride—I'm getting milk to heal Alex's ulcers! I zipped down our driveway, a metal milk can dangling from my handlebar, and after gliding a few miles down the road that borders the gulf, I turned inland onto a sandy path flanked by vast stretches of parasol pines. The pines had shed much during the summer, forming thick carpets of needles, which were hazardous and fun to slide on. To be absolutely sure of obtaining milk, my mission had to take place toward dusk, when the cows had just been brought in from the fields and been placed in the milk barn. The setting sun filtered aslant through the trees, dappling with gold the brown, satiny floor. I enjoyed the stillness of the forest, broken only by the *whish* of my tires on the thick carpet of pine needles, the cling-clang of the

Francine picking grapes in the south of France in October 1940.
(The scars on her forehead were caused by the recent car accident in Tours.)

empty milk can against the metal of my handlebar, the twitter of birds being quieted to sleep by the last rays of slanting sun. After a few miles, the
pines became sparser and I came into a clearing, and the farm suddenly
came into view at the end of a dirt path on the right. I dismounted my bicycle and walked it to the dairy barn, where a few children had already
started to queue up, waiting for the farmer to arrive.

As the sun began to brush the horizon, the farmer came out of the
dairy barn, a slow-moving, distrustful man. When it was my turn, he
poured four ladlefuls of milk from his pail into my can, then carefully
counted the change I had taken out of the pocket of my shorts before returning it to me. The easy part of the mission had been accomplished:
Now I had to get home without spilling the milk and without getting too
scared of the dark.

For as a child I believed in ghosts, and I was terrified of the darkness
hours, which, I had been led to believe, betokened all kinds of ghoulish presences. This was yet another phobia once induced by my father: His strategy
had been to toughen me up by instilling fears in me—such as my terror of
his driving too fast—and then, with luck, helping me to overcome them. As
the autumn days shortened through October and November, much of my
journey was undertaken in the dark, and I was terrified of crossing the isolated pine forest. As I set forth from the farm, I switched on the light on
top of my handlebar. While pedaling, I tried to concentrate on the yellow
circle of light glowing just ahead of my front tire, hoping that it would
safeguard me from the forest's demons. I pedaled slowly, dreading any
brusque movement that would cause the milk to spill, dreading even more
the presences about me, looking steadfastly at the golden spot of light
ahead of me. But at every stirring of the wind in branches, at the rustle of
any animal on my path, great panic seized me, I imagined that a dread presence was reaching out for me, was thrusting its arms out from the very forest, about to grasp me. . . . Oh, Father, Father, I'm not afraid, see, I'm not
afraid of ghosts, I'm a good little soldier, I'm not afraid of all that you've
taught me to fear, no, the dead cannot come and claim me, I'll pedal on, I'll
look straight ahead at my circle of light until I'm gone past them. . . .

I cycled faster, milk pail lurching; the pursuers receded, I'd escaped them once more—ahead of me glimmered the lights of the main road. I reached the end of my forest lane, turned left on the main road that runs parallel to the Gulf of St. Tropez. The car traffic was sparse. A few minutes after passing the last café, I turned up our own driveway, the driveway to the best house Mother and I had ever lived in, and Alex was there to greet me, brushing his funny little mustache against my cheek as he thanked me for the milk. "*Merci*, Boubousiki," he said. ("Boubous" or "Boubousiki," interchangeably, were Russian terms of endearment Alex, Mother, and I had adopted when we began to live with one another; they created a special bond between us, singling us out as a budding family.) Alex brought the milk into the kitchen, where Maria quickly brought it to a boil to pasteurize. Then we put it into a large shallow pan to cool down quickly by dinnertime. And as we sat down at the long, hospitable oak table, the three of us and whatever migrating guests might be staying with us that week—the Lidovs, or one of Alex's friends from Les Roches days such as Jean-Pierre Fourneau and his family—I was filled with pride as Alex savored the tall glass of milk that was so essential, so the doctors had told him, to the healing of his ulcers.

By the end of November, all three of us had received our visas. John Wiley's lobbying on our behalf, the sponsoring letters from my mother's father and Simon Liberman had borne fruit. And in the first weeks of December, my mother engaged in another act of derring-do: To retrieve valuables from Alex's flat and our own that were essential to our journey to the United States, she decided to travel to Paris with a group of contrabandists—it was the only way one could then cross between the zones. We had fled the capital in such a hurry that she had left behind most of her jewelry and important papers; her strong sense of family duty also led her to worry about Aunt Sandra, Aunt Lila, and the Monestiers, and she wanted to say good-bye to them. And in view of the notorious anti-Semitism of the Vichy police, it would have been considerably riskier for Alex to undertake such a trip. (Looking back on it now, I realize that

French citizens' zany optimism concerning the military situation of June 1940 had led hundreds of thousands of Parisians to rush out of the capital in a manner quite as improvident as ours. Simone Weil and her family, for instance, filled with the same delusions and assured that "a new front" would at any minute be reconstituted north of Paris, realized on the afternoon of June 13, the day before the Germans took the city, that the very last southbound train out of Paris was about to depart; they rushed to the Gare de Lyon without even returning to their flat, leaving the city with no more than the clothes they were wearing that day.)

Mother's trip to Paris demanded that she first take the train from Nice to Vichy. Once in Vichy, she would contact a group of clandestine truckers, who for a substantial sum—roughly the present-day equivalent of two thousand dollars—crossed the frontier at night. There was no sense attempting the crossing on foot, for even at the most densely forested parts of the frontier the Germans' guard dogs could be let loose. The contrabandists picked up their passengers in a small village near Vichy and settled them in the backs of their vehicles among sacks of produce. (Potatoes and flour were the most widely used.) The interiors of the vehicles were lined with mattresses in case German border guards shot at them. The contrabandists drove the most obscure country roads, and it is probable that they used those checkpoints at which French border guards were in their pay. Once they'd reached the Paris suburbs, they let their passengers out and picked them up again five days later at another assigned location.

My mother admits to having been very scared by the ordeal. But the trip to Paris proceeded smoothly. Once she had reached the Paris suburbs, she took the subway to the Place d'Iéna, a block away from our apartment; she suffered dreadful claustrophobia on subways and had barely ever taken one in her life, but all bus service had been suspended because of the fuel shortage, and the only cars in circulation were the Germans' Mercedes. My governess, who had stayed on in our apartment to safeguard it from being requisitioned by the Germans, greeted her with tears of joy. Mother could take only two suitcases back with her on the contrabandists' return trip, and she started carefully assembling our belongings: the little valuable jewelry she had; whatever papers of my father's were of any importance; whatever clothes of hers and mine she could fit into her luggage. Last but not least, she wrapped all of the Mayakovsky letters and poems she owned into a special folder and decided to place them in a bank vault for the duration of the war. Why did she not bring them to America? I've often been asked. For the same reasons that led her to beg her mother, from 1935 on, not to mention her romance with Mayakovsky: She sensed that a strong tide of anticommunism was about to sweep the West and that upon arriving in the United States she and I might be compromised if it became known that she had been the muse of the Soviet Union's most celebrated poet.

The following morning, after taking the Mayakovsky documents to a bank, Mother proceeded up avenue Kléber toward the Etoile. Her destination was the Monestiers' flat, which was right off the Champs-Elysées. As she headed down the avenue, she heard a man's voice calling out her name. She wheeled around and saw a German officer getting out of a Mercedes. It was her old friend "Spatz" von Dincklage. "What are you doing here?" She asked him icily. "I'm doing my work," he answered. "And what is the nature of your work *now*?" Mother snapped. "Same as it's been for decades," Spatz answered, "I'm in Army intelligence." "*Tu es un vrai salaud*," my mother burst out, "you're a real bastard. You posed as a down-and-out journalist, you won all our sympathy, you seduced my best friend, and now you tell me you were spying on us all this time!" "*A la guerre comme à la guerre,*" Spatz answered and proceeded to invite Mother to dinner.

"I was vaguely tempted to accept," she admitted later, "for the simple reason that he might have offered me important information." But her patriotism and her anger quickly prevailed. "He had posed as a victim of Hitler's racism, he had worn rags, he had ridden in a beat-up thirdhand car," she would fulminate when telling the story decades later. "He had seduced Hélène Dessoffy into an affair because she had a house near France's biggest naval base, Toulon, and we'd all fallen for the bastard's line!" Moreover, there was Mother's sense of protocol. "What would it have looked like if I'd gone out to dinner with him?" she would add. "The widow of a Resistance hero riding in a German Mercedes with a top-ranking Nazi officer, I couldn't allow my concierge to see that!"

Shortly after she saw him, Spatz went on to have a notorious affair with Coco Chanel—an affair from which Chanel's career, after the liberation of Paris, barely recovered. The entire episode gave my mother a tragic sense of the extent to which Nazi espionage had infiltrated French society. It also instilled in her a dread of the entire institution of espionage: Decades later, by extension, it led her to paranoid suspicions that most Soviet visitors in the United States were KGB agents.

That first day in Paris, Mother went to Alex's studio at Villa Montmorency and rolled up as many of his canvases as she could fit into her suitcase. She went on to have dinner at Simone and André Monestier's; they already knew that my father was missing in action but had not received any further details. After sharing the facts with her favorite relatives, she fell into Simone's arms and burst into tears: "It was my fault, it was all my fault," she sobbed, "I ruined his career in the diplomatic corps, after that, he became prone to foolhardy actions, he was bent on a course of self-destruction." When my aunt Simone told me that story, many decades later, she added: "I tried to console her by reassuring her that she'd played no role whatever in your father's death, but of course your mother was in some part right."

Simone wisely waited until the 1970s, the decade before her own death, to tell me this. It led me to the following, sorrowful considerations, which I could not possibly have handled in earlier years: To what degree had Tatiana and Alex been conscious of the fact that their legendary happiness was grounded in my father's death? Or, to be superstitious, to what degree had they even caused his death by wishing it to happen? Considering their emotions decades later, I was forced to realize that Alex, being an intensely jealous man, must have hated my father for having shared a life with Mother; that he must have detested him all the more because my father belonged to a caste and embodied a system of values that Alex could never have aspired to—that of the ancient chivalric aristocracy of France, fiercely proud and prejudiced but given to extraordinary feats of valor at times of crisis. I had to accept the fact that Alex must have felt a kind of dreadful jubilation upon hearing the news of my father's death and that I would have to deal with the guilt of having loved two men who loathed each other.

Perhaps more important, I had to confront the complex emotions that my mother must have experienced upon my father's death—a perplexing blend of sorrow and liberation, further complicated by the guilt that sense of liberation brought. In her last decades, many of Tatiana's friends, commenting on the moments of great melancholy that alternated with her habitually vibrant manner, would ask me what deep sorrows in her life might have caused those more somber moods. Only recently have I realized that my mother was one of those women whose fates had been shaped by men's deaths: in her case, Mayakovsky's and my father's.

During the days Mother undertook her hazardous trip to Paris, I was sent to a boarding school in Cannes. I couldn't quite understand, at the time, why I couldn't have peacefully stayed with Alex at Sainte Maxime. But again, Mother's sense of propriety—and perhaps also my late father's injunctions about not exposing me to "the Ste Maxime crowd"—prevailed. The phrase "one does not leave one's child with one's lover" must have run through her mind. The dormitory was freezing. The meals were composed almost exclusively of sweet potatoes and small field potatoes. I direly missed Alex's carefully gleaned black-market items. He phoned me every two days to keep up my spirits and his, for by this time there was no phone communication between the Vichy and Occupied Zones, and he later told me he had worried terribly about Mother. The only other highlight of my brief boarding-school experience was that it increased my knowledge of the facts of life. The rumor I'd heard the previous year in Gujan-Mestras, I was told by a fourteen-year-old in my dorm, was absolutely true. The man *did* stick his thing into the woman's little hole to produce babies, and—far worse—he often stuck it in there just to have fun, which struck us as particularly repellent.

A week or so after my mother had returned from Paris, she came with Alex to pick me up. Why has she waited an entire week? I asked myself, sensing for the first time, with some unease, that Alex and Mother might treasure those moments they spent without me. I'd seldom been happier than upon my release. The gloom of winter had settled on the coast, but at

Va-et-Vient all was lightness and cheer. All our visas are in order! We have tickets on a boat out of Lisbon! We're ready to leave!! The rumor had spread that it was far safer to cross the Spanish frontier by train than by car, for border police on trains were less prone to persecuting Jews than their colleagues on the *routes nationales.* So even though Alex had hoarded gas coupons to get us to Spain, we decided to take one train to the Spanish frontier and then another to Madrid, whence we would leave for Lisbon. It was on the train from Nice to the Spanish frontier that I witnessed, for the first time, a bitter argument between Alex and Mother.

Mother and I are sitting on one side of the compartment, reading, and Alex is on the banquette facing us. At a stop in the vicinity of Toulouse, a man with a long beard, dressed in a long black coat, with a small round hat on the back of his head, comes into our compartment and sits down next to Alex. Alex, looking uneasy, gets up and moves over to our side of the compartment. The man in black, who had smiled politely as he'd come in, suddenly looks solemn. My mother is giving Alex angry sideways glances and saying to him in Russian, *"Pozor! Kakoe hamstvo!"* ("Shame on you! What boorishness!") She smiles ingratiatingly at the stranger, who gratefully smiles back. He rides with us for only an hour or so and exits our compartment with a small bow and a last grateful smile for my mother. She looks out of the window until the stranger is out of earshot, and then she lets Alex have it. "I've always known you were anti-Semitic!" she half shouts at him, "and you suffer from the *worst* kind of anti-Semitism, *Jewish* anti-Semitism! How rude, how boorish can you be?" Alex looks apologetic, tries to butt into her tirade, *"Mais* Boubousiki.. . . . *Je m'excuse* Boubousiki," but she continues the invective. "A nice-looking rabbi sits down next to you, and what do you do? Insult him by moving away from him! Aren't you ashamed of yourself? There's nothing worse than Jewish anti-Semitism, especially at this time of history!" Alex, stumbling for words, could not manage to soften the tongue-lashing of the blond virago whose delicate social sensibility he had offended. Her refrain "Nothing worse than Jewish anti-Semitism" would last all the way to the Spanish frontier. *"Bon, finis,"* she eventually said. "But don't you ever act that boorishly again!"

My one winter coat had been abandoned in Paris the previous summer.

So throughout the trip, I had been wearing a fur coat belonging to Alex's mother, who had left for the United States in August and had asked us to bring her coat to New York. It was stolen on the way from Hendaye to Madrid, while we stepped off the train for a minute to stretch our limbs. And as soon as we got to Madrid, where Mother immediately pleaded a migraine, Alex and I went out to look for a winter garment for me. He was determined to find me a coat similar to the one his father had bought him in London in 1921 upon arriving from Russia, when he was my age. After hours of searching, he finally found the model he desired: It was a double-breasted camel's-hair reefer a few sizes too large, hanging fairly to mid-calf because, as he put it, "you're growing very fast, and we won't have much money on the other side." He topped it off with a perfectly matched camel's-hair hat. My mother's face radiated with delight when I came into our room in my new outfit.

We had decided not to engage in any holiday celebrations until we were on the boat, and we spent an uneventful Christmas Eve in Madrid. My most terrifying recollection of our exodus is that of boarding the train that would take us from Madrid to Lisbon. Rumors abounded that the Spanish government might at any moment expel all refugees from the country and force them to return to France, and at the Madrid train station panic prevailed. The teeming crowds—thousands of exiles from all parts of Europe—gave the space a biblical, end-of-the-world aura. Highly ambivalent about the legion of foreign refugees it was being forced to accommodate, the Spanish government had not adjusted train schedules to meet the fugitives' needs. We found hordes of exiles camping on the floor of the waiting rooms, their possessions stuffed into tied-up blankets or carpets as well as suitcases; they were expecting to take the same train to Lisbon as we. Alex had bought our tickets from the concierge at the Madrid Ritz, tipping heavily, of course, to secure the purchase. But such was the pandemonium, so dense the crowds, that tickets had become meaningless. Railroad officials were nowhere to be seen. Refugees not speaking a word of Spanish, waving tickets or other credentials in a futile pantomime, tried to persuade stony-faced, indifferent policemen to give them access to the platforms. Hundreds of small children had lost their parents in the crush and walked about the station weeping, an equal number of adults paced the platforms, crying out their children's names.

Moreover, no signs for the next train to Lisbon were in sight, and the police had no idea of the trains' schedules. "The hotel, let's return to the hotel," my mother began to moan as we fought our way through the dense crowd. "Let's turn back, I'm suffocating," she repeated, suffering, as usual, from the panic caused by claustrophobia. "We must get on that train," Alex replied firmly. "But the train doesn't seem to exist," Mother moaned. "They've probably canceled it!" "It exists, it exists," Alex said grimly. Suddenly, a voice announced on the loudspeaker, in Spanish: "All aboard! Madrid-Lisbon express on track twenty-four, leaving in seven minutes." We picked up our bags and ran to get in line amid the swarming crowd. But nothing so orderly was possible. Instead, we were caught in a shouting mass of humanity that was rushing toward the platforms, crying out lost relatives' names in a half dozen languages. "*Sauve qui peut,*" Alex muttered, and we followed him as he tried to shove his way through the crowd. Making little headway, he turned to me and whispered, "Pretend you're sick." He continued shoving, holding his suitcases over his shoulders, now shouting "*Enfant malade, enfant malade!*"

I played this suddenly assigned role to the hilt, limping like Quasimodo and coughing pitifully, the way I imagined Camille must have coughed in her death scene, deliberately stumbling several times over the hem of my long coat. The gambit worked. Enough persons were moved by my plight to make room for us, and we finally reached the platform, which was as densely seething with crowds as the waiting rooms. But my mother's panic grew more intense upon her first glimpse of our train. It was already packed beyond capacity by those who had arrived hours early to secure seats; some travelers, crammed twenty to a compartment, held their worldly possessions on the windows' rim or even sat on the edges of windows, their legs dangling out of the train; and hundreds of additional refugees were attempting to climb into the cars. "I'm not getting in there," Mother cried out to Alex, "I refuse." "You're getting in," Alex shouted firmly, "this may be the last train in months!" "No no no," my mother shouted back, beginning to weep. We were now standing a foot away from the train, and the locomotive had begun to make threatening hissing sounds. "*Boubous,* get in," Alex shouted again. "No no no no," my mother sobbed. He turned to me. "Frosinka, you get in first!" Suitcases in hand, I managed to climb the first two steps, wrangling my way past some Polish refugees by muttering some dimly remembered phrases in their language; once firmly established on the train, I held my hand out to my mother. "Maman, come with me!" I shouted as the train began to pull very slowly out of the station. Alex walked beside the train, pushing my sobbing mother from behind, and managed to lift her to the first step. I tugged her up the rest of way. Alex got onto the stairs himself, hauling the rest of the baggage. As he joined us, the engine gave a hoot and started to pick up speed, leaving hundreds of shouting, weeping refugees stranded on the platform. We had made it out of Madrid.

"Where do we go next? " I asked Alex.

"Right to the left, into the WC," he whispered back. It was an inspired decision. No one had yet opted for spending the night standing over the train's toilet. I tugged my trembling, panicked mother into the tiny, reeking space. And as Alex struggled through all the cars in a futile search for a more comfortable site, Mother and I remained there until the following morning, leaning against its walls, occasionally nodding off for a few seconds, forced to watch hundreds of passengers of both genders relieve themselves.

Thus it was that we finally reached Lisbon. By the last days of December, we had boarded our ship. It was a pleasure yacht called the *Carvalho Araujo*, which had never gone farther than the Azores and was making its maiden voyage to New York. My mother and I had been assigned a cabin on the lower deck; Alex was to share a cabin on the top deck with a noted French flutist, René Le Roy, whose charm and culture had immediately led Mother and Alex to befriend him. In a matter of hours, it was decided that the four of us would share all meals together. The tiny ship lurched terribly on the storm-tossed winter seas, and within two days some reshuffling of bunks had taken place. My mother and Le Roy were very prone to seasickness, whereas Alex and I remained perfect sailors in the roughest seas. So to accommodate my mother, it was decided that she would share the more comfortable upper-deck cabin with Le Roy, while Alex came down to share the lower cabin with me. I felt my mother was per-

Tatiana, Alex and Francine sailing to the United States in 1941.
Francine wears the camel's hair coat bought by Alex before the departure.

fectly safe with Le Roy—brought up in her world, I may have vaguely known the meaning of "homosexual" before I fully knew the meaning of "mistress" or "lover"—and the accommodation struck me as perfect. At night, when it was time to go to bed, Alex would put a pillow over his eyes and say, "You can get undressed, I'm not looking," which made me feel very grown-up. My new life with Alex and Mother seemed to consist of a series of equally unconventional arrangements that I found charming.

I remember our passage on the *Carvalho Araujo,* which took a whopping two weeks, in a blaze of gold and of music. Before dinner, René Le Roy often uplifted the storm-tossed passengers' morale by playing the flute parts of Bach's Brandenburg Concertos. His performances were held in the dining room, where vitrines were filled with delicate lace-patterned gold jewelry of Portuguese provenance, encrusted with fake diamonds, which transfixed me. My lust for them was fulfilled when my mother, who could not make up her mind which of three brooches in the vitrine she preferred, received all three of them from Alex as a New Year's present. I could then admire them, fondle them at will.

My bonds with Alex deepened yet further during our ocean crossing. Beyond her distaste for the ship's British cooking, my mother was too seasick to eat, and for one meal out of two she stayed in her cabin, drinking broth. Le Roy often started the meal with Alex and me, turned pale, and left to join Mother in their double-bunked room. Most days, Alex and I remained alone at our table, feasting on three large meals and feeling very superior. Throughout the icy January rains and terrible swells, when half of the passengers were absent from the dining room, we remained at our table, devouring all the bland delicacies that were meant to be good for Alex's ulcer diet: cream soups, chicken and mashed potatoes, custards and trifles. It was during those weeks spent lurching toward the United States that I learned my first words of English from Alex, which explains why my adopted language, for the next few years, was tainted with his British public-school accent. "Hoow duuu you duuu, chaaaaarmed to meet you," I repeated after him during our solitary, gorging dinners.

For decades to come, these highlights of our exodus to the United States formed a strong conspiratorial bond between Alex and me—the bond of intensely shared memory. "Do you remember that incredible train ride between Madrid and Lisbon?" we'd still ask each other thirty, forty years after our arrival in the promised land. "And how we went out to purchase that camel coat when *Mamasha's* mink coat was stolen. . . ." "And René Le Roy playing his flute in the dining room of the *Carvalho Araujo.* . . ."

PART TWO

The New World

"To live is such an art, to feel is such a career."
—HENRY JAMES, *The Tragic Muse*

Alexei Evgenevich Iacovleff, Francine's grandfather, in his
Cadets uniform, St. Petersburg, ca. 1900.

TWELVE

Rochester, New York

In a photograph I've had since early childhood, my maternal grand-father, Alexei Evgenevich Iacovleff, is shown in his mother's St. Peters-burg apartment at the age of nineteen, indolently reclining in an ornately tasseled damask chair. He is dressed in the uniform of the Imperial Cadets. A very long cigarette holder is poised in one hand, a white kid glove held limply in the other; a fashionable pince-nez perches on his nose; his boots, polished to bronze gleam, stretch nonchalantly over a Turk-ish carpet. The mirrored wall behind him reflects the quantity of rich stuffs—brocade, moire, ormolu, ebony, cut glass—that fill his mother's turn-of-the-century drawing room. The photograph well conjures up his life as a privileged young playboy of St. Petersburg society: the smell of rare Turkish tobacco, gambling rooms in early-morning hours, women, women, cards, and dice, the hedonism of a gentry beginning its fall into doom.

There seems to have been a restless, nomadic streak among the Iacovleff men. Although he was trained, after his cadet days, as an archi-tect and engineer, my grandfather's early life was marked with quite as much adventure and recklessness as that of his younger brother, Sasha. He married a beautiful, ambitious, coquettish woman, my grandmother, who liked nothing more than to surround herself with ardent admirers and play them off against one another. Assigned by the imperial government to design opera houses in different regions of Russia, he changed habitations every three or four years, a swift turnover in those days when a home was lived in by the same family for generations. The dashing Alexei Evgenevich was one of the first persons in his country to own a car and to pilot a glider plane of his own, a commodity that he seems to have handled in a somewhat slapdash manner. But my grandfather's love of risk was above all reflected in his passion for gambling. How often, whether working in St. Petersburg, in Vologda, in Penza, had he won the equivalent of a month's pay in seven minutes and, carried away by the greedy hope that he could double that sum, lost all that he'd just gained. How often, after losing several months' worth of salary, had he staked his last fifty-ruble note in an attempt to recoup the losses and wasted it all again. How often, staggering out of a casino after a rich night, had Alexei Evgenevich given half of his new banknotes away to whatever beggars he met between the casino and his lodgings and sunk the rest, the following week, into another eccentric venture—such as financing the first glider flight between Moscow and St. Petersburg. And how many times, finding himself in a new city with one ruble in his pocket, not knowing whether he'd have anything to eat that day, had he staked that last coin and made some two thousand rubles in the following hour, suddenly able to order champagne in the best restaurants and acquaint himself with some actresses.

Alexei Evgenevich's wife—my grandmother—remonstrated, threatened, deplored. These Iacovleffs! she fulminated, what a group of derelicts! The Aistovs never carried on like that, she might add, holding up as an example her own father, the admirable company director of the Marinsky Imperial Ballet, who'd worked at one institution, lived in one house, for his entire life and had never so much as touched a pair of dice. Succumbing to her pleas after some particularly ill-advised folly, Grandfather Iacovleff had occasionally imposed periods of abstinence on his gaming; but during those moments he seldom ceased hearing the treasured sounds of his addiction—the clink of scattered money on the baccarat, blackjack, roulette table, the croupier's siren voice crying out *"trente trois et un, rouge, impair, manque!"* Might one count the times this rake had resolved to give up his vice forever as soon as he won back what he'd just lost, yet reneged on his promise? Swung through the chaotic emotional cycles involved in games of chance—apprehension, elation, dread—the gambler's psyche does not crave respite from such frenzied sequences but strives for still more chaos, still more cyclones of the spirit. And even as Alexei Evgenevich became the head of a family, he could not seem to conquer his passion for that fatal seductress he later referred to, in his American years, as Lady Luck.

Much has been written about gambling, less about the particularly reckless habits of Russian gamblers. To label my grandfather's actions "decadent" or "irrational" would reveal a total ignorance of Russians' curious attitude toward money—an attitude that to some degree pervaded every member of my Russian family. For in the view of the Russian intelligentsia and nobility, amassing capital—that skill considered so virtuous in the "civilized" West—was a rather vulgar activity, which should be engaged in only by the merchant classes. As Dostoevsky (himself an addict of the gaming table) put it, better than anyone else, the Russian is reckless with his money because he has an all-too-Christian compulsion against the very principle of accumulating it. "Not only is the Russian incapable of amassing capital," he writes in his classic novella *The Gambler*, "but he dissipates it in a reckless and unseemly way, and looks at that art of dissipation as a worthy, even a noble trait. Hence his propensity for gambling." Musing on the recklessness of Russians' spending, he adds: "Is there a notion more repellent than to subordinate the eternal soul of a human being created in God's image to the accumulation of capital, as the Germans are so skillful at doing?" In sum: Any Russian being chastised about squandering his money too quickly might well answer "Blast the money! The quicker the better!"

According to the Iacovleff family's official line, the reason for my grandfather's sudden departure from Russia in 1915 is that he had patented a revolutionary new automobile tire, which necessitated a kind of rubber not found in Russia. That tale always struck me as inane. I suspect, rather, that he had run up huge debts, too often reneged on his promise to give up gambling, and solved his dilemma by abandoning his family and taking flight. All we know is that in 1915 he traveled directly east, via Siberia, to China, with the intention of migrating, eventually, to the United

States. Freed from all family censures, able once more to frolic at will with Lady Luck, he gave full rein to his addiction. For two or three years, the elegant vagabond lived in Shanghai, where a large community of Russian exiles had begun to gather—he had so radically cut all ties to his family that he did not even know his favorite sibling, Sasha, was in the Far East in precisely those same years. Being fluent in French and German, when he had lost at the casino he supported himself for weeks or months at a time by serving as a tutor to the children of more fortunate exiles or interpreting for visiting dignitaries. After a winning streak, he would buy an expensive horse and, accompanied by a guide, ramble through the Gobi Desert for a few months until his money ran out, enjoying "the beauties of nature"— always his favorite pastime when he was not at the gaming table.

Thus did Alexei Evgenevich Iacovleff, a very tall, slender man with an aquiline face of unusual beauty, squander his life until an October midnight in 1917. As he stood in front of a Shanghai casino after having once more gambled his last cent away, he heard news of the Russian Revolution and was filled with the rueful awareness that he might never be able to go home again. He leaned against the wall of the casino, lit up a cigarette, and continued standing there, the probable loss of Russia heavy in his heart. And right there on the steps of the casino . . . I'll tell the incident in his own words, as he shared it with me several decades later:

It was the first winter of the Revolution. I knew that if something extraordinary did not happen I'd take up that pistol they'd trained me to use so well in cadets' school, and . . . I needn't say. A Russian of my acquaintance came up to me—he was as desperate as I, we'd had a bit to drink, we stood around commiserating about our losses. Suddenly, an elegant carriage drives up to the casino. A woman leans her head out of the window—she's very beautiful, heavily veiled. "You look frozen, come into my carriage," she says in slightly accented French. We get in, she drives us to her flat, she gives us still more champagne and brandy, we spend a curious night with her. In the morning, as we're about to leave her flat, she asks us what we want most in the world. Our answer is that we want to go to the United States. She orders her coachman to drive us back to our respective lodgings, and before we leave her she hands us both an envelope.... They each contained the equivalent of several thousand dollars! We left for America a few weeks later.

So he arrived in San Francisco in 1918, a single man with still no interest whatever in life beyond gambling and the occasional exploration of "the beauties of nature." A large Russian community had also gathered in California, and Alexei Evgenevich continued his hapless habits of yore: In his unlucky weeks at the gaming table, he took various short-term jobs as tutor or translator or even as garage mechanic; in his luckier ones, he roved about California, savoring its Sierras, its northern lakes, its southern deserts. So it went for a few years, until 1922, when, after a particularly heavy loss at the baccarat table, he walked into a San Francisco department store in hopes of finding employment, for a change, as a salesman. It is there that fate was again most kind to him, introducing him to a winsome young Russian woman named Zinaida. A tiny, slender creature ten years his junior, she had come in to buy a blouse and, having detected a Russian accent in his speech, addressed him as he stood in line at the employment office. ("Women always did this," he said decades later with a weary sigh. "They found me handsome, they grabbed at me.") Zina had fled her homeland with her widowed mother in the very first weeks of the revolution; here she was in San Francisco, a registered nurse at the local hospital, with enough earnings saved to soon move into a house of her own. Alexei Evgenevich was taken with his compatriot's sweetness and charm. And "Zinochka," as she was later called in our family, was determined to get her man. She soon offered Alexei her hard-won savings on the condition that he give up gambling and return to his original vocation: engineering.

For some reason—perhaps the vagabond had finally wearied—he accepted. A week or so before they married, Zina suggested that to make life easier, he might change his name to some more pronounceable Yankee form. This, too, he readily agreed to do. Thus it was that Alexei Evgenevich Iacovleff became Alexis ("Al") Jackson and began to live the plain proletarian life invoked by his new name. With Zina's mother in tow, the Jacksons moved to

Rochester, New York, where, Zina had learned, there were openings at the local Kodak plant. Grandfather landed a minor engineering job on the production line where the cameras were assembled, the same job at which he was still working decades later—never once having asked for a promotion or even a raise—when the time came to retire. For most ambition, desire, and life force seemed to have been drained out of him when he stopped his long tryst with Lady Luck. She had been his one true love, and upon being forced to give her up he became a sedate, inert, perhaps a broken man.

A reformed gambler can be a tragic sight: He will not give evidence of the physical deterioration caused by alcohol or drugs; he will remain, to all appearances, intact. Yet look at his eyes: Whatever ardor, curiosity, strength of will they once expressed may well be gone. They will often have that listlessness, and above all that deep solitude, which characterized my grandfather's gaze. That very aura of derring-do that had made him so thrilling and seductive to women was suddenly drained out of him. From the time he married his Zinochka and settled down to a risk-free Yankee life, Al Jackson had no goal whatever but to make ends meet. Once his addiction was wrenched from him, he had no yearning for accomplishment, a better car, a larger income, no ambition for anything beyond the security of sitting evening after evening, year after year, by his coal grate, reading *Popular Mechanics* or listening for hours on end to his beloved radio.

For nine years after their father's departure from Russia, my mother and her sister, Ludmila, did not receive any news from him whatever, did not learn about any of these turns in his fate. It was only in 1924 that Babushka finally caught up with her vagrant American son. In a stern letter from Paris, where she had lived since 1922 after her emigration from Russia, she reminded him that he had abandoned a family back home: You left two daughters in Russia who love you, miss you; do something about them! As soon as my grandfather answered her missive, Babushka, very proud of her detective work, immediately reported to her granddaughters in Penza.

"My Dear and Most Beloved Grand-Daughters, your father has been found!" So begins Babushka's letter to Tatiana and Ludmilla, dated

August 1924. "A Russian priest helped us to find each other. Papa writes that he very often sent letters, both to you and to me, but never received an answer."

(In time-honored Russian tradition, the derelict male is being called to order by a powerful, dominating female who thrusts him out of his indolence; how many such women have I seen throughout Russia, remonstrating and bullying their sons and husbands as they chase them out of bars and gambling dens and the smug refuge of their sofas.)

"He's so happy that we've found each other at last," Babushka's letter continues. "He had no idea that Aunt Sandra and I were living abroad. He's had a very difficult time because he was only allowed to take 500 rubles out of Russia, and he's had to get along all this time without any steady material support. He now feels very concerned that you have a steady source of funds. Soon I'm sure that we can all manage to go and see him."

(Par for the course, the Russian gambler, upon being forced to confront his trespasses and his years of neglect, is swamped by a tide of self-reproach, offers eternal love and his last pennies to the poor children he's left behind, and asks them to share whatever humble home is his.)

"He has remarried and has a five-month-old son, Evgeny. He says that he thinks of you all the more often since his child was born because he so loved looking after you and indulging you when you were little girls. . . . [I]ndeed I particularly remember that when Lilechka cried only Papa was able to calm her. He very very much wanted to find you, and us."

Remorse on draft, like German beer.

This was the individual—Alexei Evgenevich Iacovleff, alias Al Jackson, former architect of the czar's opera houses, now a blue-collar worker at the Kodak Company—who was waiting for us on the morning of January 8, 1941, as our boat landed at the Brooklyn docks: the *Carvalho Araujo* was too small to dock at Manhattan's Hudson piers, and our hearts had sunk as we approached a grim area of small red houses instead of Manhattan's fabled skyscrapers.

Even at the age of ten, within a few seconds of being in my grandfather's presence I could sense some of the ways in which he differed radically from the other Iacovleffs I had known. The family's physical carapace was all there,

New York Herald Tribune, *January 9, 1941: Tatiana and Francine photographed as they arrive in the United States after "stormy voyage."*

reminding me poignantly of Aunt Sandra and Uncle Sasha—long, lean limbs, narrow, fine-boned face, almond-hued eyes, rich baritone voice speaking exquisite prerevolutionary Russian. But he was far taller and more gaunt than any Iacovleffs I'd known, looking curiously mournful in his six-feet-four frame. And hovering over his bushy, graying mustache, his aquiline nose, were eyes whose gaze had nothing of Sasha's swift slyness, or Mother's intensity, or Aunt Sandra's and Babushka's soulfulness. They were filled, instead, with a melancholy apathy, with the emptiness of resignation. But before I could give it any more thought, the reunion was occurring.

A half century later, I'm still obsessed by the curious fatefulness of this meeting: my mother, my grandfather, embracing again after a separation of twenty-six years.

I've often tried to imagine the emotions each of them experienced that morning. There was a curious parallelism of ages: the wan exile waiting for the thirty-five-year-old daughter he had last seen when she was nine years old, about the same age as the child, so strikingly resembling her, whose hand she was now clutching. And the young blond widow looking down at the crowd below to find the sixty-year-old father whom she had last seen as a dashing thirty-four-year-old gambler. The striking Iacovleff physique, of course, speeded the recognition: They found each other within a few seconds of our reaching the bottom of the gangplank. "*Papasha!*" my mother exclaimed. "*Detka!* [little girl!]," the tall mustached stranger sobbed out as they fell into each other's arms. "*Zdravstvuite, Dedushka* [Hello, Grandfather]," I said in turn, out of docile mimicry, when he turned to embrace me.

Standing at the side of Alexis Jackson was another member of our new American family, Simon Liberman, Alex's father. I had never met him before, and upon our first embrace I had a wave of sympathy for him far keener than any I felt for my grandfather. Simon's compact, rotund solidity, the sheer cunning and determination he emanated, were both awesome and very reassuring. His swift, rather Oriental eyes darted swiftly over us and sized up our situation, and he immediately took action. "Porters!" he called out, slipping a few dollars to a man standing on the dock who instantly summoned a colleague and took charge of all our bags. With a swift, authoritative step he walked over to a customs official, narrated some dramatic detail of our arrival, made flattering comments about the Customs Service, and within twenty minutes we were on the way, long before any other passengers. As we got into his chauffeured limousine, tiny, powerful Simon Isaevich now smiled warmly at us, his owlish, spectacled face radiant over his big fur-collared coat. Alex's mother was home with a migraine, he said—Alex had predicted that this would be her way of signaling her continuing disapproval of my mother. Sitting next to Simon was my grandfather, his chin still quavering a bit with emotion, his mild, perplexed eyes locked into a perpetual expression of surprise—he may not have been exposed in decades to the kinds of luxuries Simon enjoyed doling out. The car swerved across the Brooklyn Bridge and the first true symbols of the promised land—Manhattan's skyscrapers—finally came into view. Simon beamed with delight as we three refugees exclaimed and admired.

Once in Manhattan, we went straightaway to Simon's duplex at 4 East Sixty-fourth Street, a lush habitation where, I instantly decided, I would spend as much time as possible. It was decorated in darkly warm, luxurious textures: brown velvet couches, cashmere throws, zebra and leopard skin rugs, several of Uncle Sasha's portraits of Henriette. It was also replete with the newest American gadgets, and I was immediately hypnotized by the workings of a wireless radio, the tiniest I'd ever seen, which became my talisman for the day. As I played with it—the adults were huddled in a corner, talking in hushed tones—Henriette came down, making a dramatic descent of the stairs; and after an effusive, tear-laced embrace of her son and a glacial greeting to my mother and me, she asked about her fur coat. "These idiots lost my fur coat!" she wailed in several languages upon hearing that it had been stolen on our way to Madrid, *"Ces crétins ont perdu ma fourrure!"* She thereupon climbed back upstairs with swift, angry steps, not to reappear.

It was time for lunch, which was served by a black housekeeper in a bright pink apron. My grandfather sat silently through the meal, eating faster than anyone else, continuing to cast astonished glances at all that surrounded him. I concentrated on Simon. He sat across from me, his short neck almost buried in his sturdy shoulders, looking at me through his thick glasses with a smile of warm approbation, which was akin to the purr of a solid, contented cat. After lunch, it was time to go on to what Mother and Alex kept referring to as "the hotel." Simon stayed home to rest, having put us into a cab with our sparse luggage. My grandfather in tow, we drove to the Windsor Hotel on West Fifty-eighth Street, the manager of which was a friend of Simon's; after a brief session at the registration desk, we went upstairs to Alex and Mother's rooms, which were on the same floor, discreetly located down the corridor from each other.

My memories of the next few hours are far hazier than those of the earlier part of the day—they are muffled, most probably, by the shock of the news I received. For shortly after arriving at the Windsor Hotel I learned that I was not destined to stay on at the hotel with my mother and Alex. I was informed, rather, that I was to leave that very evening with my grandfather for Rochester, New York, where I would remain until further notice. I must have been totally stunned by this news. It was certainly the most painful moment I'd known in life thus far. It is possible that I wept grievously upon leaving my beloved new guardians; on the other hand, I was already so skilled at the art of concealment that I may well have repressed all tears. However the three of us parted, some eight hours after arriving in the United States I found myself in the third-class carriage of a night train bound for Rochester, New York, being taken by a total stranger, my grandfather, to a city I'd never heard of until that very afternoon, clutching, as my only reassurance, the little suitcase I'd brought from France. Looking at it in retrospect, from Mother and Alex's point of view it all seems perfectly lucid. Seeing the material hardships of their own childhoods, their principal priority was to see me adequately lodged and fed—to consider my psychic needs might still have seemed like an extravagance. Moreover, once all uncertainties and persecutions lay behind them, the lovers were finally free to tend exclusively to their own happiness. Now that we were all safe, I was again being looked on as a lost parcel of sorts, as I had been the previous summer of the debacle of France—SOS, burdensome child here, needs to be forwarded somewhere, who'll take care of her? Ah, how marvelous! *Papasha* will take her away!

It was a stone-hard, uncomfortable, vinyl-lined train seat I sat on all the way to Rochester, of a discomfort and ugliness I'd never before experienced. Thinking back with longing to the plush, velvety textures of French trains, my body aching terribly after a few hours, I began to contemplate my options: This whole deal might not be as utterly catastrophic as it seemed. Out there in Rochester, there might be people to be charmed—Dedushka's wife, his son—there might be a job to be done.

Sliding about on the disgusting vinyl seat, I tried to size up the mustached stranger sitting across from me. He would sleep for a half hour or so at a time, his head slumped on one of his shoulders, his body rocking with the lurching of the car, and then wake with a jolt and set his astonished eyes on me. For that was my grandfather's most characteristic expression, an air of startlement, the eyes saying, "What, there's a world out there? And I belong to it? And you've got something to do with me?" He would give me a timid, surprised smile, pat my knee with a gruffly whispered *"Detka,"* and go back to sleep. So my night was spent: staring at the gently snoring stranger in the opposite seat, fuming, pondering the disgrace of my exile. We arrived in Rochester a half hour or so after first light. I sat glumly through the cab ride from the station, wondering whether his home would be as dismal as the train ride. The cab drove slowly down a treeless street in the Rochester suburbs lined with several hundred drably identical habitations and stopped at one particularly dreary lodging. *"My doma,"* my grandfather said as he paid the driver and lifted my suitcase out of the cab, "we're home."

I slouched behind him in my long camel's-hair coat, cursing the day I was born. Hadn't I been a model child? Had I offended Mother and Alex in some way I was not aware of? The very ground—whatever of it peeked out under the dirty strips of snow—was ugly in this place, it had neither the snazziness of a city nor the beauty of the country, there wasn't a bush around, not to speak of trees. . . . I was close to tears as I slumped behind my grandfather, up the three steps of his grim house. But then the front door burst open, and my spirits suddenly lifted. A tiny slender brunette with brilliant blue eyes, wearing a bright red sweater—she was only three or four inches taller than I—ran out and enfolded me in her arms. "Frosinka," she cried out in Russian. "What a treasure! At last you've come to us! I who always wanted a daughter!" This was Zina, my grandfather's second wife, whose half-weeping, half-laughing state clearly displayed great joy. Behind her stood her mother, Ekaterina Ivanovna, a stout woman in her sixties, still dressed in the flowered kerchief and thick woolen stockings traditional to Russian peasantry, who also beamed at me radiantly.

Reassured that things might be endurable for a while, I followed Zina into her bleak little house, of which I was immediately given a tour. Going up the narrow, uncarpeted stairs, you reached a landing that accessed the house's only bathroom and three small bedrooms, one of which was occupied by Zina's mother, the second by Grandfather and Zina, the third by their sixteen-year-old son Eugene or "Jika." Downstairs were a kitchen; a tiny dining area; a living room, the principal furnishings of which were two easy chairs set on either side of a coal grate, and a sofa on which Zina had placed pillows, sheets, and blankets. "Yours," she said radiantly, "your own bed." "Not even a room of my own," I moaned to myself. But her sweetness again allayed that dismay. A big snowstorm was predicted for the following day. And that very afternoon Zina, who did not drive, gleefully persuaded my grandfather to go out shopping and buy me a snowsuit—it was navy blue with red piping, and I found it so novel and delightful that I insisted on keeping it on, day and night, for the next few days.

For the following many weeks, I became Zinochka's and Katia Ivanovna's shadow, following them on their daily routine: doing the breakfast dishes, making the beds, dusting the house, laundering, ironing. The two women were readily given to tears, and their lamentations were particularly abundant on the heaviest workday of the week, Monday, wash day. It was then that every feature of bygone life in Russia—its dachas and green pastures, the glory of its nature, its music and its cuisine—tended to be most longingly recalled, most tearfully compared to the drab tedium of their Rochester life. "Servants bringing us tea at every hour, such emerald lawns, such orchards!" Zina would sob as she ironed Grandfather's shirts, pointing to the narrow backyard, identical to some three hundred adjoining ones, where the muddy ground lay like mangled flesh under the dirty bandage of the melting snow. A rusty car motor, Eugene's abandoned summer project, lay decaying on the ground. The laundry lines of every family in the neighborhood were going up that afternoon, flapping desolately in the icy wind. My companions would go on to deplore the bleak monotony Alexis Jackson imposed on his family, his apathy and indifference, his failure even to ask for a promotion or a raise in all the years he had been working for Kodak. I fully sympathized with them, for I'd realized after a few days that the Jacksons never traveled or entertained or dropped in on anyone; that they seldom read anything beyond the local paper and *Popular Mechanics;* that after dinner Grandfather just listened to his radio and chomped on his toothpick, Zina and her mother sighed and mended garments, and Eugene loped upstairs to do his science experiments. So I joined readily in their tears, concealing as ever my worries about my father but pretending, instead, to mourn all the splendors I, too, had left behind on another continent: the elegance of our Paris flat, the radiance of Alex's villa, the beauty and excitement of the Mediterranean.

In the afternoon, when most of the day's chores were done, I enjoyed my only respite from the monotony of the Jacksons' life: I turned on the

Rochester, 1941, clockwise from lower right: Tatiana's half-brother, Jika; Tatiana; Grandfather; unknown woman; Francine; Tatiana's stepmother, Zina; Zina's mother, 1941.

radio and took my daily English lesson by listening to the soaps. For improved diction and enlarged vocabulary, I rehearsed the parting lines from a large variety of shows: *Our Gal Sunday, Life Can Be Beautiful, Woman in White, When a Girl Marries, Young Doctor Malone.* "What will Nancy do? Will she tell Dr. Malone about her suspicions?" At 3:30 or so, the peaceful concentration of my task was broken by Jika's return from school. A loutish youth with a savage laugh who excelled at pulling radios apart and putting them together again, he made a point of totally ignoring me, vexed that the women's attention was now so centered on me. Very occasionally—when he was coming down with a cold or a bad snowstorm was predicted for the afternoon—Grandfather came home earlier than usual and found the women weeping over their domestic tasks. He stood at the threshold of the kitchen, majestic, disdainful, and thundered at us with his most violent Russian word: *"Erunda!"* he shouted. "Nonsense! Nonsense, this women's tears!" He walked away, his head bent, his frame incongruously fine-boned and aristocratic under the loose folds of his faded blue work clothes. We might continue to whimper as we hovered over the day's wash. He would walk back to the doorsill, more threatening this time. *"Erunda!* Siberia for this women's folly! My slippers! When is dinner?"

For when it was a normal day and he came back from the factory at 5:30, Alexis Jackson's habit was to eat directly upon coming home—he wanted his dinner "on the table" within a few minutes of arriving. *"Obed gotov?"* "Is dinner ready?" he would query loudly upon walking into the house. As Zina scurried anxiously about the kitchen, he slumped into the armchair, exclusively reserved for him, which stood by the coal grate; he tossed off his shoes, thrust his feet into the slippers that Zina had prepared for him, and unfolded his copy of the Rochester *Democrat and Chronicle.* By this time Jika had galloped down the stairs and slumped into the chair opposite his father's, looking at him with an air of glum expectation. *"Zdravstvuy, maly,"* "Hello, young one," Grandfather greeted his son curtly. When all was ready for supper, Zina would meekly call us in for the meal, which usually began—this was a particularly bizarre detail to a foreigner's eyes—with a goblet of Del Monte canned fruit. It proceeded to some potatoes and stew swimming in a fecal gravy—roast was reserved for Sundays—and often ended with bowls of trembling multiflavored Jell-Os, which Zina had lovingly cut up into small square cubes for a decorative effect. Grandfather was one of those very thin men who can eat vast quantities without ever putting on any weight, and he gulped his food down with noisy proletarian slurpings, greedily and hungrily, as if he had to catch a train. Whatever conversation there was at the Jacksons' meals was held in Russian, in part because Zina's mother had never learned a word of English, in part because Grandfather, to his credit, thought a mastery of Russian might be beneficial to his son—it was one of the few parcels of his Russian past he had not discarded or forgotten. But throughout most meals, silence hung over the table like an ax, occasionally relieved by an exchange of information about the weather forecast or by father and son comparing the relative merits of various brands of radio batteries.

I perused the members of my current family as they put away their dinner, attempting to decode the peculiar brand of joylessness that suffused this morose fellow—my grandfather—whom family legend had presented as an irresistibly seductive playboy. I never once saw him laugh, and his smile, if such there was, radiated little else than a wan, jaded indifference. Yet his melancholy, I came to understand in the following months, did not reveal any sense of failure—since he had stopped gambling, he had never desired anything enough to experience failure. His was a sadness, rather, which had to do with the tragedy of living in a desire-free world. Most baffling of all, in my eyes, was his total lack of that longing for distinction and achievement that had suffused that entire side of my family: Sasha, my mother, even Sandra and Babushka. All such aspirations, to him, seemed to be as much of an *erunda*—trifling, meaningless nonsense—as religion or women's tears; and it was for this reason that even at a tender age I saw him as something of a traitor to our family.

Yet after dinner, which due to the speed of his eating was over shortly after 6:00, Dedushka did regain a bit of sparkle. He loped to his chair, started chomping on his toothpick, and gave himself wholeheartedly to the only occupation that still brought a gleam of life to his vacant eyes: listening to the radio. "This is H. V. Kaltenborn!" a voice boomed out of the box as he fiddled gently with the dials of his favorite machine. "President Roosevelt orders twenty-four-hour shifts on war production. . . . King Carol of Rumania and Magda Lupescu are said to be in Chile. . . . thousands of islanders flee Crete." The content of the messages emitted by the wooden box meant little to him: In his eyes, contemporary events were yet another *erunda*. It was the sheer marvel and intricate working of the machine that mattered, its triumph over time and space. Tinkering with the dials, figuring out how clear the reception could become with the proper tuning, how many stations were available on any one night, he clucked his tongue admiringly, saying, "Fantah-stic, fantah-stic what the radio can do." He listened to it religiously until our nine o'clock bedtime, surrounded by his subdued family—Jika tinkering with some science project, Zina and her mother repairing some torn sheet or worn garment, I eagerly continuing, through Grandfather's radio programs, the English studies I'd started that afternoon with the soaps. Having delighted to *Orphans of Divorce,* and *The Road of Life,* before going upstairs to bed, he inevitably put an end to the evening with a curt statement concerning the fact that it was only two more days— or three or four—to *Major Bowes' Amateur Hour,* which was the high point of his week, and which brought out whatever zest was still left in him.

Major Bowes' Amateur Hour, which went on the radio every Saturday at eight o'clock, consisted of amateur performers whose opportunities to present their talents to the public were determined by the revolutions of an enormous wheel of fortune set in a New York radio station. The amateurs, hundreds of them—accompanied by trained dogs or ventriloquist para-keets, equipped with xylophones or electric guitars—sat in an audience hall holding numbered lottery tickets. The rotations of the wheel, which shuf-fled duplicates of their tickets at great speed, dictated the selection of con-testants and their chances to make their marks upon the world. My grandfather paced the living room for a good half an hour before the pro-gram, in expectation. Then he sat down in his chair a few minutes before the show in order to be able to shout in unison with the announcer, at eight o'clock sharp, the leitmotif of the program: "Lady Luck, there she goes! Where she stops nobody knows!" He shouted it hoarsely, with a desperate, flailing motion of his arms, as if he were briefly greeting an old flame who had been his life's passion, and the shout always startled me greatly, for it was the only time of the week when he raised his voice above its habitually hol-low timbre, when his stooped frame showed any passion or animation.

The show began. During the following hour, chomping on his tooth-pick, his eyes half closed with pleasure, Grandfather listened reverently to triplets from Nebraska singing from *La Bohème,* to drum majorettes per-forming "Yankee Doodle" with their toes. He sighed with contentment af-ter each number, and as the wheel of fortune spun around to choose the next contestant, he loudly repeated those expressions that seemed to have been his favorites in the English language: "Put eet there, Lady Luck! Where she stops nobody knows!" Major Bowes's wheel of fortune, I realized during my stay in Rochester, was the closest link the old gambler still had to his beloved, abandoned vice.

On very rare occasions, and only on an evening when Major Bowes was not on the air, my grandfather might offer me some soliloquy that had to do with his Russian past. Such discourses were often interspersed with phrases spoken in the antiquated French he'd learned in the 1880s at the knee of his governesses, a French as quaint and faded as a lovely glove kept for years in a dusty drawer. One of these musings—it occurred on an evening when he'd caught me looking at the photograph of him as a cadet in St. Petersburg—went somewhat as follows:

> Stare on, *chère petite*, stare on! You must wonder whether that is really me, the elegant fop, the *fripouille* you see in this picture. . . . And don't you and your mother wish I still looked like that, don't you wish you'd found some elegant lord prancing for you at the pier when you landed in America last month. . . . Your mother must think my life is very boring. She's as ambitious as she's beautiful—I saw that from the moment she got off that ship a few weeks ago, *mon Dieu comme elle me rappelle sa propre mère*. . . . I don't know what she thinks she'll get out of America: Success, fame, money, where does it all lead to?? All a big bother, a big bore, all *erunda!* For me—equality, none of your European nonsense, none of your titles, your *belles manières*, your heroism, your wars. . . . This is what I like here—democracy! Relax! Put it there, Major Bowes, everyone an equal chance!

He picked at his teeth again and spat into the coal grate. And for the rest of my life that double image of my grandfather—the bored young Adonis in the photograph, the inert egalitarian aging before me—led me to look on indolence as the most cardinal of sins.

In the following years, Mother and Alex shipped me out to sleep on a few other living-room couches, but of all of these makeshift beds the Jacksons' was by far the worst. While I was in Rochester, Mother and Alex

Tatiana, Alex and Francine in 1941, a few months after they arrived in the United States.

phoned me twice each week from New York. But their most loving words did not soothe the terror of my nights, which mark the beginning of the insomnia that has plagued me much of my life. As soon as I put my head on the pillow, a flood of tears overcame me. Why, why had they sent me away? I'd be like a shadow in the house when I returned to them, I'd eat next to nothing, make not a breath of noise if only they took me back. . . . Moreover, the cloak of silence with which I muffled all issues concerning my father—my anxiety about his condition and his where-abouts—weighed increasingly on me day by day. There was still no one I could trust with my secret. Oh, if he could only give me a sign, a sign of life. I had promised him, and myself, to be patient, but how long could his secret mission last? Couldn't there be any respite to it, couldn't he take two days' leave in Malta, say, during which he could go to a post office and mail me a letter? He did not know our precise address in the States, but he could reach us through the Dessoffys—they had not budged from their house in the Vichy Zone, Mother had communicated with them since she'd reached New York, Father could get in touch with me at any time through them . . . in short, the possibility of my father's survival, over the months, was growing increasingly tenuous and more improbable and was demanding an increasingly arduous act of faith.

Finally, finally, in the middle of March I was called back to New York. I traveled labeled and tagged, like a package, with the help of the Travelers Aid Society, which specialized in shipping parentless children from one part of the country to another. My mother and Alex stood at the exit of the train at Grand Central Terminal, frantically waving a huge stuffed panda bear in the way of a greeting. I thought I would be joining Mother and Alex at their hotel, but once more that was not to be. Sometime in the late spring they would move into new apartments on Central Park South, they explained, but for the time being all was still "too disorganized" for me to live with them; they were too busy settling into their first American jobs. They had arranged for me to stay in Greenwich Village with their friends Justin and Patricia Greene, who had redecorated an entire room for me to live in and who had also arranged for me to go to a wonderful New York City school. Pat Greene would help me to settle at school, Mother said—she could help me with my homework, do all kinds of things for me that she, Mother, was incapable of doing.

Although initially disconcerted that I could not be with Mother and Alex, I was intrigued by the notion of finally going to school again and overjoyed by the prospect of a room of my own. Moreover, Justin Greene, a tall, sandy-haired medical doctor and psychiatrist who had been a frequent caller of Mother's before the war, when he had interned in a Paris hospital, was a familiar and beloved figure. So after a night spent on a folding bed in Mother's hotel room, it was with a certain anticipation that I accompanied the Greenes downtown to my new home. This time, my mother's choice could not have been wiser. My memory of the months spent with the Greenes are among the most radiant of my youth. Pat Greene was a soft-spoken twenty-six-year-old girl from Salt Lake City with a heart of gold and a sly sense of humor; Justin, also a merry, endlessly cheerful person, spoke fluent French and was there to help out whenever my barely nascent English or Pat's rusty high-school French failed us. The Greenes had married the year before and had recently moved into a beautiful little brownstone at 23 West Eleventh Street. And their kindness to me was so great, the aura of happiness and serenity they created so memorable, that a decade later, upon finishing college and finally being able to move into a flat of my own, I was determined to find a lodging on that very same block. Although by that time they had moved uptown and were raising a large family of their own, I spent a blissful two years in a dank one-room cellar flat a few doors down from where I'd lived with the Greenes, reliving my happiness with them every time I passed their former house.

My room at the Greenes' was on the second floor of their brownstone and looked out over a quiet garden. They had painted it a ravishing hue of sky blue and refinished an iron bedstead in the same color. The fits of nightly tears that had seized me in Rochester greatly abated. And I soon knew that if I decided to break my silence and talk about my father, the Greenes would be the only persons I could turn to. My anxiety may also have been quelled by the fact that I was now kept busy at an admirable school. Pat Greene had arranged a scholarship for me at the Spence School on East Ninety-first Street, of which she was a graduate. Every morning, my alarm clock would ring at 7:30, and by ten of eight I would be in the kitchen, putting away whatever breakfast bleary-eyed Pat, still in her nightdress, had thrown together for me—both Greenes were night owls, and had trouble keeping to any punctual early-morning schedule. Justin himself was barely dressed by 8:00 A.M., when it was time to jump into his car and race uptown, trying desperately to make it to Spence by 8:20, when assembly began. Despite the anxiety caused by these hectic mornings, the Greenes and I derived great conspiratorial merriness from our shared mayhem, and I rose every day with the most immense joy, eager to be surrounded with the extraordinary warmth and hospitality that my classmates and teachers had lavished on me from the second I had walked into the school, plunked into the second half of fifth grade.

In March 1941, I was the first and only refugee to have been admitted to Spence, and I still spoke little English beyond the phrases I'd memorized in Rochester from listening to soap operas—"What will Nancy do? Will she tell Dr. Malone?" But lack of English was no great obstacle, for among New York's upper classes in 1941 Francophilia reigned triumphant. Over half of the girls in my class—there were only twelve of us in the fifth grade—had French governesses. They enjoyed showing off their knowledge of my language, competed with one another as to whose pronunciation I judged best, and introduced me proudly to their mothers, many of whom were also fluent in French. I was cherished and fought over and became a mascot of sorts—when I went to classmates' homes after school, their mothers would put little French flags on cupcakes and cookies to let me know where their hearts lay. Moreover, having been tutored at home all of my life, I found great fascination in learning about my classmates' often colorful family lives. There was Cornelia, whose uncle, the actor Monty Woolley, upon staging a two-ring wedding ceremony with his boyfriend, was said to have trained his poodle to walk on his hind legs to serve as ring bearer. There was Audrey, daughter of a Greek-American businessman, a forthright, sunny girl with a dazzling smile who gave me the nickname I was to retain throughout my seven years at Spence, "Nikki"—she had initially used a Greek version of my name, "Francinikki," as a token of her affection. There was Julia, a jovial sort with a mop of straight blond hair and a wanton, somewhat hysterical laugh who came from a terribly staid WASP family and particularly astonished me by telling me that she had had sex with her older brother. "It's terrific," she'd comment about the episodes with one of her wild laughs, which were accompanied by a slightly vulgar motion of her palm across her face, as if she were wiping spittle from her mouth. The tale of incest might not have been imagined: Beginning with late adolescence, Julia had her share of nervous breakdowns.

Pat Greene, who was studying at the Art Students League, had hired a huge, slow-moving Alsatian woman, a Madame Gaspamont, to pick me up at school every day. And I must have been enjoying the athletic activities imposed on me at Spence, for I found a great source of fun in running away from Madame as fast as I could, hiding behind buildings and then pouncing on the astonished, anxious woman with a resounding yowl. Pat, who remembers me as "a gay, very stalwart child who never complained and hid her inner feelings to a worrisome degree," would get home shortly after I did and help me with my brief fifth-grade homework. In the later afternoon, we played dominoes or cards or a simplistic game Pat had invented for me, which I particularly cherished: Sitting at the living-room window that looked out on West Eleventh Street, we piled up a heap of matches on a tray. I got a match for every man we saw walk by, Pat got a match for each of the women who passed by—and guess who won?

And then there were the evenings, which were particularly glamorous when the Greenes entertained, which was with some frequency. It was the first time, I believe, that I was asked to attend adult dinner parties and sit at table. There was soft candlelight in the pale-green dining room over-looking the back garden, Pat's fine family silver and china, delicious food, and gracious, animated talk. And the Greenes' calm, fruitful lives, on the street I believed to be the finest in New York, offered me a model, for many years to come, of life-as-it-should-be.

As for Mother and Alex, how were they faring in our first months of exile? They came to dinner every few weeks at the Greenes' or took me out to tea, and during these reunions my mother's gaze rested lovingly, worriedly on me—she seems to have sensed how difficult it would be for her to have me at home. And after all, without me she and Alex were prospering.

THIRTEEN

The Authentic Journal of Society, Fashion, and the Ceremonial Side of Life

It had been far easier for Mother than for Alex to land a job in the United States. Contacts, how their lives thrived on contacts! Three days after arriving in New York, they met a prominent society woman named Helen Hoguet, the wife of a New York doctor; she worked on commission for Henri Bendel, persuading her acquaintances to buy their clothes there. An ardent Francophile, Helen had immediately taken up Tatiana's cause and arranged for her to design hats at Bendel for seventy-five dollars a week. As attested by Cole Porter's "You're the top . . . you're a Bendel bonnet," that store seemed to have been noted for its headgear. Tatiana's contract with Bendel stipulated that her *nom de chapeau* would be "Countess du Plessix"— in the tide of pro-European sentiment that swept New York during World War II, celebrities of the beauty and fashion world frequently took on exotic titles to sell their wares. Think of "Countess" Mara shirts and ties, "Countess" Alexandra de Markoff's and "Princess" Helena Rubinstein's cosmetics. So Mother was grateful to be making three hundred dollars a month, though even with the addition of the two hundred Simon Liberman was giving Alex each month, the salary barely sufficed for the young couple's needs.

The reestablishment of Alex's career in magazine publishing was to be considerably more arduous. He knew that he had to get a job to bring Tatiana the comfort and luxury essential to her happiness. However, he also had to make peace with his parents and accustom them to the idea that he was not going to be a full-time artist. Simon and Henriette had imagined that upon moving to New York their son would continue to be an *artiste peintre*, the vocation they had been urging him to follow since his schooldays and which he had pursued since the mid-1930s, when he'd left his job at *Vu*. If it seems strange that the Libermans were so eager for their only son to devote himself to art, a calling that high-bourgeois parents in other cultures tend to disapprove of, it should be remembered that a cult of the artistic vocation is integral to the Russian tradition, particularly in the intelligentsia. Henriette, as we've seen, had encouraged her beloved son to be a painter since he'd been a small child. Over the years, she'd totally persuaded Simon that it was their son's true calling, and the stipend Simon started giving Alex upon his arrival in New York was clearly intended to encourage him in his painting career. Alex, however, found this sum very modest in the light of all the luxuries Liberman *père* lavished on himself and his wife: the Fifth Avenue penthouse, Henriette's furs and jewelry. Notwithstanding the fact that his father had recently lost quite a bit of money through unwise investment, might the paltriness of his two-hundred-dollar allowance have also been part of his parents' strategy to estrange him from Tatiana? He soon realized that at some time in the near future he had to cease depending on them.

So in order to pacify his parents, for the first weeks of his stay in New York Alex hid his true intentions. He bought himself an easel and a batch of oil paints and set them up in his tiny studio flat on Central Park South, which had a beautiful view of the park. And he shrewdly invited his father to pose for his portrait, hoping to reassure Simon about the fervor of his calling as an artist. But as he painted his father—I lived for years with this life-size, slickly realistic portrait—all kinds of emotions and schemes were going on in Alex's mind: Of course he couldn't meet his needs through painting; of course Tatiana's penchants for comfort and luxury, as well as his own, which were quite as great as hers, were the first priorities he had to attend to.

So on the sly, Alex started looking for his first American job. Irene Lidova had given him a letter of introduction to Alexei Brodovich, the revered art director of *Harper's Bazaar*. A former cavalry officer in the White Russian Army, Brodovich's revolutionary views of design had been inspired by the Russian Constructivist avant-garde artists who immigrated to Paris after 1918. He was also an inspired teacher. He had become famous for hiring Europe's and America's most gifted photographers and giving them free rein in *Harper's Bazaar*, the typography and layouts of which were renowned for their modernism and elegance. Brodovich asked Alex to draft some sample pages for women's shoe designs. Alex complied, bringing in some layouts—juxtapositions of shoes and women's faces that he was the first to describe, in later years, as perfectly awful. Understandably, Brodovich rejected Alex's work, and the men never communicated again, nodding coolly to each other at a distance the few times they met. (Brodovich was a frugal, reclusive scholar, totally dedicated to his art and to his teaching career, who seldom ventured into the café society milieus through which Alex built his reputation.)

But then, a few weeks after his arrival, Alex heard that his old friend and boss from *Vu* magazine days, Lucien Vogel, had also immigrated to New York in recent months. He was working as an adviser to Condé Nast, the powerful founder and director of Condé Nast Publications. Vogel had been a friend and collaborator of Nast's in prewar days. (Nast had bought Vogel's fashion magazine, *Jardin des modes*, and had added it to his own roster of publications, *House and Garden*, *Glamour*, and *Vogue*, the last of which already had several foreign-language editions.) Alex knew that Vogel might provide a good introduction to the country's preeminent publisher of luxury magazines. Alex and Vogel had lunch together, and on the twenty-eighth of January Vogel wrote Nast the following letter, which gives interesting insights on how Mother and Alex wished their relationship to be perceived in New York society. (The many misspellings are attributable to Vogel's notorious absentmindedness.)

Dear Condé:

  Alexandre Liebermann [sic] *was one of the best of my former collaborators, and was with me for many years as art director and lay-out man for VU.*

He has just arrived in New York, and I think I should let you know about him, since he is a young artist who has a great deal of talent, sound technical knowledge and excellent taste.

Alexandre Libermann was educated in the most aristocratic of the French collèges, École des Roches. He speaks English as well as he speaks French.

He arrived here with Mme du Plessis [sic], who is the niece of the painter Yacovlev, a great friend of mine before his death. Mme du Plessis lost her husband at the time of the collapse of France. He was an officer in the Air Corps and was brought down by the Spanish over Gibraltar when he was on his way to join the de Gaulle army. . . .

Mme du Plessis, who had been separated from her husband for several years, is a talented hat designer. She found a position as milliner with Bendel two days after her arrival.

Perhaps you would be interested in knowing Alexandre Liebermann. He intends either to reenter the publishing field or to go into window display, in which he is also very gifted.

Cordially yours

Lucien Vogel

Alex was not very optimistic about the outcome of Vogel's introduction. How could Alex's brief stint as art director of *Vu* impress Condé Nast? As they waited for an answer from the publisher, Alex and Mother went to a dinner party where Alex renewed his acquaintance with another Russian émigré, Iva Sergeyevich Voidato-Patcevitch, "Pat" for short. A strikingly handsome Russian aristocrat with a great talent for finances, Patcevitch had served as Nast's principal financial adviser for more than a decade and had single-handedly rescued the company from

Alex Liberman's portrait of his father, Simon, finished in New York in 1942.

its post-Depression doldrums. Until 1940, Patcevitch's home base had been in Paris, where Nast had large investments, and Alex had briefly met him in Paris's prewar publishing milieu. Patcevitch immediately told Alex that he should join him at Condé Nast and promised to arrange an interview with the legendary art director of all three Condé Nast magazines, Mehemed Agha.

Dr. Agha, as he insisted on being called, was known at the Condé Nast offices as the Terrible Turk. A portly, monocled graduate of the Bauhaus who had been born in Russia of Turkish parents, Agha was brought to the United States by Condé Nast to modernize the look of his magazines. And from 1929 on he was as respected for his avant-garde views as he was dreaded for his sarcastic wit and violent temper, which led him to alienate numerous coworkers. Frank Crowninshield, *Vanity Fair*'s urbane editor, complained that Agha had so inflated his power that "an additional floor had to be engaged in the Graybar building in order to prevent him from bulging out of the windows, growing through the roof, or occupying the elevator shafts." Carmel Snow, *Vogue*'s New York editor until 1932, found Agha's sarcasm intolerable, and her dislike for him may have been a major factor in her defection to *Vogue*'s chief competitor, *Harper's Bazaar*. This was the awesome individual—"Agha the Terrible Turk"—who upon Patcevitch's recommendation curtly received Alex in his offices, and in an arrogant and disdainful tone told him to report for work in the art department the following Monday.

Monday came, and Alex was assigned a double-page spread of fashion drawings. He spent most of the week on this assignment, and on Friday was called into Agha's office. Agha pointed out several dreadful flaws in Alex's layout and tersely told him that he was "not good enough for *Vogue*." Crushed, Alex collected his paltry paycheck and went back to the Windsor Hotel in midafternoon, despondent. It might be even more difficult than he had feared to find a job in the United States. But shortly before 5:00 P.M. a call came from Condé Nast's own office. Patcevitch had apparently urged his boss to interview Alex himself, and Alex was asked by Nast's secretary to report to Nast's office first thing Monday morning.

A short, painfully shy, balding man with small eyes and rimless pince-nez glasses, Condé Nast, who was then in his sixties, was later described by one of his mistresses as having "the vivacity of a stuffed moose head." But in spite of his dire lack of personal charisma, Nast's revolutionary views of journalism were as influential as those of his principal competitor, William Randolph Hearst. His own publishing career had begun at the turn of the century, when, as a manager of *Collier's Weekly*, Nast was responsible for the magazine's original twenty-thousand-subscriber circulation passing the half-million mark. When he left *Collier's* in 1909 to build his own empire, the first magazine Nast bought was *Vogue*. It had been founded a decade and a half earlier with the backing of Cornelius Vanderbilt and other wealthy socialites and had announced itself as "the authentic journal of society, fashion and the ceremonial side of life." Thirty years later, by the time Alex first met him, Nast had built up a publishing empire rivaled only, in its time, by Hearst's and Time-Life.

Sitting at his desk in an immense office in the Graybar Building, at 420 Lexington Avenue, Nast received Alex with exquisite politeness; Alex instantly realized that Nast had no idea that Agha had already hired and fired him. They talked about various cosmopolitan issues—Alex's experiences at *Vu*, the fall of France, French publishing in general. After a half hour of cordial conversation, Alex showed Nast a gold medal diploma he had won in the 1930s for magazine design, upon which Nast said, "Well, a man like you must be on *Vogue!*" He asked to have Dr. Agha sent for and told him he wished Alex to be in *Vogue's* art department. "Yes, Mr. Nast," Agha said. "Dr. Agha never said a word, I never said a word, and that's how I started at *Vogue*," Alex said later. Having been hired, fired, and rehired in the space of seven days, Alex started working in *Vogue's* art department in February 1941 for a salary of $150 a month—precisely half of what Mother was earning at Bendel. Sitting in the layout department on the nineteenth floor of the Graybar Building—there were six other designers in the room, all of them senior to him—he was to cohabit in *Vogue's* art department with Dr. Agha for almost two more years. And throughout much of that time, the two men sustained civil but very cool relations, never letting anyone know about the encounter they'd had before Nast's intervention.

Notwithstanding his thoroughly asocial manner, Nast was a keen judge of personality, and another secret of his success was his judicious choice of editors. In 1914, he had assigned Edna Woolman Chase to be editor of the magazine, and she reigned over it, the Queen Victoria of twentieth-century fashion publishing, until well after World War II. A small, formal, iron-willed puritanical woman who had been brought up by her Quaker grand-parents and had begun at *Vogue* in a clerical position when she was eighteen, she had an unfailing instinct for her very elitist readers' tastes. Under her rule, the latest fashion reports from Paris alternated with news of who had died, was born, married, or made a debut into New York's WASP gentry. Until the 1940s, the magazine even devoted a section to this society's do-mestic pets. Most editors were themselves well-born women working for tiny wages (among them were Barbara Cushing Mortimer, later known as Babe Paley, and the future New Jersey congresswoman Millicent Fenwick). And they readily abided by Mrs. Chase's stern sumptuary codes, which de-manded that all editors wear hats and white gloves in the office and that they never be seen, even on the hottest day, in open-toed shoes.

It is chiefly to the personal relationship he quickly established with *Vogue*'s principal forces—Condé Nast and Edna Chase—that Alex owed his swift promotions within the ranks of the magazine's art department. He im-mediately charmed both of them by that formal yet cordial Brittanic man-ner he had acquired at British public school—it impressed Americans as being very "aristocratic," and he could turn it on and off like a faucet. "He had a great gift for jumping into the lap of power, he very soon became Mrs. Chase's pet," said former travel editor Despina Messinesi, recently deceased at ninety-three, who joined the magazine a year before Alex. "Why I even re-member Alex working in his shirtsleeves in summer, he was certainly the only person on the floor whom Mrs. Chase ever *allowed* to work in his shirt-sleeves." Alex equally impressed Nast because he was a veteran of French news journalism, and the publisher knew that *Vogue* should start placing far greater emphasis on world news and cultural events if it was to survive the stiff competition being offered by *Harper's Bazaar*. So as he worked in the lay-out room on the nineteenth floor of the Graybar Building, Alex was fre-quently called into Nast's office, where he was asked to join Mrs. Chase, Agha, and several other top editors in picking out a *Vogue* cover. Nast would

Alex charming the ladies at a Vogue *party, November 1943. At center,
editor Bettina Ballard; at right, editor Muriel Maxwell. Photograph by Serge Balkin.*

ask Alex which of the possible photographs he preferred. Upon hearing the
junior staffer's verdict, Nast would say, "I, too, like this one best," and that's
the photo that was inevitably used.

Moreover, within a few weeks after Alex had arrived at *Vogue*, one of his
own layouts was accepted for the cover, which at that time did not have a
fixed logo. For the May 15 edition, the editors had chosen a Horst P. Horst
photo of a girl in a bathing suit balancing a red beach ball on her feet. Alex,
playing around with the image, suddenly realized that the beach ball could
substitute for the "o" in *Vogue*. Today, his design may look corny and utterly
inane. But in 1941, Frank Crowninshield, whose *Vanity Fair* magazine had
been incorporated into *Vogue* in 1936 and who now served as *Vogue*'s cultural
editor, was terribly impressed by the image. He complimented Alex on it as
he walked by Alex's desk and then popped into Nast's office and told him
that there was a new "genius" in the art department. So Alex, with a cover

Alex's first cover design for American Vogue, spring of 1941.
The photograph of the model is by Horst P. Horst

on his record, now had a far firmer foothold in the hierarchy of the art department. And he had a new friend in Frank Crowninshield, known as "Crowny," who often invited him to lunch at New York's most exclusive men's club, the Knickerbocker, and thoroughly briefed him on who was who in New York's social and cultural scene.

But curiously, Alex's brilliant debut at *Vogue* in no way satisfied his parents. A few months after he joined the magazine, Simon Liberman, probably egged on by Henriette, whose visions of Alex-as-great-artist were being undermined, must have announced that he was discontinuing the two hundred dollars a month he had been sending his son. This withdrawal of support seems to have been followed by statements of concern about Alex overworking himself at Condé Nast. (In the following thirty-five years, his mother constantly stated such worries—"You're killing yourself through your magazine work.") For in the late spring of 1941, Alex wrote the following anguished letter to his father.

Moi rodnoi,

I've just received your letter. It is a pity that you worry about me, I don't look all that bad. Unfortunately, in the last three days I got ill with laryngitis and couldn't talk. Now it's also turned into a sinus infection and it all tires me.

Speaking about work and exhaustion, I disagree with you and with Mother. We live in such hard times that one is happy to have some kind of firm support; it is important for me to work on something definite, to belong to a large organization—God only help me to succeed. For then I can start painting again and live a different life. Believe me, 80% of my exhaustion has nothing to do with Condé Nast, but with my financial problems. It's hard for me to admit, but psychologically I always need a feeling of security. *When I started working at Condé Nast and still had your support I felt "free." I felt* independent *and didn't worry whether the bosses liked my work or not. I took things lightly. But when you put a stop to all support I began to feel that every Vogue lay-out was a life and death question for me, and I'd spend sleepless nights worrying about the next day.*

This is one side to my worries, the other is less serious. It has to do with the current reality of our life. We can barely get by on $600 a month, we have to pay all our debts, buy clothes, we have to get settled. . . . [T]his puts me in a terrible *situation. I thought of selling something, but I have nothing to sell. Tatiana also has nothing left.*

I think that when there is only one son, who never wants to hurt you or cause problems, then $200 a month for him and his family is not that terrible. It seems to me that you should not want to know WHAT I am doing with this money, painting or working at Condé Nast. I'm healthy in mind and body, I'm young, I'll still create a lot.

Rodnoi, I know that you've recently had difficult times . . . but why should we be the victims? T. and I work in order not to hang around your neck. Can you imagine what it would have been like if we depended on you and asked you to to-tally support us? I'm presently asking you for a loan of $500–$600. Look on it strictly as a loan, and in the next 6 months you need not give me anything. It will be the same as if you gave me $100 each month. . . .

Forgive the desperation of this letter, but it might help us to better understand each other. T. and I began with our reserves, but each time T. or F. go to the doc-tor, it is a shock to our budget. I have no coat, no shoes, I can't afford such things. I have to pay the lawyer and the doctors. I can't even buy myself a new easel.

All right, enough! I'll stay home another week because of my cold. I'm paint-ing on weekends, Tatiana is working, Francine goes to school.

I kiss you so tenderly, and I pray to God that you understand me and not make it hard on yourself when everything can be so simple.

Yours,

Shura.

Needless to say, over the next few years Simon and Henriette's constant blackmailing and bullying of their son only aggravated Alex's ulcers, with nearly fatal results.

In June 1941, a few days after classes ended at Spence, I was sent back to live with Mother at 230 Central Park South—Pat Greene was going to Salt Lake City to see her family, and Justin was to join her there for a few weeks of vacation. After the challenge and excitement of school and all the amusements Pat had generated after school hours, Central Park South felt very dreary and lonely. Our little flat looked out on the bottom of Columbus Circle, and on a building that displayed a ribbon of neon lights that gave the world news. Mother had set up a dining area in the tiny hallway, furnishing it with a glass-and-metal table and matching chairs purchased at Macy's garden-furniture department. (The entire thirty-five-dollar set is in use to this day in my son's country house.) A great part of our small living room was occupied by a deep, wide couch upholstered in beige damask that served as Mother's bed—a gift from her friend Irena Wiley—and an upright piano. ("How can one entertain properly without a piano?") Parallel to the living room was an even smaller space that was my bedroom, with twin beds covered in a beige leaf print I hated. The whole flat was painted a brash, blinding white and exuded an aseptic, chilly gaiety.

When Mother left for work in the morning, a tall, warm black woman named Sally Robinson, whom she had hired as housekeeper, came to watch me; and within twenty-four hours of coming home I started wondering how Sally and I would manage to spend our time during all those hours alone. I instantly started reading *Gone with the Wind*. Having only had a few months of schooling in the States, I still read English more slowly than French, and I remember starting shortly before 10:00 A.M., when Mother went to work, and continuing straight on until her return at 6:00 P.M., chewing on a sandwich at midday upon Sally's orders. When Mother and Alex went out, which was four nights out of five, Sally and I either went to the movies or played dominoes, the only game I'd managed to teach her. Or else I just sat at the window, staring at the bright ribbon of world news circling about the top of the old General Motors building, anxiously studying the international events.

For throughout those early summer weeks in New York, I was growing aware of the fact that I was reaching some kind of anniversary with my father—it was just about a year now since he had communicated with me. Even while reading or hanging out with Sally, I kept focused on that band of swirling news emanating from the tallest building on Columbus Circle: "Germany Invades USSR. . . . Mussolini announces he will occupy Greece. . . . Anti-Vichy riots in Syria." Syria, Syria is the country Father had been posted to in the winter of 1939–1940, he was an expert on Syria, that might still be the site of his current mission! His assignment there might last the whole span of the war; his duty toward the Allied cause was far mightier than his duty toward me; I must retain my patience. He might be in hiding four, five years—he might not come back for a decade! Or else he might come back sometime soon, any time now, for just one day's leave, one day of perfect communion with me. . . . The phone would ring some evening as I sat alone in our apartment, staring at the headlines on the top of the nearby building—"Finland declares war on USSR"—it would be Father on the phone, he would beckon me to some secret meting place: by the side of a certain lake in Central Park, in front of a Vermeer at the Metropolitan Museum. He would have temporarily left his air-force uniform for a worn flannel suit, he would look thin and careworn, I would embrace him as I reassured him of the fervor of my faith in him. . . . We would talk thus for an hour, our hands clasped, discussing our future together, the end of the war, the happiness we would share together in our little house in the south of France. . . . I would be satisfied with such a brief meeting, I would be resigned to the idea that after a last embrace he would fly back to his mission the very same day. . . . "Pssst, miss, you're not concentrating!" Sally would snap as I lost another round of dominoes. "What's wrong with you, miss, you're increasingly absentminded!" I startled back to reality, determined to maintain my silence, my holy silence, the essential, sacred silence that would help carry my father to safety.

Life was more cheerful on those rare occasions when Mother and Alex stayed home for dinner—well, not exactly stayed home, they hated staying home; it was more cheerful on those rare nights when they were not engaged and took me out to dinner. That was a cause for great celebration, for we always went to the Automat, the treasured Automat on Fifty-seventh Street between Sixth and Seventh avenues, which was perhaps my favorite place in New York along with the Greenes' house. Hurray, Mother and Alex are all mine tonight! Before we left home, Alex would ready the quarters and nickels needed to acquire the goodies of our choice and give each of us a handful of coins. We'd leave our bleached little flats at 230 Central Park South and walk arm in arm down Seventh Avenue, acting out our rarely played script of Loving Little Family. Still remembering the hunger we'd experienced a few months before, we always chose a table splunk in the middle of the room, better to examine that sumptuous wall of living food—the iceberg-and-Jell-O salads glimmering in their glass cages, the dozens of cream of broccoli soups and apple cobblers, the coquettish chicken potpies with little emerald peas twinkling behind the doors of their vitrines. Sharp clink of our coins going into the slots, soft whirr of the little glass doors as they magically opened to yield their treasures. I have no memory of what we ever chose as our main course. I only recall beginnings and endings: chicken noodle soups, apple and cherry pies, and particularly the hunks of coconut cakes with acres of gooey white icing, which I carefully consumed before the cake itself, pleading, after I'd finished the icing, that I was full. I remember, too, the few friends who occasionally joined us at the Automat, such as Yvonne Alberti, a spinsterish lady, cousin of Irena Wiley and therefore cherished by Mother. She had late in life married a mustached Spanish equestrian named Manolo, who could even make a horse walk up long flights of steps and was said to be a bit of a sponger. But mostly it was just the three of us at the Automat, the tenderly smiling Us. "Boubous," my mother would say to Alex, "look how she's eating!" And my guardians would exchange their glances of new world, bright world happiness, recording the pride and pleasure and amusement they took in the happily growing child.

Only a few weeks after I'd returned from the Greenes' and had begun to spend my days moping at home, with nothing much to look forward to beyond another installment of Scarlett O'Hara, Gitta Sereny, the eighteen-year-old Hungarian girl who had been with us at Villandry, arrived dramatically from Europe—someone always seemed to come to Mother's rescue. Mother eagerly invited her to stay with us for as long as she wished in exchange for helping Sally, who did all the cooking and cleaning, to take care of me. For the next months, Gitta, who had recently defied fascist border police to walk across the Pyrenees into Spain and had hitchhiked much of the way to Lisbon, could do no wrong in my mother's eyes. ("She is a heroine!") Gitta at eighteen was a robust, awesomely precocious brunette with dark hair, blazing eyes, and a very ringing laugh that exhibited her uneven but sparklingly white teeth. Her manner was aggressively forthright; she was quadrilingual and had a distinct interest in playing an active role in other people's lives. She also had a special sense of mission about children—about rescuing them, counseling them, figuring them out: Decades later, upon becoming a celebrated journalist, she would do groundbreaking research on the fate of children in Nazi concentration camps. And in June 1941 it somehow dawned on her that I sorely needed her help. I had liked her at Villandry, and as she began to share my room at Central Park South I started looking on her as an older sister—very powerful and wise and a potential dispenser of that forbidden knowledge that precocious ten-year-olds are eager to acquire or at least be exposed to. "Too bad I'm not married when I smell so good!" she would say to me as she lay in her bubble bath, eyeing me carefully to see how much I knew about the basics of life.

So during those summer weeks, Gitta and I went to the planetarium and the Frick Museum and the Bronx Zoo and the movies. On hot days, we took the train to Jones Beach, and she helped me to perfect the swimming strokes I had learned with Alex the previous summer. When we stayed home in the evenings—Mother and Alex went out more often than ever after Gitta's arrival—we played gin rummy, and I read aloud to her from *Gone with the Wind* to improve my pronunciation, or else we prepared for one of Mother's wonderful parties.

For by the time I came back to live with Mother in June 1941, she had already started holding her noted soirees. As much as she loathed crowds in public places, pleading that they caused her to suffer panic attacks, like most Russians she dreaded, above all else, to be alone. And she simply did not understand the meaning of the phrase "too many people," as long as they were all under *her* roof. At her own parties, no crowd was ever too vast, no table ever too full. "*La Formule,*" as she referred to her recipe for a successful social gathering, was to invite as many people as possible for 8:30 or 9:00 P.M., so as to make sure that they had already had dinner and wouldn't expect more than a drink and a cheese plate, then simply let them loose upon one another. "Of course, of course," her voice would trill for a few days before each event, "bring all the friends you want." Neither Alex nor

Mother touched a drop of liquor—his ulcer diet forbade it, and at that time Mother was indifferent to it. But even in those first American months of very straitened finances—Alex's letter to his father attests to our penury, and our prodigal hospitality could not have escaped his parents' attention—champagne and Scotch flowed freely on those evenings, Gitta and I were ordered to get into our best clothes in order to open the door, and Sally had been retained after-hours to keep rinsing the glasses.

In 1941 and 1942, our first year in the United States, Mother's party list inevitably included the diaphanous blond beauty Claude Alphand, whose husband, Hervé, would later serve as France's ambassador to Washington. A great patriot and an ardent proselytizer for the Free French, Mme Alphand brought her guitar to all gatherings, and one particular song in her repertoire inevitably brought tears to the eyes of homesick émigré guests: *"Je tire ma révérence, et m'en vais au hasard, sur les routes de France, de France et de Navarre."* Alternating with her as provider of musical entertainment was a hugely tall, wheezing Franco-Russian exile named Georges de Svirsky, "Zizi" for short. A close friend of Uncle Sasha who made a vague living as an interior decorator, he had met Mother in Paris just after she'd arrived from Russia. Like many Russians who dabble in music, he played the piano at many soirees in exchange for booze and meals. He was particularly fascinating to me because he had lived for two decades, and was to continue to do so for several more, with two women at once. They were sisters—a wispy, simpering blonde named Mout and a sharp-witted, Cupid-mouthed brunette named Follette—and for years this intriguing triad made other émigré New Yorkers' living arrangements seem morbidly dull. "But it's the happiest family I know of," Mother exclaimed when anyone questioned her about Zizi's ménage à trois. "The two girls take turns with him, and everyone is absolutely satisfied!"

Zizi seemed to have only three numbers in his piano repertoire, and he played all of them in his own highly idiosyncratic arrangements: Bach's "Jesu, Joy of Man's Desiring," the march from Prokofiev's *The Love for Three Oranges*, and the coronation scene from *Boris Godunov*. He played very stooped over, breathing heavily, his eyes twelve inches from the keys. And even as a ten-year-old I had trouble concentrating on the music because Zizi's loud, gruff wheezing interrupted it dreadfully, while his long, unkempt gray hair often obscured the keys, causing him to strike many wrong notes. Yet Mother sat rapt through his performances, loyally maintaining that her friend's arrangements of those three pieces were unequaled in power and beauty.

There were many other Russians in attendance. In 1941, our closest friend in the Russian émigré community was Countess Elena Shuvalov, whose hard-drinking, chronically unemployed husband, Peter, was a direct descendant of the Shuvalovs who for centuries had served the czars as high-ranking government officials. "Aunt" Elena was a sharp-featured woman with keen blue eyes and blond hair in a stark bun; she supported her family by running Saks Fifth Avenue's ready-to-wear hat salon, and in the next years her son, Andrew ("Andriusha"), two years younger than I, would be a close friend. There was also Sasha de Manziarly, a half-Russian, half-French diplomat who had lost a leg in World War I, was currently serving at Free French headquarters in New York, and, like Claude Alphand, was a gifted guitarist, singer, and seducer. And there was the half-Russian, half-German Countess Ada Mohl, a stately, alabaster-skinned beauty whose blond hair was done into a hugely tall beehive and who had special cachet in our eyes because she was said to be the mistress of Anthony Eden, whom my mother and I considered to be the world's handsomest man.

It was among such people, at moments of maximum mayhem—Sasha de Manziarly or Claude Alphand belting out their songs among a group of fellow exiles who sat pell-mell on the floor of our tiny living room or huddled by the dozen on the couch—that Mother was most truly in her element. Unsure as she was of her talents or even of her powers of seduction, she knew for certain that no one could gather other human beings more gaily, skillfully, and economically than she. As she sat in a corner of the room, usually on a high upholstered stool so as to show off her long, beautiful legs and better survey her gathering, the satisfaction of success glowed in her eyes. And the happy commotion she instinctively brought to our frugal little flat—the noise, the music, the smoke, the clinking glasses, the animated talk and laughter—created an aura of Homeric hospitality that I long for to this day.

Tatiana and Salvador Dalí out on the town in the late 1940s.

It must be emphasized that entertaining, to my mother, was far more than a mere amusement. It was a civic duty of sorts born out of the venerable, parareligious Russian tradition of communality—however little I have, the gods will punish me if I do not share my roof, my food with others. This proclivity to largesse seems to have been traditional in Russia for centuries. "Numbers of families, lately prosperous and wealthy, are yearly reduced to beggary by hospitality as ruinous and meaningless as that of Timon of Athens in his unregenerate days," the author E. B. Lanin, author of the wonderful book *Russian Characteristics*, wrote in 1892. "Every Russian, whatever his social position, his means, or his needs . . . deems it a sacred duty to entertain his friends and relations. . . . [M]any spend their last borrowed coin upon these ruinous merry-makings . . . filling whole streets with impatient creditors."

But Mother's innate impulse toward lavish hospitality and her keen in-

terest in others were certainly not traits Alex shared. He looked on entertaining exclusively as an important career move. His guest list came solely
from two groups: those members of the Condé Nast staff who could assist
his career, and those acquaintances made since his arrival in the United
States who might eventually be of aid in the rescue of his often disastrous
finances. Prominent among Alex's favorites was a genial, very wealthy
Franco-American couple named Beatrice and Fernand Leval, whom he and
Mother met at a dinner party a few weeks after their arrival in New York.
Beatrice was a pert, fine-boned woman from a prominent Jewish family
who had been schooled in France, had taken her college degree in art history, and had already started a beautiful collection of French Impressionist
paintings. Fernand, half Swiss and half French, a tall, hulking man with red
hair and shy, kind eyes, headed the Dreyfus Frères office in New York. Both
Levals, upon first impression, had thoroughly disliked Tatiana and Alex,
finding them intolerably pushy. (In the next decades, this opinion was to be
shared by many prominent members of New York society, including the
William Paleys, whose opprobrium would much vex Alex.)

But a few weeks after their first meeting in February 1941, Tatiana and
Beatrice had tea alone. This time, Beatrice was totally charmed by Mother's
generosity, culture, and what she called "her wonderfully uninhibited Russian
stream of consciousness." Since then, the four had grown to be close friends,
the Levals had become steadies at all of the Libermans' gatherings, and for
the next two decades Fernand was often called on to loan Alex money when
our family finances skirted yet another catastrophe. Yet however useful guests
such as the Levals proved to be, I don't recall Alex having a good time at his
own parties. He simply hovered dutifully in the background with his charming, inscrutable smile, making sure that guests were properly introduced and
had their glasses filled, remaining affable yet totally aloof.

I return to the summer of 1941.
    At the end of July, it was time to take our summer vacation, on Long Is-
land, where Mother, Alex, and the Vogels had rented a cottage together for
the month of August; Gitta was to join us later in the month. Our first sum-

mer home in the United States was at Sands Point, a few miles from Port Washington, and cost $550 for the month—$275 for each of the couples. A plain white cottage with green trimming, surrounded by a large lawn, it had the advantage of being a few hundred yards from the beach and only a few miles away from the expansive estate Beatrice and Fernand Leval had rented for the summer. It must have had six small bedrooms: the Vogels occupied one; Gitta and I another; some weekend guests, usually Pat and Justin Greene, the third; Sally the fourth; and due to Mother's sense of propriety, she and Alex occupied the other two rooms, for until their official marriage in November 1942 they always slept in separate rooms.

During our weekends on Long Island, Mother created outdoor versions of the soirees she'd had at Central Park South. When I look at photographs of our Sands Point house, I see dozens of French and Russian refugees and a smattering of Francophile Americans—the Levals, the Greenes—sitting about a sunny lawn, glasses in hand, huddled in conversation, I suspect, about the course of the war. I see radiantly affable, mustached Peter Hoguet, our first American doctor, who had lost an arm in a car accident and whose wife had arranged for Mother's job at Bendel. I inevitably see Simon and Henriette, whose own summer house was a half hour away and who had now become more or less resigned to Alex's job at Condé Nast and to the permanence of Mother in Alex's life: Simon sits lordly and pensive in a lawn chair, Henriette reclines kittenishly on the grass, her thighs as provocatively bared as those of a teenager on the make. Also in evidence is one of Henriette's many former lovers, tall, imposing Lucien Vogel, now balding, dandyish, a pipe inevitably clenched in his mouth, and his big, noisy wife, Cosette, who always became the center of attention at mealtimes because of her predilection for the science of pendulums. All food, she believed, had to pass the pendulum test before it could be safely consumed. As tall and majestic as her husband, with graying blond hair in a tight bun, yellowish teeth, and a huge masculine laugh, she stood over the dish of food to be tested, holding a long metal chain at the end of which a small globe was attached. If the pendulum swung clockwise, the food was fit to eat. If it swung counterclockwise, she advised that it be thrown out. No one dared contradict her, for she had been, for decades, one of her country's most prominent culinary

Alex Liberman shortly after arriving in the United States, 1941.

authorities—her series of books, *Les Recettes de Cosette,* had more or less the same standing in France as Julia Child's do on these shores.

Also frequently seen in these summer photos are Eugene ("Jika") Jackson, my mother's half brother. So fervent was Mother's sense of family that notwithstanding her father's decades of negligence, she had instantly taken his entire American clan under her wing. She particularly adored her stepmother, Zina, whom she declared to be "a true saint," and had embarked on the difficult mission of making Jika's manners "more European" and eventually getting him into a fine college. Whom else do I see among the guests spread out on the lawn, lounging in chaise longues, in that green uncertain void that was the second summer of the war? Spectacled, chain-smoking Jacques Lebeau, a French brain surgeon who had been Justin Greene's closest friend during their student days in Paris and who a few months later would recross the Atlantic to join de Gaulle's headquarters in London; Marcel Vertès and René Bouché, fashion artists who would have great vogue into the 1950s. There's a curious sense of suspension about this crowd, of both anxiety and expectation: In August 1941, who knew when the war in Europe would end? Who could even be sure that the Allies would prevail? How many of these friends spread out on a Long Island lawn knew whether they could ever in their lifetimes return to France?

Looking at picture albums of that first American summer, two photos stand out. In one, my mother is pointing, laughing, to a barbecue pit on which a piece of meat is cooking. And this ushers in a recollection that is all the more charged because it is beset with tastes and smells as well as sounds: Making one of her frequent lewd puns, my mother is saying,

"*Barbe-au-cu*," "bearded ass," and the phrase is accompanied by the pungent smell of charcoal-grilled steak. "I like my steak *au bleu*," I also hear her saying, by which she meant ultrarare: Barbecued steak was the first Yankee culinary custom she adopted, so it became a standard Saturday-night treat at Sands Point. And when I recall that summer, the taste of my mother's "*barbe-au-cu*"—my first American madeleine—comes poignantly back to me: smoking-hot coal-black grit of the meat's surface on my tongue, followed quickly by the cool, dank, near rawness of the meat inside, pursued in turn by the violent sting of Gulden's dry mustard, mixed into a paste with a bit of water, a condiment which for decades accompanied any beef that Mother and Alex ever ate.

Another shot that particularly strikes me: As Lucien Vogel bends deeply over his Leica, and his wife Cosette holds her pendulum over a dish of food, and a dozen exiles mill about them, glasses in hand, talking and laughing, I sit on the edge of a chaise longue, quite away from the rest of the crowd, away and very separate. There is a book on my lap, as usual, but in this photo I'm not even reading it. My arms rest on my knees, my shoulders are hunched, my eyes are cast down to the ground. I'm looking, in fact, ever so isolated, even in despair—as I might well have been, for it was in that month of August 1941, more than one year after the fact, that I finally learned about my father's death.

Soon after we had moved into the Sands Point house, my mother seemed to have been seized by one of her sudden panics concerning me—"*Mon Dieu!*" so this panic attack seems to have gone, "that child does not yet know about her father's death!" I suspect this concern came to her at that particular moment because it was the first time since we'd stepped off the boat that she and I were spending time together round the clock. There followed a confused series of actions, the substance of which varies a bit from witness to witness, that brought my childhood innocence to an end. For the sake of chronology, I'll begin with Pat Greene's.

"As soon as she got to Sands Point, Tatiana realized that someone had to tell you the truth," Pat Greene, now a very spry ninety, said to me in 2003.

*Tatiana and Francine in August 1941 at the summer
cottage in Sands Point, Long Island.*

She was absolutely incapable of telling you about your father's
death herself, so she started looking right and left for people who
might tell you instead. The way she went about it was rather disorganized and hysterical, she'd grab Beatrice Leval and say, "Would
you tell her, please?" and Beatrice, terrified, would demur, and then
she'd say, "I'll ask Gitta, where's Gitta?" Well, Gitta wasn't there
that first week in Long Island, so she asked me to talk to you. I
didn't want to either. But Justin, all along, had been appalled that
notwithstanding his prodding Tatiana hadn't told you anything.

He'd begun to realize that she was so terrified she would never do it herself. . . . His instinct as a psychiatrist was that it would be better if a woman spoke to you, so then he persuaded me to tell you.

Pat offered me these recollections as we sat in her living room in Houston, where she had recently moved to live near the oldest of her four sons.

I remember breaking the news to you on the beach, soon after we'd come out of the water. It was a hot sunny day, we'd taken a swim together, and as we came out of the water I said something like, "I'm so, so sorry that you lost your father in this terrible war." And you know what? You pretended not to have heard. You didn't say a word, you just went back towards your mother and her friends, she was having one of her beach parties, and before I knew it you were absorbed in her crowd. Then that evening, Tatiana turned to me and asked me, "Did you tell her?" And I said, "Yes, but it didn't register." And she grew very annoyed, she said, "Why didn't Justin report that to me?" And then she put her head into her hands and said, "I can't do it myself, I just can't." Gitta was arriving the following day, so I guess she decided to wait for Gitta, for that's the last I heard of it until the storm was over.

Then there's Gitta's version. Upon arriving from Europe earlier that summer, Gitta had been appalled to learn that I had not yet been told the truth about my father, which she had heard the previous summer at Villandry. "I told Tatiana repeatedly, 'You can't do this, you must tell her,' but she kept saying 'I can't, I can't hurt her that way.' 'But you're hurting her far more this way,' I told her, 'somewhere inside she knows he's dead, but she's fighting to keep him alive.'"

Speaking to me in 2003 in London, Gitta Sereny, O.B.E., now in her early eighties and one of Europe's most distinguished journalists, told me that when she came to stay with us at Sands Point in the second week of

August, Mother said to her, "Could you do it? Please tell her." Gitta kept reiterating that this was Tatiana's job, but one morning, after an hour or so of heated argument, she reluctantly agreed to do it that evening. "I don't want to be here when it happens," Mother said. So she called the Levals and arranged for her and Alex to have dinner and spend the night at their summer home, ten minutes away.

Alone with me, soon after supper, Gitta told me about my father's death. "I tried to do it as gently as possible, but I didn't hedge," she recalls today. My reaction, as Gitta tells it, was far less violent than my mother had feared. "It was as if deep down you knew all about it, but didn't want to admit it, " she told me. "Perhaps it was even a relief for you to hear it . . . you cried, but not uncontrollably. I put you to bed. You went to sleep by eleven, after a final bout of crying. I sat up in a chair next to your bed for a while to be sure that you'd be all right, but to my amazement you slept very deeply, peacefully." As Gitta remembers it, Tatiana and Alex reappeared shortly after 8:00 A.M. the following morning. I jumped out of my chair and flew into my mother's arms, according to Gitta, and Tatiana held me and cried, sobbing, "Ma chérie, ma chérie," and we went off by ourselves for a while while Alex sat down and had coffee with Gitta. "Alors, ça va?" he asked Gitta. "Ça n'a pas été trop terrible?"

My own memory adheres quite closely to the two women's accounts. I recollect some confrontation with Pat Greene shortly after we had come out of the water on a bright, sunny summer day—her phrase of condolence, and the sun sparkling on the water as she spoke it, and the grit of coarse sand under my feet, and the deep, rich green of the pines overhead, and my retreat into sullen silence. And I recall Gitta, a few evenings later— I know it was after dark—giving me the same information, but more directly, bluntly; and I recollect as if it had occurred yesterday the storm of tears that overcame me and that also overwhelmed Mother as she ran to me the following morning and wrapped me in her arms. "Why didn't *you* tell me?" I remember sobbing, repeating the word "*you*," "why didn't *you, you, you* tell me?" "I'm sorry, I'm sorry, I didn't know how," she wept. We sobbed like equals that morning, like the two lost children we both were. The terrifying thing is that from then on Mother was seldom able to recapture my trust. And we spent the rest of our lives—she lived on for another half century—

not ever having any kind of a true emotional encounter again. We would continue to skirt each other, rather, like two wary lionesses, occasionally pawing or nuzzling each other in token of affection but rigorously avoiding any confrontation that would even begin to approach in intensity the one we had shared that summer day in Long Island.

Seeing how completely he had taken over our lives by then, Alex's total absence from these events of August 1941 may be striking; but there's no way he could have played a role in them, seeing that they had to do with the death of a man he hated but barely knew. And I imagine him staying carefully on the sidelines, urging Mother to find some messenger to do the dirty work for her. For from the moment his fate was permanently linked to ours, one of Alex's central goals in life was to protect Mother from any harsh crises that came our way, to shelter her from reality as assiduously as he satisfied her most outlandish whims. From that day on, any unpleasant task that had to do with me—be it caring for my illnesses, scolding me for poor grades, expressing criticism of an indecorous boyfriend, or censoring the use of lipstick—was taken on exclusively by Alex. Tatiana was his idol, the princess in the ivory tower who must at all costs be protected from all human concerns or pain, and this strategy of protection, which I happily participated in, would be a principal dynamic of our family life for the following half century.

However, I should also give Alex's secondhand version of the August 1941 events. He was forced to confront them in the years following my mother's death, when one of his recent biographers, Dodie Kazanjian, reported to him at length on her own conversations with Gitta Sereny. When confronted with Gitta's version of the Sands Point episode, Alex vigorously denied that Gitta had ever been delegated to act as the news bearer of my father's death. My mother wanted to eventually do it herself, he said, in her own due time. (One wonders how many years she might have allowed me to retain my illusions.) And both she and Alex were "surprised and quite annoyed," in Alex's words, to learn that Gitta had taken the task upon herself.

What is unfortunate is that for many decades my diplomatic need for constantly accommodating Mother and Alex, my dread of alienating their love in any way, led me blindly to accept their version. I blamed Gitta

Sereny for being a meddler and interloper in this situation and dealt most unfairly with her in my first, fictional rendering of the events. Only recently have I begun to understand that I owe her immense gratitude for sharing news with me that Mother and Alex might have broken to me with far less diplomacy or psychological grace. I might have been a considerably more confused, wounded woman without Gitta Sereny's help. And I have tried to apologize to her for any kind of pain I might have caused her by a rendering that was clearly molded by Mother's and Alex's cowardice and evolved during those years when I still remained, emotionally, their slave.

.

FOURTEEN

In the East Seventies

In the autumn of 1941, as I was beginning sixth grade, we had to leave Central Park South, where we'd had only a six-month lease. I suspect Mother and Alex wanted to live at closer quarters to each other, so we moved on to a floor-through in a brownstone on Seventy-third Street, between Lexington and Park. Here Mother and I had a little three-room flat on the front of the building. Alex's one-room studio, which had a separate entrance but was on the same landing, looked out on the back garden.

Before we moved into the new flat, I had to go into exile once more. The apartments have to be totally repainted! It will take us at least a month and a half! I was sent to lodge, this time, with a couple I barely knew named Eugene and Marguerite Leytess, who lived in the east eighties. Eugene was a short, genial, bespectacled Russian Jew who had made good money in the copper trade. His wife was a stout, highly painted Romanian with a short temper and frequent fits of melancholy. She had a son from an earlier marriage, Jerome, who was a year or so older than I and attended the Lycée Français. Theirs was a two-bedroom flat, and for the second time in six months I was forced to sleep on a living-room couch. At 10:00 P.M., when everyone had retired for the night, I made up my bed with sheets and blankets kept in the coat closet, and at 7:15 A.M., as I was getting ready to go to

Spence, I unmade it and stored the sheets away again. The Leytesses' attitude toward me was one of benign tolerance. Jerome and I were at an age when boys and girls are very shy toward the opposite gender, and we barely addressed a word to each other during the months I lived with his parents. I spent most of my time hovering on a little chair behind a Chinese screen in the living room, attempting to read and do my homework without disturbing my hosts, and was called in, rather coolly, when meals were ready. I was treated with greater deference than the man/insect in Kafka's "Metamorphosis" but with not much greater warmth. It was a period when most members of the émigré community traded favors with one another: The Leytesses seemed to sense that Mother and Alex were about to become an important couple on the New York scene and were getting insurance on the glamorous pair's goodwill by inviting me to stay.

As I went to bed on the Leytesses' living-room couch, the nightly fits of tears that had beset me in Rochester resumed. Now that I was in full knowledge of his death, I cried for my father, of course, my emotions all the rawer because they had to be nursed in isolation, away from all close friends and loved ones. But I also cried for reasons that I didn't then begin to understand: The week my birthday came around—I turned eleven that September—I woke several times in fits of tears that verged on hysteria, filled with the anxiety that I was growing very *old*. "I'm decaying with time," my reasoning seems to have gone. "I'm eleven now. I'm growing so old that I can die any time." At times of self-reflection—as close as an eleven-year-old can get to self-reflection—I asked myself whether I was afraid of dying or actually contemplating an act of self-destruction. It's only decades later, upon rereading Sigmund Freud's epochal essay "Mourning and Melancholia," that I realized the link between my unresolved mourning for my father and my obsessions with death. During those months at the Leytesses', my only way to allay my depressions was to harbor illusions about my father's survival. As soon as I went to bed, I pressed to my ear a little wireless radio that Simon Liberman had given me, and I listened to news of the war. Perhaps Gitta Sereny and Pat Greene and Mother had all been wrong; perhaps my father's mission was so secret that he wouldn't be allowed to write anyone for years, in the fall of 1941 the Allies were fighting it out in many regions of North Africa—my father was a special-ist in that area, he might still be among them. . . . So I continued secretly to dream and lie.

My exile at the Leytesses' finally came to an end. I moved into Mother's freshly painted flat at 125 East Seventy-third Street. What a joy, when I tip-toed out of my room at 8:00 A.M. to take myself to Spence, to see Mother asleep in the room next to mine! She would be snoring lightly, her baby pil-low nested on top of her blond hair, her long, red-nailed fingers resting on top of the coverlet. I had no need to muffle my footsteps, for she took very strong sleeping pills and would not wake until her alarm clock rang at 9:00 A.M. Upon the dot of that hour, Alex, who had set his clock to quarter of, would rush to her side with her little breakfast tray; this consisted of a pint-size cup of very strong instant Nescafé lightly dosed with milk—she would always spurn the freshly brewed kind—and a "biscotte" with jam, which she barely touched. (This breakfast ritual continued, unchanged, for half a century.) In part for reasons of frail health—his ulcers, her migraines—Alex and Mother were finicky about getting every second of sleep they could have after their evenings on the town. They still went out five nights out of six—"It is absolutely essential to our careers, darling"—and grew cross if their morning schedules, which were geared to dressing at top speed and getting to their offices by ten, were in the least bit disturbed. So my principal way of communicating with my sleeping mother was to stand in front of her bed and stare at her with the same kind of wordless reverence that had swept over me when I was a much smaller girl in Paris and had crouched in her mirrored bathroom as she sat at her vanity, occasionally blowing me cool, distant kisses.

I was often reprimanded for being late to school, but I found it hard, having just turned eleven, to pull myself together in the morning. For one thing, I stayed up late all the nights Mother and Alex were out for dinner. I had a wonderful time reading, listening to music, and practicing my bal-let steps by the hour to Karl Maria von Weber's "The Specter of the Rose"—piano and ballet lessons were de rigueur in my family, whatever our penury. I was very proud of being the only girl in my class allowed to stay home by herself at night, and I didn't go to bed until I heard Alex and

Mother entering the front door, when I slid quickly into bed, pretending to have been asleep for hours. I was equally proud of being the only one among my friends whose mother had a full-time job, and I looked on Alex and Mother's hectic social schedule as another part of their hardworking lives. But since I'd seldom had much to eat since noon the day before—needless to say, my guardians' schedule did not include any breakfast ritual for me—I woke up in a state of great exhaustion each morning and took a taxi to school, thus using up all my allowance by midweek.

It was during those months at Seventy-third Street that the embarrassing issue of nourishment first came up in our fledgling family. Sally had taken the winter off to be with her aging sister in the Midwest. Mother had hired a part-time housekeeper named Magda, a cheerful red-haired Romanian in her middle years who came at noon and left at five, leaving dinner for me on the stove. But I had no inclination to heat up a meal and sit down to it all by myself, preferring to nibble on cheese and crackers or open cans of my favorite food, canned fruit. As for the dinner left for me on the stove, I threw part of it away so as to pretend I'd eaten some of it and left the rest in the icebox for Magda to take home. Mother and Alex, to whom the kitchen was unknown territory, were oblivious to my ruse, and Magda, if she noticed, didn't say anything. Thus it was that at the age of eleven and a half, I came down with a severe case of anemia and malnutrition.

By February 1942, I was feeling increasingly listless in the mornings. But I had an iron will and a fairly manic reserve of nervous energy and no other premonitions of ill health, until the day I began fainting in school. The first time was in math class, when I went to the blackboard to do a five-figure addition. Everything before me suddenly started spinning around before turning totally dark, and I came to in the school nurse's office, smelling lavender-scented salts. "Shouldn't you go home?" Nurse asked. "Is there anything wrong with your health?" "Oh, I'm just fine, I'll go right back to class. I'm just growing very fast," I said cheerfully. "Yes," she agreed, "it may just be growing pains." "It's just growing pains," I parroted gleefully to my classmates. "I'm growing so fast."

But the following week I fainted again during morning study period in the library. This time, the concerned nurse was finishing a phone call to

Mother at Bendel just as I came to. "Your mother didn't understand the word 'faint,'" she reported, perplexed by Mother's very minimal grasp of the English language. "Is there anyone else I can call?" Immensely relieved that Mother hadn't gotten the gist of it—Alex and I were still perfecting our strategy of protecting Mother from anything that would disturb her— I gave the nurse Alex's number: "My mother's *friend*," I said, moving my eyebrows expressively to communicate my sense of that word. So the nurse called Alex at *Vogue* to say, "Francine has fainted for the second time this week," and Alex, abiding to our tactics, said, "Don't let her mother know, I'll be right over." He indeed arrived twenty minutes later, expressing immense love and concern, as he did upon any crisis I faced. He took me home, saw me into bed, and spent an hour with me until Magda arrived. "Be sure she has a good lunch," he said to Magda as he was preparing to leave. "She just loves her school lunches." He came in to give me a hug. "I've made an appointment with Dr. Kling, darling," he said. "I'm sure you're fine—you're just growing so fast." "Don't tell Mother!" I begged. "Don't worry," he said, "I'll just tell her you've had dizzy spells."

I read with delight throughout that day as Magda brought me trays of soup and sandwiches. Made to feel important and interesting by Alex's devotion and love, I dozed on and off, enchanted by the prospect of an appointment with wonderful Dr. Kling.

Dr. André Kling, who was to remain our family doctor for the next two decades, was a genial, handsome Viennese Jew with the most suave bedside manner in town. A twice-divorced, childless bachelor with a roving eye, he treated me with great deference and affection, as if I were the child he'd most love to have as his own. And as the three of us came into his office—it was 10:00 A.M., and Mother was glancing nervously at her watch, terrified that she'd miss a customer at Bendel—he insisted on taking me alone into his examining room, where he proceeded to question me at length about my schedule and my eating habits.

"You're very skinny again," he commented as he bumped around my chest and stomach. "Could you give me a precise rundown of your diet?"

This is a question I had to answer most cautiously. For I was so happy to be living with Mother and Alex again, so dreading the prospect of being sent off to yet other strangers' couches, that I'd rather have disappeared into the wall than have the doctor accuse them of any negligence. I needed to put the blame squarely on my own shoulders, then and there. So I told the doctor that I'd been a very bad girl, that I'd lied to Mother and Alex, that a delicious dinner was always left on top of the stove for me but that it had been my habit to throw half of it away and open a can of fruit. "What about breakfast?" he asked impassively. Well, no, there was no breakfast at home, I said. Alex brought Mother her coffee at nine, and by that time I was already at school. "So in fact you do not eat anything but canned fruit between lunch on a Tuesday and lunch on the following day?" he persisted. "I guess not," I said. "But I'm never hungry." "Incredible," he murmured. "You must have breakfast, sweetheart," he said in his lilting, Viennese-accented English, "you're suffering from malnutrition. Breakfast is very important for a growing girl." "Well, maybe something can be left for me in the icebox. Please, please don't let Alex and Mother get up any earlier to take care of me," I pleaded. "Promise, Doctor, promise?" "Promees Tohmees," he repeated, attempting to mimic American schoolgirl talk.

After drawing blood from my arm, the doctor went back into his office to rejoin Mother and Alex, and as I got dressed I caught peeks of the three of them through a crack in the door. Watching Alex and Mother listening to the doctor's urbane remonstrances ("a high-strung eleven-year-old with a record of frail childhood health who has recently lived through a severe emotional upheaval cannot be left on her own like this"), I saw an expression come upon their faces that I would observe innumerable times over the following half century whenever their conduct was in the least way faulted. It was an air of charmed agreement, as if to say, "Why, you're reading our minds—this is exactly what we were just *about* to do!" "This is *precisely* what we were about to arrange," Mother said excitedly to the doctor. "We were about to ask Magda to stay until seven-thirty to give Frosinka her dinner." "This has gone on for five months," Doctor Kling said a little sternly. "But we're just *beginning* to get organized, *cher* André!" my mother moaned, with that gesture of both her hands to her brow ("It's all too much for me"), which intimated that reality was getting uncomfortably close to her.

So the good doctor went about fulfilling his goal. In a consummately diplomatic way that put my guardians into a state of mild alarm yet did not let them feel guilty of any major negligence, he succeeded in communicating his message: *Someone* had to be there to supervise my evening meal. The upshot of our visit was that Magda, who was delighted to earn a little additional income and be fed dinner, was hired to stay for an extra three hours into the evening. And before she left for the night, she was on orders to fix me some instant breakfast—glasses of freshly squeezed juice and milkshake that I, in turn, was requested to consume before going to school in the morning.

Doctor Kling had his own suave methods of blackmailing me and had made me promise that in exchange for his not upsetting my guardians' schedule, I'd turn my light out promptly at ten every night. What with Magda there every evening and my new early-to-bed regime, within a month I'd put on a few pounds and bounced out of my room every morning with unprecedented energy, scooting past my mother's bed and running over to Park Avenue to catch the 8:00 A.M. Spence bus. Within two months of our first visit to Dr. Kling, I received the finest report card I'd yet had at school, and a month later still, barely a year after I'd arrived to the United States not speaking a word of English, I found myself to be the winner of Spence's lower-school spelling bee. (I was still on scholarship, as I'd remain for years, and a group of Spence mothers, certain that we'd invented our émigré credentials to have access to financial aid, descended on Mother at Bendel to check her out. They found a shy blond woman in a dim, cramped workroom who spoke barely a word of English, and decamped with profound apologies.)

One of my most vivid memories of Seventy-third Street, where we lived between the fall of 1941 and the winter of 1942, through my sixth grade and into the beginning of my seventh, is of watching a spectacular fight between Alex and Mother.

It must be her birthday, May 7, 1942. We are standing in Alex's little studio flat at the back of our floor-through, giving Mother her presents. I have just offered her a pair of bookends I've made for her in arts-and-crafts class, triangular blocks of wood that I'd painted a bright hue of shocking pink modeled on the packaging of Schiaparelli's perfume Shocking, Mother's favorite scent that year. She has accepted this gift with pride and emotion— "You made this yourself! How did you know shocking pink was my favorite color? I adore them!" So I breathe with relief, basking in her pleasure.

Now it's Alex's turn. Clearly terrified, his mustache trembling, he is holding a little black jewelry box in his hand. She frowns suspiciously even as he hands it to her. Alex and I know her to have extremely finicky tastes in jewelry. I, too, hold my breath, panicked for my beloved Alex.

She opens the box, and frowns even more ferociously as the gift comes into view. "*Mais c'est minable!*" she exclaims. "It is pathetic!" I rush over to her side to examine the contested object. It's a very pretty, rather conventional brooch—an aquamarine of rectangular shape, about an inch by an inch and a half, embedded in a very pretty setting of gold lace filigree. But Mother does not even take the pin out of its box. She snaps the box shut, and with a stream of imprecations hurls it across the room, aiming at Alex's face. I watch the flying object, poignantly recalling that earlier tantrum of hers when she had thrown a telephone book across the room at my father in our Paris flat. "How could you not know that this is just the kind of object I *detest?*" she shouts at Alex in our familiar blend of French and Russian. "Have you even looked at it carefully? I bet you didn't even *buy* it yourself! I bet you asked someone else's *secretary* to buy it for you!!" Alex has sought refuge in an armchair in a corner of the room and is looking like a contrite, punished child. "I did buy it myself," he says. "I thought it was beautiful." "You can't possibly think it's beautiful," Mother cries. "It looks, it looks . . ."—she searches for the proper word, "*Indian,* that's what it looks like!" And she marches out of the room, toward her own quarters a few yards away from his. In keeping with her distaste for any culture not safely grounded in the European West, "Indian" is as negative an epithet as she can summon.

I run up to Alex to embrace him, putting my head on his chest. He is so angelic to us, and he must be so hurt! Moreover, he's spent money on that brooch, and we're so broke! He pats my cheek, picks up the rejected item off the floor. "These moods don't last long with her," he whispers. A few minutes later, we tiptoe fearfully into her room. She is lying on top of her bed, reading Chekhov's short stories. "Admirable!" she exclaims, pointing to the book. "Utterly admirable!" She goes on to suggest that we celebrate by all going to the Automat together. The brooch is not alluded to until the end of the dinner, when, as we sit contentedly over our apple pies and coconut layer cakes, she turns to him wistfully and says, "All I ever want from you for my birthday is a dozen red roses. . . . Remember the red roses you used to send me in Paris?" Not too long after this incident, I began to understand that red roses had played the same role in Mother and Alex's erotic lexicon, ever since the beginning of their liaison, as the cattleyas that Swann sends Odette, in Proust's *Swann's Way*, after each of their trysts. And from that year on, for the following half century, a dozen red roses appeared at Mother's bedside on the mornings of her every birthday. Decades later I realized that red roses had also been the flowers that Mayakovsky had arranged to send her weekly after his departure from Paris.

I have equally vivid recollections of Seventy-third Street that have to do with my own emotional upheavals. Memory one: It is evening, and Mother and I are in the cubbyhole dressing room that stands between my bedroom and our shared bathroom, a space with walls that my mother has totally covered with mirrors. She is observing herself carefully in them, as usual, as she gets dressed to go out for dinner. As is often my habit, while leafing through a book I should be reading for school I'm sitting on the dressing room's one chair, watching her fix her hair and her face and choose items from her little collection of costume jewelry. With no warning, as she puts on an earring and continues to stare at herself in the mirror, she suddenly says, "Alex and I are thinking of having a baby, wouldn't you like that?" I break out into a tempest of tears, which lasts well into the evening, letting tears replace the words I do not dare to speak, which would go something like this: I insist on remaining the single, adored daughter, I refuse having anyone share that privilege, I want to remain The One! And the word "baby" is never mentioned again.

Years later, I learned that Mother did not particularly want another child, that she had dutifully asked me the question upon Alex's and Gitta Sereny's insistence. Gitta, who seems to have served as a minister of communication in our family, reports that earlier that very year Alex had approached her in the following manner: "Gitta, dear, could you please ask Tatiana if we can have a baby together?" "But how can *I* ask her that, Alex?" Gitta demurred. "It's up to you to ask her that." "I can't," Alex said sheepishly. "I just can't talk to her about such things." "Well if you can't, no one else can," Gitta said. "Please, Gitta, you have no idea how hard it is to speak to her about anything," Alex pleaded. (He would later tell Gitta that whenever he wanted to discuss any issue of substance with Tatiana, she would snap at him, saying, "So you want to have another of your Jewish conversations?" Part of their great happiness together, so Alex would later rationalize it, is that they never shared serious talk.)

So once again Gitta reluctantly agreed to do liaison duty in our family. She reports that when she broached the issue with my mother, asking her whether she was thinking of having another child, my mother came back at her with this bizarre response: "And why should I have another child? To bring another Jew into the world?" "We all know she was the opposite of an anti-Semite," Gitta commented recently as she recalled the episode. "Making a brazen, offensive statement—sexual, racial—was often her weird way of terminating a conversation she found too intimate."

Memory two of our days at Seventy-third Street is from a few weeks or months later: It is a Sunday afternoon, and I'm being taken for one of my favorite treats: hot chocolate at Rumpelmayer's on Central Park South, our first refuge from the war, a site past which we still walk with a certain triumphant nostalgia. Throughout our walk toward Rumpelmayer's, I've been holding Alex's hand rather than Mother's, telling him about some details of my English and history classes that are particularly intriguing and whose substance only he can grasp; whereas Mother seems very bored with anything that has to do with my schooling, he always has a way of making me

feel delectably important, whatever issue we're discussing. I glow with pleasure as we sit down at Rumpelmayer's—red velvet seats and draperies, walls
upholstered in dark lush fabrics, a treasured setting I shall search for in
other cities throughout my life. The steaming chocolate is brought in,
topped by its mound of whipped cream. Mother stares at me with her shy,
loving eyes; she suddenly clears her throat and says, in Russian, "We have
something to ask you." And Alex adds, in French, "We wonder what you'd
think if *maman* and I were to get married." I drop my spoon and start weeping. I sob uncontrollably, the tears flooding and ruining my hot chocolate.
The tears are all the more painful because I cannot figure out why I am
weeping—I love this man, he has become an even more stalwart center of
my life than Mother, so why am I crying? I am a didactically logical, Cartesian child—"she always wants to know all the reasons," people say. I weep
all the harder because I cannot stand my confusion, my lack of clarity. To
the pain and astonishment of my guardians, I weep into the night and, secretly, for weeks to come whenever I recall that conversation. The true
source of that particular upheaval became clear only many years later, when,
rereading *Hamlet* with a fastidiousness that can come only in adult years, I
lingered on the following line: "The funeral bak'd meats did coldly furnish
forth the marriage tables." Meaning: My guardians' purported remarriage
was uncomfortably close to my father's death; the deep love I had so hastily
transferred to Alex implicated me in the guilt of their union; their wedding
news confirmed a death that I was decades away from totally accepting. But
it might be that my Cartesian streak also deepened my crisis that day: How
screwed up could their sense of sequence get? I might well have wondered.
First they ask me whether they should have a baby, and *then* they ask me
whether they should get married? That may have been too much for a severely rational eleven-year-old to handle.

But life on Seventy-third Street had its joyful moments, too. Of particular pleasure to me—even more, ironically, than to Mother and Alex—
was the custom we began, that year, of sharing weekly dinners at the home

of Alex's father. The visits occurred on Thursday evenings, when our house-keeper, Magda, was off. Shortly after our arrival in New York, Simon Liberman had lost a considerable part of his fortune through an ill-advised investment and had moved to a smaller flat on Fifth Avenue, a few blocks uptown from Spence. Every Thursday after school I gleefully walked up to his home, did my homework as quickly as I could, and then settled down to a long talk with this gentle, contemplative scholar for whom I'd had a surge of tenderness and sympathy from the instant we'd met. Mother and Alex wouldn't get to his house until six-thirty or so, so the afternoons Simon and I spent together were wonderfully serene and unhurried, steeped in the time-lessness of mutual understanding. Beyond his exotic history as a fearless rev-olutionary, as a prominent economist, as an adventurous traveler who umpteen times had crossed the steppes of Russia, the reason Simon Liber-man wove a particular spell on me in the early 1940s was this: He was fin-ishing a book that was to be called *Building Lenin's Russia*, and he was perhaps the first person I'd known whom I thought of as *a writer*. Every one of his words was to be treasured, scrutinized, remembered. I'd always been attracted to philosophy and religion, and Simon had been an intimate friend of the Russian philosopher Nikolai Berdyaev, to whom he had offered considerable material support after Berdyaev's emigration from the Soviet Union in 1927. Simon began to expound Berdyaev's ideas to me when I turned thirteen or so, and they carried a greater ring of truth, in my Utopian adolescent years, than any other view of life I'd been presented thus far.

The Berdyaevian philosophy proposed by Simon was a brand of Chris-tian personalism, which had immeasurable influence on his son, Alex (or, let's say, on Alex's earlier incarnations), and has remained part of my credo to this day. Berdyaev believed in a benevolent Divine Will, immanent rather than transcendent, which demands each of us to strive for the greatest pos-sible fulfillment of our innate potential. Evil and all forms of social ills are always the result of potential that remains unfulfilled. In Berdyaev's religious existentialist view, we can realize ourselves only through interdependence and communion with other humans, and the only good society is an egali-tarian one that fosters compassionate relationships among all its individual members. Such were some of the views propounded by Simon Liberman as he sat in his study overlooking Central Park, talking in his gentle, almost whispering voice, his hands crossed over his knees, occasionally cocking his head from side to side, owl-like, to emphasize a point. Later, as I approached my fourteenth year, he frequently stood up as he talked and went to his shelf to pull out books for me—one particularly affecting work was Kierkegaard's *Fear and Trembling*, which eventually became the subject of my senior thesis at Barnard College. My readings of Berdyaev and Kierkegaard and my weekly talks with Simon were my principal spiritual training, my only way of continuing the religious education I'd begun as a child with my Roman Catholic father and my Russian Orthodox Babushka.

So went the first half of my afternoons with the gentle scholar Simon Liberman. Then in the second half of our visits . . . this is so curious, so unconnected: In the second half of our afternoon visits, I danced for him. He would put a Russian recording on his Victrola—preferably some wild, fast-paced tzigane song—and I became a fiery gypsy, twirled a scarf and whirled and leaped about his study, blending ballet and Russian folk dancing inspired by my particular love for the ballet *Scheherazade*. My friend clapped his hands and laughed, saying, "Faster! Faster!" He stamped his feet to the music and cried, "You have such talent!" He clapped some more and swayed in rhythm to the music, his eyes gleaming with pleasure behind the round, scholarly glasses. I may have danced to release some primal energies that needed unleashing after such serious adult talk; or it might have been my way of thanking him, in the most immediate and seductive way at hand, for the great adulthood he'd conferred on me through his conversation; or it might even have been some symbolic dance of seduction that had to do with my love for Alex, which I expressed by weaving a spell on his father. When I danced for Simon those many afternoons of my early adolescence, I danced with a certain taste of danger, too, beginning to sense the perils of the world in which Alex and Mother moved: that siren world of fashion, that domain of constant seduction, replete with perilous and facile lures, in which the principal conflicts among us, in the following decades, were to be played out.

．　　．　　．

There was another great source of delight during the year we lived at Seventy-third Street: our first American Christmas, which we spent in Washington, D.C., with John and Irena Wiley, a couple whom I revered more than any of Mother's close friends. John Wiley, an American diplomat who in 1934 had married my mother's closest chum from Warsaw days, Irena Baruch, had served in Moscow under William Bullitt in the mid-1930s, and had gone on to be chief of the American diplomatic mission in Vienna in 1938. He was an Indiana Quaker, a tall, stately, spectacled, genial fellow full of mischievous fun and ironic witticisms. Unlike most Quakers, he was a great connoisseur of wines and a Cordon Bleu–trained chef and also a very heavy drinker. A second-generation foreign-service officer, he had been born in Bordeaux, where his father had been serving as consul, and had been brought up all over Europe, speaking numerous languages.

John and his exotic wife, Irena, a painter and sculptor, were deliriously in love with each other and enjoyed the kind of idyllic marriage that every romantic girl dreams of re-creating in her own life. Irena Wiley, a niece of the great economist Bernard Baruch, was the daughter of affluent Polish Jewish intellectuals. She had been brought up by French and British governesses, had studied sculpture in London, Paris, and Rome, and was fluent in as many languages as John. "You don't speak Romanian?" Irena and John had twitted me ever since I could remember. "There's no reason not to know Romanian." As genial as her husband and endlessly affectionate toward her friends, Irena was my mother's height and equally imposing, with very long black hair tied into a simple bun, flawless olive skin, and slanting, almost Asiatic, almond eyes. Her center of gravity was totally different from that of most other westerners—she glided rather than walked, with slow, mellifluous movements, a bit stooped over, like a cat searching for yet another place in which to curl up. She chain-smoked, like John, through a long black cigarette holder, and, like John, who spoke in a basso profundo several tones below Chaliapin's, her low, melodious voice had been made gravelly by nicotine.

John and Irena were the most thrilling people I knew. They were adventurous, reckless, endlessly curious, and cultivated. When on vacation, they would ride dozens of hours on barely passable dirt roads to visit obscure medieval churches or sleep wrapped in blankets, under the stars, in the ruins of Persepolis or Baalbek. And they throbbed with recent history. While stationed in Moscow in 1935, at the beginning of the great purges, they had sat a few yards away from Joseph Stalin as he reviewed a May Day parade, had seen close friends arrested at the dinner table who never reappeared. (The Moscow experience later turned John into an intractable Cold Warrior, and he was in part responsible for the excessive anti-Soviet paranoia that marked my mother until the end of her life.) The Wileys had also seen Hitler ride into Vienna at the time of the Anschluss, and a few days later had visited with Sigmund Freud in his study in Vienna, offering to spirit him to Great Britain on the next plane. Upon being recalled to Washington in 1941, they had smuggled a manuscript of Father Teilhard de Chardin's *The Divine Milieu* out of Japanese-occupied Beijing. Indeed, next to the Wileys my notably cosmopolitan parents seemed provincial and sadly limited. Uncle John and Aunt Irena, as I'd called them since I'd first known them in prewar Paris, amply returned my affection: Their greatest sorrow was to have been childless. And perhaps because they sensed the vulnerability caused by my childhood's upheavals, they lavished on me, until the end of their lives, abundant affection and advice.

From the summer of 1941, when Uncle John, like most American diplomats posted in Europe, was recalled to the State Department, to 1945, when he would be assigned ambassador to Colombia, the Wileys lived in their brownstone in Georgetown. This is where we joined them for Christmas in 1941, a fortnight after Pearl Harbor and the United States' entry into war. As we arrived at their snug, welcoming house filled with treasures from the Orient, I was assigned the task of masterminding the lighting of their huge Christmas tree, which reached to the ceiling. Those were the days when trees were lit with real candles, which were set into little metal holders that clamped onto the tree's branches, and I planned the spectacle for those hours of the evening in which the room was sure to be occupied. Aunt Irena and Uncle John were born educators, and they reached out to me with fervor and generosity—never before had I felt so integrated into adults' lives, so firmly placed at the center of their world. Did I want to see the Jefferson or Lincoln Memorial this morning, or was I in favor of a little ride down the Potomac? What recording would I like them to play next, Mozart or Chopin?

So the Wileys surrounded me with respect, with admiration—it is rare and marvelous for a child to be admired—and their home felt like a nest warmer and more nourishing than Alex and Mother's. It was while basking in the Wileys' affection, in fact, that I perceived the first glimmerings of any kind of a vocation. On New Year's Eve, upon coming home from a party at their friend Cissy Patterson's—my first past-midnight outing ever—I slid into my bed in the cozy study/guest room that stood off the Wileys' living room. At my request, Aunt Irena had put on a recording of Beethoven's Violin Concerto for my bedtime music. As its first measures rang out, the grown-ups came in one by one to give me a kiss and tuck me in, Uncle John last with a gallant peck on my wrist, reminding me yet once more that there was "no reason not to know Romanian." I was listening, I believe, to Fritz Kreisler's rendering of the concerto. I closed my eyes as the grown-ups were exchanging their last few words in the room next door: Uncle John was commenting on the meeting President Roosevelt was having with Winston Churchill in Washington that very week; its principal achievement was the creation of a Combined Chiefs of Staff, which would unite the British and American high commands . . . then everyone parted for the night, and I allowed the music to invade me. A few minutes into Kreisler's cadenza, I was suddenly filled with a sense of the beauty and wonder of the future. I had often doubted our survival during the arduous past year, and now I suddenly knew a future could actually occur. But the cadenza was also filling me with what I can call only a sense of destiny: It was demanding me to strive and to make my mark upon the world—it was intimating that with the proper striving I could achieve. Over the past days, the Wileys had expressed their great faith in me, as no one else had since my father's disappearance, and there and then I decided that I wasn't going to let them down. So I fell asleep immersed in the Wileys' affection and trust, cradled in the music, filled with new determination for the future, offering God gratitude for our survival, for my guardians' erratic but abundant warmth, and for the love and loyalty of friends such as the Wileys. I woke happily into the first morning of 1942, certain that the New World would bring my fledgling family all kinds of joys and surprises—which indeed it would, for in 1942 Mother and Alex began to fulfill their ambitions to rise to eminence in the New World.

The political events of 1942, however, turned out to be heartrending to anyone supporting the Allied cause. On the Russian front, German armies advanced southward into the Caucasus and laid siege to Stalingrad, where the battle raged for many months, leading hundreds of thousands of Russian civilians to die of hunger. In North Africa that summer, Rommel's forces dealt heavy blows to British troops at Tobruk and forced a humiliating retreat, which would be stopped only at El Alamein. A few months later, on November 8, the Allied forces that landed in Morocco under the command of Dwight D. Eisenhower and George Patton met unexpectedly stiff resistance from German armies. And two days later, Germany retaliated in a way that brought sorrow to every French émigré: Coming home from school on November 11, 1942, I was about to put my key in the door of our house when I saw the front-page headline of the *New York World-Telegram* lying on the threshold: "German Troops Sweep into Vichy France." Oh no no no, I wept as the ardent patriot I was. They were occupying the south of France—not an inch of my country's sacred soil was now free; nothing of France was left beyond that community of men who'd pledged to continue the fight, whom my father had almost succeeded in joining. I summoned up my childhood heroes—Clovis, Charlemagne, Joan of Arc, Henry IV—to return and save our country, I also wept hard as the child I still was: They had invaded Va-et-Vient and overrun those joyous sunlit acres in which I'd spent some of the happiest months of my life. What would become of the house, of Maria? Would anything, anyone survive? I thought of my blue bicycle, of my proud, scary ride to the farm to fetch Alex's milk, of all the joys we'd shared in a free France, and the child and the patriot wept together.

FIFTEEN

Saks Fifth Avenue and Condé Nast

In the 1940s and 1950s, no Manhattan store, with the possible exception of Bergdorf Goodman, more grandly characterized American elegance than Saks Fifth Avenue. And in those decades, no area of this lavish realm better epitomized American high style than the Salon Moderne on Saks's third floor, a suite of rooms walled with Louis XV boiseries and pale-blue damask, which was looked on as the mecca of women's custom-made fashions. Originally founded in the 1930s, the Salon Moderne was directed by a tall, blond, willowy dress designer called Sophie of Saks, who throughout the prewar years had made it a showcase for Paris-imported clothes. For in private life, Sophie was the wife of Adam Gimbel, Saks Fifth Avenue's founder and president, an ardent Francophile who made a point of reading one book a week in French and, upon the onset of World War II, began to suffer withdrawal pains from his beloved Paris. Upon the cessation of trade imposed by wartime, Sophie had started to design a line of her own custom-made clothes. But both Gimbels desperately wished to recapture the Salon's prewar European cachet; and in 1942, when they met the lively, beautiful émigré milliner Tatiana du Plessix, who was currently working at Henri Bendel, they sensed that they might have the winning ticket.

Hats were big business in those years, for throughout the history of fashion millinery styles have changed at a far faster pace than those of any other vestment—think of the phrase "old hat." One of *Vogue*'s retired fashion editors estimates that during the 1940s she and her colleagues acquired a minimum of ten new hats each season to remain in style, giving the last year's bunch to their maids. So a polished talent such as Tatiana's was in great demand. Upon meeting her and being impressed by her skills and cosmopolitan éclat, Sophie and Adam Gimbel offered her a job making hats for the Salon Moderne, upping her Bendel salary to $125 per week. "Don't ever learn English, you'll sell more hats that way," Adam Gimbel told Mother, and she more than amply followed his advice.

Gimbel's decision to blend his wife's talents with Tatiana's was a dazzling success. Within a few years, Sophie's only competitors in American made-to-order clothes would be Mainbocher and Hattie Carnegie, and Tatiana's only possible rivals were Lily Daché and John Fredericks. Sophie and Tatiana's motley crew of customers included stars such as Claudette Colbert, Marlene Dietrich, Madeleine Carroll, Irene Dunne, and Edith Piaf; the socialites Mrs. E. F. Hutton, Mrs. Pierre Du Pont, Mrs. James Van Allen, and Mrs. Charles Henry of Philadelphia; assorted magnates such as Estée Lauder, Betsy Bloomingdale, Mrs. Darryl Zanuck, Mrs. Walter Annenberg and her daughter, Enid Haupt, Harriet Deutch (heir to the Rosenwald-Sears-Roebuck fortune), and Anita May (wife of the founder of the May company.)

Tatiana and Sophie's talents complemented each other perfectly. Tatiana's spry creations added a dash of intrigue and wit to Sophie's very traditional comme il faut elegance; a typical touch of her whimsy was to garnish a winter hat with a thermometer or a tiny revolving weather vane in lieu of the traditional feather. Yet her headgear remained ideally suited to 1940s ultrafeminine tastes, for she designed with an intimate sense of women's needs, aiming to make them both seductive and comfortable. Tatiana's fame, according to *The Christian Science Monitor*, was based on the fact that "[her] hats, whether they are large or reduced to almost nothing at all—have a way of fitting on the head. Tatiana . . . blends imagination with a taste for color and material and an unfailing sense of how her hats will look and feel when they are put on." By contrast, "Lily Daché's and John Fredericks's designs were far more outlandish and contrived," says cultural historian Rosamond

Bernier, who bought a half-dozen hats from my mother in 1945. "Tatiana's were never outré, her taste was impeccable, and she had a laser eye for what was most becoming to your particular features."

Both Sophie and Tatiana, who became the closest of friends, were workaholics and rarely went out at noon, so they lunched every day in Sophie's office. Helen O'Hagan, who was then the Salon Moderne's press officer, relates that both Sophie and Tatiana loved to talk, but even at those office lunches Tatiana tried to remain the center of attention. "She carried on about whom she'd met at dinner parties that week and who should be sat where at different kinds of social functions," O'Hagan says. "Then the two of them would discuss their bridge game for the following Saturdays and Sundays, whom they'd enlisted to play. When Tatiana had hogged the stage for a bit too long Sophie would lean over and poke her knee and say 'Tats, enough! Let someone else speak!'" Even during lunch, O'Hagan relates, Tatiana always sat in a chair that directly faced the Salon Moderne's entrance, keeping it wide open so that she could quickly jump up and catch any customer who wandered into the salon at lunchtime.

When a client did come in, the dictatorial Tatiana seldom let her choose a hat. She allowed no fingering or perusing of models: She immediately imposed her preference, and that was that. "Tatiana simply brought something out and said, 'Thees ees hat for you,'" said our close family friend Ethel Woodward de Croisset, who frequented the salon in the late 1940s. "And then she put it on your head and made a loud one-word comment in French, such as 'Formidable!' or 'Divin!'"

But my mother's success as arbiter of fashion was based on cultural and social skills that far transcended her craft as a designer. Like Elsa Schiaparelli, who created some of the 1930s' most inventive headgear, Mother had studied sculpture before learning the millinery trade. Steeped in art history under Uncle Sasha's tutelage, Tatiana raided some of the world's most beautiful paintings for her designs: She modeled many of her snoods and wimples upon the coifs of the women in Vermeer, her favorite painter of all time; Velázquez and Goya were equally constant sources of inspiration ("Passementerie trimming brought a Spanish look to a bicorne of black Persian," *The New York Times* said in its review of Tatiana's fall 1950 collection. "The

Tatiana in the early 1940s, publicity shot for Saks Fifth Avenue.

Spanish note is a favorite with this designer.") The floral abundance of Russian folk art and the highly charged aesthetic of Russian Orthodox liturgy may have been equally powerful influences in her work, as they were in her penchant for mammoth costume jewelry. Moreover, hats were always more regimented by social protocol than any other vestment, and Tatiana's stint as a diplomat's wife had enabled her to master a code that was still central to midcentury elegance: the fittingness of each chapeau to a particular social occasion. Her expansive character was also ideally suited to becoming an all-

Tatiana in 1948 making hats in the hot, cramped workroom at Saks Fifth Avenue.
Photo by Constantin Joffe.

around adviser and confessor for hundreds of New York women. Not unlike hairdressers, who often become their clients' closest confidants, she was a gifted cosmetician and lay psychiatrist: An important source of her success was that she was able to convince plain women that they were beautiful. "I listen to problems and solve by putting flowers on heads," she used to say about her customers. "They parade out of salon full of confidence, like prize racehorses."

However lavish the decor and opulent the customers of her Salon Moderne, my mother's workshop at Saks Fifth Avenue was more akin to a Dickensian nineteenth-century sweatshop. Located in the extreme right corner of the third floor, close to the elevators, not far from where Gaultier, Ungaro et al. currently hang their wares, it was a dark, low-ceilinged room, with no cross-ventilation, that in summer became barely tolerable. At either end of two long horizontal worktables there sat some twelve seamstresses who executed my mother's designs. Tatiana had to produce sixty models each year, thirty for the spring collection, thirty for the fall. The atmosphere of her atelier was made electric by her concentration and her awesome speed of execution, but it always remained serene. She was notoriously generous and thoughtful with her assistants, immediately sending them home when they were beginning a cold or had child-care problems; they were awed and endlessly amused by her. And each time I came into Tatiana's peaceful, industrious workroom, I felt a comforting sense of continuity from seeing that she designed her creations in precisely the same way she had in Paris: Ethereal, ruby-lipped, black-clad Mother sat alongside her workers at one end of the long tables, holding a bunch of pins in her mouth, staring at her reflection in a large stand-up mirror as she cut and sculpted felts and draped voiles and jerseys onto her blond hair. My most striking memory of Mother at work has to do with the delicacy and uncanny swiftness of her fingers. However crippled and clawlike her right hand, which remained misshapen by her nearly fatal car accident, it flew over the cloth as rapidly as a hummingbird, fashioning the most delicate pleats, crimps, flutings, and tucks with the deftness of a microsurgeon.

By the fall of 1942, a few months after Tatiana had started to work at Saks, Alex's career at Condé Nast also began to take off. Once again, he received a crucial promotion by playing all the right cards, charming all the right people.

In the spring of 1942, Condé Nast, who had a serious heart condition that he wished to keep absolutely secret, dictated a confidential letter to his secretary naming Iva Patcevitch to succeed him as president of the company in the event of his death. I suspect Alex was informed of the contents of that letter, or perhaps he simply sensed what was in the air. All I know is that he must have started to pay his court to Patcevitch that very spring, for it was in June of 1942 that Pat and his regal, British-born wife, Nada, materialized in my life. I was staying at the house near Port Jefferson we had rented that particular summer, being minded by our housekeeper, Sally, and had gone out for a walk to the village. "The Patcevitches have arrived!" Sally called

VOGUE

Decorating Issue

TASTE and TASTE

in fashions and furniture

Price 35 Cents
40 Cents In Canada

April 15, 1945
Incorporating Vanity Fair

April 1945, a few weeks before the end of World War II,
Vogue cover with Tatiana hats. Photo by John Rawlings.

out to me as I returned. "They're looking for you! Go down and find them
at the beach." The house was set on top of a high dune, and I ran down the
steep flight of wooden stairs to the beach, excited to have some company
on a weekday. A few hundred yards down the shore, a handsome couple
was walking toward me, waving. As we reached one another, they stooped

down to embrace me, expressing great joy in my company, and I remembered having seen them once or twice at Alex and Mother's earlier that year. From then on, Uncle Pat and Aunt Nada, as I was bidden to call them, became an indissoluble part of our lives.

It was already clear that Pat, once he had assumed the directorship of Condé Nast, would rise to a higher social and economic position in New York society than any other Russian émigré of his generation. So no wonder that Alex saw to it that he and Pat become best friends and no wonder that he urged Mother to become best friends with his boss's wife, the notoriously difficult Nada. The Patcevitches spent a great deal of time at Port Jefferson that summer of 1942, where Pat taught me chess and Nada helped me with my summer homework—they were yet another of those child-loving, childless couples who looked on me for some years as an adopted daughter. The result of this new intimacy was that shortly after Condé's death on September 19, 1942, when Pat became president of the company, Alex became one of *Vogue*'s two art editors: The other one—Arthur Weiser, the longest-tenured person in the art department—had been there for a whopping twenty-three years. In view of the fact that Alex had worked at the magazine for only twenty months, the promotion Pat offered Alex was remarkable.

Having seethed at Alex ever since his decision to fire him had been unintentionally countermanded by Nast, and having been further enraged by Alex's privileged standing at the magazine, *Vogue*'s art director, the Terrible Turk, Dr. Agha, was of course incensed by this promotion. Agha nursed his griefs in silence until December of 1942: A military draft was expected in those months, and Agha hoped that Alex, like many other young men at the magazine, might be called to military service. But alas for Agha, in December Alex was classified 4F because of his ulcers. So early in 1943, Agha marched into Patcevitch's office and issued an ultimatum: "Either Liberman goes," he said, "or I go." Agha, however, seemed to have vastly overestimated his popularity at Condé Nast, which, to his surprise, turned out to be zilch: It had been undermined by his cynical and haughty manner and by the extravagant salary he had been demanding—$40,000, the equivalent of nearly a half-million dollars in our time. Pat's decision was a rapid one. A few days later, he announced Agha's resignation and offered the thirty-year-old

Alexander Liberman another promotion by appointing him to take Agha's place as *Vogue*'s art director.

Within a few months, *Vogue* had acquired a far more modernist style. To use Alex's own phrase, it had more of a "cinematic flow." Titles and captions, now printed in tabloid-style typeface, became far more immediate and more informative—as Condé Nast had wished, Alex was moving *Vogue* in the direction of a news magazine. Alex was helped by the historical moment, for the United States' entry into war necessitated more serious content, brought hundreds of thousands of women into the workforce, and imposed a novel informality and democracy on women's clothes. American designers such as Claire McCardell and even, in the higher price brackets, Valentina were emphasizing fluidity and spontaneity over elitist hauteur. Alex, a protofeminist if ever there was one, believed in making a magazine for women who worked, and he was the right man at the right time, for, as he put it, "the war destroyed old fantasies of leisure." Alongside staid European talents such as George Huyningen-Huene and Horst P. Horst, Alex hired young American photographers such as John Rawlings and Frances McClaughlin to give zest to the new, informal fashions.

Alex also recruited a *Life* magazine news photographer, Gjon Mili, who had been boldly exploring the technique of strobe lighting, to do fashion shoots. Startled readers suddenly saw models pushing shopping carts in supermarkets or running down the beach beneath an arc of water drops. In the following years, he equally encouraged Erwin Blumenfeld, another European refugee who like Alex had rebelled against "visions of loveliness," to apply his bold techniques of solarization to fashion photographs, resulting in some of the most avant-garde covers *Vogue* had yet run. Above all, the entire magazine became more politicized, more in touch with current events. As soon as he began to run the show at *Vogue*, Alex talked the cautious, tradition-bound Edna Chase into publishing Cecil Beaton's pictures of bombed-out sites in London. He assigned the great photographer Lee Miller, a friend of his and of Tatiana's since prewar days, to cover the war in Europe. She became one of the first correspondents to document, in pictures, the tragedy of the Nazis' death camps, and perhaps Alex's finest, most courageous act of persuasion was to convince Mrs. Chase to publish them.

Country lunch in France, early 1950s. From left to right, Gitta Sereny Honeyman,
Irving Penn, Tatiana and Francine, Don Honeyman, Aunt Sandra Iacovleff.

Finally, there was Alex's discovery and advocacy of a young American
photographer named Irving Penn, whose career was one of Alex's finest
achievements. In the early 1940s, Penn, a very private man with a gentle,
self-effacing manner, was an aspiring painter who had been supporting
himself as art director of Saks Fifth Avenue, a job arranged for him by his
favorite teacher at art school, Alexei Brodovich. With an uncanny sense of
Penn's great gifts, Alex hired the diffident young artist in 1943 as his personal
assistant, with the special assignment of thinking up ideas for *Vogue* covers.
However the photographers to whom Penn presented his suggestions—
Horst, Blumenfeld, Rawlings, Beaton—kept turning his ideas down. So Alex
suggested that Penn take those pictures himself, gave him a space in the *Vogue*
studio adjoining the Condé Nast office, and hired an assistant who would
help him master the eight-by-ten studio camera. The resulting pictures—
marked with Penn's fastidiously premeditated compositions, his austere clarity of vision, and his highly innovative methods of printing—turned out to
be the most groundbreaking images of the 1940s. Alex's astute insight into
Penn's potential gifts as a photographer and his championing of him were

all the more remarkable because of the formidable opposition initially shown to Penn's work by Mrs. Chase and the rest of the magazine's editorial staff. It took only a few years to prove Alex right: By the 1950s, Penn was being recognized as one of the most original and powerful photographers of his time.

Throughout the following decades, Alex continued to offer Penn unflinching support as he branched out from his early still lifes to a great variety of genres: There were his portraits of celebrities—also thought of as "shocking" by the rest of the *Vogue* staff—taken against backdrops of worn, scuffed carpets. There were the documentary photos of ethnic groups from all over the world—Peru, Extremadura, New Guinea, Tibet—posed against the stark white walls of the portable studios with which Penn traveled throughout four continents. ("Go to the other side of the world and bring us back something delectable for the Christmas issue," Alex told Penn every summer. "I'll save you fourteen pages.") And there were the fashion shots with which *Vogue* more violently subverted traditional notions of the "ladylike" than did any other women's magazine of its time: a girl sitting on a bar stool, her shoes kicked off, her hair as rumpled as if she'd just gotten out of bed; a woman delicately removing a shred of tobacco from her tongue. Praising such typical images of Penn's oeuvre for revealing "the imperfections of actual life," Alex championed, and helped to create, a great American artist.

Over the years, Penn also became as close a friend as Alex had in the world, although in Penn's view it was very difficult to be "close" to Alex. "He wasn't a person of true relationships," Penn told me a few years after Alex's death. "We were professional friends. It was a relationship of mutual need. . . . People were useful to him or they were not. . . . I was useful. But did I really get to know him in our fifty years of almost daily collaboration? At those moments over lunch when I felt we'd finally made some kind of close contact he'd look at his watch and get that funny look in his eyes which let me know that he had to see someone more important."

"However, what a wonderful collaborator he was, I miss him terribly," Penn added. "We could laugh together at the absurdity of the world we worked in, and I so enjoyed it when he told me off: 'Why did you send me that lousy picture?' He was usually right. Now I live alone in a tower of success, with no one to laugh with me."

One odd aspect of my parents' careers was that Mother never had an inkling of what Alex's life at Condé Nast was like and did not want to know. Not once during Alex's half century at the company did she ever visit his office. "Why go, I know just what ees like," she'd growl when asked about her lack of interest in his work life. "Ees like one beeg ice cube." And Alex's office was indeed a bare white cube, the glacial austerity of which I always associated with his Calvinist upbringing. There stood nothing in it beyond a few chairs and a black Parsons table swept clear of everything but a pad of white paper and one sharpened pencil; there were seldom any mementos or artworks in sight (in the earlier years he kept a photo of Mother in a drawer, and in later decades he hung a few pictures of his public sculptures on the wall.) Alex was notoriously fussy about maintaining this icy order. Si Newhouse, who in Alex's last thirty years was his closest associate, reports that the only time he experienced Alex's bad temper was on an occasion when he put his coffee mug on Alex's desk. "Take that away!" Alex cried out. "There was a strange Puritan squeamishness about him," Si recalls.

There was an instance in which Mother's Oriental aloofness from Alex's working life worked to her detriment—the one time in their decades of married life when Alex was rumored to have an affair. The lady in view was Brigitte Tichenor, *Vogue*'s accessories editor, a long-stemmed British-born beauty with large azure eyes and sumptuous black hair. I was then a young working woman just out of college, and, having set her cap at Alex, she did everything to use me as a bridge to him, lunching and dining me assiduously to find out which breach in his marriage she could rush into. This tactic having utterly failed, Tichenor started the rumor mill going by inviting Alex repeatedly to very long lunches at Chambord—the then most-fashionable restaurant—at which she held him for more than two hours by talking to him exclusively about his paintings, which no one else in those years seemed interested in discussing. ("Here was this cultivated, beautiful woman paying court to me," Alex candidly recalled years later. "It was novel, and rather agreeable.") One summer, unable to get him out for a night on the town after a year of wooing, Tichenor boarded the same boat to France as the Libermans. This is where Tatiana finally received news of the lady's assault—she heard about it from Philippe de Croisset, a very close friend who headed Condé Nast's French branch and who had heard an office rumor that Alex was about to divorce Tatiana for Tichenor. Mother's shrewd countertactic was to be utterly charming to the interloper, who, seeing no hope in sight, finally abandoned her pursuit and partied for the rest of the sea voyage with a younger crowd in cabin class.

Even though Alex was probably the youngest art director in New York when Patcevitch entrusted him with the design of *Vogue*, he exuded self-confidence and was popular with the great majority of the staff. The ultimate democrat, he was unfailingly thoughtful and prodigally generous toward the more menial workers on the staff—secretaries, technicians, company chauffeurs—who all revered him. There were two particular terms in Alex's charm factory that he used as tools of seduction: one was "noble," the other was "dear friend." "This is a *noble* cover," he'd say to John Rawlings in praise of a shot of bathing suits for a summer issue. "This is a *noble* layout," he'd say about a pleasant double page of winter boots executed by an underling in the art department. ("Every time he used the word 'noble' I felt, *yuck*," said the late Richard Avedon, who had no love lost for Alex and was one of several who derided the word.) As for the dreaded phrase "Dear Friend," it was used by Alex when he had a particularly harsh criticism to dole out. "You curled up in your boots as soon as you heard those two words," says Lord Snowdon, who as Anthony Armstrong-Jones worked extensively with Alex in the 1960s and '70s. "They might take the following form—'Dear friend, you know how deeply I admire you, but those last photographs of yours were a total disaster.'" "When he said 'Dear friend,' you knew you were in deep shit," said Helmut Newton, one of the many experimental photographers whose work Alex championed early in their careers, and who appreciated Alex's love for pornography. (Alex's hero was Larry Flynt, Newton reports, and Alex often repeated Flynt's motto, "Show the Pink," when sending Newton out to a shoot.)

Alex's relations with persons in the company's higher power structure were more complex. Within a few years, several of the Silver Fox's colleagues detected darker sides of his character, which had to do with the extremely calculated way in which he kowtowed to people who were useful to him. "Alex instantly jumped into the lap of anyone who enabled him to increase his power," says Rosamond Bernier, whose friendship with the Libermans went back to 1944. "His charm was in operation full-time toward those whose support he needed." "No one knew better than Alex which way the wind was blowing," says Daniel Salem, a close associate who was Condé Nast's chief financial officer for some thirty years. "He rarely displayed any true conviction or loyalty of any kind, he tended to go for whatever was useful to him, and perhaps this is what made him so indestructible."

Gitta Sereny was struck by Alex's extreme emphasis on every kind of outward appearance. In 1949, Gitta married an American photographer working for *Vogue* in London, Donald Honeyman. After Honeyman was called back to the magazine's New York office in 1952, soon after their first child was born, the young couple, whose finances were strained, took an apartment at Riverside Drive and West 101st Street. "Alex was totally appalled by that address," Gitta recalls, "'You're mad, Gitta,' he told me over lunch the day after we'd signed the lease. 'Do you want Don to make a career at *Vogue*? He'll never make it if you're not living on the east side.'" "How do you expect us to live on the east side on our tiny income?" Gitta asked Alex. "There's always the bank," coolly answered Alex, who for many years lived on loans from his company and his friends.

Colleagues were also struck by Alex's byzantine talent for self-promotion. "He was as arduous a self-promoter as you can meet," says Snowdon, "very slippery, like an eel, always wheeling and dealing for himself." Even Si Newhouse, his boss of later years, who for four decades was inseparable from Alex, admits that there was "much calculation and self-interest" in the way the Silver Fox ran his life. And some midcentury colleagues in the fashion world who truly disliked Alex even denied—not very convincingly—that he had any originality in his career as art director. "He was a totally false, utterly unoriginal man," says Pierre Bergé, the brilliant Parisian who founded the Yves Saint-Laurent couture house and ran it for many decades, and was a close friend of Tatiana's. "He never had an idea of his own. He swiped ideas from everyone else. Even his typography, his journalistic ideas—he got them all from Brodovich. Now *there* was a man with vision!"

Tatiana, by contrast, was seen as a far more authentic person. "Whereas Alex's warmth was often Machiavellian and feigned, Tatiana's warmth was totally genuine," says Gray Foy, who as the lifelong companion of Leo Lerman, Condé Nast's principal cultural adviser, was close to the Libermans for more than fifty years. "Tatiana was frequently hurtful but utterly forthright, she was incapable of subterfuge. . . . Hers was a straight road with a few cul-de-sacs, whereas Alex followed a map full of secret labyrinths."

Finally, most of Alex's colleagues can elaborate on his extreme capriciousness and on his occasional streak of nastiness. "He was an incredible perfectionist, but this perfectionism could make him terribly volatile," says Mary-Jane Poole, who worked in Alex's office in the mid- and late 1940s and even remembers bringing him, at 11:00 A.M., the daily glass of milk he needed for his ulcers. "He enjoyed tearing up an entire issue of *Vogue* on a Friday afternoon, forcing the editors to work at the office throughout the weekend to abide by his whims. And he also had his moments of cruelty—to create excitement, he would torture editors by pitting them against each other and watch them fight it out." Tina Brown, whom Alex chose to be editor of *Vanity Fair*, speaks of his "destructive, Salieri-like streak." "Just as Salieri was jealous of Mozart," she notes, "Alex was often envious of people of true talent. . . . When he sensed that someone had risen too high in the esteem of Si Newhouse, for instance, he'd say to me, 'So-and-so is second-rate, I must go and plant the poison.' And inevitably, he'd achieve a measure of success."

The more sensitive Condé Nast staffers could be deeply wounded by Alex's machinations. "There was a definite streak of sadism in him," said Despina Messinesi.

He was the most underhanded man imaginable, and he could also be brutal, he could say terrible things to you face-to-face, his voice, his expression never changed as he criticized you, which made it all the worse, he'd make you feel very stupid, make you feel like a worm. It was not unusual to see people coming out of his office crying. . . . At times he would humiliate people publicly, too, he would make them sink to the floor. . . . It may all have been done in order to make them work harder, but he did have a highly unusual ability to be intentionally mean.

"And yet the following day," Messinesi added nostalgically, "he could be very sweet and remember that your mother had been sick."

Needless to say, it is only the Dr. Jekyll aspect of his character—the prodigally kind and tender one—that Alex displayed to Mother and me when we began to live as a true family in our new home, at 173 East Seventieth Street. "Didn't we have the luck of the devil finding him," Mother whispered tenderly to me every few months for the following many decades, when he was out of earshot. "Didn't we have the most amazing luck?"

SIXTEEN

Our Home I

Our brownstone on Seventieth Street, which we moved into in December 1942 and in which Tatiana and Alex remained for nearly a half century, was the first place in which I came to know a genuine, relatively traditional two-parent family. It was the house in which I celebrated all Christmases between my twelfth and my twenty-third year, the house in which I studied for all school exams and wrote out my college applications, the house in which my friends and I had our first drinking bouts and nursed our first hangovers, the house from which I evicted my first rejected lovers, the house in which I was courted by my husband, the house in which we celebrated our marriage, the house from which I left for the hospital to give birth to each of our children. It was also the house from which Alex and Tatiana, in their last decades, left for their numerous stays in hospitals, the house from which my mother would leave a final time to die in the solitude of an intensive-care unit. It was the site in which I experienced most rites of passage, and to this day 173 East Seventieth Street remains a radiant center of my universe, the place where most of my dreams occur, a habitation I still cannot pass, sixty years later, without a pang of intense nostalgia. For it is the house in which three nomads, scattered for decades by wars and revolutions, found their first resting place and their first roots.

173 East Seventieth Street is one of those traditional east-side brownstones of 1920s vintage, the first floor of which lies slightly below street level: One descends three steps toward two doors that, in our time, were painted white—on the left was the service door, flanked by a window that gives into the kitchen. To the right was the entrance door, through which one accessed a vestibule, the right wall of which held a large mirror, under which was set a small baroque console. This piece of furniture already brings up a precise memory, because it is on that console that I first read the news of Alex's and Mother's marriage.

I believe we spent our first night at Seventieth Street on a Sunday of November 1942. The following afternoon, as I came home from school a bit later than usual—at 4:30, after ballet class—I found a half dozen or so telegrams on the console, a few of them already opened. I glanced at them and saw phrases such as "Felicitations on your wedding day and all affectionate wishes" and "All fondest wishes dearest Tatiana and Alex and decades of happiness." I was stunned, hurt, enraged. They'd off and gotten married earlier that very day, without telling me a word, without inviting me to the ceremony—once more they'd excluded me! I was angry rather than sad, but in my habitually diplomatic way I concealed my feelings, composed myself for their arrival, and greeted them with smiles and my own tender felicitations. It is only years later that I realized how hilariously Mother's often hypocritical sense of protocol had dictated the timing. Now that she was about to live virtually under the same roof as Alex, share the same entrance door, it was de rigueur that they be officially married.

There's another detail of Alex's and Mother's wedding, related by their only witnesses, Beatrice and Fernand Leval, which is telling of my mother's compulsively workaholic nature: To follow the brief legal ritual downtown, the Levals had organized a little wedding lunch at the Pavillon restaurant. My mother did not attend it. She was expecting a "very important client" at 2:00 P.M.—a Hollywood producer who, she hoped, would commission her to make hats for his next film—and she did not want to run the risk of being a second late. Sentiment be damned! Alex, Beatrice, and Fernand held the wedding celebration without her.

Back to my house tour: Walking past the console down a short corridor,

Alex, Tatiana, Francine and the housekeeper Sally,
shortly after moving to Seventieth Street.

straight ahead of you was the dining room, a space mostly furnished, for the next decade, with the same white metal table and chairs that "my parents"— I can finally call them that—had bought at Macy's upon our arrival in the States. The floor of the dining room was covered in a vinyl that emulated marble; walls were painted a stark white, as they were throughout the house; at the far end of the room was a large, multipane window that looked out onto one of those charming little gardens common to Upper East Side houses. Its windowseat was upholstered in, of course, white vinyl, and to the left of that was a large comfortable chair, covered, uncharacteristically, in a gray cloth fabric, in which Alex took his breakfast every morning.

Shortly after we had moved to the house—I was then twelve—it became a habit for Alex and me to have breakfast together in the dining room on Saturdays and Sundays—my mother would linger in bed until

noon or so, reading a book or catching up on world news through French-
and Russian-language newspapers. So it was Alex and I alone, he sitting by
the window with his little tray of Cream of Wheat and tea, and I at the
round white metal table in the middle of the room. And the occasions
we shared in that dining room were the most cherished moments of my
youth. For over the years, as he listened with intense interest to any issue I
brought up, fixing his green gaze on me as if my problems were the only ones
that would concern him throughout that entire morning, I increasingly
looked on him as a confidant as well as a role model, and offered him a kind
of blind trust that I would not confer on anyone else for a long time to
come.

At times, these were mainly educational encounters, at which Alex
quizzed me on diverse facts of history or literature, searching out just how
much I was learning at Spence; once his queries were answered, he'd recommend a few books he felt I should read that semester to round out my education. (They were often hopelessly dated duds, such as R. D. Blackmore's
Lorna Doone, which had captivated him as a romantic thirteen-year-old in
British boarding school.) At other times, our reunions in the dining-room
became joint ventures of exploration and decision making, such as that
spring morning of 1951, before my last year of college, when he suggested
I take a break from the summer jobs I'd had since graduating from Spence
and go to summer school instead. As we were discussing this over the Sunday papers, our eyes simultaneously came across an ad for Black Mountain
College's summer session: That's it! we exclaimed together upon perusing the
roster of artists and writers who were teaching there that year: Robert
Motherwell, Ben Shahn, Charles Olson among them. The Black Mountain
experience was to change my life.

As I grew older, the dining room served as a ground for Alex's attempts
to explore my inner state of mind: It was there that he inquired into my
relationship with such-and-such a man and, later, probed my attitudes
toward my work and, after my marriage, posed questions concerning my
children's conduct and education. This room was indeed the site of our
most private, sensitive encounters. I cannot forget, for instance, the sight of
Alex, in the autumn of 1956, sitting in his chair by the dining-room win-

dow every morning, waiting for me to return from my daily 7:00 A.M. sessions at the psychoanalyst's. I was twenty-six and had just spent two tormented years in France that had been plagued by poor health, unrewarding jobs, and a disastrous love affair. Having decided I must go into treatment, Alex had arranged for me to see a rigorous Freudian. Although he'd developed a habit, as his position at Condé Nast grew more exalted, of leaving the house before 8:00 A.M. to get to the office before any of his colleagues, during those months he somehow felt a need to check up on me each morning. As I came home he sat on his chair by the window, his hands meekly folded on the briefcase that rested on his lap. He would look at me a bit shyly, as if to say, "I hope you won't think I'm probing," and ask, "How did it go today?" "Oh excellently," I'd inevitably reply to make him happy, even after I'd lain on the couch bawling for an entire hour or raging silently at the doctor. Only after such an exchange did Alex pat his briefcase firmly, saying, "Good, good," and go off to Condé Nast after giving me a kiss, looking very satisfied. The deep interest Alex took in my sessions with Dr. Norvell Lamarr, of blessed memory, led me to think that notwithstanding his assertions that he had never felt the need for analysis, he might have secretly missed it and had a vicarious satisfaction from carefully observing the progress of mine.

Upon my getting married and moving to Connecticut, Alex and Mother decreed that my old childhood room on the third floor was to serve as my growing family's pied-à-terre whenever we came to New York. They would turn out to be the most fanatically devoted of grandparents; and the Seventieth Street dining room became the training-ground for my own children's manners and provided the setting for many legends about the uncouthness of their early youth. Recalled and giggled about until Alex's last months of life, for instance, was that lunchtime when my younger son, Luke, a noted carnivore even at the age of five, signaled his rebellion against the rigorous this-fork-that-spoon protocol imposed by my mother, who had been trying to teach him how to serve himself daintily from the platter when it was passed to him by her butler. When the platter finally reached his left shoulder, Luke simply leaned down and sank his teeth into the leg of lamb, lifting it a few inches off the platter. For a few more years, my mother decided to fix the children's plates herself, but Alex, who greatly enjoyed recalling the anarchic moments of his own childhood, gleefully belabored the incident for decades.

The dining room at Seventieth Street was of course indivisible from its adjacent kitchen. Both were run by the marvelously stern Mabel Moses, who in the company of her seductive husband, Matthew, took over the household the day we moved in. Mabel was then thirty-one—as of this writing she is ninety-three and thrives in retirement in Las Vegas. She was a spectacled, slender-waisted, yet solidly built woman with hair neatly tucked into a big, round bun, who exuded energy and determination. Mabel was laconic and chronically distrustful. She did not have a ready smile and could be very dour, preferring to signal her approval or disapproval through facial expressions, such as mimicking people's uppitiness with a raise of her brow and a twitch of her mouth. But if you truly pleased her with some good news, she would burst into peals of throaty, jovial laughter, stomping her feet and shouting, "Get out of here!" ("I just became editor of the school paper, Mabel." "Get out of here!" *Stomp stomp.* "Cleve and I just got engaged, Mabel." "Get out of here!" *Stomp stomp.*) Like most good cooks, Mabel was maddeningly set in her ways: Every spoon and fork had to be left precisely in their habitual places—"Don't you mess with *my* kitchen" was her refrain to me for over four decades whenever I'd come in to have a taste of her delicious fare. For Mabel was an exceptionally talented chef, versatile enough to have assimilated any number of French and Russian dishes into her originally Yankee repertoire. Within six months of being in our employ she was making the most succulent beef Stroganoff in town, cutting up the highest-quality fillet into long, thin strips which she sauteed very briefly before finishing them off with strong broth, sour cream, and dill. Her *gigot aux flageolets*, punctuated with enough paper-thin slices of garlic to faintly perfume the entire roast, was also a marvel. Her roast beef and Yorkshire pudding were of equal perfection, the batter rising to five brown inches. Needless to say, her American staple dishes, such as southern fried chicken, which Mother adored, were as peerless as her robustly fragrant apple pie, the flaky and featherlight crust of which haunts my culinary imagination to this day.

As a teenager, I was not interested in kitchen skills, believing that they would be unfitting to my "liberated" woman's life. But how many other skills did Mabel teach me in the bargain! She was yet another adopted parent to me, stern but doting—"There hadn't been much mothering in her life," she'd explain to my friends decades later, "so I decided to take over." She taught me how to rinse my hair with vinegar to give it proper sheen; to handle my periods, an issue my mother would have been hopelessly evasive about; and

The one and only, beloved Mabel Moses.

to keep boys at bay. ("Don't you do no foolish stuff with my baby," she would growl at any suitor who looked as if he might have a trace of libidinal impulse toward me.) She was the only driving teacher I ever had, and I still think of her when I tap the brake pedal very lightly when going down a snowy hill or dim my lights when driving through a thick fog. She taught me to moderate my alcohol intake, and upon episodes that she found out long before my hectically busy parents, she gave me my first scoldings about using it to excess. Although she herself was a teetotaler, when I hadn't managed to hold my booze properly—a frequent problem among my peers in the Eisenhower

era—she became a walking encyclopedia of hangover cures. Mabel even taught me to write thank-you notes, offering me, the Christmas I turned sixteen, my first set of engraved stationery. This was a skill I could never have learned from my seignorial parents, who actually enjoyed boasting—such was their arrogance—that they had never once written a thank-you note to anyone. (This uncouthness hardly went unnoticed by their acquaintances. Many were the January evenings when, sitting alone at home, I'd have to field calls from Mrs. So-and-So, irately asking whether the Libermans had received the chocolates, the begonias, the crystal vase, which had been shipped to them at Christmas. My parents greeted my reports of such calls—I'd usually cover for them, saying, "Why I'm *sure* they didn't receive it"—with disdainful shrugs.)

Mabel did not initially come to us alone. Her husband, Matthew, was an ultrasuave, very pale Negro with considerable intellectual aspirations, as hedonistic and unctuously ingratiating as Mabel was offish and austere. He took painting lessons with Alex and asked me to lend him all the novels I'd read for school, of which Maupassant's were his favorites. He was very fond of his drink, a habit perhaps abetted by the considerable amount of leisure time he enjoyed when my parents were at work—a typical vision of the Moseses in our kitchen had Matthew sitting at the table by the window that gave out upon the street, smoking and reading his literary classics, while Mabel, all in white, stood by the stove, chopping, peeling, stirring. Matthew was also a reckless womanizer and was booted out of our household during my college years when my parents discovered that he had seduced, or been seduced by, one of my mother's canasta partners. (Mabel divorced him shortly afterward.) He lasted long enough, however, to cultivate my lifelong interest in black popular music, which began in my fourteenth year, when Matthew and Mabel started taking me to the Savoy Ballroom on Saturday nights. By the time I was fifteen, the Savoy—still off-limits for most whites in the late 1940s—had become my way of initiating many friends into the Harlem experience. John-Michael Montias, a favorite escort of my early adolescence, recalls one such Harlem adventure: "We were gyrating deliriously on the dance floor, the only white couple there, when I suddenly pulled you aside and pointed to the entrance and said, 'Watch out!' Your parents were standing at the entrance of the Savoy with a tall, cape-swathed Englishman, Cecil Beaton." John-Michael reports that we beat it to a side exit just in time, and my parents remained certain, for the rest of their lives, that they had been the first white New Yorkers to "discover" Harlem in the 1940s.

In my beloved Mabel's lexicon, my mother was known as "The Madam," I was referred to as "The Baby," and Alex was known as "The Boss." Boss indeed he was, for my mother was as incapable of calling a carpenter or plumber or hiring a cleaning woman as she was of overseeing my homework. And so with the same cool aplomb with which he checked on my report cards, booked all our dentists and doctors, imposed my curfew hours—a severe midnight all the way through high school—it was Alex alone who dealt with the occasionally decomposing roof, peeling walls, leaking pipes, and sometimes derelict domestic help. A true househusband before the word came into being, performing all the duties that Mother was too impatient or too bored to carry out, he would continue to function as the exclusive head of household into the final decades when he became chairman of Condé Nast, all the while nurturing his flourishing careers as painter, sculptor, and photographer. He clearly relished being both my mother's Superman and the absolute slave of her whims. He also enjoyed brandishing his virtues of domesticity and fidelity—though some of his colleagues found it in dubious taste, it always remained part of his PR image to vaunt his marital constancy and to boast that he had "never, never once," as he always put it, been tempted by another woman. ("How quaint to brag that he's never even looked at another woman!" the editor of French *Vogue* burst out once in the 1960s, when his devotion to Mother had become something of a publishing-world legend. "There's something rather vulgar about such a boast.")

One of Alex's domestic achievements, after the departure of Matthew Moses, was to hire a series of male household helpers who were as trustworthy as Mabel and could survive her imperious manner. Matthew's first replacement was a reclusive Frenchman from Brittany named Jean, a mysterious creature with no apparent friends or mistresses. A man of painstaking neatness and cleanliness, he came to us in 1951 or so, the year Elena Shuvalov's family vacated the fourth-floor apartment they had been renting from us since we'd moved into Seventieth Street. Jean lived in one of the two little bedrooms up there, a space he maintained in a state of monastic order. After returning from an outing of an hour and a half on his one day off, Sunday—we presumed he'd gone to Mass—for the rest of the day he remained in his room. The only sound we ever heard emerging from that space was a mild fluttering of little papers, as if he were wrapping many tiny objects in tissue or leafing quickly through a book of very thin pages. He was highly literate, with a rich store of biblical quotations that were applicable to any number of situations and often served to express his disapproval of the occasionally messy state of my own quarters. My college friends, when they came to stay at Seventieth Street, were hardly models of neatness. Upon such occasions, Jean would stand at the doorway of my room, examine the mayhem with a horrified air, and then, hands clasped, eyes turned skyward, exclaim, *"Sodome et Gomorrhe!"*

The dining room—and-kitchen complex presided over by Mabel and, during part of her long tenure, by Jean was the true power center of the house, the site that was crucial to my parents' social ascendance. For the noontime Saturday meals that were held at the Libermans' from the late 1940s on may well have been New York's first "power lunches" in the contemporary sense of that phrase. At their table, graced by Mabel's spectacular cuisine and our fine collection of wines (which were acquired, mostly as presents, from French vintners of our acquaintance), my parents charmed the prominent Parisians and New Yorkers who helped them to rise into the highest circles of the art and fashion world. Salvador Dalí, who notwithstanding his poses was a far nicer man and a more loyal friend than he's been made out to be, was trotted out every few weeks for show. Soon to be added was the Hollywood set, such as the designer Gilbert Adrian and his winsome, diminutive wife, Janet Gaynor, whose sweet voice had the pitch of a twelve-year-old's and who upon becoming Tatiana's client brought more of her silver-screen acquaintances to the salon: Claudette Colbert, Irene Dunne, Madeleine Carroll. By the late 1940s, there was also the international fashion, art, and entertainment crowd: Christian Dior, Hubert de Givenchy, Zizi Jeanmaire, Roland Petit, Patricia Lopez-Willshaw with her husband, her lover, and her husband's lover, and eventually "le génie Saint-Laurent," upon whom Mother doted. And there was the enduring roster of moneylenders, wealthy New York couples who periodically bailed out Alex at times of particularly straitened finances. Among them were the Levals; finance tycoon George ("Grisha") Gregory and his wife, Lydia, who had emigrated from the Soviet Union in 1932—Lydia's friendship with Tatiana was made all the closer by the fact that she had been an acquaintance of Mayakovsky in the year previous to his death; and Charlie and Genia Zadok, who served a double purpose: Charlie, who as chairman of the Saks Fifth Avenue/

The living room at Seventieth Street, late 1950s.

Gimbel's complex was Mother's boss, was also one of New York's most prominent collectors of contemporary art and so was particularly fawned upon by Alex.

Alex began to paint again on weekends in the late 1940s, and as he attempted to place his works in galleries, bands of art critics and dealers started to appear at their weekend lunches: Clement Greenberg, Harold Rosenberg, Betty Parsons, Andre Emmerich, Thomas Hess. And in the 1960s, as Alex began to show his work and strove to be accepted as an artist, the Libermans also began to collect the Big Artists at their table. Such were some of the guests who were *"réchauffés,"* "warmed up," as my parents put it, at the dining-room table, before being taken upstairs to the living room to be finished off with coffee and liqueurs.

East wall of the library at Seventieth Street, mid-1950s. The Légers were given to Alex when he photographed the painter for The Artist in His Studio.

As you walked up the first flight of stairs at 173 East Seventieth Street, your hand perhaps gliding on a round banister gleaming with high-gloss white enamel paint, you came upon a landing that gave, on the right, onto a spacious living room and, to the left, onto a room that over the years alternated as a library and as Alex's studio. The living room, accessed by a large oval-shaped doorway into which were set two large sliding doors, was an almost square room. Its three large windows, which looked out north upon the garden, were hung with a translucent gauze curtain that gently filtered the abundant light. Immediately to the left of the entrance was a love seat upholstered in white vinyl, and in the middle of that wall was a fireplace, which was used often in winter. ("Fireplace without logs," so

Tatiana at home at 173 East Seventieth Street,
photographed by Erwin Blumenfeld in the early 1940s.

Tatiana and Francine in the living room at Seventieth Street
sitting in front of a Dalí signed to Tatiana, 1944.

ran one of Mother's axioms, "is like man without erection.") An eighteenth-century Louis XV armchair that had stood in my father's study in our Paris apartment was set between the fireplace and the window, underneath which were bookshelves filled with volumes exclusively in French. (Their covers were all white or beige, as French editions still tend to be—Mother allowed no American books in that room because most would have ruined her beige-and-white color scheme.) To the right of the window there stood, from 1943 on, a large three-panel screen by Marcel Vertès depicting scantily clad women sporting Mother's hats. Most of the room's right wall was taken up by a large, deep Chinese-style settee upholstered in ivory damask and the two low, matching chaises flanking it—gifts from the Wileys, who had brought the set back from Beijing. These seating arrangements provided a perfect foil for mother's love of being photographed. Dressed in black satin pantsuits and hung with clanging jewelry, she often reclined on that couch, odalisquelike, as she posed for most every photographer of note who ever worked for Alex—Horst, Rawlings, Blumenfeld, Beaton—looking, in turn, bemusedly tender, icily impassive, or downright menacing.

Works by contemporary artists began to accrete on our walls within a few years of our moving to Seventieth Street. In 1943, Alex acquired an ink-and-wash abstraction entitled *She-Wolf* by a little-known painter named Jackson Pollock: He had attended an auction held at Knoedler to benefit a charitable cause and was appalled to hear the crowd tittering with laughter as the work came up. Infuriated that any artist's work should be derided, Alex bought it on the spot for $150. The collection grew by leaps and bounds after 1947, when Alex and Mother started to return to France for six weeks of the summer to attend the Paris fashion collections and to take a few weeks' vacation in Italy and at Va-et-Vient. It was then that Alex began his project of photographing the studios of all the major twentieth-century French artists (and the artists themselves, if they were still alive). Most of the photographs were published in *Vogue* and eventually were assembled into an epochal work of art-historical documentation, *The Artist in His Studio.*

Braque, Matisse, Picasso, Giacometti, Villon, Léger were just a few of the scores of artists to be documented by Alex in the following decade. Most of these masters gave Alex a "souvenir" or two in exchange for the privilege of seeing their work published in *Vogue.* (Léger, being an old friend of his mother's, was particularly generous: He told Alex to choose any black-and-white works he wished for fifty dollars, and he let a large gouache study for *La Grande parade* go for five hundred.) In the case of the stingier artists, such as Matisse or Picasso, Alex usually managed to wheedle something out of them for a few hundred dollars. Thus, by the late 1950s the walls of the Libermans' second floor were hung with a powerful collection of pictures, mostly works on paper, from which decades later, after my mother's death, Alex was able to make an immense profit.

But apart from the pleasure I took in these artworks, the living room was my least favorite part of the house. It had unhappy associations with my first year at Seventieth Street. In early December of 1942, soon after moving in, I'd nurtured a fantasy of our first Christmas in the new house, a fantasy admittedly as corny as the popular images—the covers of *The Saturday Evening Post* and of *Ladies' Home Journal*—from which it was derived. I imagined walking down Fifth Avenue just before the holiday carrying beautifully wrapped gifts for my parents, setting them prettily under the tree, carrying up the logs from the basement for a perfect fire. On Christmas Eve, we'd have some dinner brought in by the charming, impoverished Russian nobleman, Prince Trubetskoi, who eked out a tiny living catering Russian food such as blinis or cutlets Pozharskie. (His ways were as improvident as ours—upon delivering the food, he'd accept our invitation to tea and keep his taxi waiting for a half hour, ensuring the lack of any profit whatsoever.) We'd take our dinner up on trays—so my daydream continued—and share it as we sat in front of the blazing fire, just loving one another and taking turns opening our presents and reading Dickens. (How I thought my mother and Dickens were compatible remains a mystery.)

As Mabel used to put it whenever I was harboring an illusion, "Wake up, girl!" From that first Yuletide at Seventieth Street, I realized that such a fantasy was strictly chimerical; that Christmas, to them, would be yet one more occasion to heighten their status in society by holding large, glitzy gatherings. Our Yuletide parties, in fact, came to be particularly noted for Mother's insistence that everyone who set foot into our house receive a beautifully wrapped gift. So beginning on December 22, Alex and Mother and I gathered at the dining-room table in front of scores of sensibly priced presents—baubles purchased at Saks with Mother's discount, freebies acquired by Alex from *Vogue*'s beauty or jewelry departments. We sat there into the wee hours, wrapping the goodies and writing out the accompanying cards. Mother, who insisted on this frenzy but continued to plead her bad right arm as an excuse never to write again, would dictate to us: "*Boubouziki, écrivez! 'A Jane, Joyeux Noel, Tatiana et Alex.' 'A Cher Fernand, nos voeux les plus affectueux.'*" Alex and I would translate the greetings into English if need be and write long past midnight, while she wrapped the baubles in gold foil paper and finished them off with fancy knots of white satin ribbon. (The style of her Christmas wrappings remained the same until the end of her life—over the decades she hoarded so much white satin ribbon, so many dozens of gold paper rolls, that their leftovers stand in my closet to this day.)

So from the 1940s on, our Christmases became among the most fabulous in town, further enhancing the Libermans' reputation as the city's most charming and generous hosts. Living, in time-honored Russian fashion, in a state of perpetual debt, subsisting on the Levals' or the Gregorys' borrowed money, our dentists, doctors', and carpenters' bills yet unpaid, we placed beautifully wrapped gifts for some eighty persons under our ten-foot Christmas tree. Toward midnight, when the *distribution des cadeaux*, as we called it, began, I would constantly be sent into the bathroom to rewrap and relabel, for an unannounced friend, a gift someone else had brought us a few minutes earlier. So fabled, in fact, was the discrepancy between my parents' penury and their lavishness that fellow exiles even invented a Russian word to describe their zany form of prodigality: "*Libermánshchestvo.*"

By the early 1950s, when the original Yuletide party had set the model for gatherings held on many occasions throughout the year and "East Seventieth" had become a three-star Michelin stop on the international set's road map, the array of celebrities assembled at one of the Libermans' gatherings might include the following luminaries: Yul Brynner, a full-blooded Russian who had immigrated to the United States via Constantinople and had taken a great shine to Mother; Viola and Raymond Loewy, the industrial designer who had altered the look of midcentury America, from its Coca-Cola bottles to its Studebakers; Charles Addams and his ethereal harpist wife, Daphne; the writers John and Jane Gunther, who were summer neighbors and close friends of the former director of the Museum of Modern Art, Alfred Barr Jr. (the connection would prove most useful when Alex would relaunch his painting career); the birdlike Russian-born fashion designer Valentina, who lived for decades in a ménage à trois with her manager/husband, George Schlee, and his notoriously reclusive mistress of long standing, Greta Garbo; and from the fifties on, when her reputation as a collaborationist and as Spatz's wartime lover had faded, nasty-faced Coco Chanel, from whose mean little mouth a Gauloise was perpetually hanging. Whatever other Paris fashion tycoons were in town—Christian Dior,

Jacques Fath, Jean Balmain, Jean Dessés—would also attend. (The only exception was the aristocratic Cristóbal Balenciaga, who thought the Libermans were arriviste rabble and was seen solely in the company of Alex's archrival, Diana Vreeland of *Harper's Bazaar.*) This very partial listing should not exclude Marlene Dietrich, Mother's closest friend throughout the 1950s and 1960s, who made a point of appearing at the Libermans' parties in the plainest working clothes—jeans and a turtleneck, or even the white nursemaid's uniform she donned when wheeling her grandchildren's stroller to Central Park.

As for colleagues of Alex's from Condé Nast invited to Christmas Eve and any other parties, beyond the ever-present Leo Lerman, they would inevitably include Jessica Daves, a plump, plain, shy woman who in the 1950s succeeded Edna Woolman Chase as *Vogue's* editor in chief; Jessica used to absentmindedly chew canapés through the veils of the little black hats she always wore, creating a gooey mess of tuna fish or chopped liver, her hat gradually descending upon her face until she realized her gaffe and ran into the nearest bathroom, moaning, to clean up. There was also Babs Rawlings, *Vogue's* chief fashion editor, whose mouth was a gash of electric pink, whose platinum hair—touched up with a soupçon of clear boot polish to give it extra sheen and tightness—was swept vertically upward, like that of a cartoon character undergoing electric shock. She had extraordinarily beautiful, narrow feet, which she exhibited in open sandals throughout the coldest winter days, and always came in the company of her two long-haired dachshunds and of her husband, the gifted photographer John Rawlings, a man of exquisite physical beauty and immense politeness. Babs's manner was to jostle, strut, and clatter her way through any crowd, playing to the hilt the role of fashion oracle, making dramatic announcements about the season's fashion trends: "Small heads are *in* this year!" "Hems up by *at least* three inches this fall!" Also in evidence was photographer Horst P. Horst, a solidly built, genial German refugee with a crew cut who was the first to give me lessons in ballroom dancing; having discovered, when I was still a preteen, that I loved the fox-trot, he would have me put my feet on top of his own very wide, size-eleven shoes whenever one of our house warblers strummed a guitar, and off we'd go. Far quieter guests were Irving Penn and his beautiful, angelic wife, Lisa Fonssagrives, a couple of legendary devotion, who rushed home after half an hour to their son and their secluded Long Island house; and the equally reclusive Erwin Blumenfeld, an intellectual with a barbed black wit who never spent more than twenty minutes at any such philistine gathering.

And at the center of this multitude, of course, there was Mother, the group's centrifugal force: she whirled among her crowd like a tornado, beckoning the waiters to refill guests' glasses, making flamboyantly provocative cultural pronouncements—"Dostoevsky ees nothing but journalist"; "Everybody know women's brains are smaller than men's." She also bullied and advised: "Your hair awful thees natural color, return to platinum"; "You found dress at Bloomingdale's? Bloomingdale's ees for sheets." She often made shockingly outré comments: "I can tell by the way your wife walk," she declared to the dumbfounded Andre Emmerich, "whether she has clitoral or vaginal orgasm." Seldom had any such declarations made me feel more wretched than on a rainy evening during my college years, when I was trying to sneak upstairs to my room in the company of my Bryn Mawr roommate, who was still wearing her plastic raincoat. Mother immediately spied us and called out to my terrified friend in her most commandeering tone: "Take off raincoat! Eet look like contraceptive!"

The kinds of music played at our parties changed in the late forties, when Zizi de Svirsky, Claude Alphand, and Sasha de Manziarly returned permanently to France. After their departure, Mother's singing star was Prince David Chavchavadze, whose mother, Nina, was née Romanoff—"David is therefore of *royal* blood," my mother never tired of stressing. He often spent the night on our living-room couch when he was on army leave in the 1940s and later, when he finished his education at Yale. He was a handsome, impish second-generation émigré, six years my elder, on whom I had a fierce crush throughout my early adolescence; accompanying himself on guitar, he sang a stirring repertoire of Russian songs, mostly martial, patriotic ones such as "Moskva Moia," "Katiusha," and "Stenka Razin."

The most vivid memories I have of our Seventieth Street living room, in fact, are associated with its *Russianness:* the music that filled it from the late 1940s on; the White Russian colonels Mother engaged, in my teens, to make me memorize Russian poetry (to this day, thanks to her precaution, I can still recite the first stanzas of Pushkin's "Ruslan i Ludmila": *"Na luko-moria doub zelenyi /zlataia tsep na duby tom"*); and last but hardly least, the marathon weekend gambling sessions that took place on weekends. By 11:00 A.M. on any Saturday the Libermans were not holding a star-studded lunch, two bridge tables were set up in the near end of the living room. A half hour later, there would be Alex and Tatiana and Sophie Gimbel and Grisha and Lydia Gregory and a rotating roster of other players, slapping at the cards until 6:00 P.M., when everyone dispersed to run off to their respective evenings on the town. Silence reigned in the house throughout such Saturdays, interrupted mostly by the gentle whirring of cards being shuffled and an occasional shout, in any of three languages, of "I double!" or "I pass."

The favored games were bridge and, later, canasta. Extra guests occasionally came to play backgammon with Alex. Unlike Mother and Uncle Pat, who were fairly cautious players and dreaded losing money, Alex loved to gamble for high stakes and boasted that he was one of those desperate Dostoevskian gamblers who (not unlike my grandfather) are always ready to stake their last dollar on earth. Oscar de la Renta, who found the Libermans to have more "mystery and magic" than anyone he'd ever met, played weekend backgammon with Alex for many years and reports that the thrill of taking terrible risks far outweighed any discomfort he may have felt over losing large sums. "For over a decade Alex regularly and with enormous cheer lost several hundred dollars a week to me," says Oscar, a notoriously brilliant player. "He liked to joke that over the years he'd just about paid for my swimming pool."

This compulsive gambling, which also persisted from morning to night on summer weekends on Long Island during the years in which the Libermans shared a vacation home with the Patcevitches, had the result of somewhat severing me from my parents during my adolescence: Realizing that they had no time for me on the only two days on which we could have enjoyed some family life, I happily grafted myself onto other families, first those of my school chums and, during my first two years in college, the tribe of my sweet, handsome fiancé, Peter Burgard. Peter was the stepson of the great baritone Lawrence Tibbett, who had raised him as his own child. There were so many children by so many marriages in this prodigal, hard-drinking clan that the Tibbetts found it easiest to give total precedence to their offsprings' proclivities and whims. The Tibbetts' household was my first experience of a youth-centered family; and for two years their genial hospitality offered me the sense of nesting I'd missed with my busy parents and enough expensive dining, hangovers, and front-row opera seats to last me a lifetime.

Back to our own living room: the Libermans' prodigality toward outsiders led Seventieth Street to be known as a "typically Russian" household. And yet, did their hospitality give their parties that ambience of coziness, of gemütlichkeit, which Russians are so fabled for? Not in everyone's view. Kathleen Blumenfeld, whom Alex had hired to run the *Vogue* studios (she was the daughter-in-law of Erwin, the photographer), felt that my parents' gatherings were "totally artificial, exclusively devised to impress New Yorkers with the Libermans' hit parade of acquaintances." "Those functions were devoid of any sense of intimacy whatever, they were made glacial by everyone's terror of Tatiana," she told me recently. "Everyone I know felt very estranged. And yet you kept going because it had become central to the New York scene."

Finally, how did Alex truly feel about such gatherings? During these events, he usually hovered at the edge of the room like a high-class maître d', looking affable and yet utterly detached, and after Mother's death I realized that he, too, had loathed them. That he considered himself to be a man with no friends. That most other humans bored him to death. That he had a chilling lack of interest in them. That he looked on hospitality as merely serviceable, as another boring expedient that humored Mother and helped him to climb the power ladder. Later, he seems to have particularly hated the way my mother had encouraged my husband and me to have our own friends to Seventieth Street whenever we were in town. For throughout those years in which my childhood room remained our New York home, upon those innumerable occasions when we were going out to a restaurant with friends, Mother would be virtually offended if we did not invite them to Seventieth Street before dinner. One of the first phrases Alex spoke to me a few hours after my mother's death—it was barked rather than spoken and served as my first intimation of the terrifying changes that were about to come over him—was: "No more inviting people to my house, ever again!"

This leads me back to the time I was sixteen, when I was being courted by the only Russian beau I ever inherited from my mother's milieu and who, ironically, tested Alex's patience more than any of my other gentleman callers. Prince George Vassiltchikov was a twenty-eight-year-old Russian émigré who like most Russian noblemen had been brought up by French, German, and British nannies and was equally fluent in all four languages. First exiled in Lithuania and then in France, he served in the French resistance during the war. And after the liberation his linguistic skills brought him to the attention of the military authorities establishing the Nuremberg trials, of which he became one of a team that pioneered the system of instantaneous interpretation. His sister, Princess Tatiana Metternich, was a close friend of Elena Shuvalov, who introduced him to the Libermans in 1946 when he arrived in New York to serve as an interpreter at the newly founded United Nations. "Georgie," as he was known to all, was a compact, leonine man with a mane of blond hair and long-lashed blue eyes, handsome in a slightly dissolute Slavic way; his intelligence, culture, and wit remained unmarred by his tremendous stutter in four languages. The marvel about Georgie, however, was that as soon as he began to speak into a microphone, the stutter totally disappeared and he wound in and out of French, Russian, German, English more mellifluously than any other member of the UN's large staff of translators: He apparently needed an audience of thousands in order to perform the simplest linguistic act.

Our difference in ages, twelve years, and the fact that Georgie belonged to a very fast social set, which I enthusiastically adopted—divorcées with shady Latin American lovers, frequently drugged central European nobility—seemed to bring Alex no end of worry. I went steady with Georgie for the last two years of high school, and—seeing the hours we kept and the amount of alcohol we consumed—I myself am amazed that I made it out of Spence and into Bryn Mawr. Although it would have been extremely easy for Georgie to take advantage of me, and although he acted toward me, in my mother's favorite phrase, like a "perfect gentleman," we did indulge in some very heavy petting. Mother must have been fully as cognizant of that fact as Alex, but for the simple reason that Georgie was a *Prince* and that his older sister, to boot, was Princess *Metternich,* our dalliance did not bother her in the least. Confronted with the possibility of such a brilliant match ("It's more than nobility, it's almost royalty," she said when talking of the Vassiltchikov family), crests and coronets danced with such frenzy in her imagination that she did not seem to care a whit about what the rascal did with my body.

So it was Alex who took the brunt of all the worrying. I suspect that his father's past as a socialist militant made him secretly distrustful of high-ranking Russian nobility. And beyond his unease about Georgie's aristocratic origins, he was clearly terrified that his teenage daughter might be seduced by a twenty-eight-year-old roué. "Czarist rabble!" I once heard him mutter about Georgie as he shooed me upstairs at the stroke of midnight. Never did Alex behave as a more possessive paterfamilias, in fact, than during the two winters I went out with Georgie. Upon our return from each one of our dates, he was up and waiting for us, sitting on the white plastic settee to the left of the living-room door, his mustache twitching impatiently as he pretended to read a book. As soon as we came up the stairs, he would dismiss Georgie icily with a *"Proshchaite"* ("Good night") and direct me, with a severe nod of the head, to go straight upstairs to bed. Over a half century later, Georgie, who is now living, wheelchair bound, in a small village in Switzerland, told me that in all his years of courting young women he had never encountered a father as aggressively possessive about a daughter as Alex. "I always imagined he kept a shotgun under his bathrobe as he sat there in the living room," he recalled dreamily. As I looked back on these episodes decades later, I realized that Alex had worried increasingly about me as I grew into womanhood and that this depth of concern was not only linked to his affection for me: It also had to do with his great unease about all things sexual, whomever they pertained to—an unease that could occasionally border on the hysterical.

So the living room at Seventieth Street at which my parents' parties and Alex's policing of my love life took place was not a cozy room; it was on the contrary a showroom of sorts such as couturiers or car dealers have, both glacially impersonal and somewhat kitschy. It was a place for ogling and evaluating the products at hand, be they beauteous guests, their hideous or divine clothes, their adequate or tragic men, or my own boyfriends.

For Mother, too, would make her tours of inspection in the living room. Nothing entertained her more than meeting new people and showing off her often laser-sharp insights into human character. Year after year, she would sweep down the stairs with feigned casualness when I entertained potential beaux—or later, as a married woman, my husband's and my friends. During our predinner Cokes or martinis, she pretended she was going down to the kitchen to get some tea yet kept her eyebrows suggestively raised, as if to say, "Can I just look in for a minute?" I buckled under her gaze and inevitably asked her in. "I'll only stay a second," she'd coyly say. And she'd plunk herself on the white plastic settee, exchanging a few mundanities about the weather or about the kind of restaurant or party we were headed for. After a few minutes, she would go upstairs again, and there would be some discreet muttering in my parents' room: She was giving Alex her report. Unlike Alex's rigid scrutinies, there was nothing possessive about Mother's investigations. They were solely incited by her endless curiosity about human beings and her desire to impress me once more with the infallible veracity of her insights. "Nice enough," she would say the following day, or, "They'll bore you to death in two weeks," or, even more threateningly, "Be careful!" If the visitors turned out to fall into either of the two last categories, she would exclaim triumphantly, "You see, you see, I'm always right!" "Your mother's always right," Alex would meekly repeat if he was in the same room, this phrase being one of the easiest ways of pacifying her.

It was just this kind of maternal perusal that the thirty-nine-year-old American artist Cleve Gray underwent in the fall of 1957, a few weeks after I'd returned from my wretched few years in Paris. I was then twenty-six. We'd met at a Sunday lunch in Connecticut, where he lived, and had gone out a few times since then, meeting in midtown for reasons of convenience. By the time he made his first visit to Seventieth Street, Mother just had a suspicion that something was up. Perhaps because his French was far better than that of other callers, Cleve Gray was the only one to decipher the reports Mother gave to Alex upstairs. *"Boubous,"* he recalled hearing her say upon his first visit, *"il est charmant, et* pas *du tout pédéraste!"* Some three months later, in February of 1957, Cleve Gray stood by the window of the same living room, asking Alex for my hand in marriage. "It is a marriage made in heaven," Alex said, his mustache trembling with emotion, and this time, he, too, was dead right.

Irving Penn: "Mr. and Mrs. Alexander Liberman with Francine du Plessix, February 1948."

SEVENTEEN

Our Home II

Whenever you climbed from the second to the third floor at Seventieth Street, you'd pass one of Mother's frequent touches of decorating whimsy, a charming Neapolitan cherub of painted wood, nestled at the bend of the stairs. On the walls of the stairwell were hung black-and-white works by lesser masters of the Libermans' milieu: portraits and *Vogue* illustrations by René Bouché, Eric, Felix Topolski, and even drawings of mine from my days at the Art Students' League, which I had attended in my late teens. Once at the landing, you saw, at the right, the door to my parents' room, which gave onto the garden, and, at the left, the one to my room, which looked out on Seventieth Street.

Whereas the living room was a place for public scrutiny, for flaunting and impressing, I associated my parents' room with Alex's inner gazing and with my mother's narcissism. For its altar and centerpiece was the glaringly lit dressing table that stood dead in the middle of the far wall, between the two windows hung in thick pale-gray linen. The very surface of the table was mirrored, the wall all around it was mirrored, and on either side of the table were multitiered lamps of leaf-patterned white metal that each took three lightbulbs. The dressing table was made all the more shrinelike by the fourteen-piece silver cosmetic set, engraved with the viscountal crest, that

338

had stood in Mother's electric-blue bathroom in Paris and had followed us into exile. At either side of the room were two identical double beds, the sideboards of which were upholstered in gray satin damask. At the far end of Mother's bed were bookshelves holding her large collection of Russian-language books. At the far end of Alex's was a desk upon which he kept memorandums about the week's engagements and also his more sentimental possessions: photographs of his mother and father and of Mother and me and also an album of photographs of Venice I had taken when I was sixteen, during our first trip abroad after the war, and which remained on his desk until he vacated the house in 1991. Photography had been the first art for which I'd had a strong inclination, and I'd dedicated the album to him, on the flyleaf: *"A mon Alex adoré, mes premiers efforts."* This object's sentimental appeal, I imagine, was that it served as one more link between us: In his early adolescence, as in mine, photography had served as a first artistic calling.

The pictures hanging about the walls of my parents' room had exclusively to do with the family: the one sanguine Alex had done of me, age eight, when I had gone to his Paris studio to pose for him in my tutu; by the 1960s, Alex's photos of my sons, and portraits of all six of us by friends such as Bouché, Vertès, Irena Wiley; and still later, my own children's first artistic efforts. When I open the door of my memory to this room I see, first of all, Alex lying on his back on the bed to the right, his hands folded on his stomach, his eyes half closed in rest but never in sleep or else wide-open, gazing straight at the space ahead of him. He would take this rest every day of the week between six and seven, regardless of whether or not he was going out to dinner. He would seek refuge upstairs for even lengthier times on the nights he and Mother were *not* going out to avoid the stream of visitors she entertained in the predinner hours. I respected this retreat of Alex's. I remained aware that he was an invalid who'd several times struggled for his life and whose health needed to be protected from my mother's insatiable need for human company, human noise.

The same door of memory, when it focuses on Mother, frames her as she sits at her dressing table, painting her face, or arranging her hair with the same absorption as she had in her Paris bathroom, except that as she gets older she looks at herself more critically, with diminishing satisfaction. There are night tables by each of their beds: His is very neat and denuded, holding merely a glass of water and whatever magazines he's reading that week, for whatever medications he takes are kept hidden in a closet of his bathroom; he does not like to have it known that he takes them—never once have I seen him swallow a pill in public. Her night table, however, is laden with foreign-language magazines and prescription drugs. The French publications she keeps by her bed are *Match, Evènements de Paris,* and *Jours de France.* (The latter are heavily laced with gossip concerning the high jinks of European nobility—the engagements and divorces of the Spanish or Belgian royal princesses, the ball gowns worn by the queen of Holland during the king of Sweden's visit.) Mother will never learn English well enough to peruse *The New York Times* or to read more than a few paragraphs of any book I'll ever write, and as she will get older the language of exile will annoy and weary her increasingly. As for Mother's medications, they are all kept on the second shelf of her night table, dozens of them: Their principal intents are to wake her up, to allay her migraines and other real or alleged pains, and to help her get to sleep. She has been addicted to this sequential regimen—stimulant, powerful painkiller, sedative—ever since I can remember, possibly beginning it after her near-fatal car accident of 1936. She is notoriously addicted to her pills, she hides nothing of her habit, in fact she flaunts it and proselytizes it. Upon hearing any friend complain of fatigue in the morning, she will say, "But just do as I do! Take a Dexedrine in the morning—there's nothing like it! You'll feel on top of the world!" "You're afraid you won't sleep at night?" she adds if her acquaintance voices hesitations. "Well then, take a Nembutal when you go to bed—you'll sleep like a log! I've been taking both for most of my life!"

So efficacious was her proselytizing that she briefly converted me, though as a rebellious teen I was hardly eager to adopt any of Mother's practices. It began at the end of my junior year at Spence. I must have talked about the importance of my spring exams, which would be crucial to the process of college applications. I was intent on getting into Bryn Mawr, and she must have felt my keen obsession to succeed, for one night as I was boning up on Milton she stole into my room and handed me a little round, white pill: "Take it before the exam," she said. "You'll see, it'll do marvels for you." I indeed felt unusually lucid throughout my exam and was impressed not only by the result, an A+, but by the fluency, the exhilarated ease with which my ideas poured out. I stress "impressed," rather than "seduced." For the sense of being "speeded up" did not suit me. I was high-strung enough already, with an uncomfortably fast resting pulse, and the experience unsettled me, even frightened me. So from then on and into my last two college years, when I transferred to Barnard, I occasionally accepted a pill from Mother before an English or philosophy exam. For reasons of fetishism or perhaps good sense, I reserved the "speedies," as I called such pills, for those subjects, sensing that taking them for math or even history might be counterproductive. And it was with an air of disappointment that she would see me marching off to the latter exams without her talisman. "Are you really *sure* you don't want one?"

The same process inevitably led Mother to convert me to sleeping pills. The severe bouts of insomnia I'd had since my father's death occasionally returned, and when I was sixteen or so she must have been kept up by the sound of my pacing about long past midnight. For one night she came into my room holding yet another kind of pill, yellow this time, and said, with some annoyance, "Instead of creating this pandemonium, please take this and go to sleep!" This habit, alas, was far more pernicious. By the time I was nineteen, I was taking Nembutal once or twice a week, whenever sleep did not readily come to me. And by the time I'd worked for a few months at my first postcollege job, I was totally addicted: I handled the midnight-to-8:00 A.M. shift at United Press, writing radio bulletins, and lived in a basement-level studio on West Eleventh Street. The tensions of the work—it was in 1953, during the McCarthy hearings—were compounded by the stress of the intolerably noisy trucks that reverberated through my little room, and I doubled, tripled my doses of preceding years.

My mother's habit of pushing her pills on me could well have turned out to be disastrous. It took a happy marriage and a move to a serenely calm rural site for me to kick the barbiturate habit. And it took me many more years to admit to myself that Mother had been hooked on drugs for much of her life, that drugs may have been at the heart of her exuberant energy and dynamism and charm and, yes, success. In the late 1960s, when I'd begun to suspect that the pills were also having a perilous effect on her health and observed the gusto with which she started to consume alcohol after her retirement, I tried to talk about it to Alex and encountered an impenetrable wall of denial. He, of course, had known about her addictions all along. But just as adamantly as he'd protected her, all those decades, from the reality of the world, shielding her from any worrisome information, he now protected her reputation as a model of purity and uprightness. "I don't know what you're talking about," he'd say icily, his mustache twitching with an almost villainous snarl. "She takes an absolutely *normal* amount of medications."

But *pace* on my mother's peddling and addictions and Alex's devious enablement of them. Part of the Libermans' arrogant charm, part of the power they emanated, was their projection of endless self-confidence. The tactics they used to uphold the myth of their perfect marriage were similar to those used to erect the Soviet government's propaganda facade: No chink in the perfect society must ever be admitted, even if it was clearly perceived by all outside observers. Like the gang in the Kremlin, the Libermans exuded an absolute assurance that in every possible area of their life—in every one of their habits and proclivities—they had made the most perfect choices, had created the greatest achievable harmony.

I cannot leave my parents' beloved bedroom—the room I went into on a morning of my fifteenth year to hear Alex whisper, "My father died last night," the room in which he added, a few seconds later, "We don't become adults until our parents have died," the room that my husband and I entered to announce that we were expecting our first child—without recalling a few incidents that reinforce my sense of Alex and Mother's minimal libido, perhaps, even, of their sexual naïveté.

Incident one: Considerably more sophisticated than my parents realize, I'm in my late teens, and Alex has called me to his studio in the library for "a little talk." It must be 1949 or so, for his first minimalist pictures are hanging on the walls, pristine black circles on white ground. I'm sitting on a high stool, my back to the window, facing him. Gently, very methodically, with a tinge of embarrassment in his voice and with his lips faintly, priggishly pursed, he outlines the various measures a woman can take to avoid becoming pregnant. "There are condoms," he says, "certain rubber objects, which men can put on their . . . dum-dums, you know . . . you understand," he adds, perhaps beginning to sense my expertise on such issues, though like most aspects of my private life I carefully guard it from my parents' voyeurism. "There are diaphragms, which women can use and which I believe are *quite* comfortable. There is the possibility of the man withdrawing before orgasm . . . a time-honored tactic!" he adds, attempting a smile. "But the best method of all," he continues, and only then does his voice take on a tone of clarion enthusiasm, "there is *abstinence!*" Some seconds pass, he may be observing what that last, buoyantly offered option is having on me. "It might be very beautiful for you to retain your virginity until you get married," he quietly offers. Another wait, and then he adds, "Your mother has often refused herself, made herself unavailable, and that is an absolutely central part of her great magic. . . ." "I already have a diaphragm," I shoot back.

Incident two: The following episode, which occurred three decades later, some twenty-five years into my marriage, also reveals Alex's extremely close relationship to my husband in the decades that preceded my mother's death. Cleve and I are encountering some common sexual difficulties related to his cardiac medications. Upon a visit to New York, Cleve tells me he has related the details of our vicissitudes to Alex. I'm irate at this disclosure. For whereas I've been using a strategy of filial secrecy since my teens, my husband tends to open our lives to Alex's frequent questioning in the same manner in which he once allowed the meddling of his own invasive parents, and we often clash about our filial tactics. So I let him have it, but the harm is done, and it is with apprehension that I drop in on Alex during his daily rest on his bed. "Hello, darling," he says. "I'm sorry about your troubles." I mutter something about the nonimportance of it all, yet he wants to explore it further. "But listen," he says. "One can very well come to orgasm without an erection." "Without an erection?" I ask, incredulous, and then add, teasing, "That's a good one!" "I assure you," he insists with that tone of annoyance that always appears when I've contradicted him. In such instances, he has the habit of repeating a statement, breaking up his sentence into syllabic units for purposes of emphasis. "You-can-ver-y-well-have-an-or-gasm-with-out-an-er-ec-tion," he repeats. The notion sounds wackily medieval, recalling the edicts of heretical religious sects that approved only those forms of sexual contact that excluded penetration. But this time around I don't argue it. I simply bid him goodnight with a kiss on the cheek (which he accepts grudgingly, as if still smarting from my sarcasm) and leave his room, thinking, Boy, that's the wackiest one I've heard from him yet.

Memory now bids me to move across the third-floor landing and into my own quarters.

When you came into my room, the first piece of furniture you saw, splunk between the two windows, was the large white desk at which I worked throughout six years of Spence and four years of college. The rest of the furnishings were inconsequential: chintz-covered twin beds, a white chest of drawers, a white dressing table placed between the two mirrored doors that gave out to the bathroom and to the hallway. It is at this big 1920s-vintage desk, which Mother bought at auction a dirty brown and painted glossy white, that I studied for my exams, dreamed of a variety of vocations, scribbled in my first journals, wrote my first infatuated missives to diverse Lotharios at Exeter and St. Paul's, pinned up photos of my various heroes and crushes (de Gaulle, Anthony Eden, Rita Hayworth), that I first read Dostoevsky novels, and wrote my undergraduate thesis on Kierkegaard. It is also in this room and at this desk that I ceased to mourn my own blood father, thus learning to forget if not to reject him.

In his pivotal essay "Mourning and Melancholia" (the original and far more eloquent title is "Traüer Arbeit," "the work of mourning"), Sigmund Freud constantly reminds us that grieving for a loved one is a hard, slow, patient labor, a meticulous process that must be carried out over a far longer amount of time than contemporary society tends to allot us. Crucial to this toil, Freud tells us, is our careful examination—"piecemeal," as he puts it— of each association, each place and belonging once shared with the departed.

(Don't hasten to put his/her clothes away; continue to polish his/her silver.) Equally essential are those traditional gestures of ritualized grief (memorial services, visits to a grave or commemorative site) that confirm the absence of the dead one. In this "slow, long drawn-out, . . . and gradual work of severance," Freud writes, "each single one of the memories and situations of expectancy which demonstrate the libido's attachment to the lost object is met by reality's verdict that the object no longer exists."

What happens if the enormous energy available for the labor of grief does not find its proper tools or associations? It can become what Freud calls "pathological mourning." Like those spirits of the dead in Greek literature who, if improperly mourned, often return to cause mischief—devastating crops, destroying whole towns—the psychic energies of mourning can wreak grievous harm if they're repressed. They tend to turn inward in a dangerous process of self-devouring (as when we say that we "eat our heart out"). They can metamorphose into what we now call depression, a condition for which Freud preferred the more resonant, tradition-laden term "melancholia." And, most tragically, they can give rise to self-hatred and self-destruction: "This delusion of inferiority is completed by sleeplessness . . . and by a suppression of the instinct which compels every living thing to cling to life."

Rereading Freud over the years, I finally understood the full emotional context of the nightly fits of weeping that had plagued me in the first two years after my father's death. For in my particular case of mourning, there were precise historical and geographical obstacles to my performing any of those ritualized gestures needed, as Freud puts it, "to confirm the absence of the dead one." His burial site—a vast military cemetery on Gibraltar—lay thousands of miles across the ocean and was made further unreachable by war. Moreover, the fact that Alex hated every association with my father restrained my mother and me from ever mentioning him and encouraged us to erase most every trace of the warrior lying in his military grave thousands of miles across the ocean.

But the depressions and fits of tears that overcame me in Rochester and on other strangers' beds may have also been caused, in some part, by the manner in which Mother and Alex had constantly shunted me away during our first two years in the United States. For as soon as I settled into my bright, cheerful room at Seventieth Street, which gave me my first true sense of rootedness and permanence, my grief was greatly becalmed. As my new parents gambled, laughed, dined, and entertained the years away, as I watched them seek the company of the powerful, talented, and wealthy, I began to play their game, I began to forget with them, for it was by far the easier and lazier path. We were the newly minted family off to a phenomenal start in the new country, and I had already transferred to my charming, generous stepfather much of the affection I had borne to the dead warrior. I now joined my new parents in their memory-destroying dance, I collaborated like a traitor, I came to know the euphoria of burying the past rather than burying the dead. As for my nightly terrors, by mid- to late adolescence they were efficiently repressed, waning apace with most memories of my father, with most conscious interest in his life or death.

In 1948, as a freshman at Bryn Mawr, I landed the role of Ismene in a college production of Jean Anouilh's *Antigone*. (It was the only time my parents came to visit me at college—they declared my performance to be terrific and for some years deplored that I was not following my true calling for the stage.) As I sat in my room at Seventieth Street on a weekend home, studying Ismene's lines, here were some of the themes, recently clarified by a course in Western civ, that ran through my mind: Antigone, custodian of primeval ritual observances, confronts her uncle Creon, the archetypal male technocrat who is ready to violate any divine law that stands in his way for the sake of political expediency. Having put Antigone's brother to death on grounds of treason, Creon has forbidden him all traditional burial rites. Against the advice of her accommodating sister, Ismene, Antigone safeguards her dead brother from suffering the greatest dishonor in Greek society: being "left unburied, food for the wild dogs and wheeling vultures." Following the dictates of her conscience and of the Greek religion, she offers her brother the burial rites forbidden him by Creon and suffers the consequences, going to her own grave "unsung, unwed." Female hearth versus male polis: As I memorize my lines, a proto-Marxist and militantly secular tomboy, I sympathize totally with the docile, panicky Ismene, even enjoying moments of approval for the tyrant Creon. Prosperity and survival above all! The forces of progress must prevail! Antigone, in my eyes, is an unintelligibly archaic creature, morbid and freakish in her addiction to rites that I find antiquated, meaningless. How I disdain Antigone when she tells Ismene, "You've chosen to live, and I to die." How I relish the moments when I chide my sister for venturing on "hopeless quests," for being "much possessed by death."

Only decades later did I grasp the link between Ismene's limp obedience to Creon and my own cowardice toward the rites and rights of a dead one lost in war. Only recently have I realized that the role of Ismene, "that beauteous measure of the ordinary," as Kierkegaard describes her, was the one my mother and I had played together for some years. And I would continue to play it for decades to come.

The year after my rendering of Ismene, I received an unsettling letter from Uncle André and Aunt Simone Monestier, with whom I'd visited at length for the two previous summers I'd returned to France. They were informing me that my father's body, which had been buried in Gibraltar, was about to be repatriated, that his remains were due back at the ancestral vault in Brittany the coming July, that the entire du Plessix family was gathering for the final burial; everyone, of course, expected me to come. I recall the exact spot on which I stood in my New York bedroom as I read this missive, the precise quality of the April light slanting through my window. I remember a sense of being fiercely assaulted by that letter, of being threatened in some very private space of me, which I now realize was the site of an inchoate, deeply sunken grief: How dare they ask me to cross the ocean and appear on such-and-such a day for an abstract and tedious family duty! I remember thinking those very words: "tedious," "abstract."

So even though I fully planned to be in France that summer, I wrote back to the Monestiers telling them not to expect me; I crassly lied and said I could not leave the States that year. "Thank you for letting me know darling ones," I wrote. "There's no way I can make it. I'm so glad you'll be there"—by which I meant, Thanks for minding my business, just take care of it without me, don't bother me with memory. That is one cycle of emotions I lived through in my room on Seventieth Street. And what incentives my parents and their friends gave me for silencing and burying my grief! What a good time we had together, whenever they gave me time!

The addition of the Patcevitches to our family greatly enhanced the merriness of my youth. Iva Patcevitch, the Russian émigré who in the fall of 1942 succeeded Nast as president of Condé Nast, was the son of a high official in the czarist government who had been the governor of Tula Province. A man of myriad gifts with an uncanny talent for finances, his capacity to charm others quite equaled Alex's, and he embodied, in the eyes of New York society, the most glamorous values of the old Russian aristocracy. A cadet at the St. Petersburg Naval Academy at the time the revolution broke out, Pat arrived in New York in the early 1920s. He was brought to Nast's attention by the tycoon's daughter, Natica, who had met the young émigré at a party. Pat was immediately hired and played a crucial role in holding the company together during the depression.

Uncle Patsy, as I called him, who lavished affection and generosity on me throughout my adolescence, was an exquisitely beautiful piece of work. His aquiline features were graced by long-lashed eyes of deep turquoise blue and topped by a mane of platinum hair that had grown silvery very prematurely, in his twenties. He was a gifted athlete who moved with a sinuous, Nijinskian walk, and his gorgeous physique, which he particularly flaunted in summer by wearing extravagantly minimal bikinis, recalled a perfectly chiseled Fabergé object. There were few things in life he couldn't do well. He knew reams of poetry in three languages. He played the piano beautifully and was a specialist in the most arcane areas of Russian music— César Cui was a particular favorite. A chess champion in his youth, he was equally unbeatable at most any parlor or lawn game you can imagine— dominoes, backgammon, croquet. He was a stupendous ballroom dancer, played marvelous squash, was an exceptional chef and gardener, and did it

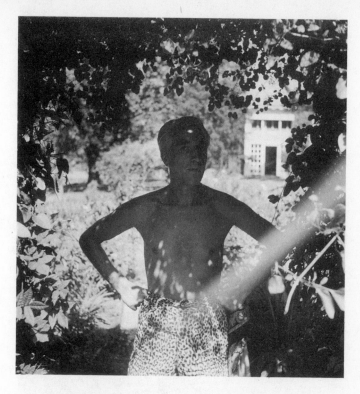

*Iva S. Patcevitch ("Uncle Pat") at the summer estate in Stony Brook,
Long Island, which he shared with us from 1944 to 1947.*

all with no apparent effort, with more *sprezzatura* than any male seducer I've
ever met.

Luxury and extravagant comfort were essential, as they were to Alex, to
make Pat feel secure. Even in his early, impoverished first seasons in New
York, Pat booked two seats whenever he went alone to the theater in
winter—the second seat was for his coat. Throughout much of his life, he
carried in his vest pocket a miniature gold swizzle stick from Cartier designed to remove excess bubbles from his champagne. Pat's rarefied aesthetic
sense would have deterred him from taking a wife whose beauty and style
were less than very grand. And, indeed, Nada Patcevitch was an austerely
handsome woman who, although she would later suffer much from her hus-

Tatiana and Alex on the terrace of our summer house in Stony Brook, 1946.

band's innumerable seductions, had been, in the 1930s, one of England's great beauties.

Yet beneath the surface of Pat's hauntingly beautiful physique, his ready, flirtatious wit, his superficial but glittering, multifaceted culture, lay a rigorously disciplined character. An indefatigable worker, in every way moderate with the exception of his ambition and his phenomenal libido,

Pat had every possible attribute needed for the presidency of a prestigious publishing company. Like Alex and many other successful émigrés, he was also a considerable snob, and in no way did the two men complement each other better than in their very disparate forms of snobbery. Alex was strictly an achievement and fame snob. Pat had the genetic snobbism of a finicky horse or dog breeder: He went for caste and blue-blooded lineage, fawning on old New York WASP grandes dames such as Mrs. Cornelius Vanderbilt, Jr., or Mrs. John Hay Whitney, to whom Alex would never have given the time of day.

In 1943, the year after Port Jefferson, the Patcevitch-Liberman clan began to share a vacation house every summer, a habit they were to continue for the following four years. After a problematic rental in Greenwich, Connecticut, at a property whose pond was filled with leeches and where poison ivy took its toll on all, we shared three consecutive summers in a wonderful house in Stony Brook, Long Island, a rambling colonial structure that we came to look on as a second home. Owned by a grand Catholic family that had come into hard times, it overlooked an inlet of Long Island Sound; the house was surrounded by large lawns and had a private squash court. A multitude of children had inhabited the house in the last generation. And apart from the master bedroom, which the Patcevitches occupied, the living quarters had been divided into many small, monastic chambers, which enabled my parents and the Patcevitches to entertain successive waves of houseguests. Since Nada was the only adult in our extended family who did not work, it was there that she and I kept each other company while Mother, Alex, and Uncle Pat were in the city. How lucky Mother had been to find yet another substitute mom for me! Gitta Sereny had a full-time job these days and was visiting us only on occasional weekends.

For the next few years, as Pat and Alex went about their own bonding rituals—discussing Condé Nast by the hour, playing squash and chess—Mother and Nada were inseparable, proclaiming that they were not only each other's best friends but "like sisters." Indeed, they were both tall, generous, cultivated, imperious women who terrified their husbands into satisfying their every whim, and for the following seasons they copied every

detail of each other's style: They swept up their blond hair in similar classic rolls, used the same hues of ruby-red lipstick and nail polish, chose a
"twin" look for summer wear (shorts and men's shirtwaists tied just above
the midriff), wore equal amounts of barbaric jewelry to the beach, and aped
each other's way of laughing (slightly bent over at the waist, right hand over
the heart, *hee hee hee*). But although Tatiana had become Nada's best friend
upon Alex's orders and for a few years seemed attached to her, she and
Nada were very different women. Mother—a true nester—was deeply attached to her home, loathed traveling, and declared that she would leave
Seventieth Street only feet first; Nada was one of those British dilettante
expatriates to whom lightly learned wanderings—be it in Afghanistan, Tibet, or North Africa—were an essential part of their identities. Mother
was a dedicated career woman who finished every professional task with ex-
acting perfectionism; Nada's desk was littered with two decades' worth of
unfinished travel essays, unfinished short stories, barely begun novels.

Their physiques were equally distinct. My amply proportioned mother
was a Juno-esque size-sixteen earth goddess; the delicate, skittish Nada was
a virginal Diana whose great violet eyes surmounted a sharply aquiline nose
and a thin, distinctly unsensuous mouth. She was five feet nine and wore a
size ten, and it soon became an ideal of mine to achieve that borderline
emaciation that characterized Nada's frigid style, an effort much encouraged by the two women. "Don't you think we should begin to watch her
weight, Taniousha dear?" Nada would say to Mother as they tallied up the
week's report about me. "Absolutely Nadiousha, I'll tell Sally to cut out the
apple pie." "And the breasts are growing awfully big. . . ." "There's always
plastic surgery," Mother would answer reassuringly.

An average Stony Brook summer weekday: When I enter Nada's room,
she is sitting up in bed, her makeup already applied with exquisite skill, offering her morning's litany of complaints as Sally stands over her breakfast
tray. ("Ooh, those breasts," Sally used to whisper to me. "I can't stand looking at those breasts, like little dead frogs.") The toast is soggy, Nada is
singing out into the morning, the war is still on and you can't travel anywhere, my volume of Cyril Connolly has disappeared, and you haven't

thanked me properly, you little horror, for that bathing suit I bought you yesterday. Then every morning after gripe time came that procession which was the central ritual of our day: Nada with her baskets, her beach mat, her oils, her slender amethyst-charged arms leading the way to our little inlet beach for our daily sunbath. These are still the years when any fashionable woman's summer life is focused on achieving the darkest, most cancerous tan possible. On August weekends, when Mother is on vacation full-time with us, she and Nada and I spread out our arms and legs side by side for Pat and Alex to judge, asking, "Who's the darkest of us all?" For this purpose, week after week Nada and I lie there with the stillness of sacrificial victims, turning our bodies by a few degrees an hour to achieve maximum exposure to the sun, occasionally taking an hour off to move to the bulrushes to the left of the beach, where we could take off our swimsuits and, as Nada put it, "tan the whole package."

And then we'd turn to our reading. From the time I'd been a small girl, I'd been happy to lie on a beach by the hour with a book, but at Stony Brook there were many interruptions, for Aunt Nada liked to talk to me during our sunning sessions, dredging up her recollections, her accounts of innumerable unfinished projects. For Nada's mind—oh, heavens, it resembled an exploded emporium, or one of those Third World towns in which half-built hotels stand rusting in the middle of trafficked squares. She would read me excerpts from her unfinished novels or short stories, one of which, I recall, had the opening sentence "Her dream lapped about her like a warm bath." At other times she would discuss one of her unfinished historical studies—a history of the papacy or of Mayan sculpture. Or else scraps of her past came tumbling out of her chatter: her presentation at Court, when she had been dreadfully ashamed to have dropped her handkerchief before the queen; Bucharest in the twenties, Baden-Baden in the thirties, when she had been courted by the earl of so-and-so, the duke of this-and-that; the glacial, indifferent mother who let a nanny do all the bringing up; that nanny's ghoulish, man-hating humor; that favorite couplet of Nanny's, which Nada repeated to me weekly, Nanny's idea of great fun: "Pray tell me Ma, what is that mess / That looks like raspberry jam? / Hush hush my child that is your pa / Run over by the tram." How Nada laughed at that, her thin torso shaking on her beach mat, her carefully painted lips curling savagely over her white teeth.

By the time the Patcevitches were firmly established in our lives, just after Pat's ascension to power, he had fallen out of love with Nada and gone on to many other pursuits. With genteel diligence they tried to hide their divisions during their last years together. On Friday nights, Pat's arrival in Stony Brook with my parents was attended by barrages of endearments—Beloved Nadiusha! Patsy, darling! He would often bring her some jeweled bauble to wear as a token of his repentance, and there would be much public hugging, accompanied by oohs and ahs from that weekend's audience: "How superb, what style Patsy always has!" Yet I was always aware of the dread between Nada and Pat—their bitter mutterings in the bedroom a wall away from mine, the banging of their bedroom door as he left to sleep in an empty guest room. A very pretty, bright twenty-four-year-old divorcée who was spending a summer weekend with us in 1944, Peggy Riley (who was to enter New York cultural history as the distinguished essayist and lecturer Rosamond Bernier), tells the following story: It was a Sunday night, she needed a ride back from Stony Brook to New York, so she accepted Pat's offer to drive her into town. Their trip was slowed by heavy traffic, and once in the city, Pat asked Peggy to come up to his flat in order to telephone Nada, who was in a perpetual state of nerves whenever he drove without her. He waited until after he had made his call and reassured his wife that he was safely in Manhattan to make a lunge for the pretty Peggy. "That was Pat all over," Rosamond told me recently as we shared memories of that decade. "He had to make that call to Nada first, like a good little boy, before pouncing on you." Bauble after repentant bauble came Nada's way, the most memorable of them being a three-inch-high "dog collar" of tourmalines and small diamonds, which covered the entire height of her slender neck down to the edge of her frail shoulders and remained her stylistic trademark, not unlike my mother's macelike garnet ring, until her marriage, and her New York life, came to an end.

Nada and Francine in the squash court of the summer house in Stony Brook.

Each summer spent in the Stony Brook house yields one or two memories that stand out above all others.

Nineteen forty-four: The summer's emotions center on the Allied landing on Normandy and our armies' march toward Paris. Ensconced in our summer home since early July with old Sally to keep house for us, Nada and I have tacked up a large map of western Europe on the wall of the dining room; armed with pushpins, we daily track the Allies' progress eastward and southward from Omaha Beach. Nada, who like Pat has spent half of her wanderer's life in France, is fully as excited as I am. Those *sales Boches* will soon be kicked out, we rejoice every day, our beloved Paris will be freed before the summer's over! However unpolitical they are, Alex, Mother, Uncle Pat are equally jubilant—Paris, for all of us, is still the center of the universe, our emotional heartland, the mecca from which all culture and civil-

355

ity flow. On an early August weekend, the Libermans and Patcevitches have assembled a large number of friends for Sunday lunch. It is a typical *Liber-mánshchestvo* table, groaning with food, ablaze with laughter and trilingual talk. Edna Woolman Chase has brought her daughter, the peppy writer Ilka Chase; the sparkling Peggy Riley is here with her lover, a tall, brooding Russian photographer named Constantin ("Kostia") Joffe; Aunt Elena Shuvalov hovers over her son Andriusha, who's about to leave for Exeter; our dear friend Albert ("Albie") Kornfeld, the editor of *House and Garden* magazine, has just regaled us with a tale of how he took the *Queen Mary* for the single purpose of abiding by his mother's wishes that her ashes be scattered in midocean. ("What do you *think* I'm doing?" he snapped at the nosy steward who burst into the cabin to ask why Albie was leaning perilously out of his porthole. "I'm scattering Mother!") Also present are our principal financial supporters, Beatrice and Fernand Leval, and our nostalgic warblers, Claude Alphand and Sasha de Manziarly, the latter of whom has always been a special friend to me.

The table—a wooden plank has been set up outdoors on top of a trestle to accommodate sixteen people—is drenched in sunshine, the wine is flowing, and as we feast on Sally's southern fried chicken and blueberry pie the talk soon centers on one speculation: When will our beloved Paris be liberated? The Allies are marching southward toward the Sarthe, Sasha de Manziarly announces; they might reach Le Mans next week; their next goal will be the Loire. Many at the table are pessimistic: The Germans' resistance has often been stiffer than expected, a lot of blood is yet to be shed. Mother is always the greatest pessimist of all, a trait Alex traces to all the tragedies she's witnessed. "They'll never be in Paris before October," she announces glumly. "Not a chance! *Les Boches* will fight like savages!" But on this perfect summer day, most of the guests opt for a more moderate view, and before I know it—this is, after all, a predominantly Russian table—everyone is taking bets. "I bet anyone one hundred dollars that Paris will be liberated by September 10," says Sasha de Manziarly. "I bet you one hundred dollars not before September 15!" Alex calls out. "Two hundred dollars that it will be earlier, by the fifth!" says Pat, always ready to raise the stakes.

But I've been listening to the radio as compulsively as I'd listened to it three years ago as a ten-year-old, when I was still nursing delusions about my father's death, and I think they're all crazy—they're underestimating the heroism of resistance fighters who're staging uprisings all over France. "Paris will be liberated by August 26!" I speak up. "Any thirteen-year-old who accurately predicts that date deserves a bracelet from Cartier," Sasha de Manziarly says. "Are you putting your bets on August 26, young lady?" "Most definitely," I answer. "Cartier it'll be," Sasha announces. Mother, Nada, and Pat glow with pride at their darling's precociousness. Alex's mustache twitches with mild displeasure—he's always wary of my being the center of attention, and he disapproves of my being offered jewelry by any man, for whatever reason.

Sure enough, in the following weeks the Allies sweep southward and eastward so swiftly that Nada and I are repositioning our pushpins twice a day. On August 17, American troops take Orléans, on August 19 they cross the Seine at Mantes, and on that same day resistance units stage insurrections all over Paris, capturing the Hotel de Ville and all post offices. Our armies reach Paris on the twenty-fifth, one day before I'd predicted it. At 6:00 P.M., Free French forces led by General Leclerc come marching up the Champs Elysées, and a few hours later my idol, Charles de Gaulle, rides into the city on top of a tank. The entire family is still assembled at Stony Brook. Mother and I, Pat and Nada weep and hug one another with joy, and Alex, who until the end of his life we will never once see cry, is opening champagne for everyone, his mustache trembling with emotion.

A few weeks later, as we're resettled at Seventieth Street, Mother begins to establish phone contact with a few relatives in Paris: Aunt Sandra, Aunt Lila, the Monestiers, all have survived the Occupation safely. And sure enough, during my first weeks back at Spence, a little black box is delivered to me from Cartier. The gallant Sasha has kept his word and has sent me a beautiful gold bracelet. For some years—until it disappears during a hotel stay, perhaps stolen, perhaps left behind in a moment of sensual abandon— it remains my most prized possession, a perennial reminder of my motherland's liberation.

. . .

That was the historic summer of 1944. My two most vivid memories of the summer of 1946—I was then fifteen, going on sixteen—are the following: Aunt Nada and Uncle Pat offered me, as a gift for my upcoming birthday, a luxury I'd craved for several years and which my parents hadn't been able to afford: time at a horseback-riding summer camp in Steamboat Springs, Colorado, which my classmates at Spence had raved about. Alas, I enjoyed very little of this treat. At the end of my second week, my horse bolted while crossing a mountain trail, I fell onto my right side and splintered my collarbone into some thirteen pieces. An angelic camp counselor accompanied me on the small, shaking mountain train that connected Steamboat Springs to Denver—the most physically painful experience of my life, including childbirth—and booked me into Denver Children's Hospital. She kindly spent a night by my bedside to see me through the first of what would be five rounds of surgery. After she left me to resume her duties, I was on my own. My parents phoned every few days for the next fortnight to send their love. But this did not minimize the extraordinary bouts of depression that swept over me each time I woke from the successive anesthesias, which were still of the chloroform-mask kind: Coming to after each of these ordeals, lying in a ward filled with sobbing children, I wept not out of some indefinite sorrow, as I did in earlier years, but out of solitude and distinct physical pain. Yet not a shred of blame was in my thoughts. Not until many years later, when narrating this episode to others—"You mean they didn't fly out?" startled friends would say—did I begin to think it odd that Mother and Alex felt no need to be with me. For back then, age fifteen, I was already so used to fending on my own that the thought did not once occur.

My other vivid memory of Stony Brook in 1946 has to do with Mother and Alex asking me to pose in the nude. For over half a century I seem to have repressed the memory of that episode, which resurfaced only after my mother's death in 1991, when I came into possession of several boxes of photographs that had been stored at Seventieth Street. I don't recall the words my parents used to talk me into posing—I only know it was suggested to me on an August morning as the three of us sat alone at break-fast, and I particularly recall the soothing, almost obsequious tone in which Mother kept repeating, "We'll all go down there together, Frosinka, dar-ling, we're all doing this *together*." "There" was that spot on our little inlet beach, to the left of the house, in whose tall bulrushes Nada and I used to sunbathe naked. "We'll stand around in the bulrushes together, where it's so pretty," Alex said gently, his green eyes pleading. "Is that okay with you, darling?" "Why, sure, I guess so," I answered, vaguely pleased and flattered and yet apprehensive. All three of us were prudish about our bodies, the project did not seem at all natural, yet as soon as they proposed it I wanted to do it immediately, that very morning, in order to have it over with.

So the three of us trooped toward the bulrushes, and Alex loaded his film as I took off my bathing suit, feeling, at that particular moment, vaguely offended. Was this *right*? Was it *honorable* of any mom and dad to photograph their daughter stark naked on the beach? What would Aunt Nada and Uncle Pat think of this? What if someone outside of the family were to see these shots, someone at Alex's office? Alex never developed his own film—what would the guys in the darkroom think? Once my clothes were off and Alex started shooting, my parents grew particularly solicitous and tender. "Are you all right, darling, are you comfortable?" Alex asked. "You look ravishing!" Mother exclaimed. Alex believed passionately in waste ("American civilization is built on waste," he'd say grandly, "on glori-ous, glorious waste"), and he always used numerous rolls of film for any picture he ever shot. As his camera clicked through dozens of rolls, I stood there in the bulrushes, turning my head this way and that, attempting to look both languid and regal, feeling both embarrassed and proud. And then to my relief it was all over, and we went back to the house, where Uncle Pat and Aunt Nada were reading *The New York Times* on the terrace. The pose was never mentioned again, the pictures never discussed—in fact, I seem to have repressed the memory so efficiently that years later it never even surfaced in any conversations with my shrink.

So upon first seeing the pictures in 1991, I began to wonder what light this incident shed upon my parents' characters. Were they being sentimen-tal, attempting to preserve a trace of my childhood before it was totally

Marlene Dietrich portrait autographed to Francine, 1948.

swamped by womanhood? Or did these two persons of minimal libido look on the session as a sexual stimulant of sorts? This was the first inkling I had of my parents' strong streak of voyeurism; to what degree, I mused, was this a deviant act? Alex would live on for eight years after I discovered these pictures, and it is a reflection on both of our characters that I would never have dreamed of mentioning them to him. When in a jocular mood, however, I have often thought with bemusement of all the contemporary women who, coming upon such family mementoes, might have sued their aging stepfathers for a handsome sum on grounds of sexual misconduct.

How volatile my parents' world was! In the summer of 1947—the year we all returned to Europe for our vacations, the first year we did not share a summer home with the Patcevitches—Pat and Nada separated. Pat had fallen in love with Marlene Dietrich, who swiftly replaced Nada as Alex and Mother's best friend. For the following two decades, Nada went on to live in innumerable warm climes—Corsica, Sardinia, Mexico, the Dordogne, a score of Greek islands—perennially dissatisfied, never staying put for more than a year or two. During those years, I kept up with her through Christmas cards and called her or lunched with her on the infrequent occasions she visited whatever city I was living in, Paris or New York. Nada had been a most difficult woman, and I was the first to have been harassed by her neuroses. But I was grateful for her demanding generosity and for the motherly role she had tried to play (however awkwardly) during some crucial years of my adolescence.

Yet I noticed that from the time Nada was officially separated from Pat, my parents never once returned her calls. Throughout most of those post-Nada years, I was kept too busy by college, jobs, and romances to fully plumb the extent of the Libermans' betrayal: In their brutally pragmatic ethic, the woman whom my mother had looked on as her "twin sister" had lost all meaning in their lives once she ceased to be the boss's wife. As I grew older, I realized that I had witnessed, through Nada, one of many similar acts of abandonment that marked the Libermans' careers.

On the occasions we met after her divorce, Nada proved to be far too proud to hold forth on my parents' disloyalty. "How are *they*?" she'd ask knowingly, with a sad smile. "I often think of *them*, of my so-called *sister*." She'd add in a wry, ironic tone, "Is she happy enough?" Nada died in Greece in the 1960s after a long illness, leaving me in her will whatever little jewelry she had left—much of it dismantled amethysts and tourmalines—from Pat's dowry of guilt.

In the following years, Mother was indeed happy enough in the company of the friend she grew to love, for some years, above all others, Marlene

Dietrich. I first met Marlene at a beachside cottage on the north shore of Long Island, which Pat had rented in the fall of 1948, a few months after his divorce from Nada came through. In my first sighting of the star, she stood barefoot at the stove, cooking an elaborate dinner. Her blond hair was tousled with studied casualness, her makeup so artfully applied as to be invisible, and her naked legs were topped by one of Pat's impeccably tailored Sulka shirts. It was Marlene's habit, when cooking for friends, to elaborate on the ingredients essential to the dish she was making. Discussing the half cup of brandy she considered essential to a proper *boeuf bourguignon*, she bent over toward a low shelf to reach the bottle and revealed the only fabric, other than her cotton shirt, that adorned her nakedness that day: the string of a hygienic tampon, dangling demurely between the legendary legs.

Holy mackerel, I said to myself, no underpants! This woman is so glamorous that she can get away with anything! Eager, like any self-respecting teenager, to hone my own potential for glam, I instantly disposed of all former icons of female allure. Into the wastebasket went photos of the unambiguously female sex goddess Rita Hayworth, my screen idol since age twelve. I now thrilled to Marlene's dusky temptress roles in films such as *Shanghai Express*, to her *Blue Angel*'s Lola Lola, who drives men equally batty as tuxedo-clad cross-dresser and glitzy, garter-baring vamp; and above all, to live footage of her career's most heroic incarnation: Marlene in U.S. Army uniform, taking huge risks to boost our soldiers' morale by belting out "Boys in the Backroom" near the front lines. My parents, needless to say, were equally stricken. They marveled at the manner in which she blended the personae of bisexual adventuress and devoted down-to-earth grandmother. They dined out for years on accounts of the way Marlene repaired her fragile glass-beaded cabaret dresses herself on an ancient sewing machine, and of the manner in which, when cooking a meal for friends, she insisted on serving them in a white apron, refusing to sit down with them at table. For the following two decades, Marlene fulfilled—spectacularly so—the Libermans' deep need to be steeped in fame and glamour.

· · ·

Such were the principal happenings at our summer home. My own room on Seventieth Street, which I described earlier in this chapter, is bound to be linked to the tenuous relationship I maintained with my mother during my growth into womanhood. And within this complex process, one moment in the fall of 1946 is particularly significant—the time I told my mother I was having my first period.

I did not menstruate until the age of sixteen. For some three years, as my classmates, one after the other, periodically hosted the "visitor," as we daintily called it at Spence, I played a delicate make-believe game, every four weeks punctually dropping the excuse card into the little black box at the gym, savvily chatting about tampons, pads, cramps, oooooh, pass me the Midol, I have the worst cramps. I had no one with whom to share my dreadful secret: Mother had never approached the issue; Alex had proffered some vague information, but this was one set of worries I could not bring myself to share with him—worries that my period might *never* come, that I could never have children, that I was doomed to be barren and useless to society . . . and then one day, late in the fall of my junior year, the period arrived. I welcomed it directly after basketball practice and rushed home to Seventieth Street. I ran into my bathroom, pulled down my pants, and sat on the toilet, admiring at leisure the longed-for streak of pink. It must have been just before six, for Mother came in from Saks and opened the bathroom door, staring at me, as she occasionally did upon returning from work, with that shy, inquisitive glance that was meant to ask, "Is everything okay?" "Maman, I have the period!!" I exclaimed. But I don't know how to handle it, I added, most of the girls use pads, some use tampons, but that idea kind of scares me, do you, have you, ever used tampons, is that what I should try to use. . . . She stared at me, deadpan, and said, "Oh, sure, I can put anything up there—tennis balls, anything!" And then she fled the bathroom, my chaste blond goddess, utter terror in her eyes.

So I was again left, in my new happiness, with the task of decoding her complex messages. By now I was a precociously literary, symbol-savvy teenager beginning to look at colleges. What was that business about "balls"? Men have balls—was she trying to tell me how many men could get in there, or, conversely, was she intimating that she was the one in the family who had the balls? Or was she trying to prove how "modern" and "progressive" she was, prodding me to accept my sexuality forthrightly and have fewer hang-ups about it than she did? If so, she succeeded. But this was the weirdest one she'd pulled on me yet.

EIGHTEEN

Remaining in Fashion

I t was in my bedroom at Seventieth Street, at our summer house in Stony Brook, and most particularly from her workroom at Saks Fifth Avenue, that Tatiana waged a battle familiar to all mothers but particularly arduous in our case: the struggle over her daughter's adolescent body.

As a tot, I'd felt painfully unnoticed, but as I came to puberty I grew to know the opposite misery: Mother's constant observation of my bodily surface. Her criticisms were all too biased by the numerous hang-ups she had about her own body, particularly about her breasts, which had been direly misshapen—so she never tired repeating—by nine months of nursing me. ("What else could I do, in *Warsaw*?") So from my thirteenth year on, her sartorial commandments went somewhat like this: "You and I can't wear belts, *chérie*, our breasts are too big"; "We can't wear red shoes, our feet are too wide"; "Can't you always keep that curl in your hair? It's so much more becoming than when it's straight." Such scrutinies reached their critical mass at those longed-for and dreaded moments when we had to shop for my clothes, which due to our limited finances we bought exclusively at Saks because of Mother's large discount.

The first years after we'd moved to Seventieth Street—1942–1944, when I was twelve and thirteen—had passed without any major sartorial tensions. I had been in seventh and eighth grades, living in an exclusively fe-male world, going through crushes on older girls, learning to handle the crushes even younger girls had on me. I had three close friends in those years, who each fulfilled a different range of emotional needs: the exquis-itely pretty, highly popular Nadine was half-French and half-Russian and understood me in every possible way; Jeannette was a wiry vixen with sav-agely gleaming braces who was the class's outstanding athlete and whose support was essential to my being included in the class's inner circle of power; Jane was a heavyset girl with large breasts and big, dreamy blue eyes who was obsessed with the notion of being "creative." With Jeannette and Nadine I indulged in trading cards, a pastime taken up by only a chosen few. With Jane, I read Kahlil Gibran and went compulsively to the opera every Saturday afternoon of the season, paying fifty cents for standing room, clutching a little red volume entitled *The Story of a Hundred Operas*, which Jane and I consulted with the fervor with which young Red Guards later memorized the sayings of Chairman Mao.

But there came that time when we had all turned fourteen, and Spence decreed that all members of our freshman class must acquire a long evening frock for the occasion of our rite of passage into East Coast preppie pu-berty, the Groton–St. Mark's Christmas dance. Nadine's and Jane's mothers had done their duty months ahead of time, and since October I'd been ad-miring the gowns in their closets, scrumptious visions of pink organza ruf-fles and sherbet-hued tulles. I, too, had been asking Mother since the beginning of the term to go shopping for the dress, but week after week she'd put it off, saying she was too busy. Finally, on a Thursday in late No-vember, she consented to the expedition and asked me to meet her at Saks after school.

Every normal child is a conformist, and as I get to Mother's workroom I've already created the dress of my dreams, pink or blue and very flounced, a skirt perhaps scattered, like Jane's, with a few multicolored paillettes. I'm not ready for the following scenario. Looking at the clock, leaving orders with her assistants to page her instantly if a customer should appear—"We be back in twenty-five minutes!"—Mother clutches my hand as she pulls me headlong down Saks's grim, gray service stairs toward the junior misses' department two floors below. "Pssst! Pssst!" she whistles as we emerge onto the floor, her impatience, her frantic pace, created, I realized only years later, by her daily dose of Benzedrine. "Salesgirl! Queeck!" she cries out. She is known throughout the store, so help instantly arrives—Countess du Plessix, what can we do for *you*? "She must have dress for evening, long, black!!" she commands. "But Maman, I don't want black," I gasp. "I want pink or blue—I hate black." "Ridiculous!" she answers. "Black is *only* color for evening." "But Maman. . . ."

Alas, she is already at the junior misses' evening wear rack, going speedily through the garments, pushing back a half dozen dresses I crave, crave to try on—to see how they feel, to try out their flowers and flounces on my detestable body, to compare them to Jeannette's and Jane's gowns, to at least describe them to my chums—but Mother is already way ahead of me, triumphantly holding up her definitive choice. It minimizes the bosom all right—bodice of stark black velvet, sad little skirt of black-and-white plaid organdy, cap sleeves to match. It is mannish, it is nunnish—in sum, it's a lemon. "We try on!" she orders. And she rushes me into a dressing room, undoes my belt, helps me to whip off my sweater, and now it is on, this dud of a dress. As she exclaims "*Quelle élégance! Divin! Un rêve!!*" I stare at myself dejectedly in the mirror. I loathe this dress. I'm ashamed of it. I'm still too young to return to this delectable floor without an adult, and I long to linger here another half hour to try on the pink and powder-blue possibilities on the rack. "Maman, can't I try this—" "There you go again, you want to try on the whole store!" She is running out of the dressing room, black-and-white monstrosity in hand, and I don't persist, I pliantly acquiesce, for her love has been so hard-won that the smallest confrontation could destroy it.

The working day is over, and we go home to Seventieth Street, Mother triumphant about the day's purchase. "We must show Alex!" she exclaims when we hear his key turning in the front door. The three of us assemble in my room, where there are full-length mirrors on both doors, and while they whisper about the day's events at their respective offices I go into my bathroom to try on the monstrosity. "How elegant! How very perfect, darling," Alex exclaims as I emerge, having been thoroughly briefed, I imagine, on the opposition I put up. "Your mother is *always* right!" So I am stuck with the lemon of a dress. And a few weeks later, when the famous Christmas dance takes place, I am stranded for the entire evening with an acne-ridden Groton ninth-grader who may be too shy to approach any of the prettily flounced babes on the floor and bores me throughout with detailed descriptions of his chemistry experiments. That very Christmas, Pat and Nada, sensing my loathing for the black rag, came to the rescue by offering me a sequined turquoise number with which I sailed into self-assured stardom at several ensuing festivities. Over time, however, I have often puzzled over Mother's imposition of her own stark blackness on my first evening frock: Was she denying my sexuality because it made me into a rival? Or was she, however unwittingly, imposing her own deep sexual hang-ups on me?

This reminds me of another fashion expedition of my youth, one that was relatively peaceful but equally filled with sexual ambiguity: It was when Mother bought me my first pair of trousers. Pants were a big issue for her. She'd always looked at herself as "emancipated" because she had started wearing trousers in the 1920s, when they were indeed bold symbols of women's sexual liberation. And just as her fashion sense had been arrested somewhere between the Riviera thirties and the wartime forties, so her notion of chicly liberated women was frozen around the notion that "they wear pants." So as I stood in the dressing room a year or so after "the visitor" arrived, trying on my first pair of slacks, Mother stared at me with that gaze of admiration which it was my highest goal in life to glean and said, "Divine! You must *always* wear pants!" And she carried on about my skinny hips, so much more elegant than her size sixteen; why ever bother with a skirt? From then on, for the next half century, "You must always wear pants" became mother's most often repeated sartorial refrain—her way of saying, so I decoded it, that it was I who must wear the pants in my family, just the way she had in hers. "You must wear pants," I later realized, was Tatiana's version of that central talismanic phrase with which every mother attempts to retain some control over her daughter, be it through verbal symbols such as "You're killing me" or "I won't argue any more" or by the Queen of the Night's high-F aria in *The Magic Flute*, which, in my feminist reading of the opera, is the hypnotic refrain that keeps her daughter Tamina under her spell.

But, ah, we did have some good times, Mother and I. The best moments we shared were on those days when I was on a school vacation from Spence and picked her up at Saks to go to lunch at the Hamburger Heaven on Fifty-first Street between Madison and Fifth, across from St. Patrick's Cathedral. "Thirty-five minutes!" she would proclaim, looking at the clock, as we once more rushed from her workroom down the gray service stairs. We sat on the childlike high chairs and winked at each other conspiratorially as the waitresses snapped the little trays over our knees. Food was very important to Mother, as it is to most survivors of famines, and unlike Nada and many other fashion plates she was not that concerned about remaining svelte. She ate heartily and lustily, and in the prime of her health she continued to relish basic American food: steak and hamburgers ultra-rare, corn on the cob, apple pie (apple "pee," she called it, deliberately retaining her amusing mauling of the language). We both ordered our meat extrarare and lathered it with all the wonderful American junk—pickles, ketchup—that still symbolized the paradise of our adopted country, topping it all off with lemon-meringue pie. And I won my victories by trying to be interesting, forcing Mother to stretch out our time to forty, forty-five minutes. I reached that goal by questioning her about who was coming for hat fittings that afternoon—Very important, she'd answer, looking at her watch, Irene Dunne and Claudette! And she would expound on what "look" she was trying to impose on each of those clients. We never discussed school, for she always feared that such talk would reveal her profound ignorance of all educational matters, and throughout the seven years I was at Spence she never visited it until my graduation day. Yet admixed with my great awe and dread of her, the sense of *chosenness* I enjoyed during those times together—Mother is giving me thirty-five minutes of her precious time!—gave me the greatest happiness I knew in my adolescence. Indeed, those moments we shared were all the more luminous because they were rare and hard-won, because she imbued them with her own special radiance of warmth and wit. They made me strive all the harder for Mother's love and led me to overlook, rather breezily, her busyness and occasional negligence.

Throughout history, hats have been more freighted with associations of sexuality, authority, and status than any other vestment that comes to mind. It was the earliest and most potent symbol of leadership devised by man: coif of Egyptian pharaoh, bishop's miter, medieval crown, headdress denoting military status or police control—and, conversely, the doffing of hat as an essential sign of respect in church, court, and society.

But hats and the general etiquette of headgear were also powerful tools for subjugating women's sexuality. While a male's abundant hair was a flaunted and esteemed symbol of sexual potency, for a woman to show her hair unbound was a sign of emotional imbalance (Ophelia) or promiscuity (Mary Magdalen). And from the beginning of recorded history, women in most cultures were required to cover their heads in public, often even at home, with veils, wimples, bonnets, or coifs. Into the first decades of our own century, hats, except upon formal evening occasions, remained essential emblems of female modesty, and a woman emerging from her house *en cheveux*, hatless, was seen as lower class or morally suspect. These sumptuary codes were somewhat relaxed after World War I and further loosened after World War II, but hats still remained obligatory for formal daytime occasions—lunches, business meetings, church. "It was even a sign of rank to wear them to the office," says cultural historian Rosamund Bernier, a former client of Mother's. "Whereas *Vogue's* secretarial staff had to take their hats off upon arrival, editors wore them throughout working hours, staring at their typewriters right through their veils . . . soon after I joined the magazine, I was told that if I wanted to keep my job it was advisable to buy a hat from Tatiana—they cost ninety-five dollars, a week's salary."

Might my awe and dread of Tatiana have been deepened by this symbolic freight of caste, etiquette, and paramilitary order (Mother as policeman of the body?) Would I have cloaked her with an equally potent aura of *authority* if she had been America's leading designer, say, of swimwear (Madame Cole of California) or of just plain dresses (Claire McCardell, Anne Fogarty)? Who knows.

"The attachment to the mother is bound to perish," Sigmund Freud wrote, specifically discussing daughters' relationship to their mothers, "precisely because it was the first and was so intense. The attitude of love probably comes to grief from the disappointments that are unavoidable and from the accumulation of occasions for aggression." Dr. Freud never did give us girls much of a chance to bond. What his writings on this issue have helped me to realize, however, is the byzantine complexities of daughters' struggle for independence from their mothers. A boy has a relatively easy time of it, achieving the necessary separation from his first love object—mother— by identifying with his father. But since a gender-role identity is equally essential to the development of a healthy female psyche, a girl faces the paradoxical task of having to detach herself from her mother *while continuing to identify with her to some degree.* And this ambiguous process of disentanglement is all the more complex if the mother is a high priestess of the very rite that every teenager wants to master above all others: seduction.

Between my thirteenth and eighteenth years, when I left home for college, Mother inevitably talked me into passing canapés to the world-class fashion icons (Babe Paley, Gloria Guinness), the members of *Vogue*'s sartorially exquisite editorial staff, and the dozens of meticulously starved fashion models who attended the Libermans' gatherings at Seventieth Street. Mother always wanted me to appear at her parties—not that many professional women had children those days, and as I grew up and became more "presentable," as she put it, she increasingly wished to show me off. Just before such events, after perusing every inch of my bodily surface—"Not that sweater again, your breasts are too *large*"; "How many times have I told you that your face is too *wide* for straight hair?"—she propelled me into the living room with a shove at the small of the back and the following command: "*Charmes!*" ("Charm!" in the imperative tense.)

Beyond exposure to the confusing and often triadic sexual arrangements prevalent in any milieu of high style ("no, *chérie*, Alexis de Rédé is Arturo Lopez-Willshaw's lover, not Patricia's"), the chimeric world of couture in which both Mother and Alex moved is bound to have complex effects on any adolescent girl. For she is confronted with those arbiters of seduction who dictate the fall and rise of hems in the West; who advise hundreds of thousands of women on how to comb their hair, improve their figures, seduce their men, feed their guests; who proclaim the gospel of instant gratification with headlines such as "Needed Immediately for Winter! The Bold, Courageous Trapeze!" or "Essential for Evening: Banana Velvet, Fabulous with Sables!" And however we may rage against such tyrannical frivolity, we tend to be bewitched by its goodies. The problem is exacerbated if our fashion-icon parents are as seductive as mine were, and if we have to work as hard as I did for their affection and attention. So well into my twenties I whirled through several contradictory cycles—periods of servile obedience to my parents' swank milieu, followed by cycles of turbulent rebellion against it.

My last years at Spence were still those of servility. I spent much of my energy trying to meet the demanding standards set by the Libermans and my summer mom, Nada. During my weekend escapes from the Seventieth Street gambling den, I wasted a good part of my time looking for contraptions—chest-flattening bras, feet-shrinking shoes—that would purge me of those bodily details so banned by the fashionable. I engaged in numerous diets that might help me to resemble the ghoulishly emaciated models who flocked to Mother's parties: three days of buttermilk and soda water, three days of hard-boiled eggs and tomatoes, three days of stewed prunes and tea. Attempting to hone my measurements to the faddish thirty-four/twenty-four/thirty-four inches, I went to health clubs and stood in archaic pummeling machines, which have left permanent marks. My desire for emaciation, I later realized, was based on a need to simultaneously please Mother and differentiate myself from her: While slavishly emulating the prevalent standards of style for which she was a conduit, I was fashioning my body to be as dissimilar as possible from her own voluptuous frame. What tormented misunderstandings occur between mothers and daughters! A great deal of my own insecurity was based on my feeling that, compared to Tatiana and her ravishing women friends, I was dreadfully plain; meanwhile, her growing affection for me was fed by the satisfaction that I was becoming increasingly "presentable" and was also turning into what *she* would have liked to have been: a school-smart, tomboy skinny "intellectual."

So I was a very divided soul: Inwardly, very secretly, often feeling faint from my diets, while graciously continuing to smile and pass canapés to Elsa Maxwell, Jacques Balmain, Hubert de Givenchy, I was carving out a future for myself radically dissimilar to my parents' lives. I, Francine Ludmilla Pauline Anne-Marie du Plessix, wanted to marry a country gentleman who would liberate me from all this shit. I'd continued to have a strong religious streak, and I dreamed of settling down with a scholarly, somewhat mystical gentleman farmer who wrote poetry or novels on the side, like the fellows in *Country Life* photographs with captions that say "Mr. and Mrs. Tertius Waugh and their five delightful children." No more howling white rooms and ice-hard white furniture and freaky women who plastered their hair down with black shoe polish and decreed, "The Toreador look! Small heads are in this fall." No, no, I yearned for a snug Tudor parsonagelike country home with dark wood paneling, chintz curtains, ottomans tufted in deep burgundy, cozy kitchens where I would put up blackberry jam much of the summer while listening to my husband talk about St. Paul's view of the resurrection and the eschatology of the Patristic Fathers. . . . That was all in preparation for my next cycle of rebellion against Them, my cherished parents.

M y first two college years were spent at Bryn Mawr, my second two at Barnard, when I often came home to reoccupy my room at Seventieth Street. I seem to have flirted, during those years, with a variety of possible careers as drastically different from my parents' as possible. I began as a medievalist, dallied midway with physics and premed, ended up majoring in philosophy and religion, and came close to entering Union Theological Seminary for a graduate degree in divinity ("*Ça fait très bien de s'occuper de Dieu,*"

"It's very elegant to busy oneself with God" was Mother's comment about that possibility). And at the end of my junior and senior years in Barnard I enrolled for summer sessions at Black Mountain College, a community whose zeitgeist—rebellion against every form of established order, political or aesthetic—would thrust my antiparental cycle into full gear.

At Black Mountain, I occasionally smoked pot, sat entranced through John Cage's Zen-anarchist lectures, played strip poker with Bob Rauschenberg, and particularly appalled my mother by wearing leather motorcycle jackets and chopping my hair as short and jagged as a contemporary punk's. ("She has *shaved* herself!" Mother cried. "You look like Port Authority Terminal," moaned Alex, who had never been to an American bus or train station in his life but had published Gjon Mili's daunting photos of them in *Vogue.*) The summer after graduation, I bought a thirdhand Plymouth with the money earned from winning Barnard's Creative Writing Prize, drove to New Orleans, and spent two months in a haze of bourbon, hanging out with jazz clarinetists, and playing poker with a Communist Party cell (a salubrious experience: their humorlessness quickly inoculated me against the CP). I wasn't good about staying in touch with Mother and Alex that summer. And Alex, fretting about the possibility of my becoming a fallen woman and a communist to boot, telephoned Mabel from the south of France, ordering her to fly to New Orleans and check up on me. Mabel, thrilled with the free trip, found me living in a one-room flat on Bourbon Street, "full of beans and hanging out with very different folk," as her diplomatic report to the Boss and the Madam was phrased. Her trip was an education for me: Determined to give her a good time, I packed her into my car and took her for a three-day sightseeing trip of the bayou country, throughout which time we had to stay in "colored folks' motels," as such institutions then called themselves, in order to remain together.

I returned to New York and worked for two years as a reporter on the overnight shift of the United Press radio desk, writing "World in Briefs" on murders, earthquakes, corn futures, and the latest developments in the Joseph McCarthy hearings. A hardworking tomboy—hadn't my mother prepped me for being just that?—I was the only woman on the UP's graveyard shift, relishing the martinis consumed at 8:00 A.M. in Third Avenue bars with my male colleagues. I went home to a basement room in the West Village that I shared with my dearest friend at Bryn Mawr, Joanna Rose, who was then working as a model on Seventh Avenue. My moving out of her house struck Mother as a personal affront, upsetting her so much that she took to her bed for three days, demanding morphine for an alleged migraine, and would never even deign visit my downtown quarters. However, Alex, always the peacemaker, did come down to the Village during my first fortnight there and reported to her that it was "a dignified, even distinguished location," which restored a measure of peace between Mother and daughter for the rest of my stay in New York.

I n the mid-1950s—the feminine, unquestioning Eisenhower fifties, the last golden years of the standards of beauty and elegance that had shaped my mother's vocation—Tatiana of Saks's career flourished as never before. "Nothing goes to a woman's head like a hat by our own Tatiana," the Saks in-house magazine boasted. "Her magnificent creations are the delight of our most particular customers." *The New York Times*'s Virginia Pope wrote that Tatiana's designs display "both wit and wisdom" and praised their "soigné look" and "well-groomed charm." Mother's hats were so popular that in 1955 Saks decided that she must produce a ready-to-wear line alongside her custom designs and sent her on the road to promote her creations in its midwestern branches. "Tatiana—so much the vogue!" an ad in *The New York Times* announced. "Charming for Easter but prophetic for summer are three black diamonds from her newest collection, the More-Hat Look . . . the Deep-Mushroom, shadowy sheer or all-velvet . . . the Theater Chignon. . . . Now available in all our out-of-town stores."

I was not that much in touch with the prime of Tatiana's career. For at the age of twenty-three I had moved to Paris. And I had upped the ante in my new cycle of filial compliance—my gambit, this time, was to secure my mother's love by emulating the life *she* had led at that age. With Alex and Mother's help, I got a job with France's leading fashion magazine, *Elle*, and set out to conquer precisely that same glittering beau monde Mother had wished to conquer forty years before as a young refugee from Russia. I sat in the showrooms of Chanel, Patou, Givenchy, and Dior, taking notes on the tweeds and tulles paraded at collection time. Living in a tiny, somber room on the Ile Saint-Louis, down to a bare 110 pounds and verging on anorexia, I masterminded fashion sittings, pinned dresses on zonked-out models, wrote fashion captions, which said, "Balenciaga's newest chemise surprise! False double hem, single-breasted buttoning down the side." Like Mother in the 1930s, I scrambled to get invited to the Rothschilds' dinners and borrowed dresses from couture houses to attend them. ("Angel, do you have a little number to lend me for the evening? . . . Brown chiffon size six, oh, thank you.") In sum, I was trying to replay my mother's success on precisely her own past turf, the siren Paris.

In those years, my correspondence with my parents reflected my fear that their success, their bonds with important friends, far superseded their need for me. "*Maman adorée,*" so one letter of spring 1955 reads, "I am crazed, crazed with joy at the prospect of accompanying you to Rome this summer. . . . I beg you not to change your mind. . . . I'm not so much thrilled by the prospect of Rome . . . as by the notion that it will be the only way we can be *quietly* together. . . . You and Alex remain, as you've always been, the center of my existence." And then there were the missives in which I stated my solidarity in practicing *their* trade, couture (a vocation for which I felt increasingly unfit). "Monday the major hustling begins," I wrote in 1955 as I covered the winter collections for *Elle.* "Three major collections a day to cover and then fashion shoots late into the night. . . . I'm in the photo studio where I'm going to live through the rest of the week, preparing the color pages, which are made before the collections begin in an atmosphere of atomic secrecy—a messenger just arrived from Dior in an armored truck, pistols in each hand, with the suit we're using on the cover."

My frequently caustic descriptions of the Paris fashion scene and of Paris high society in the mid-fifties seemed to impress Mother immensely. Her crippled hand had always served as an excuse for never writing more than a few phrases, so her habit was to cable me rather than write or else to jot a few words at the end of Alex's infrequent missives. But in the autumn of 1955 she must have found a pal willing to take dictation from her or hired a secretary, for I received a perfectly typed three-page letter from her in which she hints, for the first time, that I might be "a writer." "Your long letter from . . . the Ile Saint Louis is, quite simply, a *chef d'oeuvre* of contemporary prose. And you're totally mistaken if you think that it was too long, for I had Alex read it to me three evenings in a row."

But however thrilled my mother was by my modest success in her world of fashion and by my promising literary style, nothing delighted her more than the man I was going out with during my last year in Paris. In this particular mimesis of Tatiana I had aspired to be courted by barons and counts, as she had, and I bettered her: I ended up going steady—how corny can you get?—with an alcoholic prince. No earlier accomplishments of mine—no A+ college exams or Creative Writing Awards—evoked such a surge of maternal approval as I received during my affair with that particular cad. Every writer I know relishes above all others one particular line of their crafting. And my own favorite, from my novel *Lovers and Tyrants,* tartly resumes the subtext of my two-year stay in Paris in the 1950s: "fucking goons for mom." For what was I really doing with that ridiculous prince, with my borrowed finery and my absurd bouffant hair, with my meticulously underfed mannequin's body, with a fashion career that led me into deep depressions? I was running toward the arms of the beloved couple whose love I'd been trying to conquer ever since my father's death, I was running as fast as I could, like a track star on speed, toward their affection and approval, all the time shouting, "I'm just like you now, please pay attention, pay attention at last. . . ."

And then in the middle of that race, I went kerplunk. I woke up one morning, delirious, with a 105-degree temperature and internal hemorrhages and was declared to have one of the more extreme cases of mononucleosis on record. Doctors prescribed total rest for two months and partial rest for at least another year. I returned to the United States in the autumn of 1956 to pursue my convalescence, and this homecoming requires a stylistic note: As I stood on the boat deck, waving to the emotional parents waiting impatiently for me on land below, I was wearing a Chanel suit of pink and gray tweed, which they had offered me as a present a few weeks earlier for my twenty-sixth birthday. The first and last item of haute couture I would ever own, it marked the end of my life in fashion. A few months later, it was in this particular outfit that I met my future husband, the reclusive, contemplative painter Cleve Gray, and redeemed my life by setting forth on that quiet rural existence, in a snug, dark house, which I had dreamed of since childhood.

For Cleve Gray was to be the savior of my adulthood, just the way Alex had been the savior of my youth. While loving and admiring Tatiana and Alex, he remained critical of them and was generally appalled by the world of fashion; he understood the various ways in which my path in life must diverge from theirs; he honored and encouraged our differences while never trespassing on my filial affection. The spoiled child of an obsessively doting, neurasthenic mother who would have made a shambles of a less stalwart son, he had lost much of his youthful arrogance during four years' service in World War II, yet was still plagued by many problems—a tendency to passivity and reclusiveness, a blend of shyness and great impatience, occasional lack of social skills. But there was a sterling integrity and depth to him, which it was never in my hustling parents' character to possess: Radically—at times pitifully—devoid of any self-promoting impulses, he was as guileless, as incapable of advancing his own ends, as Alex was skilled at that art. He was as loyal as my parents were fickle, as wary of appearances as they were haunted by them, as indifferent to social status as they were obsessed by it. And through his probity and tenderness he offered me a greater self-assurance and stability than I had ever dreamed of achieving. A summa cum laude graduate of Princeton in art history, his learning in the very field in which my parents thought they excelled was far deeper than theirs. And both my parents, initially taken by his handsomeness and wonderful manners, soon recognized his superiority in many areas of culture and of general common sense, and grew to adore him for the remarkable human being he was.

The texture of filial and maternal bonds can be greatly altered by a daughter's marriage. What was wondrous about my definitive farewell to the world of fashion and my new life was that my relations with Mother gradually improved. Perhaps we had been greater rivals than I'd ever realized for

Alex's love and the world's attention. Though I'd been more or less self-reliant since I'd left college, perhaps it was also a relief to my parents—as Tatiana had coolly said about her own mother—to have "one less mouth to feed." Moreover, there was a strong streak of traditionalism in my eccentric parents, and they may have wished, above all, for their daughter to "make a good match" with a man they approved of. Within months, Mother was boasting to her friends that Cleve was "the world's *best* son-in-law"—it helped that he was Jewish, spoke fluent French, had landed on Normandy Beach a few weeks after D-Day, and had been the first GI to call on Picasso and Gertrude Stein right after the liberation of Paris, all her rather simplistic hierarchy of manly valor.

I went on to have two sons, born sixteen months apart. And as meticulously as I had crafted a body, a quiet country life, a marriage, a decor radically different from Tatiana's, I offered my children all that I had not received from her in my youth: I drove daily car pools, made dinner for them most nights of the week, gave them their first skiing and tennis lessons, tried to offer them constant companionship, constant conversation. If my relations with Tatiana reached an unprecedented level of serenity in those years, it may also be because I was continuing to fulfill most mothers' secret wish: the desire that their daughters not repeat their mistakes, that they better them in every aspect of the art of living.

Through my children, I also grew more aware of Tatiana's Confucian streak, her potential for family dutifulness. Both she and Alex adored their grandsons from the start, and I was amused and gratified to see that they lavished far more attention on them than they had on me—perhaps they had been mellowed by their success, by the achievement of most of their ambitions. They could not see enough of my children and were thrilled to call off dinner parties in order to babysit for them. An abiding memory: Mother running up the stairs upon coming home from Saks the first time I brought my first baby to Seventieth Street, rushing into our room shouting, *"Il est là! Il est là!"* and sweeping the six-week-old into her arms, repeatedly cooing, *"Joli garçon! Joli garçon!"* She grew to be hilariously competitive about my children, as she was about most aspects of life. They worshiped her, and at the age of three my oldest son, Thaddeus, repeatedly announced, "I'm going to marry Grandma when I grow up." How she rubbed *that* in—"He wants to marry *me*, not his mother."

Our friendship was not without its difficulties. Unable to master more than a few paragraphs in English, in the following decades Tatiana was never able to read more than a few pages of my writings beyond those that were translated into French. She grew proud of me solely on the basis of hearsay that I was achieving "a reputation." Moreover, I'd saved my soul and my sanity by carving out a private world that she could not invade and incorporate into her great kingdom, and I had to keep my frontiers closely guarded. My husband and I visited my parents almost weekly. But if Mother could have had her way she would have had us perpetually under her all-engulfing control, attending the same parties she and Alex attended, joining them in all the summer sites they vacationed in every year: Va-et-Vient, Ischia, Venice, the Lido. Our one capitulation to her wishes, a month spent at Va-et-Vient with our children in 1965, turned out as wretchedly as I'd feared: We couldn't stand my parents' hectic social pace, and they, in turn, constantly derided our need for seclusion. So from then on, I politely said no to most of her varied offers and demands. No, Maman *chérie*, we can't join you at the Lido next summer; no, Mother, don't make a copy of your Dior suit for me, it is simply too formal for my kind of life; no, we can't join you at the April in Paris ball next month.

Thaddeus and Luke Gray playing doctor with "Grandpa Liberman," 1963.

In the first months of my marriage, my husband, whose life would have been far easier if he had said no early on to his own extremely invasive parents, asked me, "Why do you always say no to your mother?" Within a year, he'd understood enough to cease asking the question. And over time, Mother was also wise enough to realize that my achievements had depended on my ability to carve out a realm of my own. So we visited across our borders, hugging profusely but still somewhat armed, able to discuss my children's education, whatever books we'd both read in French, the illness and death of old friends.

I t is ironic that my career took off the very year Mother's declined. In the spring of 1965, just as I was submitting my first pieces to *The New Yorker*, the ax fell on Ta-

Tatiana and her first grandson, Thaddeus, on our Connecticut terrace, summer 1960.

tiana of Saks. To all appearances, her trade seemed to be flourishing. "Tatiana's hats are works of art in themselves," a Saks press release had boasted the previous fall. "Prim, Proper and Pretty," the Chicago *Sun-Times* praised her last collection. "Tatiana specializes in the Bow Geste," Lois Long had written in her *New Yorker* column "On and Off the Avenue," praising the way in which the designer's "massed bows of inch-wide black satin ribbon give a charming, bunchy look to basically neat shapes." Yet Saks's management decided that the hat department of the Salon Moderne was losing too much money. And with no great ceremony, Tatiana was fired by her friend Adam Gimbel—due to the general demise of custom-design fashions, Sophie of Saks, who, miraculously, remained Mother's close friend, was to close the Salon Moderne altogether four years later.

What I find most astounding about Tatiana's twenty-three-year tenure at Saks is that not even at the zenith of her career was she ever offered a raise and that she never dared to ask for one. This timidity concerning money, which she shared with her father, was part of her Old World culture, her grande dame quality—talk of personal finances was far more taboo to her than talk of sex. It also had to do with her self-demeaning modesty. For however well she sold, Mother never thought she was selling enough. "I'm not worth more than they're giving me," she told Alex whenever he urged her to ask Adam Gimbel for a raise. And so the fabulous Tatiana of Saks ended her career receiving the same salary she had been offered more than two decades earlier as a refugee—a little more than eleven thousand dollars a year. Moreover, upon retiring she never even received a pension. "She's a countess," Gimbel told my stepfather when he got up his courage to raise the issue, "and everyone knows you're well off now."

The demise of Tatiana's calling in the early and mid-1960s had deep roots in the culture at large, for it was based on the sudden obsolescence of the hat, a singular chapter in the annals of Western fashion, which was provoked by innumerable socioeconomic factors. A small sampling: the general process of democratization ignited by the Kennedy era and the consequent blurring of class distinctions that hats had always delineated (Jack Kennedy, one might note, was the first presidential candidate of the century to campaign without a hat); the first stirrings of a feminist movement, which rebelled vociferously against the dictatorship of fashion; the rising influence of the young, who had always been exempted from the wearing of hats. By the late 1960s, the only persons showing enthusiasm for headgear were members of the counterculture, whose eccentric varieties of symbolic hats—coonskin caps, Che Guevara berets, calico pioneer sunbonnets, Native American headbands—mainly served to express sympathy for oppressed political and racial minorities, for much that was tribal, ethnic, primitive.

However flamboyant her facade, Tatiana's aesthetic had been one of quiet elitist moderation, of seductive yet tamed femininity. And nothing could have been more abhorrent to her than the forthright, egalitarian sensuality that accompanied the demise of the hat and was reflected in the high fashion magazines that had been her bibles since her youth: Helmut Newton's lascivious Valkyries, Deborah Turbeville's shots of seemingly masturbating girls. Some years after her retirement, she shyly brought out an album of her press clips to look at with me—John Rawlings or Horst P. Horst photographs of daintily groomed Jean Patchett modeling Tatiana's exquisite boaters, bretons, toques. "Don't women still want fashions that are *becoming*, like mine were?" she wistfully asked me.

My heart always aches when I imagine the dejection Mother must have suffered upon the last Friday of work, upon the first Monday of having to stay home. In 1965, she was only fifty-nine, still filled with volcanic energy. Her habit of hard daily work, pursued since the age of nineteen, must have been quite as addictive as any drug she ever took; and its cessation must have been as anguishing as her father's giving up his gambling. If I had to live my life over again, I would try to visit with her more often in those first years of her retirement, to praise the valor of her career, to make her sense that in her moments of affliction her often intractable daughter was her best pal, her most loyal admirer. If I had another life to live, I would be a pure *friend* of Tatiana, enjoying a comradeship unburdened by the inevitable debris of mother-daughter relations. What a gigantic appetite and gift she had for friendship! She might occasionally play by Alex's brutal rules of social pragmatism, as she had by abandoning the difficult Nada, but her true loyalties, radically unlike his, extended far, far beyond New York's "useful" persons. It included dozens of friends from the 1940s and a number of charity cases—down-and-out Russians, meek and very boring little Quaker ladies sent her by the Wileys—whom she fed and sheltered because they had been put in her care.

In the years that followed her retirement, I also discovered other dimensions of that dutifulness toward family, which she was displaying so passionately to her grandchildren. By then, she had persuaded Alex to support quite a few of her down-and-out relatives. The Libermans sent monthly stipends to my great-aunt Sandra, who upon reaching her mid-sixties had to retire from the music school where she had taught voice for several decades. They equally supported my grandfather, whose wife, the sweet Zinochka who had been so kind to me in Rochester, had died of cancer in 1958. Mother and Alex then invited him to live with them at Seventieth Street, and he occupied my old childhood room on the third floor for more than two years, until a hearty, comely middle-aged French woman fell head over heels in love with the handsome old man and whisked him off to her bed-and-breakfast in the Hudson Valley. Moreover, throughout the 1950s and 1960s my parents also gave financial aid to my mother's half brother, Eugene "Jika" Jackson, who now had a family of his own but could work only part-time after a debilitating car accident. And for a while they even sent several thousand dollars a year to my father's cousin, Uncle André Monestier, whose fortunes had never recovered from the economic havoc wrought by World War II.

Another family grief had befallen Mother shortly before her retirement. It was in tragically timed circumstances that she heard in 1963 about the death of her mother, Lyubov Nikolaevna Orlova. In the late 1950s, correspondence between the United States and the Soviet Union, although far improved since the Stalin era, was still haphazard. One letter out of four may have reached its destination, and Soviet citizens could still get into trouble for corresponding with a "capitalist power." Still, some Soviets and westerners took their chances. Mother's sister, Lila, who then lived in Paris, began to write their mother in 1957, with no ill effect, but I much doubt if she informed my mother that she'd resumed the correspondence, for the sisters, over the years, had strayed far apart. Moreover, Mother was totally under the sway of her beloved John Wiley, a protégé of John Foster Dulles who had persuaded her that it was highly dangerous to write to Russia. Mother, who had her own share of paranoia about the Soviet Union, took his advice as gospel truth.

Compound this with a certain lazy, self-protective streak in my mother's character and with the difficulties presented by writing with an impaired right arm: Tatiana did not contact her mother until April of 1963, after John Wiley had reluctantly given her the green light. She finally wrote, giving news of the past eighteen years since the war's end, news of my growing up, of my marriage, of my children, sending photographs of all of us. A month or so later, she received a note from her stepfather, telling her that Lyubov Nikolaevna had died of heart failure the very day before Tatiana's letter arrived. True to the stoical narcissism that runs through most women in my Russian family, my grandmother had gone to the hairdresser the morning of her death, come home, sat down in her favorite armchair, and passed on.

It doesn't get much more Greek than that, does it? Only a few weeks before, Lyubov Nikolaevna had complained to Lila—as she'd complained for the previous six years—about Mother's silence. I inherited my grandmother's letters upon Lila's own death in the late 1990s and have read the following maternal cris de coeur: "Could you think of a few good reasons why Tatiana does not write to me?" "If you see Francine and her little children, will you please write me all about them?" "I've never been so hurt by anything as by Taniousha's silence." Tatiana might well have defied John Wiley's counsel if Lila had passed on such comments, and her letters could have offered my grandmother a great solace in her last years. But an intractable paranoia informed the sisters' relations. Mother told me about her loss one afternoon when I came in from Connecticut. She was sitting on the Chinese sofa, looking unusually pensive, and waved me over to sit by her. "I wrote to my mother for the first time in many years," she said impassively, "she died the day before my letter arrived." It was the first time in my life that she had even mentioned her mother without my solicitation. She stood up, sadness in her eyes, blew me a kiss, and walked up to her room.

So that is another instance when I should have tried to restore tenderness, made a greater effort to offer some consolation. But this sudden allusion to a mother whom she'd never mentioned, with whom I'd always assumed she'd had glacial relations, caught me off guard.

Moreover I was living the self-absorbed pace of most women in their thirties—raising my children, while also increasingly writing about and working for political causes, so much so that in the late 1960s my heavy involvement in the antiwar movement was to create yet new sources of tension between Tatiana and me. True to her émigré origins even then, as tourism and student exchanges between the United States and the USSR had begun to flourish, she remained archaically opposed to any détente with the communist world. As far as she was concerned, the only good commie was a dead commie, and on the basis of what she had read in New York's leading Russian-language paper, *Novoye Russkoye Slovo*, she was gung ho on the Vietnam War. My husband was as fervent an antiwar activist as I, and her opposition to our views grew particularly vociferous whenever she drank—a teetotaler all of her life, after retirement she had begun to indulge more and more heavily. During our visits to New York, as she watched Cleve designing Eugene McCarthy posters or heard me making phone calls about some forthcoming peace rally, she would scowl at us over her Scotch or her glass of Bordeaux, growling, "You sell out to Hanoi? You play into hands of Vietcong?"

But can we ever invent an ideal parent? In those very years, returning from an antiwar demonstration in Washington, D.C., in the company of Cleve and Dick Avedon, I mused nostalgically: "What would I have been like if I'd had a mother who would have *understood* me . . . like Hannah Arendt, say?" "You'd have become a fashion model," Avedon answered, deadpan.

As a rebellious offspring of the best-dressed crowd, I should end this chapter with a last note on my thrifty, unmodish attitude toward clothes and on my sentimental concern for carefully preserving any present my parents have ever given me: I so lovingly maintained the jacket of the Chanel suit in which I met my husband that in the fall of 1994 I wore it to the christening of our first grandchild.

NINETEEN

The Artist in His Studios

I must now explain how Alex began to paint again.

In March of 1946, at the age of thirty-three, he had suffered the first ulcer hemorrhage he'd had since the age of seventeen, and again he had nearly bled to death. He was ordered to stop working for two months. I was on spring vacation from Spence during a few weeks of his convalescence. Mabel was on maternity leave, Sally could come for only a few hours a day, so it was up to me to cook most of Alex's meals—if the desolate pap of a severe ulcer diet can be called a meal: His all-white regimen consisted mostly of breast of chicken, mashed potatoes, rice, Cream of Wheat, vanilla junket. I took immense pride in cooking for Alex and always tried to give his food a festive touch by putting a tiny green object at the center of the whiteness—a green pea, a teeny sprig of parsley. During that spring break, I did little else than shop for my parents, sit home and read Dostoevsky, and cook. At the appointed time for his lunch—1:00 P.M.—I would bring Alex his tray. He would be lying on his bed on the right side of the room, reading, propped up against several pillows. "Hello, darling," he'd say, however tired or sleepy he was. Sitting up a bit—in the first weeks after his hemorrhage, the effort was visible—he would squeeze my hand, say, "Thank you, my love," and ask me what I'd done or read that morning.

Before disappearing, I'd kiss him on the top of his head, aware, as I remained throughout my youth, that beyond the fact that I adored him, this man may well have saved my life.

It had been a stressful and eventful year for Alex. In January, his father had died of cancer, leaving barely a cent to anyone—by that time, Simon's business earnings had sharply declined. His mother, Henriette, had been more exasperating than ever since Simon's death. (We all breathed a sigh of

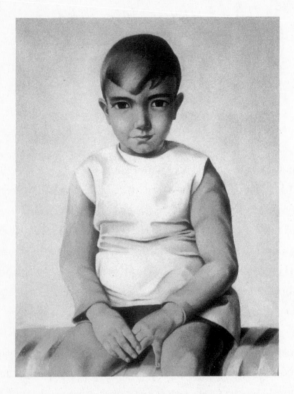

Alex's "Yellow Boy" (portrait of Liuba Krasin's son),
painted in Paris in 1938.

relief the following year, when she returned to live in Paris.) Moreover, that very year, shortly after Alex had become an American citizen, the lease on our Seventieth Street house had expired, and Alex had taken a large loan from Condé Nast to buy it, retaining the Shuvalov family as our upstairs tenants. But the most important factor in Alex's illness, I believe, was that his success as a whiz kid of American fashion publishing had left him no time to paint: Beyond the very academic portrait he had done of his father upon arriving in the States in 1941, Alex had not picked up a paintbrush for five years, totally repressing what he looked on as his true vocation. The summer after his illness, he decided to take a longer summer break than usual and accepted an invitation for us to visit the Levals in July at their house on Martha's Vineyard. Alex had had no time whatever to travel in the States, and it was in a little fishing town on the Vineyard, seemingly inspired by the impact of a totally novel site, that he suddenly went to an art store and bought himself a folding easel, some brushes, and oils.

Alex was particularly captivated by the fishing boats on Menemsha Bay and the area's misty marine light. Setting up his easel amid the lobster pots, he started painting landscapes with brushstrokes far looser, far more liberated than those on his tight, academic canvases of the prewar years. The pleasure of making art again seemed to be infectious. As soon as we returned to Stony Brook for our August vacation, Alex set up his easel in the gallery area of the squash court, dropped out of Mother's and Uncle Pat's card games, and began a six-hour-a-day studio regimen. He painted flowers that Mother arranged from the garden; landscapes of the water view from our house; a portrait of me—the first he had done since 1938, when Mother had first brought us together—that still bore traces of Iacovleff's slick realism. That very fall, upon returning to Seventieth Street, Alex transformed our second-floor library into a studio and began quietly to paint on weekends whenever there was a respite from his social life, showing his work to no one beyond Mother and me.

Alex's next breakthrough occurred in the summer of 1947, when he made his first postwar trip to Venice. The Libermans took a room at the Gritti Hotel, across the Grand Canal from Santa Maria della Salute, and Alex began obsessively to paint the view from his window, working with gouache on paper, limning the play of light on the church's domes and voluted arches at various times of day. After two weeks in Venice, they drove on to Sainte Maxime. They had joyfully reclaimed Va-et-Vient, which had been only faintly damaged by the German occupation, the previous sum-

Alexander Liberman, "Santa Maria della Salute,"
Venice, oil on canvas, painted in 1948.

mer. Maria, the housekeeper, had been there to welcome them, weeping with emotion. They were so happy with this summer vacation schedule—two weeks apiece in Venice and Va-et-Vient—that they continued it for many years.

In the following winters, Alex gave an increasing amount of time on weekends to his painting. In his attempt to express an original vision, he felt he had to experiment with a vast variety of styles. And in the ensuing three years, he traveled his way through the history of modern art with what one can only call a vertiginous journalistic speed: Experimenting with Expressionism, Impressionism, Pointillism, he "worked out his admirations," as he put it, for the artists whom he considered the greatest modern masters. A 1948 painting inspired by attending a recital by Vladimir Horowitz is an unabashed gloss on Braque. A tortured self-portrait done in the same year is an equally shameless pastiche of Van Gogh. In a 1949 portrait of me done while I was home from Bryn Mawr, the technique of distortion is strikingly similar to Chaïm Soutine's. This eerily swift change of pace was characteristic of Alex's gypsyish restlessness and his extraordinary facility.

But the late 1940s were also a period of spiritual and aesthetic search for him. He was rebelling against the stranglehold of Cubism on French twentieth-century art. He had begun to admire the work of American Abstract Expressionists, such as Rothko, Pollock, and Newman, but he thought their painterliness was still more "European" than the style he was hoping to evolve for himself. He also disliked the New York School's autobiographical impulse. For in those years he was fond of quoting a saying of Pascal that had been a motto of sorts during his Calvinist education at Les Roches: *"Le moi est haissable,"* "The ego is hateful." He dreamed of the possibility of creating an art that would be utterly impersonal and that would also be akin to music or drama in its repeatability.

Ultimately, the landscapes Alex painted of Venice's Grand Canal were most instrumental in nudging him toward abstraction. He had rendered the shimmering play of light on water by large thick dots of white gouache applied directly from his tube onto the canvas, and in 1949 these pointillistic daubs, greatly expanded in scale, took on a life of their own. He began to paint jagged, abstracted round shapes that recalled Monet's suns or volcanic craters. But these forms still bore too many traces of Impressionism and Expressionism for his taste. Later that year, his "revulsion for the personal," as he phrased it, inspired the creation of large-format circles, drawn to geometric precision with large compasses, for which he abandoned all traditional materials. Instead of using canvas, he turned to Masonite or aluminum panels. Instead of oil, he employed commercial high-gloss enamel, which created a hard, reflective sheen akin to that of refrigerator or automobile paint. He dubbed his style "Circlism," and in a statement drawn up a few years later for the Museum of Modern Art archives he explained it in the following manner:

> *I consider the circle the simplest, purest element of visual research. The circle is the common property of the two infinites, from the immense sun to the infinitesimal atom. . . . [A]bove all the circle is the purest symbol because it is instantly visible in its totality.*

By the early 1950s, Alex had evolved a system whereby his hard-line circle paintings could be created in his absence by an assistant working from maquettes. Still very weakened by his ulcers, he may have been searching for art forms through which his vision could be perpetuated in case he grew too ill to execute them himself. He is also likely to have been inspired by the Suprematist and Constructivist art that flourished in Russia in the 1910s and 1920s. And his preoccupation with art as an indestructible idea rather than a perishable object (which the art critic Barbara Rose, in her 1983 book on Alex, reads as a neo-Platonic concept) might well be traced to his traumatic experience of the century's greatest historical upheavals. Whatever motivated him, there is no doubt that he was making some of the first Minimalist art in our time. In fact, one of his breakthrough paintings of 1949, long before that "ism" had entered our vocabulary, was a white circle, finely drawn on a four-foot black square, called *Minimum.*

But one should emphasize the extreme isolation in which Alex was making this kind of hard-edge geometric art. He was working in direct opposition to the 1950s New York art scene, which was totally dominated by action painting. (In those years, the only American artist of Alex's generation to be working with geometric forms was Ellsworth Kelly, who remained in Paris until the mid-fifties.) Did Alex have any community of friends or colleagues with whom he could discuss his work? None whatsoever. His immediate entourage—Uncle Pat, Marlene Dietrich, the Levals—thought his abstractions to be amusing nonsense. Given his superhuman schedule as media mogul, househusband, and weekend artist, Alex had not had a second in which to hang out with those American painters who were transforming the art of our time—Pollock, Rothko, Motherwell, Ad Reinhardt. As for my mother, she was not fond of the company of artists unless they had reached phenomenal renown, such as Picasso or Dalí or her compatriot Chagall. Moreover, however extensive her culture, her tastes in the visual arts were downright reactionary. Her favorite painter was still Vermeer—the artist she kept urging Alex to emulate even into the 1950s. She had barely progressed beyond Impressionism, had been appalled when Alex started moving beyond his realistic portraits and his pretty landscapes, and like the rest of her milieu thought Alex's circles were, as she put it, "a lot of bunk."

In fact, it is ironic that the greatest enthusiasm elicited by Alex's paintings in the early 1950s came from the radical artists whom I had met at Black Mountain in the summers of 1951 and 1952. My closest friends there had been John Cage, Merce Cunningham, and Bob Rauschenberg, and we visited together at Seventieth Street after the end of the 1951 summer session. They were all enthused by Alex's experiments with the circle and returned often to visit him in subsequent years, when I was living in Paris. Alex was particularly taken with Cage, whose system of chance notation he occasionally emulated in his own system of composing circles, and he always remained grateful to these artists for offering him such encouragement at the beginning of his career as a Minimalist.

"Two Circles," enamel on masonite, exhibited at the Guggenheim Museum's "Younger American Painters" exhibition in 1954.

So here was Alex during weekday office hours, managing a group of magazines that shouted headlines such as "Hems up three inches, absolutely!" Here he was on weekday nights being a socialite. And here he was on weekends, creating, in often painful isolation, some of the decade's boldest art. The critic Clement Greenberg and the artist Barnett Newman came to his studio in 1953, stayed a long time, drank a great deal, but did nothing to help him, and he did not see them again for some years. In those same months, the dealer Sidney Janis visited Alex and told him he should do ballet decors. There was only one breakthrough in the solitude Alex suffered during that decade as an artist: In 1954 James Johnson Sweeney chose one of his Minimalist canvases—a stark image of two black circles on white—for a group show at the Guggenheim Museum entitled *Younger American Painters*. It was the only painting Alex was to exhibit before 1960, and it gave him a taste of the stigma his publishing career was to cast on his artistic vocation for a long time to come: *Time* dismissed Alex's Guggenheim piece as "a pristine nothing . . . by the art director of Conde Nast magazines."

It is in the context of this solitude that Alex started the series of photographs of the School of Paris painters that were ultimately assembled into his book *The Artist in His Studio.*

Over the years, Alex had developed a kind of self-protective contempt for his work at Condé Nast. He sensed that it was the only course he could have taken to assure his and my mother's needs for comfort and security—needs dictated by their chronically poor health and by the traumatic deracinations of their youths. He felt that the financial security brought by his job also liberated his art (or so he rationalized it) from marketplace constraints, from the whims of critics and art collectors. He often told me that his identity as an artist made him feel superior to much of the magazine world, and this gave him the kind of unquestioning self-confidence every good editor needs. So all the while, he looked on painting—his own and others'—as a kind of ideal realm, which could serve as a shelter from the shallow glitz of the fashion world. And in the summer of 1948, when, during his yearly vacation in France, a mutual acquaintance proposed that Alex go to photograph Georges Braque at his home on the Normandy coast, Alex jumped at the idea. He had long regretted not having met the School of Paris painters in the prewar years, and he saw it as a good chance to catch up with them. He found his visit with Braque so enriching that in the following four summers he photographed more than a dozen other artists and also documented the studios of several artists no longer alive, such as Cézanne, Monet, and Kandinsky.

Like the painting vocation Alex had just begun to resume, his chronicling of these pioneers of twentieth-century modernism was initially a totally private project, a very personal investigation into what, as he put it himself, "my life would have been like if I had devoted it completely to painting." He worked on it for four years without any intent whatsoever of publishing it. In fact, his chronicles may have served as a dialogue with the inner artist buried in his Faustian personality, the artist his mother had so insistently urged him to be. They can be seen as a meditation on the suffering and dedication all too often required by true artists and by their wives—that very suffering and dedication which Alex had not felt able to undertake.

In the late 1940s and early 1950s, I accompanied Alex on several of his visits to artists' studios and observed his working manner at close hand. It was above all else marked by the truly religious respect he had for art—a respect inherited from the Russian culture in which his parents had been steeped, a culture that adulated art to a greater degree than any other tradition in the West. It was also marked by a humility and egolessness I'd never observed in any other aspect of Alex's life or work. Similarly to Henri Cartier-Bresson, whom he may well have admired more than any other photographer of his generation, Alex worked very quietly and unobtrusively, with a handheld Leica, never using a tripod, making do with whatever light was available. He kept his stays brief—an hour or so—and returned year after year if he felt he needed more shots to make his documentation complete. The courtesy and respect with which he approached his subjects was returned—he was always welcomed back.

By coincidence, I accompanied Alex on his first visits to Braque and Giacometti, the two painters whose lifestyles, respectively, impressed him and appalled him the most. Braque, an amiable, elegant man who was sixty-six years old upon the first of four visits Alex paid him, struck him as being the "great lord" of contemporary art. He was totally awed by the blend of elegance and efficacy that characterized both Braque's home and his living space. "Braque has raised the material comfort of the artist to its highest possible degree," he wrote in *The Artist in His Studio*. "The conception of his studios is grand and noble. They are like the throne rooms of Renaissance princes. There is no outward show of luxury, but luxury is everywhere—luxury is in the peace of Braque's life, in its spaciousness and quiet. . . . Life seems to center around him. . . . He has solved the material problems of creation." And as we rode back to Paris from Normandy that afternoon in 1948, I detected a nostalgic gleam in Alex's eyes as he chatted effusively about details of our visit—Have you ever seen a more glorious work space? Wasn't Mme. Braque so charming and witty? Did you see the way she shelters and nurtures him? Isn't their life ideal? However efficiently he rationalized his need to work at Condé Nast, over the years I witnessed several such moments when Alex observed a balance of dedication and material comfort in the life of another artist and felt his own glamorous existence sadly wanting.

At the opposite pole of the Braque experience was our visit to Giacometti, who lived with his wife in one tiny, slovenly room that served as living room, bedroom, kitchen, and bath. Here was a man who insisted on a totally needless discomfort—Giacometti was already selling his work quite well but chose to retain the original squalor of his early career for what seemed to be talismanic reasons. Alex was particularly appalled by the grim dustiness, if not filth, of his surroundings: So terrified was Giacometti of imperiling his creative process that no scrap of plaster, no pencil shaving was ever allowed to be thrown out. "Perhaps there is a superstitious need to prolong the mood of his creative inspiration," Alex mused in *The Artist in His Studio.* "To relocate to improved quarters might cut the thread, alter the radioactive effect of the surroundings that have produced so many masterpieces." Needless to say, Alex began to express his horror of Giacometti's surroundings the second we left his studio. "Have you ever seen anything more squalid?" he burst out. "That beautiful young wife, the poor girl . . . What does it all mean?" "Thank God your mother didn't come along on this visit!" he added.

Alex's documentation of contemporary artists might never have had a public viewing without Irving Penn, who in 1952 encouraged him to publish some of these photographs in *Vogue,* along with accompanying essays, the first drafts of which I edited from Alex's longhand notes. (In succeeding years, Alex never felt any scruples about publishing his own photographs or any chronicles relating to him in his magazines. "They begged me to do it," he'd say coyly about his colleagues each time his work or photographs of his home came out in *Vogue's, House and Garden's,* or *Vanity Fair's* pages. In the 1980s, *Vanity Fair* would devote twenty-four pages to a new edition of "The Artist in His Studio.")

The "Artist in the Studio" series was eventually exhibited at MOMA in 1959 and acclaimed as unique documents on the pioneers of a heroic epoch who were on the verge of vanishing. They were also seen as the first

Portrait of Giacometti in his studio, from Alex's book
The Artist in His Studio.

photographic studies of contemporary artists that focused with equal intensity on the nitty-gritty details of artists' methods and materials as on their personalities. The success of the exhibition led directly to the publication of a book in 1960 by Viking Press, which received enthusiastic reviews and went through numerous editions.

As for Alex's own view of these photos, it is important to note that he did *not* look on photography as a true art form. A photo, to him, was only a record of reality and did not qualify as art because it was incapable of evoking "the intangible, the visionary and the metaphysical." The phrase was characteristic of Alex's very religious view of art, which was grounded in the mystical aesthetics of early twentieth-century Russian thinkers such as Berdyaev, whom Alex had read a great deal in the 1940s. Religiousness indeed imbues most of Alex's references to his photographic project. He saw his visits to the artists as a series of "pilgrimages," and the painters he documented struck him as being dedicated to art like "men in religious orders." These pilgrimages, he also felt, grafted his uprooted psyche back to its origins in Russian mysticism and allowed him to reestablish contact with the concept of art as spiritual transcendence, as part of "a search for the miraculous." Alex's sense of art's spirituality may be most evident in his essay on Kandinsky: "Abstract art in its highest form," he wrote, "is an expression of man's desire to rise above subject matter into a higher realm which, like a prayer, will call upon his spiritual energy." Barbara Rose reads a heavily Slavic context into the Circlist period of Alex's work, linking it to the work of artists such as Kandinsky, Malevich, and the Czech Frantisek Kupka, all of whom had reacted against the Cartesian, rationalist basis of French Cubism, all of whom searched for a cosmic or religious dimension in their art.

So Alex, ironically, had his first public success with an art form that he did not consider to be true art. As for his paintings, they were finally given a public viewing the year after the MOMA show, when his friend and near namesake William Lieberman, a curator at the Metropolitan Museum whom he had met through Marlene, persuaded the art dealer Betty Parsons to give him an exhibition. Neither the press nor the general public took significant notice of the show. However it was a succès d'estime among a few New York artists such as Barnett Newman (who had installed it), Jasper Johns, and Robert Rauschenberg. And the one painting that sold, a tondo, went to an important source: Alfred Barr, Jr., chief curator of the Museum of Modern Art.

A s for the Libermans' social life in the 1950s, it was totally centered on Pat and Marlene. "They're like sisters," Alex said proudly about his wife and the star, as he had said, a few years earlier, about poor Nada. Mother and Alex were fascinated by the way Marlene combined the roles of glamorous seductress and industrious hausfrau, and they were captivated by the obsessive manner in which she did menial tasks for her friends: She boiled a piece of sirloin for ten hours to make a quart of beef tea for Alex when his ulcers kicked up; she insisted on repairing Mother's evening gowns herself, with a special needle she had kept in her sewing kit since leaving Berlin in 1930.

The four were inseparable, spending country weekends and summers and Christmases together, and Marlene became yet another of my parents' friends who occasionally played Mommy to me. On Christmas night of 1951, when a beau of mine from North Carolina was spending a week with us, Alex, Mother, and Uncle Pat were booked to go out to some glamorous party. "Those kids should not stay alone at Christmas!" Marlene exclaimed upon hearing our family plans. And she insisted on remaining at Seventieth Street to cook Christmas dinner for my guest and me, producing a menu which ever since has been indelibly engraved in Jonathan Williams's memory: beluga caviar with Veuve Clicquot, filet of beef, and Marlene's homemade lemon sherbet, drenched with Gerwürztraminer. "There were just the three of us, having that incredible Christmas meal in your parents' kitchen," he recalled nostalgically in a recent e-mail.

Mother's intimacy with Marlene even led the actress to meddle—with disastrous results—in my own health. For Mother confided in Marlene that I had not menstruated until the age of sixteen and had menstruated only two or three times a year since then. Marlene's Germanic sense of order was very disturbed by this news. "That is not normal!" she had exclaimed to Mother. "Marlene *chérie*, tell her that yourself," Mother pleaded. So one day as I was cramming for an exam in my third-floor room—I was twenty-one, just about to graduate from Barnard—Marlene burst in on me, saying, "Only three periods a year, sveetheart, that is not normal!" She stood at my doorsill, hands on hips, wearing the white nurse's uniform she'd donned that afternoon to wheel her grandsons to the Park. "That is not normal!" she repeated, wagging her finger like a scolding governess. "I take you to see Dr. Wilson!"

And so, the following week she packed me off to the office of the terrifying Dr. Robert Wilson, the Big Daddy of hormone-replacement therapy, who in his later bestselling book *Forever Feminine* proselytized that any hormonal deficiency was "a serious, painful and often crippling" ailment that "destroys [woman's] character along with her health" and even threatens "her relation to her family and her community." Appalled, like Marlene, by the "abnormality" of my schedule, he ordered me to come to his office three times a week for the following month for estrogen injections. Only those who have been forced to take heavy doses of pure estrogen for medical reasons will fully know the discomfort that can ensue. I put on some ten pounds in two weeks. My breasts swelled and became so painful that I could barely enter a subway at rush hour in fear that someone might brush against me. After a few days, I spotted blood around the clock, without having a true period. Without telling Mother or Marlene, I stopped Dr. Wilson's treatment after a month. As for my periods, I let nature run its course—they became as punctual as a clock some seven years later, after my first pregnancy.

Pat's idyll with Marlene lasted until the early 1950s, when the star ditched him for Michael Wilding, with whom she'd costarred in Hitchcock's *Stage Fright.* She went on to have flings with Yul Brynner and numerous other men. Marlene had been the great love of Pat's life—he'd had liaisons with the world's most beautiful women but none had hooked him as totally, as torturously, as Marlene. The severance had a devastating impact on him, and he began to rely increasingly on the Libermans for companionship. Alex encouraged him to take up painting as a therapy. Pat trudged up to Seventieth Street every Saturday morning and worked in a corner of Alex's studio, which was now on the top floor of our house, in the rooms recently vacated by the Shuvalovs. He set up his easel at the opposite end of the room from Alex, who was then doing his big enameled circles on industrial board, and painted delicate little Grandma Moses–type

Tatiana and Iva Patcevitch at the Crillon Hotel in Paris, mid-1950s.

renderings of the street below. By the mid-1950s, Pat had become so dependent on the Libermans that he sold his flat near the East River and moved into a town house Alex found for him a few doors down from our own. (The dwelling was paid for, and henceforth owned, by Condé Nast.)

In those years, Alex and Pat were more like brothers than they'd ever been. At Condé Nast, they went into each other's offices for long conferences (part of their conversation focused on Pat's recent heartbreak). In the summer, they took the same boat for France, where they attended the yearly collections and booked adjoining suites at the Ritz or the Crillon. In New York, they attended plays and concerts together and drove together to spend the weekends with Grisha and Lydia Gregory—Lydia had been a flame of Pat's in the 1940s but was now content to have his devoted friendship.

Pat's closeness to my family waned a bit, however, when he fell in love with Chesborough ("Chessy") Amory, the wife of a genial playboy, Charles

("Chas") Amory. The Amorys, who belonged to the most conservative milieus of East Coast WASP society, led distinctly separate romantic lives; and Pat, for a few years, entered into a pleasant ménage à trois with them. Notwithstanding Tatiana's and Alex's perennial distrust of the American elite's anti-Semitism, they initially got along well enough with Chessy, a tall, elegant blonde with a ready laugh and a wicked sense of humor who had been a mannequin at Mainbocher and had immediately Anglicized her new lover by referring to him as "Patrick." When I returned to New York in 1956 after two years in Paris, I found the Libermans giving undiminished attention to Marlene while trying to accommodate Pat's new family, the Amorys.

When Alex enjoyed his first artistic success in the late 1950s, his mother began pressuring him increasingly to leave his job at Condé Nast and devote himself to painting. Henriette had been living in Paris since 1947. She'd recently had to close the cottage industry she had started a decade ago, a "school of charm and manners" at which she had taught women of dubious social origins the manners of the *"grand monde"*: how to sit down on a chair, how to hold a teacup (pinky daintily held up). "It was attended by a few women from the provinces, butchers' wives," Alex once quipped. Well into her sixties now, *Mamasha* had taken to wearing very short, Brigitte Bardot–type skirts and transparent tops. She still picked up whatever willing men she could find to sleep with her, and in order to maintain her quota of conquests she had numerous face-lifts. (Alex estimated that she had seventeen abortions and seven plastic surgeries in her lifetime.) The Libermans had to pay for all of *Mamasha's* whims as well as her necessities and moreover continued to be bombarded by almost daily letters from her filled with accusations about Alex's wasted vocation and the superficiality of the fashion world they lived in—"You are my only reason for existing . . . you who carry such treasures in yourself, don't waste your energies on that inane world. . . . You only have one mission in life, that of an artist who may one day thrust his whole radiant clarity into his work."

The responsibility of financing *Mamasha's* caprices, added to the Libermans' extravagant lifestyle and their largesse to other family members, put a severe strain on their finances; and there were limits to what Alex could borrow from his firm, the generous loans of which had already kept him going for many years. It is in the context of this continuing insecurity that Alex again chose self-interest over loyalty when his employer, Condé Nast, and his closest chum, Iva Patcevitch, were faced with the greatest upheaval in the company's history.

From the 1930s to the 1950s, financial control of Condé Nast Publications had been held by Lord Camrose, the British newspaper magnate who had bailed Nast out of trouble after the crash of 1929. But in 1958, after Camrose's death, his son sold most of the family's press holdings to one Cecil King, publisher of the sex-and-scandal oriented *Daily Mirror*. Under the terms of an agreement between Camrose and Patcevitch, in the event of such a sale Condé Nast's American publishers would have a six-month grace period in which they could repurchase the stock. At that time the Condé Nast magazines were not profitable, so this task proved to be difficult. With the aid of one of the company's vice-presidents, the financial wizard Daniel Salem, Patcevitch approached companies such as *Collier's*, Time-Life, and the Cowles publications, with no success. Five months passed with no deal in sight, Patcevitch and Salem were growing desperate . . . and then suddenly, in the very last weeks of the grace period, a prosperous newspaper publisher called Samuel Newhouse suddenly materialized.

The oldest of eight children born to a Russian immigrant, the five-feet-two Samuel Newhouse dropped out of school in 1908 at thirteen, when his father's health failed, to work as a clerk for a police-court judge in Bayonne, New Jersey. His boss, Judge Hyman Lazarus, had acquired a 51 percent interest in an insignificant weekly publication, the *Bayonne Times*, with offices that adjoined his. Lazarus was much impressed with young Newhouse's intelligence and imagination. After firing a series of incompetent editors, he appointed his seventeen-year-old clerk as editor of his newspaper, asking him to "take care of it until we can get rid of it." Sam, who had worked part-time as a newsboy since the age of seven, had a keen sense for the operation and distribution of newspapers. Within a year, having indefatigably canvassed newsstands and planned aggressive advertising campaigns, Sam had gotten the *Bayonne Times* way into the black. Four years later, his paper was earning him twenty thousand dollars annually (the equivalent of $350,000 today), and he had put whatever of his siblings were of working age on his payroll. Within another decade, he had bought the *Staten Island Advance* and twenty-nine other papers in twenty-two cities, surpassing his principal rivals, Hearst and Scripps Howard, in numbers, circulation, and profits.

Early in his career, Sam Newhouse, a genial, self-effacing man, had married a beautiful, equally diminutive girl, Mitzi Epstein, who had considerable cultural ambitions and a particular passion for the theater. The daughter of a successful Seventh Avenue manufacturer, she had been brought up in comfort on Manhattan's west side and was a graduate of the Parsons School of Design. Even when they were living on Staten Island, where they raised their two sons, Donald and Samuel ("Si") Newhouse, Jr., Mitzi managed to get her husband to the theater as often as she could. In the 1940s, their fortunes flourishing, the Newhouses moved to 730 Park Avenue and fulfilled Mitzi's dream by attending first nights at every important play and opera performed in New York—their seats were always in the front row, to make sure that their view of the stage was not blocked by taller citizens. Mitzi was as fond of couture clothes as she was of the stage, and by the early 1950s she had begun to dress exclusively at Givenchy and Dior. So Sam, who adored his wife, enjoyed saying that when on a morning in 1958 Mitzi had asked him to go downstairs and buy her a fashion magazine, he had "gone out and bought *Vogue*."

Although Newhouse's purchase of Condé Nast was rumored to be a thirty-fifth wedding anniversary present for his wife, it was also a shrewd business decision. In the same months, he closed down the tony Connecticut printing plant where Condé Nast magazines had been published since the 1930s and sent them to more modern, cheaper plants in the Midwest. As a result, within nine months of his having acquired Condé Nast, the company had totally turned around and was on pace to make a million and a half dollars each year.

As for Pat, ensconced in his new ménage with the snobbish Chessy Amory, he treated Condé Nast's new owner with lordly disdain and referred to him in private as "a kibbitzer." He had realized early on that the anti-intellectual Chessy would have no social chemistry with the culturally zealous Newhouses and had begun to use Alex, the Newhouses' fellow Jew, as his principal social conduit to them. Upon first dining with the Newhouses at Pat's, Mother, who readily knew which side Alex's bread was buttered on and immediately declared Mitzi to be "irresistible," was perfectly behaved. The Libermans and the Newhouses quickly became friends and soon were dining in tête-à-tête every few weeks. Mother and Mitzi chatted happily about books, children, clothes, and servants while Sam plumbed Alex's mind on Condé Nast. As for Pat and Chessy, the latter of whom had begun to strongly dislike Tatiana because of her abiding friendship with Marlene, they were married, soon after Chessy's divorce came through, on the afternoon Kennedy was assassinated—a joyous celebration was held notwithstanding the somberness of that day's events.

As the émigré survival artist Pat adapted like a chameleon to his new wife's proclivities and pastimes—Southampton, Palm Beach, country clubs, canasta tournaments—the émigré survival artist Alex instinctively set his bets on Newhouse, becoming his confidant and right hand in the running of the company. He loved the company and the magazines, Alex explained three decades later, and he had to survive. Survive he did. In late 1962, when an overhaul of Condé Nast's old guard came about and Diana Vreeland replaced Jessica Daves as *Vogue*'s editor in chief, Newhouse promoted Alex to be editorial director of the entire Condé Nast publishing empire. By this time, my parents' estrangement from Pat was considerable. Both Mother and Alex felt that Pat's treatment of Newhouse was grotesque, and Alex, moreover, worried that it would be deeply harmful to the company. His resistance to Pat stiffened, and those twenty years when Alex and Pat had been "like brothers" and Pat had poured out his despair over Nada's tantrums or Marlene's treachery seemed a lifetime away. The transformation in Condé Nast's power structure began in the spring of 1967. One night, when Alex was having dinner at the Newhouses', Sam took Alex aside and asked him if Pat was doing a good job. "I couldn't lie," Alex explained later.

Through another blunder, Pat precipitated his own downfall a few months later, in September 1967. A Bolivian tin czar named Patiñor was giving a weeklong series of festivities at the Portuguese resort of Estoril, and every European or American jet-setter of any note wangled an invitation. The Newhouses were there, mingling with other prominent American publishing, couture, and society magnates at the Palacio Hotel—this was the kind of event at which Mitzi loved to show off her wardrobe and talk about her husband's knack for rebuilding publishing empires. There was a series of lunches, breakfasts, and cocktail parties, perhaps two dozen of them, given by various individuals from both sides of the ocean. The Newhouses were invited to every one of them, except to the cocktail party given by Chessy and Pat, which Mitzi learned about the following day from her manicurist.

The corporate consequences of this inane gaffe came two weeks later. Pat was demoted from publisher to chairman and was replaced by Sam Newhouse's oldest son, Samuel ("Si") Jr. The biggest blow to Pat, however, was to learn that he had to leave his house on Seventieth Street, after a decade there. In his habitual seignorial way, Pat had assumed that even though it was Condé Nast property, he could stay in the house indefinitely, and he had not even informed his wife, Chessy, that it did not belong to them. They were all the more mortified to hear that it was destined to be the home of Condé Nast's new publisher, Si Newhouse Jr.

In the midst of these rearrangements, Alex walked over to Pat's office and offered to submit his own resignation as an expression of support. Pat, who knew full well that this was a rhetorical gesture, reassured his colleague that the palace revolution had nothing to do with him, but their twenty-seven-year-old friendship had clearly ended. Pat and Chessy retreated in helpless rage to their homes in Southampton and Palm Beach, where they resumed playing cards seven days a week and assiduously attended the functions of clubs such as Palm Beach's Bath and Tennis Club, which, as late as the 1970s, maintained rigorous restrictions on the ethnic backgrounds of its guests, not to speak of its members.

In the 1970s, Mother and Alex started going to Palm Beach, where the Patcevitches spent most of the year, for two weeks of the winter. But during the following decade they saw Pat only once, when they ran into him on Worth Avenue. I however managed to keep old bonds somewhat alive. My husband's mother also lived in Palm Beach, and on my yearly tour of duty to her I usually looked up Pat and Chessy. Chessy inevitably welcomed me warmly, and he always effusively. In the first years of my two decades of visits, he was still the dapper Beau Brummell, tanned and silvery, ascotted and Sulka shirted, whom I'd remembered from my adolescence, lurking in corners to pounce on the next pretty girl (a sport he gave up for good when comely Chessy came into his life).

The last year I saw Pat was 1991, a few months before my mother's death and two years before his own. He was lying in his sickbed, his slender, chiseled face now as wasted as a mummy's, his voice a faint rasp, recovering from a triple bypass, which he himself and an inattentive intensive-care nurse had botched. Twenty-four hours after leaving the operating table, some wild Slavic force in Iva Sergeyevich Patcevitch resurfaced. He tore off all the wires that had been plugged into his body and ran screaming down the corridors of the hospital, shouting imprecations at the medical profession. It took him months, and much severe sedation, to recover. "How is my friend Tatiana?" he whispered in a barely audible rasp of Russian when I saw him in Palm Beach later that year, as he gave me his wasted, still ravishing smile. "How is my brother Alex?" I told him that they were just fine, even though Mother was already deeply ill. As I kissed him good-bye, looking into the larger-than-ever azure eyes, smelling the familiar fragrance of his Knize Ten, I thanked him silently for the sweetness he'd brought my youth—the riding lessons, the flounced ball gowns that had made me feel so securely feminine, the cottage in Jamaica he had rented for my husband and me as a honeymoon getaway. Whatever blunders and grievances had severed him from my parents, Uncle Patsy had been a fairy godfather of my American childhood.

Witnesses at Condé Nast have been commenting ever since on the breakup of Pat's and Alex's friendship. "I was enthralled with Patcevitch," Si told me thirty-five years later. "He was the only true White Russian I've ever encountered, a man of phenomenal elegance."

Daniel Salem, who was then Condé Nast's chief financial adviser, says, "I'm shocked to this day about how Alex behaved towards Pat. Pat had virtually created Alex's career. . . . But then Alex never fought for anyone."

I imagine that Alex's career was studded with many similar instances of disloyalty, most of which I don't even know about. I do know of one such betrayal, however, which caused Alex immense anguish. It was the dismissal, ordered by the Newhouses in 1966, of the editor in chief of French *Vogue*, Edmonde Charles-Roux, who had held that post since the immediate postwar years. Edmonde, a stately, imposing woman with an aura of the Mother Superior about her—she coiled her dark hair into a severe bun and for decades wore the same austere Balenciaga chemise, cut in a variety of fabrics according to the season—was a highly respected intellectual who came from one of France's most eminent families. Her cousins and brother had been at Les Roches in approximately the same years as Alex had. Her father, before the war, had been France's ambassador to the Vatican. Family bonds between the Libermans and Edmonde were particularly close because Sasha Iacovleff, who for many years visited with the Charles-Rouxs in Italy every summer, had been one of Edmonde's dearest friends. And until 1966, Alex had always referred to Edmonde as one of his two or three closest chums.

Edmonde's dismissal came about when she decided to use an African-American model, photographed by William Klein, on the cover of French *Vogue*. The cautiously conservative Sam Newhouse heard about the proposed cover from other staffers at the Paris office and asked Alex to insist that Edmonde use another cover. "I'm the editor of the magazine," Edmonde is reported to have said, "and this cover is staying." None of Alex's art of persuasion and none of his skill for flattery were of any avail. Edmonde stood her ground, and a few days later she learned that she had been dismissed.

This was in March 1966. In July of that year, Edmonde, whose novel, *Oublier Palerme*, was about to be published and was receiving rave advance reviews (it was already rumored to be the leading contender for the Prix Goncourt, which indeed it eventually won), received a phone call from Alex, who was on his yearly trip to Paris to attend the couture collections.

He asked if he could come to see her at her flat on the rue des Saints-Pères. "By all means," said Edmonde, whose curiosity prevailed over her pride. The rest of the story is best told in Edmonde's own words.

> I hadn't heard from him since I'd been fired, so I was curious to hear him out. And I wasn't at all prepared for the scene that followed. He rang the doorbell, I opened the door, and there he stood looking at me, and even before crossing my threshold he burst into tears—truly tumultuous, uncontrollable tears. I didn't know what to do. This wasn't just a bout of weeping, it was more akin to a *"crise de désespoir."* I led him to a chair and gave him a glass of water, he continued to sob, and finally he was able to blurt out, with great difficulty, the following words: "It was all out of my control, out of my control." So I let him sob on, I soothed him and said we could always remain friends, he stayed half an hour, we talked very little, the weeping fit eventually subsided, we've seldom seen each other again.

When Edmonde told me this story in 2002, I was flabbergasted. No one had ever seen Alex weep up to then, and my family and I are witnesses to the fact that he never cried even when my mother died. So how to explain the *"crise de désespoir"*? Perhaps this particular encounter led him to a painful realization of his own weaknesses: Edmonde stood for everything in European society that Alex could have achieved and either could not or cared not to attain: rigorous intellectual discipline, true intellectual achievement. The subtext of this episode: Alex was enough of a snob to experience great pain at the loss of an old friend—about to become famous—who was clearly his superior. He was decent enough to feel duty bound to come ask her forgiveness. And he was prideful enough to feel deeply humiliated by being impelled, for the first time in his life, to go through an act of mea culpa. Extreme snobbism, more than occasional decency, phenomenal vainglory—that was Alex in a nutshell.

In the early 1960s, Alex's art making underwent still another total transformation. This metamorphosis, like earlier ones, seemed once again to have been brought on by a grave health crisis—Alex's third and last hemorrhage. It was the worst to date, but by then there was a surgical cure. The hemorrhage occurred in late August 1962 as my parents were sailing back from Europe on the *Queen Elizabeth*. My mother phoned me one evening from the boat. "He's bleeding terribly," she said with desperation, instructing me to call their doctor and have him meet the ship. We took Alex by ambulance straight from the docks to Columbia Presbyterian. He must have realized the gravity of his condition, for after he had been stabilized, and just before his surgery, he asked to say good-bye to both of my children—my youngest, Luke, was only sixteen months old. Having tenderly kissed us all, he underwent a four-hour operation in which the vagus nerve was cut and the diseased part of the stomach taken out. It was a total success. Within a few weeks Alex was home, and a month later, as he started going to the office again for a few hours, he was instructed to drink a weak Scotch and soda before dinner to relax his stomach muscles. My mother started drinking a bit alongside him. He was fifty, she was fifty-six, and it was probably the first time alcohol had ever passed either his lips or hers. Within some months, diet regulations were even further relaxed, and he was allowed to add red wine to his regimen. My parents soon became ardent oenophiles and began to collect fine Bordeaux.

Once his health was fully restored, Alex returned to painting with increased verve, and the gypsy in him started roaming again: He made a 180-degree turn and rebelled against all that he'd stood for as an artist in the previous decade. He rejected the geometric clarity and intellectuality of his circles, seeing them as "a form of hypnotic withdrawal from the world," and turned to a radically romantic, luxuriant style. The circles' sleek, impersonal surfaces gave way to loose, jagged brushstrokes, freehand splashes, blurred, fuzzy-edged bands of color. His ulcers permanently healed, he was blessed with a whole new fund of physical energy, and his painting now became an arena for expressing private emotions. He rented a studio space a few doors down from our house, in a former funeral parlor, in order to make far larger paintings. By the mid-1960s, he was working with his canvas laid on the floor, flinging paint from buckets or swinging it around with janitors' brooms. He had borrowed that idea from Pollock, whom he now idolized.

My husband introduced him to Liquitex, a fast-drying acrylic pigment that can be applied evenly over large areas. And from Helen Frankenthaler and Barnett Newman, Alex got the idea of using unprimed cotton duck, which is sold in huge rolls and enabled him to paint on a far greater scale.

Through the radically emotive style he took on in the 1960s, the angry, stone-throwing street urchin of Alex's early youth resurfaced again. This wild inner child lurking behind Alex's polished surface had always been the persona he felt closest to and was the proudest of. Over the decades, he had repeatedly and with great gusto told us tales of the dozens of Moscow windows he had broken by hurling stones, of how he had attacked and mauled his teachers and continued to shit in his pants until the age of nine. This naughty child had been imprisoned for decades under a facade of diplomacy and decorum, and now it was suddenly liberated, allowing emotions bottled up for decades to erupt on canvas. The most estimable aspect of this tumultuous new body of work is that Alex was creating art with no concerns whatever for the market or for trends. His last show of geometric painting, in 1962, had sold out, and his dealer, Betty Parsons, was appalled to see him now abandoning the style for which he was beginning to be much esteemed. Moreover, Alex was turning to Abstract Expressionism at the time it was beginning to go out of fashion: The cutting edge was now at Pop Art and at the same austere "Op Art" Minimalism he had experimented with in the early 1950s.

The first exhibition of Alex's newly loose, romantic paintings—in 1963, the year after his surgery—sold poorly and was barely reviewed. Writing in *Art International*, the influential young critic Michael Fried referred to the new work as "refined, competent, but wholly unoriginal." By failing to persevere in his original path, by giving in to his capricious, volatile nature, Alex only aggravated his life's very greatest sorrow: the feeling that he was not taken seriously as an artist.

By the mid-1960s Alex had acquired a small group of friends in the art world. Soon after our marriage Cleve and I had brought Barnett ("Barney") Newman to visit him, and after several years of not seeing him, he

Alex painting his "Volcano" series, late 1970s, photo by Dr. William Cahan.

quickly developed a great friendship with his colleague. While exploiting whatever useful contacts Barney could offer him, Alex did esteem and love him more than any other artist of his generation. In Barney he admired an intellectual who had plumbed metaphysical and aesthetic issues at far greater depth than Alex had ever had the patience to. He also admired a man who epitomized that frugal, true artist's life, which Alex had never dared to take on— Barney got along on the salary his wife earned as a public-school teacher, lived in a drab west-side flat for twenty years without selling one painting, and did not give a hoot about what he ate or where he slept. Alex was awed and moved by the dedication and uncompromising quality which marked Newman's life and art. Throughout the 1960s, his almost daily telephone conversations with Newman, who had many dense and grandiose ideas about painting and "the Sublime," deepened Alex's sense of art as an expression of "metaphysical and spiritual transcendence," as "a call to spiritual arms."

Cleve and I had also introduced Alex to Bob Motherwell and Helen Frankenthaler, whom my mother immediately swept into her circle of intimates because they were both "well bred," as she put it, and Helen, a peerless hostess, spoke beautiful French. Alex milked the Motherwell/Frankenthaler relationship for all it was worth. In 1965, Helen generously arranged for him to have a show at Bennington College, and in 1967 she introduced him to the dealer Andre Emmerich, who began to show those sculptures of Alex's that were too large for Betty Parsons to exhibit. "Alex was a great flatterer—he tried to buy his way into being accepted as a first-generation New York School painter," Frankenthaler recently recalled. "There was an endless flow of champagne, flowers, limousines being sent for Bob and me. . . . It didn't work, because after the mid-sixties Alex's painting was utterly derivative, but we did have a good time enjoying his graciousness and allure."

Emmerich, who was to remain his dealer for a quarter of a century, didn't like Alex's later Expressionist works either and says he only showed them "out of friendship." "Alex misjudged his own capacities, he made a huge mistake in abandoning his hard-edge circle paintings," Emmerich says today. "In his arrogance he believed that all his art would be equally great, he was defeated by his own fickleness . . . if he'd stayed the course and persevered in that earlier vision he would have earned a considerable place in twentieth-century art." ("Go deeper," Alex's first art teacher, Sasha Iacovleff, had often told him.)

But Alex also had a new vocation as a sculptor of metal to attend to. It had begun while he was vacationing in 1959 at Va-et-Vient, when his housekeeper's husband, a local craftsman who made iron balconies, introduced him to welding. Alex found the experience to be awesome and very "erotic." He continued welding in the following years, whenever he and Mother spent the weekend with us in Warren, Connecticut, where my husband had lived since a decade before our marriage. We owned an old farm with several outbuildings, and Cleve, with characteristic generosity, offered Alex one of his barns and loaned him a few thousand dollars to set up a sculpture studio in it (we were all broke, but that particular year the Libermans were more broke than we were). Alex started working with his usual enthusiasm, welding elements from discarded farm machinery that had accumulated for years on the property. A year later, a local road builder and welder, William Layman, was enjoined by Cleve to help Alex make his increasingly voluminous sculptures, and eventually Layman and his two sons ended up working for him full-time. The results were promising. In 1966 the Jewish Museum, a lively showplace for cutting-edge art, gave Alex a one-man show of his sculpture.

By this time, Alex's circle paintings were also gaining in esteem. One of those canvases, *Continuous on Red*, the tondo that Alfred Barr had bought from Alex's first show at Betty Parsons, was included in a pivotal MoMA exhibition curated by William Seitz in 1965, *The Responsive Eye.* There Alex was in the company of two artists who were to achieve the highest international acclaim, Frank Stella and Ellsworth Kelly. Kelly and Stella were so taken with Alex's work that they each wrote him to suggest that they exchange pictures. Alex, habitually disdainful of correspondence, never answered their requests. With the exception of Jasper Johns and Andy Warhol, whose work he loved and began to support when they were young, Alex tended to dismiss painters who were less than very famous, which put him all the more at risk of being seen as a snobbish, dilettante socialite.

But the mid-1960s to mid-1970s were among the happiest, most successful, most productive periods of Alex's life. While being elevated to the second-highest position at Condé Nast, one rung below Newhouse, he had gained a considerable reputation as painter, sculptor, and photographer. He had seen me happily married. He enjoyed a particularly close friendship with his son-in-law—the two men visited each other's studios every few weekends to offer critiques, and the meetings always ended with Alex assuring Cleve that he was his "closest friend in the world." He had ready access, any weekend he wished, to a country getaway where he could pursue his new career in monumental sculpture. Finally, he adored his two grandsons, who worshiped him. "He had a way of talking to you that made you feel deliciously important, whether he was taking you to lunch at his power table at the Four Seasons or just chatting in the dining room at Seventieth Street," my older son, Thaddeus, recalls today. "He had the capacity to be your parent and your friend at the same time . . . no one else I've ever met had this gift." (However, the boys' relationships with Grandpa Liberman grew more complex as they reached their teens, when Alex, displaying his voyeurist streak, tended to pry a bit too arduously into the details of their love lives. "Where

Irving Penn, March 1960. Family photograph with Cleve, his mother,
and grandmother. Behind Tatiana is her father, Alexis Jackson.

are the girls?" Alex asked me with a worried, disappointed air when my sons had not brought any new young beauty home for a while.)

As for his social life, it was more publicly glamorous than ever, though he was never quite honest about the extent to which it might have damaged his reputation as an artist. In 1967, Princess Margaret and her husband, the photographer Lord Snowdon, whom Alex had befriended and begun to work with five years earlier, came to stay at Seventieth Street. My husband and I were evicted from my childhood room for the fortnight of their stay, which became a veritable publicity circus and was heavily documented in Suzy's New York *Daily News* column. "My dear they were all at the Libermans," Suzy emoted in one report. "Faye Dunaway . . . Penelope Tree, the huge-eyed modeling sensation, was there. . . . Then there was Caterine Millinaire, the Duchess of Bedford's daughter, and the cute young Marquess and Marchioness of Dufferin and Ava . . . Irene Dunne . . . Françoise de Langlade de la Renta. . . . The Charles Revsons, Salvador Dali and his ocelot and, well, you get the picture." Alex's hospitality, however, did not cut much ice with the royal couple, who seemed to resent my parents' social hustling. "It was hard for Margaret to take to Alex because he was so pushy," Snowdon, who refers to Alex as "the curator of all that's hot and shallow," recalls today. "Margaret was a very shrewd woman, and she sensed that he liked her for all the wrong reasons—she saw through the Libermans' snobbism and didn't give them the time of day."

Mother's Yves Saint-Laurent gowns, which she began to receive as presents from the young couturier when she transferred her loyalties from Dior, seldom failed to be noticed in similar society columns. As for Alex, his sumptuary style remained one of Calvinist austerity: gray or dark-blue suits made for him for decades by Stovel and Mason in London, narrow, hand-knit, navy silk ties, and pale-blue shirts, which he bought by the dozens from a shirtmaker across the street from Rome's Grand Hotel. Notwithstanding the monotony of these uniforms, he, too, won fashion-plate distinction in the mid-1960s by being named to Eugenia Sheppard's best-dressed men list, along with Fred Astaire, Cary Grant, Oleg Cassini, and the duke of Windsor.

Office, studio, society drawing rooms, and most particularly home—

Alex seemed to have a mysterious capacity for being everywhere simultaneously. "He was such an enigma," says *Vogue* editor in chief Anna Wintour, who loved Alex and looked on him as "the biggest influence I've had on my journalistic career," as "the man who believed, more deeply than anyone I've ever known, in the high quality that journalism can attain." "He was so unpredictable," Wintour recalls, "we never knew what he was going to say and do, whether he'd say yes or no to anything. He'd leave without telling anyone, arrive on the sly. . . . His uniform was both an armor and a mask; it added to his inscrutability and mystery."

"He was finickety as hell and had to control everything in sight," says Charles Churchward, another protégé of Alex who since the 1970s has served brilliantly as art director of several Condé Nast magazines. "For instance, every single photo that was to be used in an issue had to be printed to ten different sizes before he walked into the art department to supervise a layout. . . . And his appetite for work was astounding. He spent his days running up and down the stairs to supervise every one of our thirteen magazines—he had to read every manuscript, every caption before it went to press, he even insisted on approving all cover proofs."

But Churchward also corroborates that Alex's mean streak remained unabated throughout the decades. "I remember him calling in one new editor and yelling at her," Churchward relates. "'You don't know anything about fashion,' he shouted, 'will you explain what you're trying to do?' This was shouted out quite loud, and he'd on purpose kept the door of his office open and asked me to stand right outside, as if to ensure that this would be a *public* dressing-down."

Yet if the nasty Mr. Hyde in him terrified many of his coworkers, at home Alex remained the benign Dr. Jekyll and lived in a state of alarm that quite equaled the dread he inspired at Condé Nast. Throughout his decades at the company, his colleagues were amazed by the look of utter terror that came to his face when he rushed to the phone to answer a call from my mother. "She really cracked the whip, he looked on her with a blend of adoration and great fright," Wintour recalls. "It was the fate of his life to seek out the dominatrix in all his relationships with women." Most of the time, Mother was phoning to complain of some malfunction at Seventieth

Street—an icebox or air conditioner not working properly—and such an incident would impel Alex immediately to race home to handle the problem.

One particular instance of the grand, superefficient manner in which he handled every manner of domestic crisis comes to mind: On a winter evening in 1978, when out alone in New York, I broke my leg slipping on ice. Determined not to wake my parents, upon coming home I crawled up the two flights of stairs on all fours and went to bed, having taken every painkiller I found in my room. The following morning, at around 6:00 A.M., a very dear family friend phoned, close to hysterics, telling me that her husband had just died. I pacified her as best I could—the Libermans kept the phone in their room shut off at night to protect Mother's sleep—and as soon as I heard Alex's first familiar morning sounds I crawled to his door and said, "Alex, dear, Nicolas just died, and I broke my leg." Within half an hour, Alex had arranged an 8:00 A.M. appointment for me with a prominent bone surgeon; bundled me into a limo and taken me to the doctor's office; ordered another limo to take me home to the country after my leg was set; and had gone downtown to Chelsea to take care of funeral arrangements for our lost friend—all this, of course, without Mother ever waking from her drugged sleep, which usually lasted until at least 11:00 A.M. ("Didn't you and I have luck finding him!" Mother always said to me when recalling that episode. "Didn't we have the luck of the devil with Superman!")

That Alex never broke down, especially during the ailments of my mother's last years, when he himself was already deeply ill, that the stresses of his numerous duties and vocations failed to destroy him, was in itself astonishing. It was quite an act, and the phenomenon of his resilience may be in part explained by the fact that he took enormous pride in flaunting it. His colleagues never ceased to marvel at the sheer fund of energy he was drawing on for his multiple vocations. "With that background of lifelong illness, where did he find the *time* for all he did?" asks Grace Mirabella, who was *Vogue*'s editor in chief throughout most of the 1970s and 1980s. "We never figured out where that energy came from."

As a young country woman raising my children, doing my own housekeeping, and struggling to find time for a nascent vocation as a writer, Alex's everywhereness struck me as Faustian, a tad demonic. It made me un-

easy: Was he perhaps spreading himself too thin somewhere? I kept recalling a puerile quatrain, popular in the 1940s among the elite of Spence's
eighth grade, which we used to spout to one another with an icily exagger-
ated British accent:

> *They seek him here, they seek him there*
> *The Frenchies seek him everywhere*
> *Is he in heaven? Is he in hell?*
> *That damned elusive Pimpernel!*

Mother did not ponder such issues. She just referred to her husband as
Superman, assumed that Superman's energies were infinite, and treated him
accordingly.

TWENTY

Tatiana's Decline

After her retirement, Mother read more than ever, an average of three or four books each week in French and Russian. She went to Kenneth's every other day to have her hair done. For at least an hour of the morning she talked on the phone to Lydia Gregory, with whom she continued to share memories of Mayakovsky. And she also began to drink heavily. Upon my almost weekly visits to New York, I soon noticed that she was becoming one of those hard-core tipplers who develop an array of tricks to cover up their addictions. She may have picked up the habit from Marlene, who started drinking substantially in the early 1960s, when her movie career had waned and she was supporting herself through cabaret acts in Las Vegas. Whenever I arrived from the country on an afternoon when Marlene was in town, I'd see the two of them sitting in the library, enjoying their Scotches together as they shot the breeze. And on the days when I came in the morning, at 11:30 or so, I'd already find a few silver tumblers around the house half filled with concoctions of Dubonnet and vodka. (The latter, Mother may have thought, would leave less of a trace on her breath.) She would still be in her housecoat, uncombed and flushed, watering can in hand, pretending to tend her plants. "I only take this very occasionally!" she'd exclaim if I caught her sipping from one of the tumblers. "It so helps

420

my arthritis!" She went out to lunch at La Grenouille almost daily, where I suspect she had still more Dubonnet and wine, and almost every afternoon she came home to play canasta.

On late afternoons when Marlene was not in town, Mother sat majestically in her living room as she sipped on yet more Scotch or Bordeaux, receiving former clients who, bereaved by the loss of her millinery and counseling skills, continued to seek her out and open their hearts to her. Moreover, from the mid-sixties on, the many Russian artists and writers who came to the United States as visitors or exiles looked on Tatiana Yakovleva du Plessix Liberman as a revered cultural icon: Andrei Voznesensky, Evgeny Evtushenko, Mstislav Rostropovich all flocked to Seventieth Street to pay tribute to Mayakovsky's muse, Joseph Brodsky and Mikhail Baryshnikov became particularly close friends. The poets returned for innumerable visits to hear her remarkable recitations of Russian poetry, to ponder her orphic judgments on Russian literature, and to read verse at her social gatherings. The readings were not without incidents: When in her cups, Mother would often interrupt Evtushenko's or Brodsky's recitations of Russian classics to shout, "You've got that line wrong!" She would correct their mistakes and go on to finish the stanza for them, leaving only the more stalwart men to resume their reading.

Yet however eager she was to discuss his verse, she continued adamantly to refuse talking about her relationship with Mayakovsky, and she shunned all press interviews. In the 1970s, a Soviet television crew managed to trick her into speaking a bit about the poet by pretending they wished to do a show on Alex, who loved publicity of any kind and had a subtle resentment of my mother's renown. Great was his dejection when he discovered that their true purpose was to interview Tatiana, who "in order to teach those communist fools how Mayakovsky *should* be read," reluctantly agreed to recite the poet's verse for ten minutes of Soviet TV time.

The Russians started to flock to New England, too, for in 1968 the Libermans bought a house down the road from our own in Warren, Connecticut. From the beginning of my marriage to Cleve, Mother and Alex came to stay with us at least one weekend out of two, usually with a friend or more of their own in tow—what Russians travel without a retinue? They

APRIL 75¢

House & Garden
HOW TO STRETCH YOUR DOLLARS
36 pages of real life experiences
*in decorating
building
remodeling
landscaping*

*Cook Book:
HOUSE & GARDEN
VISITS JAMES BEARD'S
COOKING CLASSES*

Hillside, *the Libermans' weekend house in*
Warren, CT. Photographed by David Massey
for the cover of House and Garden.

had always dreamed of a country home of their own but were never able to afford one, and ours met all their expectations. They did all they could to be helpful, bringing delicious concoctions of Mabel's to save me from too many hours at the stove, urging us to let them babysit the boys. But the psychological weight of their presence was heavy on me. For a few years after her retirement, Mother's energies remained undiminished, and she attempted to totally run my home, even trying, on occasion, to clean my house. On a January Sunday, I came home from church with my children and found that she had swept some two inches of snow from my driveway into my living room, entirely covering the floor, and was now busy sweeping it out. "What's happening?" I cried out. She put her broom down and, hands on hips, turned her most disdainful glance on me. "Didn't you *know* that this is the only way to clean rugs? That's how we did it in Russia."

Alex's new vocation as a sculptor of welded metal and the idleness of my mother's retirement made the Libermans' visits increasingly frequent. From the midsixties on, much of the time the houseguest they brought along was Jacques Tiffeau, a then very fashionable French-born couturier. He headed a prosperous Seventh Avenue firm, Tiffeau and Busch, and won the Coty Award twice in that decade for his streamlined suit and coat designs. The son of farmers in western France, Tiffeau had learned his trade with Christian Dior, whose protégé and occasional lover he had been in the early 1950s—very few men wanted to sleep more than once with the ungainly Dior, but the kindhearted patriarch remained grateful and always helped to advance their careers. The Libermans found Tiffeau extremely useful because of his extensive cooking skills: Whatever gaps there were in Mabel's care packages were filled by his exquisite *gigots aux flageolet, clafoutis,* and *crèmes caramel.* A handsome man with powerful, hairy limbs, a macho swagger, and a marvelous sense of humor, Tiffeau was a heavy cruiser—he found his dates on Times Square or in bathhouses or in Central Park—and clearly enjoyed regaling his intimates with the seamier details of his sexual exploits, which greatly titillated my parents.

Tiffeau loved the country as much as the Libermans did. Sensing my unease at their almost weekly invasion, he talked them into seriously looking for a house of their own near us. Cleve found it for them within a few months: a spacious enough three-bedroom of 1930s vintage with a superb view, three hundred yards down the road from us. Alex so trusted Cleve's judgment that upon Cleve's description he bought it over the telephone, sight unseen. Mother and Tiffeau channeled their energies into its redecoration, painting the entire interior white, buying bright-hued chintzes for the guest bedrooms and Lucite tables and white plastic furniture for the living room—"Plastic ees forever" was one of Mother's favorite dictums. Needless to say, Alex, who had no scruples about promoting any aspect of his life, soon splashed his garishly bright Connecticut living room, which featured a couple of his paintings, onto the cover and thirty-six ensuing pages of *House and Garden.* (Our neighbor Philip Roth, who thoroughly disliked my parents, said the house reminded him of "an operating room at Mount Sinai hospital.")

Tiffeau also masterminded the landscaping of Hillside, as my parents called the house. As skilled a gardener as he was a cook, he could be found every weekend up to his wrists in dirt, planting bushes, trimming the wisteria, putting in new rose beds. The house and grounds grew to be so attractive that my parents easily convinced various friends from the couture industry—Françoise and Oscar de la Renta, Diane Von Furstenberg were among the first of them—to buy weekend houses in the Kent–New Milford–Warren area. "Isn't he a marvel?" Mother cooed every few weeks about Tiffeau. "Have you ever seen such energy and talent?" "He keeps Mother so happy!" Alex would whisper to me with that air of grateful relief he took on when all went well in his household.

By 1968, the year the Libermans started spending weekends at Hillside, Marlene was spending most of her time in Paris, so Tiffeau had also become Mother's drinking companion. The problem is that like many powerfully built men, he could hold his liquor marvelously well, whereas she got high very soon and yet insisted on drinking at his pace. He tried to boss her around, commanding her to limit herself, but she refused. "See what boys in back room will have, tell them I want same," she would say, bungling the lines of Marlene's famous song. On weekend nights in the country, when she'd been at it, on and off, since lunchtime, Mother's drinking became most evident, and it was on these occasions that Alex's nasty response to her problem first came to light. After an episode during which she'd stumbled from the kitchen, laughing uproariously, and spilled a whole pot of borscht on the dining-room table, I gathered up my courage to discuss the boozing with Alex. I cornered him as he was coming down the stairs, and said, "Is it *good* for her health to drink this much?" "Leave her alone and never mention it to me again," he snapped, with that same nasty snarl of his mustache I'd seen a decade earlier when I'd questioned her excessive use of Benzedrine, and walked away.

Startled and hurt, I brought up the issue with Tiffeau. He said he'd received an equally rude answer from Alex on the topic: "Mind your own business." So we understood that Alex wanted to deal with Mother's problem his own way, all by himself; and in his handling of it I first witnessed the sadistic streak in his character that some office colleagues had reported, for his only tactic was one of repeated, private humiliation. I was the only one to observe it, for it was all done in Russian. As she stumbled and spilled one more dish, or as her voice grew intolerably loud, he would lean toward her and angrily mutter, "*Snova nadràlas!*" "Drunk again!" There are several ways of saying "drunk" in Russian, but "*nadràlas*" is ruder than most, and, however often she'd misbehaved, I was pained by the startled, humiliated look in her eyes as she heard him speak those words.

I witnessed such covert family scenes in a state of helpless sorrow, unable to help the parents I loved, not daring to talk again to Alex in fear of alienating him. Why couldn't he have her consult a doctor, I lamented, or why couldn't he get to the root of her problem, which was idleness? Her social concerns were limited, but couldn't he suggest some philanthropic work that helped Russian émigrés, such as the Tolstoy Foundation? I now know that this was all daydreaming. I wasn't facing up to the fact that the Libermans' monumental self-absorption left them little emotional space in which to care for any social cause. I also wasn't admitting the extent to which Alex wished to remain the only center of Mother's universe. During a tête-à-tête lunch with him a few years after her retirement, I had already suggested that it would be good for her to get out of the house and get involved in some charity work. He'd shaken his head in the negative with a mysterious, sly smile and said, "No, after all these years I love the idea of her just being home, waiting for me." I thought back to a Parisian friend's comment about Alex being "very Oriental, like some sadistic grand vizier."

Yet his quandary was very real: Alex, the maestro of outward appearances and impeccable decorum, suddenly found himself with a wife who was often making an ugly spectacle of herself. His entire sense of self must have been turned topsy-turvy by Mother's metamorphoses. For the first time in his life, he was ashamed of her, and his archaic reaction to it was to deny that any problem existed. It would be charitable to say that his secrecy was just another instance of that protect-Tatiana-from-reality strategy which was at the heart of their marriage: Nothing would have embarrassed a person as hermetically private as Mother, so it could be argued, than to have her behavior become a topic of medical or even family discourse. But it is more realistic to see Alex's tactic in the context of his appetite for total control: It was essential to their marital dynamic that Tatiana remain exclusively in his sway—not I nor her closest friends nor even a doctor could interfere with any detail of their marriage's functioning. As long as Tiffeau was in the house with her, keeping her from falling down, Alex could peacefully work away in his welding studio, which, those days, seemed to be his principal concern. So life proceeded at Hillside through 1969, 1970, and 1971. Mother continued to glower at us over her drinks when Cleve and I came home from antiwar demonstrations, at which we were more than once arrested and jailed overnight. "You are for Comintern?" she muttered. "You still help Hanoi?" Alex, who did not join in Mother's confrontations but had often taken us aside to criticize our "appalling" political activities, expressed his disapproval through what we called "his mustache language." Tiffeau, whose sympathies were squarely with ours, winked at us across the table, planted wisteria, and continued to make succulent *boeuf bourguignon* on weekends.

But he was a restless man and something of an egomaniac. In 1972—by this time he had easily made a million—Tiffeau suddenly closed his New York house, feeling too threatened by his three principal competitors, Blass, Halston, and de la Renta, who had considerably more financial backing than he did. He moved to Paris, worked for a year at St. Laurent but had a falling out with its directors and drifted into a series of less satisfying jobs on both sides of the ocean. And by the mid-1970s, when it was clear that Tiffeau's success story had come to an end, the Libermans had ceased to see him. Throughout their stays in Paris or during his visits to New York, his phone calls to them went unanswered: He now belonged to the scrap heap of the Libermans' no-longer-useful friends. He was to die in 1989 in his native village—of lung cancer and not from AIDS—leaving all his possessions to a childhood acquaintance who had nursed him selflessly throughout his last years.

After Tiffeau's departure, the Libermans were bereft of a helpful friend who could entertain Mother and cook. But such gaps in the Libermans' lives never stayed unfilled for very long. Barely one month passed before another permanent houseguest appeared at Hillside—the distinguished composer and musical impresario Nicolas Nabokov, first cousin of the writer. He, too, was a wonderful cook, and moreover Mother could now boast that her domestic aide-de-camp came from one of Russia's most distinguished families.

My parents had known Nicolas Nabokov as a man-about-town for many years, and upon being wined and dined by him in the early 1970s in his apartment in the West Twenties, had witnessed his potential as a gifted houseguest. At the time he entered my parents' circle, he was a tall, dynamic, handsome man just seventy years of age with blazing, mischievous blue eyes and a shock of thick white hair. His face was made a bit eerie by its asymmetry: a severe neuralgia incurred while he was serving in the American military in World War II had altered motion in his right cheek, giving him an expression of slightly leering malice, which was in perfect keeping with his mordant, scathing wit. Nicolas was then married to his fifth wife, Dominique, a very bright, pretty French woman forty years his junior who was head over heels in love with him. My family and I frequently strolled down to my parents' house for a Saturday-night dinner or a Sunday lunch. And as Nicolas and Dominique became the Libermans' regular guests we marveled at the abundance of beef Stroganoff, cutlets Pozharski, and steaming pots of kasha that came to the table. Mother, who as she grew older sought greater than ever refuge in Russianness—Russian friends, Russian food, the Russian language—was most truly in her element with Nicolas: He was cooking the food she loved best, and with him she could also discuss every possible fine point of Russian literature. She took equally to Dominique, who became like a second daughter to her. Another benefit of the Nabokovs' presence was that Mother, fearful of ruffling the sensitivities of the elegantly abstemious Nicolas, tried to moderate her alcohol intake.

As for Alex, during the Nabokov era he went through a period in which he spoke very little. He had recently begun to suffer from a severe tremor of the hand. Obsessed as he was by appearances, he detested any outwardly visible sign of infirmity. He found a neurologist who prescribed a powerful medication that controlled the tremor to a degree, but with severe side effects of sedation and depression. After silently eating his meal, answering any questions put to him gruffly and monosyllabically, he retired to his studio, where he was making maquettes for the monumental welded sculptures being executed by the Layman family. Otherwise all went serenely at Hillside under the Nabokovs' reign, which only lasted, alas, three years. For in late 1975 Nicolas had a mild heart attack and was not well enough to travel to Connecticut every weekend. Alex started phoning all his Russian friends. "Quick, quick, find someone," he pleaded, "someone who cooks well and can keep Tatiana company!" The fellow materialized some two months after the Nabokovs' departure. His name was Gennady ("Genna") Smakov, and he remained with the Libermans for most of the years Mother still had to live. I shall discuss him further below; my present task is to document another important turning point in Mother's life.

Notwithstanding the comfort and serenity of her life—Alex's impeccable stewardship of both their town and country houses, the loving
Russian friends who attended her, her closeness to her grandsons, in whom
she took increasing pride—throughout the years after her 1965 retirement
Mother's energies and morale had deteriorated. She had steadily lost the
marvelous dynamism that characterized her when she was still Tatiana of
Saks. A great change in her very glance is manifest in photos taken of her
from the 1970s on. Her former éclat and self-assurance, or appearance
thereof, is replaced by a sad, lost, yearning stare, as if she were looking back
nostalgically to a lost treasure, lost power—her work. As for her true physical decline, it began in 1976. Having abused drugs much of her life and
alcohol for the past decade, in the spring of that year she had a mild heart
attack and was diagnosed as suffering from congenital heart failure. She
had a good scare. Alex decided that during their yearly summer trip to
Europe he and Mother should spend a longer time doing the cure in Ischia
and then go on to Venice, which they both loved. (They had sold Va-et-
Vient in the midsixties, complaining that the Riviera had been overrun by
tourists.) And Mother's doctors persuaded her to limit her drinking to red
wine, a limitation which kept her quieter and more subdued, but also more
melancholy.

Was it a coincidence that she had that heart attack while my husband and
I were taking our first trip to the Soviet Union? I doubt it. Most any recollection or association with the Soviet Union seemed to be traumatic to her.
The prospect of our voyaging to her homeland had utterly terrified her, and
she'd spent months trying to talk us out of the trip. "It's very dangerous
there!" she'd warned us. "Don't go, you'll be followed everywhere by the
KGB!" But what a sneak she was: Once she realized she couldn't dissuade us
and was reassured that we'd cable her every other day, she prepared a curious
surprise: She decided that we must finally become acquainted with the
Mayakovsky saga that had so marked her life yet which she had seldom mentioned to us. For as we arrived at Moscow's Sheremetevo Airport, we were
greeted effusively by an obsequious little man, one Vladimir Makarov, who

announced himself to be the director of the Mayakovsky Museum. Handing me a huge bouquet of flowers and weeping with emotion ("Tatiana Iakovleva's daughter returned to us! Who would hope to see such a marvel!"), he told us that he had received a cable from my mother the previous day and was determined "to help us, to serve us" for the duration of our stay.

Thankfully, we had long been booked on one of those unchangeable Intourist trips, which dictated that we spend only five days in Moscow before going on to Kiev, Odessa, Leningrad. But during our stay in Moscow, *tovarishch* Makarov, a seedy apparatchik with deep halitosis and a carpet of dandruff on his shoulders, remained attached to us from morning to night. Obviously well connected to Soviet officialdom, he whisked us away with no problem whatever from our Intourist group and proceeded to give us his own tour of Moscow. It focused mostly on lengthy visits to the Mayakovsky Museum, which was then located in the very house on Dzerzhinsky Square in which the poet committed suicide. Great was our shock when, in the museum's first room, we came upon a series of vitrines containing more than four decades' worth of family photographs: pictures of my mother's and father's marriage in 1929, of various stages of my infancy and childhood, even photos of my American family, of my husband, of our children when they were infants and toddlers. I was immediately swamped with paranoid thoughts about the KGB's role in assembling this collection (the organization was notoriously possessive about the Mayakovsky legacy). But my fears were calmed when Makarov informed me that the photographs had come from my maternal grandmother. Throughout the decades that followed her immigration to France, he told us, Tatiana had sporadically sent her mother photos of herself, of her husbands, of her growing family. And a few years after my grandmother's death in 1963, her widower, Nikolai Alexandrovich Orlov, having heard that documents concerning the poet's muse were eagerly being sought by the Mayakovsky Museum, had considered it his "citizenly duty" to send on all these photographs.

We only had one final night in Moscow at the end of our trip to Russia, and on that occasion Makarov ferreted us out again, wined and dined us tearfully, and swore his eternal friendship to us.

We left Moscow on a morning flight and arrived in New York that night. We were totally surprised, upon our return, to see Alex at Kennedy Airport. "Mother's had a mild heart attack," he said to us shortly after we embraced. I suspect he wanted to prepare us as gently as possible for the news. But he also looked perplexed, fragile—he seems to have been shaken by the realization that he and Tatiana had entered a new, very vulnerable stage of their lives. "We got all your cables," he said. "But she was still very worried about you—she's terrified of anything that has to do with the Soviet Union." We told him about the curious ambassador Mother had sent us from her past. "She seems to have cabled him the day before we left!" I said. Alex's mustache twitched imperceptibly. "She didn't tell me anything about it, she never talks to me about Mayakovsky," he said, "we never speak about her past." Even with her loved ones, I then realized, my mother was continuing to maintain a chill silence about her life's principal tragedy and grief.

After her 1976 heart attack, Mother began to capitulate, looking on herself as an invalid and asking others to treat her as such, abandoning many tasks she'd usually been able to do herself and finding her principal solace in the company of Genna Smakov. A multilingual Russian classicist, ballet historian, film critic, and belle-lettrist who had recently immigrated to the United States, he was a dark-haired man in his middle thirties with a bushy mustache, large melancholy eyes, and a manner that could be—depending on how he felt about you—exuberantly affectionate, coolly formal, or icily brusque. Coming from a generation of Soviet intellectuals who were trying to recapture the broad humanistic culture of prerevolutionary Russian scholars, he was brilliant, arrogant, conceited, devoted to his friends, and suffered

Gennady Smakov, Tatiana's closest friend in her last ten years, in 1984.

Tatiana and her grandsons, Luke and Thaddeus, late 1970s.

no fools. And he relished showing off his truly immense knowledge of literature, which enabled him to recite, from memory and in the original, hundreds of lines of Virgil, Homer, Leopardi, Heine, and Rimbaud as fluently as he recited Pushkin and Lermontov. (Joseph Brodsky, his closest friend, referred to Genna as "my personal university.") From the moment they had met, upon a visit arranged by Brodsky, Genna and Mother had felt an instant kinship, and she had immediately invited him to Connecticut for weekends. Mealtimes at Hillside now turned into veritable poetry marathons as Mother, who knew even more Russian poetry by heart than Genna, alternated stanzas of verse with him by the hour. Need I say that the Libermans had also encouraged Genna to join the family because he was as gifted a cook as Tiffeau and Nabokov? Food retains a lifelong importance for survivors of famines, and it had been one of my parents' central fixations. Alex, in fact, found Genna to be so capable for the role of country companion/chef that he began to support him financially, even renting a flat for him in a fashionable district of the Village. "Isn't he brilliant?" Mother would ask when Genna was out of earshot. "Have you ever known such culture? He will soon write a masterpiece."

A homosexual who, like Tiffeau, had indulged in some risky cruising, Genna would begin to restrict his activities when the AIDS crisis came to the fore in the early 1980s. This may have deepened Mother's attachment to him. What dominating woman hasn't delighted in her sway over a docile, symbolic son who has been somewhat castrated by social or medical circumstances? I, too, was devoted to Genna, with whom I spent many a happy hour reading Russian poetry I hadn't studied since my adolescence. He reminded me of those melancholy, impoverished aunts or cousins one finds at dinner tables in nineteenth-century Russian fiction—Turgenev particularly comes to mind. He was constantly forecasting a pessimistic future for every possible situation: the horrors of the next fortnight's weather, a typhoid epidemic about to sweep the West, the demise of democracy throughout the world. But Mother relished indulging in her own innate pessimism with him, and in his presence she enjoyed her last relatively happy years. So enamored was she of Genna that he was able to readily convert the Libermans to his own proclivities—he was a passionate Wagner fan, and though they had always detested Wagner, now Wagner blared through the house at all times of day.

Genna also gave himself airs of great importance by declaring that he was writing a biography of Tatiana. "We must work now," he would announce as he sat Mother down on the living-room couch and turned on, or pretended to turn on, his tape recorder. (Any book that dealt with one of Mayakovsky's two muses was a potential bestseller in Russia, and Genna was one of many Soviet literati who looked on Tatiana Iakovleva as a gold mine.) Throughout his friendship with Mother, however, Genna remained extremely evasive about how readily she opened her past to him. "It is most difficult to make her talk about personal matters," he admitted, holding a finger on his lips. "As for anything related to sex," he added, "she is a total cipher!"

By that time, Alex, his tremor abated, had stopped the medication that had so depressed him and had snapped out of his silent phase. But he tended to be in somber moods when in Genna's presence, in part because Genna's precious manner irritated him; in part because he felt ill at ease with true intellectuals; and in part because his interest in poetry was nil and his concern for literature was minimal—he was the first to boast that he had not read a book cover to cover since Solzhenitsyn's *The First Circle* had come out in 1968. So his conversation with his perpetual Russian guest consisted mostly of barbed exchanges. Moreover, in those years Alex's somberness might also have been provoked by me, for the simple reason that I had become a writer, a vocation that I owe almost entirely to the encouragement offered me by Cleve Gray.

My first two books—both nonfiction, one on the Catholic left and one on Hawaii—had left my parents unperturbed and only mildly proud: Nothing short of a bestseller would have satisfied the two success freaks, who reproached me for failing to promote these books vigorously enough. More complex problems arose when I published my first novel, *Lovers and Tyrants,* whose French-born heroine, Stephanie, arrives in New York in wartime after her father's death in the Free French. Like much first fiction, it was very autobiographical, and the wry, often satirical manner in which it dealt with parental figures somewhat similar to mine greatly perturbed the Libermans. I described the success-driven mother floating through Stephanie's childhood as "an industrious, aloof . . . much courted beauty" who totally invents her titles of nobility. The protagonist's power-hungry, "brilliant, staggeringly successful . . . silver-haired" stepfather is a devoted family man, much downtrodden by his wife; his mustache "trembles with emotion" when he gets all his family into the car to drive to his favorite beach in the south of France. On this beach, which Stephanie loathes, "the expanse of oiled flesh gleams in the sun with the sad splendor of quartered meat" and resembles "an estuary gleaming with fish at mating time."

But notwithstanding my generally clement tone, I committed the unpardonable sin of having Stephanie dwell at some length on her father's death and on her mother's cowardly mishandling of that loss. What affected my own mother most deeply, in fact, was my description of the manner in which Stephanie finally puts closure to her many decades of unresolved sorrow by summoning the courage to visit her father's grave. This closely paralleled the process I myself undertook in my forties: Almost thirty years after my father's death, I had suddenly felt an urgent, unprecedented need to learn all there was to know about him, and I finally acquired the courage to visit, for the very first time, the family vault in Brittany where he is buried. There is a passage in *Lovers and Tyrants* in which I describe Stephanie's first visit to her father's tomb:

> I kneel down on the sealing stone which stands between me and the dead, that separates his body from mine. . . . And then suddenly my liberation comes. I am free now, kneeling on the stone, suddenly free and shaking, my head resting against the rusty metal handle that could be lifted for our reunion. I weep, I shake, I pound at the floor with my head, I kick it, I beat it with my hands. . . . He is there, he is there, he is there. Above all else he is now allowed to live in my memory, totally restored and whole now, as if resurrected, the reality of his death accepted, faced.

In 1976, shortly after the *Lovers and Tyrants* excerpt that includes this passage was published in *The New Yorker*, I came to New York on my weekly trek. I knew that my resuscitation of the dreaded Lieutenant du Plessix, my unveiling of the many delusions and deceits would not be enthusiastically received. It was late evening. Alex, who was making himself some Ovaltine in the kitchen, gave me his kiss a bit more coolly than usual. "Mother wants to see you," he said, his mustache intimating "You don't deserve a warning, but she's not exactly at her happiest."

As I came into Mother's room, she was in bed, and sure enough she had *The New Yorker* in hand, as if to prove that she had just reread the page she was about to comment on. "This is terrifying," she said, pointing to the passage above. And then she spoke a sentence that she parsed into two distinct phrases: "How could you?" she spoke, looking at me straight in the eye. "Tell the truth this way?" she added, looking away from me and slumping lower into her bed. "I needed to tell it," I replied gently, "in order to heal myself." "Heal?" she asked, incredulous, as if the word was totally absurd. She shrugged her shoulders impatiently, lay down on her side, drew the covers over her head, and pretended to go to sleep.

I went back to the country the next morning and did not see Mother and Alex again until the following week, by which time we'd all learned that

the Book-of-the-Month Club had chosen *Lovers and Tyrants* as its main selection. My parents had to face the next phase of their quandary: How to
deal with this wretched book, now that they knew it was going to be a success? They resolved the problem in the only way they knew: They immediately started planning a party.

Yet whatever gallant facade they put up throughout those months and
for years to come, until the end of their lives whatever pride Mother and
Alex took in me remained admixed with a measure of terror and vexation:
What is this dreaded daughter going to write next? What will be next on
her list of rectifications and exposures? ("It would be so wonderful if you
stuck to *religion,* darling," Alex suggested repeatedly. "It's what you write
about best.") Coming in from the country one afternoon, I saw my mother
sitting in Alex's chair in the dining-room window, hunched over a magazine.
As she heard me enter, she shot me a long, nasty sideways glance that was
straight out of nineteenth-century rural Russia, the glance of a mean, distrustful old peasant woman seeing an interloper invade her chicken coop or
kitchen garden. What kind of dirty tricks might she be up to now? What's
the fastest way of getting her out of my yard?

They have all my sympathy. It must be wretched to have a child who
writes. I thank the stars I do not have one—what a potential invasion of
privacy, of everything I myself hold most dear! From the mid-1970s on,
my literary vocation gave a wary, bittersweet undertone to my relations with
my parents that I regretted and yet relished: It commanded their guarded
respect, and it conferred the only measure of power I'd ever had over them.
As Mabel Moses put it: "Thank God you've become a writer.... The
Madam, she never even looked at you before you wrote that book."

Since I've summoned up the image of Mabel—standing in front of me
in her white smock, hands on hips, about to break out in a big laugh and a
shout of "Get out of here!"—I should account for an alteration in the
Libermans' domestic staff that had occurred some years earlier. In 1970 or
so, when Jean, the reclusive Frenchman who had served for two decades as
my parents' majordomo, retired to France, he had been succeeded by a lithe,
spunky Spaniard named José Gomez. José was a slender Barcelonan of mid-
dling height with swift, distrustful brown eyes and a manner that tended,

with strangers, to be terse and verging on arrogance. It should be said that José was homosexual (a proclivity that could only raise the high esteem my mother had for him) but was severely closeted, and this self-censorship in itself might have caused the frequent brusqueness of his manner. Irascibility and Catalonian pride were also built into José's self-image, and one of his many idiosyncrasies was his adamant refusal to ever wear anything but jeans and a turtleneck during his working hours, even when serving at table: It was an eccentricity that Alex announced as being "suited to our democratic age and very chic" and that my impatient mother tolerated because of the uncanny swiftness with which José ran upstairs and accomplished any task she set him to.

Tasks there were, for upon turning sixty Mabel had developed some cardiac problems, and José was now charged with the beckoning of carpenters, plumbers, electricians, and other services demanded by brownstones— duties he performed with a gruff efficiency that delighted my parents and with a possessive, truly dogged devotion to the house and in particular to Alex. No errand imposed on him by "the Boss"—going to the Russian stores at Brighton Beach to pick up some Russian videotapes for Mother or scouring Manhattan to find a rare kind of French sausage—was too demanding or far-fetched. So for more than a decade, the perennially grouching José, playing Leporello to Alex's chaste Don Giovanni—"*Io non voglio più servir*"—had made life possible for the Libermans at a time of rapidly deteriorating health.

The next phase of Mother's decline took place in 1981, when she had a five-hour gallbladder operation, which kept her in the hospital for two and a half months. She suffered from most every possible complication that could have arisen. She caught pneumonia, and as soon as she recovered from it she suffered a brain infection that took weeks to clear up. She had received large doses of Demerol every four hours around the clock in the days that followed the surgery, and she insisted on continuing them throughout her hospital stay. Whenever doctors tried to decrease the frequency of her shots, she noticed the lapse; she demanded—moaning with true or alleged pain—to return to her original schedule. By the time she was ready to go home, her addiction to the drug was in full swing. I remember being struck with the fact that she thought of Demerol as nourishment. Upon one of my visits to the hospital, she was half sitting up, pushing away a bowl of Jell-O, elaborating on the pain caused by any food she tried to take. "I only need tea and *this*," she said, pointing to the needle lying on the table. "You must leave, I need the bedpan," she added brusquely, ringing for the nurse. I left the room, knowing that she was going to try and get her shot ahead of time. The gaze that followed me out of the room was weary, blank, devoid of any recognizable affection, telling me, "I don't care about the world out there, I don't care whether I ever see you again, I can no longer distinguish between you and that world I'm refusing, I have no desire left outside of this needle."

A few days before she was due to be discharged, I received a phone call from my parents' physician, Isadore Rosenfeld, a brilliant doctor capable of great dedication to his patients. "How can I get her to stop this Demerol?" he asked. "Each time I try to lower the dose, Alex says, 'Please, please keep her on it, I can't stand to see her suffering.' But I'm not allowed to keep on prescribing this stuff to her without registering her as an addict." I explained to the doctor that I'd never been able to discuss any of Mother's substance abuses with Alex; that as I'd learned during her alcoholic phase, his handling of her addictions was woven into the very texture of their marriage and was an issue he wished to deal with all by himself. "You may have to end up registering her," I said, on the brink of tears. Isadore drew an exasperated sigh. "With these kinds of dosages," he said as he hung up, "she's going to turn into a vegetable."

In order to keep Mother on her injection schedule, after she came home registered nurses were hired to live full-time at Seventieth Street; since Alex was chafing to return to his studio, the nurses also accompanied the Libermans to Connecticut on weekends. One of them, Regan, was an athletic, bluntly outspoken redhead in her midthirties with whom I played tennis early on weekend mornings, before Mother's wake-up time. Throughout those months, Regan became the only person, outside of my husband, to whom I could talk about my mother's addiction. Her attitude toward the issue was critical and devoid of all subtleties. "Your mother's the kind of person who's only happy when she's *zonked*," she'd explain as we rested between tennis sets. "Staying zonked is her main goal in life." I told Regan about the Benzedrine and Nembutal addictions of Mother's working years, the booze of her early retirement years. "Go figure," she said. "Addicts are born to be addicts."

But Regan may have been too critical for her own good and unwilling to comply with Alex's complex subterfuges, which focused on never having anyone mention—or, God forbid, discuss—Mother's addiction. Within six months, Regan had been replaced by a quiet, very dignified Filipino in her midforties, Melinda Pechangco, who had been Mother's favorite nurse during her hospital stay but had been unavailable to come home with her earlier. Melinda wore her dark hair in a neat bun and had a reserved but genial manner and a soft, chuckling laugh. One of eight children born to a health inspector on the Philippine island of Visayan, she had had as tough and demanding a training as any nurse can have: As an apprentice midwife—part of her training at nursing school—she had walked dozens of miles each day through her country's swamps, often delivering babies with implements not more sophisticated than banana leaves. Later, when she had moved to the United States, she had spent years as head nurse of intensive care units, which had become her specialty.

Yet notwithstanding her arduous life, Melinda retained a distinction and innate elegance that delighted Mother. She dressed in chic tweed suits by daytime; and on weekend evenings in Connecticut, when she accompanied my parents to social occasions at Oscar de la Renta's, she wore quiet black silk and pearls. Upon such occasions, Melinda was the soul of discretion: Insisting that she was on a strict diet, she went upstairs to watch television while the rest of the guests socialized, coming down only to fetch Mother when it was time for her Demerol shot. "What a *grande dame!*" Mother commented to me when Melinda was out of earshot. The big difference between Melinda and her predecessor is that her severe sense of propriety led her to adhere to that code of secrecy and denial with which Alex wished to camouflage Mother's habit. She privately deplored Mother's addiction—"If I'd been alone with her I could have cured her of it," she told me years later, "but with Alex around it was impossible—he was incapable of ever denying her anything she asked for." But while sternly turning down her patient's constant pleas for larger and more frequent doses, she felt it proper to follow Alex's strategy of silence.

After coming home from the hospital Mother declined to even walk around the block and refused to go out in the daytime except for a twice-a-week visit, in a limo, to Kenneth's. She became increasingly dependent on Genna, who came to Seventieth Street every few days to bring her Russian fare and the newest Russian magazines. Her passion for visiting with her grandsons remained undiminished (Thaddeus was now pursuing a career in finance; Luke had become an artist), but they reported that she occasionally dozed off in the middle of a conversation. And she still enjoyed playing canasta once or twice each week, though friends related that she was too muddled to think her way through a game; in order to keep up her spirits, they purposefully lost several games a month to her. (How Mother could fake! She pretended to me that she *always* won, and every few months she would conspiratorially hand me a check, saying, "I've just won big games, buy yourself something to wear.")

My parents also cut down on their socializing a great deal after her addiction began, and due to this novel seclusion Mother and I, during her last decade, began a curious new sartorial relationship: Whenever I visited New York to spend an evening with friends, she asked me to come into her room to say good-night after I had dressed for dinner. "*Montres toi!*" she would command, scrutinizing me at length through her bifocals, and always offering some comment, such as, "You look like bag lady today, come even closer so I can see why you look so poorly!" Or "Very nice—what would we do without shawls?" However drug-muddled her brain, she somehow rallied, became lucid and vivacious, when there was something about my getup to praise or censure: "Thank God, some curl in your hair, but why that skirt when you should always wear *pants?*" I winced under her gaze, but what else did I have to offer her? I was now her surrogate fashion plate, the sole vehicle of her narcissism, the only body she had left to exhibit and scrutinize.

TWENTY-ONE

Tatiana's Last

Throughout the 1980s, it was in the intimate quarters of my parents' country house that the subterfuges which attended Mother's drug habit and Alex's enablement of it became most obvious. And as the addiction progressed, the aura at Hillside became more and more sinister. Mother grew increasingly fussy about her diet. Barely picking at the delicacies Genna found in obscure Russian cookbooks, persuading him to cook six, eight dishes for her to try at each meal, she sat at the table in a state of crystal isolation, staring at herself every few minutes in her pocket mirror. Genna, fattened by the vast amounts of food he was forced to provide, isolated by the restrictions imposed by the AIDS epidemic and the Libermans' diminished social schedule, lolled about and whined about the boredom of country life. Alex, more cynical and distant than ever, rose out of his gloom and bristled to attention only when some issue of sexuality was raised—Was such-or-such an actress sexy? Was Napoleon secretly gay? In this hothouse world severely removed from the realities of the 1980s, mealtime conversation was restricted to Genna's and Mother's limping discussions of Russian poetry and the two men's often nasty sparring, which mostly consisted of them doing malicious imitations of each other's voices or pronouncements. In the evening, Mother's manner grew more aggressive; she hurried everyone to eat faster so she could get her 8:00 P.M. Demerol shot and retreat to the pornographic movies Alex brought up to the country every weekend (in recent years, this had been one of the Libermans' favorite leisure occupations—"Bring on the ah-ah girls," Mother would say to Alex after dinner on most nights they were alone, mimicking the porn actresses' orgiastic panting). "Who wants soup?" she'd say over dinner. "Boubous, only you're having soup—hurry up and eat it." "I don't want soup if I'm the only one to have it," Alex would demur. "But it's already in front of you," she'd agitate. "So hurry up and eat it!"

The meal was dispatched with a speed which often left guests with severe indigestion, and then would come the charade concerning Mother's evening injection. A few minutes after the dessert course, Mother, gesturing to her stomach, rose and said to Alex words to the effect of "Boubous! I didn't digest that chocolate cake, come upstairs and help me to take my medicine!" Or else, if the family meal was being held at my house, she would cough loudly throughout dinner and at the end of the meal say, "Boubous, my cough is getting worse! Please drive me home for my cough syrup!" As I watched these histrionics, I marveled at the naïveté that laced the Libermans' worldliness—a naïveté made all the more remarkable by the elaborate other measures Alex took to hide my mother's addiction. (In 2004, I contacted a young man my parents had hired in my mother's last two years to take over José's duties as majordomo. This fellow let me know that he could not speak to me because Alex had made him sign a "confidentiality agreement" as a condition of employment.)

In 1982 or so, Alex and Dr. Rosenfeld decided that Mother could get along at home without any skilled nursing care—Alex, who was spending nearly half of his large salary on the production of his sculptures, had grown terribly short of money. Except for daily visits from a health professional who administered the noon and 4:00 P.M. injections, all nurses were then dismissed, and Alex himself took charge of Mother's shots. He gave her a needle at 8:00 A.M. before he went to the office and also took care of the 8:00 P.M. and midnight injections himself. What worried me the most is that Mother woke him in the middle of the night to give her the 3:00 or 4:00 A.M. dose. Beyond my concern for Alex not getting enough sleep at a time of worsening health—he had suffered from severe diabetes for a few decades and had recently developed cardiac symptoms—I wondered how his increased involvement in her drug habit might affect the dynamic of their marriage: For the half century she'd held sway over him, it had been his principal challenge and pride and joy to tame this formidable creature by fulfilling her each and every whim. But now that the tables were turned, now that drugs gave him total power over her, might their relationship be altered by the loss of the challenge? Might she lose her old magic for Alex? And could it be that keeping Mother zonked was Alex's solution for getting her out of the way, acquiring more emotional space in which to create his art? "Alex's studio," Andre Emmerich had often said, "played the same role for him that mistresses play in other men's lives."

Throughout the years during which Mother's health began to wane, Alex was having extraordinary success in all of his vocations. A new chapter in his life had begun when he started his friendship with Si Newhouse Jr., who soon after being named chairman of Condé Nast in the mid-1960s raised Alex's salary to a half million dollars. (He hiked it to a full million in 1980.) Young Newhouse had begun seriously to collect contemporary American painting and sought out Alex as his adviser. Impressed by the excellence of Si's eye, Alex took him gallery hopping every Saturday. The fact that Si bought four Liberman paintings in addition to his Motherwells, de Koonings, and Rauschenbergs could only strengthen the two men's bonds. By the early 1970s, Alex, who had become his boss's father figure and closest friend, had also helped Si to weather the major crisis that affected Condé Nast in those years: the company's dismissal of the extravagantly eccentric Diana Vreeland, who had been *Vogue*'s editor in chief since 1962. Alex's firing of Vreeland—and his general reputation of never standing up for anyone—led the famous editor to coin one of her finest bon mots: "I've known White Russians, and I've known Red Russians, but I've never known a yellow Russian."

Unfazed (or pretending not to be) by the bad press generated by Vreeland's dismissal, Alex then enjoyed a relatively peaceful fifteen years during the tenure of his protégée, Vreeland's successor, Grace Mirabella, a breezy,

Alex and Si Newhouse at the Condé Nast offices,
early 1990s. Photo by Crosby Coughlin.

down-to-earth all-American beauty who sent *Vogue*'s sales soaring upward by featuring a return to stylish, easy clothes. "Naturalness is a kind of nobility," Alex said when praising the fresh, new style initiated by Mirabella, with whom he enjoyed one of those very close, paternal, playfully flirtatious relationships on which his ego thrived. "His munificence was so winning and wonderful," Mirabella remembers today. "He'd call you in to talk about a Paris assignment and say, 'Take the Concorde, spend a lot of money, get yourself there in the most expensive way possible, take pictures over ten times if you need to, do it all grandly.'"

Alex's legendary editorial largesse was based on a process of expansion, which from the mid-1970s on vastly increased Condé Nast's prestige and profit. ("We'd have lunch every week at the Four Seasons," Si Newhouse recalled nostalgically two decades later, "and discuss what magazine we'd start or redo next.") The first magazine launched by the company in forty years—*Self,* of 1979 vintage—was an immediate success. Next came the total revamping of *House and Garden,* the purchase and makeover of *Mademoiselle,*

Gourmet, GQ, and *Details,* and the founding of *Condé Nast Traveler.* All of these new ventures were exclusively masterminded by Alex; the most dramatic of them all was the resurrection, in the early 1980s, of *Vanity Fair* magazine, which throughout the 1920s and 1930s had been looked on as the flagship of high-class American taste. *Vanity Fair* caused particular problems because it had the image of its predecessor to both capture and transcend, and it again called upon Alex's suave firing style: Its first two editors, Richard Locke and Leo Lerman (the latter one of Alex's oldest and closest friends) were highbrows who tried to continue the original magazine's tone by publishing such writers as Clement Greenberg, Gabriel García Márquez, and Susan Sontag. They were each given notice after a few months. Lerman was replaced by the famous Tina Brown, editor in chief of Great Britain's *Tatler,* who made the magazine into a huge success by adhering to the Andy Warhol dictum that "Celebrity is the Nirvana of the masses" and by shrewdly capitalizing on the dual appeal of Hollywood and Washington, D.C. Lerman, who enjoyed referring to Alex as "that housemaid's delight," was deeply hurt by the episode. And even Tina Brown was amazed by the icy resolve with which Alex went about firing his old friend. "There did not seem to be a trace of sentiment in the way Alex turned on Leo, it struck me as deeply scary that he had no conscience about it."

Alex's next major firing was even more painful. Even though *Vogue's* circulation had thrived under Grace Mirabella, tripling in a decade, Alex and Si somehow thought the magazine needed a new look. They had begun to dread the strong competition being offered by *Elle* magazine, which Alex praised for having "no feature content, just page after page of flash" and also for making "*Vogue's* earnestness and nobility, its respect for women's intelligence, look a bit quaint." And in 1988 they had become enamored with yet another beautiful, alabaster-skinned British press wizard, Anna Wintour, who was then the editor of British *Vogue.* Her distinct style—1920-ish flapper hair and an impassive manner that unfairly earned her the name "Nuclear Wintour"—had precisely that aura of "flash" Alex wanted for *Vogue.*

Those were the years when British women were beginning to be the Korean grocers of American journalism, and it was arranged, through complex and secretive negotiations, that Wintour would come to *Vogue* to replace

Mirabella. But somewhere along the line, the secrecy code was bungled: One evening, Mirabella's husband, the distinguished surgeon William Cahan, learned about his wife's forthcoming dismissal from Liz Smith's report on the five o'clock TV news. He instantly phoned her. "Gracie," he said, "Liz Smith says you've been fired."

"I was stunned, Alex was my closest friend. I truly don't remember suspecting that anything was wrong," Mirabella remembers today. "I went down to his office, and he looked up from his desk and said, 'Grace, I'm getting old.' Did he let me down? Yes, he was a coward."

But as chairman of Condé Nast, it was Alex's job to make sure that all of his editors in chief maintained their "flash," that each of the magazines was periodically refreshed. *Self*'s circulation was slipping? Fire its original editor and replace her with another zippy Brit, Anthea Disney. Disney did not heed Liberman's advice closely enough? Fire her and hire the peppy author of *How to Make Love to a Man* and *Great Sex*, Alexandra Penney. Si wanted a magazine for men and another for trendy *young* males? Buy and revamp *GQ* and *Details*, then place a brilliant young British editor, James Truman, at *Details*'s helm. Next to come in the company's list of successes was *Allure*, which Alex concentrated on exclusively for six months of 1991. Within that short span of time, *Allure* became the fastest-growing magazine in the Condé Nast empire—a sign that Alex, almost eighty and racked by several life-threatening illnesses, was still the wizard of American fashion journalism.

Throughout the 1970s and 1980s, Alex had also been playing God in his sculpture studio. Bill Layman took Alex on foraging trips to Connecticut's junkyards, where heaps of discarded metal parts were always to be found. Automobile exhaust pipes were among the first elements they collected, and assemblages of twisted and bent pipes began to sprout up all over his lawns and ours. But it was the larger pieces—the rusted cast-iron boilers and gas storage tanks—that particularly caught Alex's imagination. By this time he was looking a great deal at the work of Mark di Suvero and was aspiring to make huge public sculptures. He immediately saw the possibility of cutting up the discarded boilers in various ways—horizontally, vertically, at a slant—and welding them together into very large-scale pieces. Layman was imaginative about all the ways one could bend, twist, shape metal objects. He crushed boiler tanks by running over them with his bulldozer. He placed sticks of dynamite into discarded boilers to blow them apart—upon one such experiment the Warren Fire Department arrived—and one of the forms created by such an explosion inspired Alex's biggest piece to date, the forty-four-foot-tall *Eve*. *Eve* and its companion, *Adam* (28 x 30 x 34 feet), were among the first in a series of monumental works that would require cranes, I beams, and other industrial machinery to be produced and were specifically made to be seen in public spaces. His work would eventually more than double in size: one of his biggest sculptures, *The Way*, measured one hundred feet long by fifty feet wide by fifty feet high. By the end of the 1970s, it could be safely said that only Robert Smithson and a few other earthworks artists had been making art in a larger scale.

Alex's venture into sculpture took a huge toll on his finances. Fabrication expenses vastly exceeded sales prices. What with the three Laymans and a crew of part-time hired hands working seven days a week, it took $360,000 each year—over half of his 1978 Condé Nast earnings—to keep the operation going. The self-confidence initially needed to make these costly works is all the more striking in view of the minimal recognition Alex had received for his art. With the exception of bouts of sarcasm from Hilton Kramer, who once referred to him as "a third rate modernist pasticheur," his almost yearly exhibitions of paintings at the Parsons Gallery were seldom if ever reviewed. A show of his work at the Corcoran Museum in Washington in 1970 had poor press—*The Washington Post*'s art critic thought it had "something that recalls the sleek and stunning pages of the magazine [Liberman] works for." Less negatively, the critic John Russell referred to Alex's sculpture as "phallic artillery." (Indeed, they were extremely sexual, with an obsessively repeated theme of penetration.)

One of the ironies of Alex's life is that although his painting meant much more to him, his sculpture gave him far greater recognition. Andre Emmerich shrewdly capitalized on the fact that the works of the two most famous public sculptors of the postwar era, Henry Moore and Alexander

Calder, had become far too expensive for most American collectors. He marketed Alex's works accordingly, pricing them at modest six figures and exhibiting dozens of them at his country house in Putnam County, New York. Commissions began to come in the early 1970s after a real-estate developer borrowed six works for an installation at Dag Hammarskjöld Plaza, at Second Avenue between Forty-sixth and Forty-seventh streets. One of them so impressed Nelson Rockefeller that he bought a large piece for his home in Pocantico Hills. By the mid-1980s, Alex had become one of the two or three most prolific public sculptors in the country. I saw his creations in city after city when I went on book or lecture tours—in front of airports and office buildings, in the midst of shopping malls. By then, there were Liberman sculptures (the list is partial) in New Haven, St. Louis, Phoenix, Albany, Seattle; in Miami, Grove Isle, and Coral Gables, Florida; in Stamford, Connecticut; Rockford, Illinois; Minneapolis, Minnesota; and Granville, Ohio; at the University of Pennsylvania campus in Philadelphia, the Greater Buffalo International Airport, the Wadsworth Atheneum in Hartford. And *Adam,* the big red sculpture that museum director Carter Brown chose to stand in front of the National Gallery in Washington in honor of the opening of the museum's east wing, had already made its own headlines: Richard Nixon, offended by the massive modernist structure when it stood at the Corcoran within view of the White House, asked that it be removed.

Alex's Adam *on the grounds of the Smithsonian Institution in Washington, DC.*

To what biographical sources can one attribute this artist's impulse to monumentality? Alex himself used to trace his obsession to his early youth in revolutionary Russia: the huge, legendary cannon standing on Red Square was one particularly vivid childhood memory; another was the sight of the temporary monuments put up in Moscow to honor heroes of the 1917 revolution—immense improvised structures, connected to the Agitprop movement, the aim of which was to inform illiterate masses through spectacular, ultra-accessible art. Bill Layman, who was at his side throughout twenty-five years of sculpture making, feels that "the challenge of that hugeness" was also an emotional outlet for all the frustrations Alex experienced at the office and at home—frustrations that were vividly reflected in the artist's everyday dealings with Layman and his team of workers.

"Early on in the 1960s, when everything seemed fine in his home life and no one else would have taken on this work, Alex was a model of courtesy and graciousness," Layman reflects today. "In the late seventies and eighties, when Tatiana became seriously impaired and his problems accumulated, he began to be far more snippy and demanding—he'd come in on a Friday night after we'd worked an eighty-hour week and say, 'I'm disappointed, nothing is ready!' We seemed to serve as his pressure valve. . . . As Tatiana's health got worse and he grew increasingly burdened, Alex would often be very brusque and cutting." Bill Layman's wife, Elaine, of whom Alex was very fond, reports that when she saw him at the shop and said words to the effect of "You seem perturbed today," he replied, "Oh, darling, if you only knew."

Nineteen eighty-seven was the most dreadful year ever experienced by our family. Early that spring, Alex was found to have a cancer of the prostate and increasingly serious cardiac problems. (He shared this diagnosis with no one beyond his immediate family and led his colleagues to believe that his long absence away from the office was caused by acute pneumonia.) A few months later, Cleve learned that he would have to undergo open-heart surgery. And in May of that year, Mother, struggling to put on her trousers for one of her afternoon canasta games, stumbled, fell, and broke her hip. There were more hospitalizations, more complications, and once again she was away for a span of weeks.

Already decimated by the effects of her addiction—her refusal to walk, her capricious diet—she now became a true invalid. Alex had allowed her Demerol dosages to escalate since Melinda had left, and they were increased yet further to manage her new level of pain. Melinda soon returned to nurse Mother full-time and was appalled by the huge increase. "When I'd left her in 1982 she was getting a 25 mg injection every four hours," she says. "When I returned in eighty-seven, it had been increased to 50 mg every *two* hours—that was the unfortunate result of having had Alex in charge: He kept capitulating to her demands of increasing her doses." In addition, electric chairlifts had to be installed on the stairways at Seventieth Street and Hillside. The difference in her demeanor was obvious to me from the moment she came home from the hospital. I was waiting for her in the hallway, stretching out my arms to embrace her. Stooped and turbaned, leaning heavily on her cane, she swept by without acknowledging me, solely obsessed by her next dose, impatiently waving her frail, veined hand toward the stairway as she called to the nurse for her injection. I thought of the mad *principessas* who shut themselves up in their Venetian palazzos, ordering the closing of shutters and doors and windows, the firing of majordomos . . . that wave of the clawlike hand was saying, Leave me be, fuck the world, I want less of it than ever, bye-bye reality I've never had much use for you but now I'm leaving you altogether, it was a gesture that marked her entrance into a tightly shuttered space structured exclusively by the geometry of her addictions.

Mother had hardly been out of hospital for a month when another grief befell my parents: They learned that Genna had AIDS. Mother's reaction to the news was very unexpected; it was one of resentment and anger. The dying are not winners; as soon as she heard that her friend was doomed, she became brusque and irritated with him—she snapped at him during meals, ordered him to eat his meat faster or wipe his mouth more often, answered his queries in a gruff, monosyllabic manner. Quite abruptly, she stopped praising him to others, ceased her habitual litany of how brilliant, remarkable he was. For he had not fulfilled her expectations, in failing to prove his genius he had caused her to lose face, and she was furious.

So the aura of Hillside grew even more dispiriting: Morose Genna flanked by brooding, wasted Mother and increasingly weary, preoccupied

Alex—in addition to Mother's health problems and his own, he now had the responsibility of making Genna's appointments with specialists, booking limousines to get him to doctors. I now sensed an increasing somberness, a cynicism in Alex's demeanor. He was beginning to go about his multiple family duties with a stern, tight-lipped efficiency, with little of that tenderness which had marked his manner in our earlier years as a family. Perhaps, I often mused, this was part of the bargain he had struck with the devil, as it were, in exchange for his Faustian versatility. Perhaps the answer to his colleagues' astonished query—"How does he *do* it all?"—was that he'd gradually severed himself emotionally from most domestic tasks, turned that part of his heart to ice. In sum, he was resigned grimly to endure whatever human beings or substances kept Mother happy, for the simple reason that what he increasingly wanted at this stage of his life was a bit of time and peace to himself.

"I had rotten luck," Genna whispered to me when I last went to see him in the little Ninth Street flat we had found for him a decade earlier. He died in August 1988, after weeks of being constantly visited by his closest friends—Joseph Brodsky, "Misha" Baryshnikov, the journalist Liuda Shtern, the Libermans—and tended by the kind nurses Alex had hired for his round-the-clock care. After Genna had passed away, I realized that Mother's earlier rage had simply been a form of denial, an emotional mode she excelled at. She soon withdrew into grieving silence and barely ate anymore. She had lost her best friend, her symbolic son, the deepest link she'd yet found to her lost Russia. Throughout the following months, I tried to console her with as much Russianness as I could, bringing her new items from the Russian bookstore, occasionally cooking Russian food for her. Without being devout, she was something of a romantic about religious matters: She loved all traditional holiday rituals and always argued that Russians were quite right in looking on Easter, rather than Christmas, as the center of the liturgical year—"Everyone's born," she'd say, "but who else rose again?"

So at the Russian Easter after Genna's death, I ordered the traditional sweets, which he had been providing her for the past decade—the rich, creamy, white *paskha* and the golden fruit-filled *kulich* cake—and brought

Tatiana's last Christmas, 1990. From left to right: Neighbor Claire Bloom,
Thaddeus, Francine, Cleve, Andrew Kamins, Luke, Tatiana, and Melinda.

them to her at Hillside. She had lost so much weight that her dentures did not fit anymore; throughout the winter, she had refused to go to the dentist to have them adjusted; her muscles were greatly weakened by her insistence on spending an increasing amount of time in bed; and by this time she could eat only soft food at best. Yet that Easter Sunday she sat up on her pillows and very, very slowly ate a goodly portion of her sweets, occasionally looking up at me with the smile of a malicious, scheming child, as if to say, "You see, I *can* eat if I want to, if it's Russian, and if it's made especially for me."

But Alex's woes did not stop at the death of Genna, who had managed his Connecticut home life for more than a decade. That same year, he had seen fit to end his relationship with the Layman family and to reorganize his entire system of producing sculptures, assigning them to a foundry on the Hudson. And that same year, his chief of staff at Condé Nast, Bob Lehmann, who had run his office for nearly twenty years, had to cease working because his own case of AIDS was progressing so fast: He died within a few months of leaving his job. Last but hardly least, a few weeks after Lehmann's death, Alex learned that his domestic helper, José, who had managed Seventieth Street for two decades, was also stricken with the disease, and that Mabel, who was approaching seventy, had to retire for her own reasons of health. So in the space of a few months, the intricate, multileveled life Alex had balanced for decades with such Machiavellian diligence—his studio, his office, his home—had collapsed. In addition, there was a delicate work of deceit to perform at Seventieth Street. (How long had he and I been at this game!) Upon briefing me about José's diagnosis, he'd decreed that for the time being Mother must not be told the truth about him.

At this point, Alex was being briefly hospitalized every few weeks for cardiac symptoms and also for a chronic anemia, occasioned by his radiation treatments, which required frequent transfusions. This did not deter him from attempting to run Seventieth Street and from taking care of Mother in his habitually dutiful way. I sat by his bed during one of his hospital stays while he offered me a peroration on what he called "the fall of the House of Usher." "What do we do? How do we live now?" he asked. Propped up on pillows, needles in his arms, he spoke with a new kind of bitterness about the fact that both Hillside and Seventieth Street were getting to be too much for him. "I can't make it work anymore," he burst out, his mustache trembling. "I dream of being able to move into a nice hassle-free apartment where I could just pick up the phone to get the plumbing fixed, or a light bulb changed. . . . It's all beginning to destroy me," he added, "but it's hopeless—Mother would rather die than move out of Seventieth Street." Nostalgically looking back to the days when Seventieth Street had been a haven of efficiency, he went on to discuss the ideal staff he could find for the house: a Mabel-type cook/housekeeper, a José-type houseman to take care of the physical details of the house. . . . I gave Alex a good-night kiss and told him I'd do all I could to help out. "Pick up the phone whenever you're in the house so Mother doesn't have to answer," he called out to me as I left his hospital room. "*Au fond, l'Anglais la fatigue,*" he added—"English tires her."

After nearly fifty years, English still tires Mother, I reflected as I walked home, but otherwise we've become a truly American family, decimated by AIDS and drugs.

A short while later, after he'd resumed his office schedule, Alex's spirits rallied a bit. He had hired a bright, competent twenty-six-year-old butler, Lance Houston, to replace José. He had found a gifted aspiring artist, Crosby Coughlin, to take on Bob Lehmann's job as head of his office staff. Equally important, he announced, an acquaintance of Joseph Brodsky and Misha Baryshnikov was on his way from Moscow to replace Genna as Mother's companion.

The new Russian friend who had been programmed for Mother, one Yuri Tyurin, was hardly a Genna: Of far shallower mind and considerably more limited culture than his predecessor, he was a small, gay man in his late forties with dark little teeth, nicotine halitosis, and a mincing, obsequiously polite ballet-master manner. He claimed to have been, in turn, a dentist, a dancer, and a television anchorman and did not speak a word of any language beyond Russian. But we didn't care what kind of Soviet corruption he'd lived on as long as he could raise Mother's spirits by spouting Russian poetry and making decent Stroganoff. And upon his first weekend at Hillside, we knew we had a winner: "He is a master chef!" Tatiana declared solemnly upon feasting—however slowly, however sparsely—on his borshch and pirozhki. After a few meals, both Libermans took me aside to sing the praises of the new Russian friend. "How do you like our wonderful new Gennochka?" Mother said dreamily. "What an angel he is, how lucky we are," Alex whispered to me as Yuri dashed upstairs to help Mother ride down in her chairlift. "I've gotten him an apartment in the Village." (Alex managed to put Yuri on the Condé Nast payroll as a "consultant," the way he had for a decade of Genna's services.) Mother slowly began to rally, suggesting *kisel* for Saturday lunch, *shchi* for Sunday dinner. Alex was thrilled to spend more time in his studio, which increasingly played the role of mistress in his life—a source of relaxation, joy, and escape.

As Mother regained a bit of strength, Yuri, visions of rubles dancing in his head, announced that he, too, would write a book about her. But he needed to get hold of the tapes Genna had recorded of his conversations with Mother—tapes in which, Yuri suspected correctly, there would be some mention of Mayakovsky. He had gone through Genna's documents, which were kept in the Seventieth Street cellar, and found nothing beyond a few pages of notes on which Genna had scribbled a list of questions and answers. ("How large was Mayakovsky's prick?" Genna asks in one such exchange. "How should I know?" Mother rages in reply. "I'm telling you for the thousandth time I never slept with him!") So Yuri started to pester Alex about Genna's tapes, and Alex remained a master of evasiveness, just as he would be, a decade later, on the issue of Mayakovsky's letters. "Perhaps my secretaries put them in a bank vault," he'd reply to Yuri's queries. "Are you sure such tapes even exist?" "Maybe Genna destroyed them before he died." So poor Yuri had to interview Mother from scratch and seems to have encountered difficulties equal to Genna's: Never a competent researcher or a fluent writer, Yuri was still trying to do a book on Mother thirteen years after her death, when he wrote me to ask for any family documents that could help him in his task.

(Only after Alex's death did Genna's tapes resurface: They'd been in Alex's office desk all the time, in a clearly marked envelope, and were sent to me along with other contents of his office files. They helped me to understand the difficulties Genna had faced as he had "worked" with Mother in the 1980s: His entire body of research—the only result of those years of "interviewing" her—consisted of some three and a half hours of conversation. They are often made unintelligible by the muddling effect of drugs on Mother's mind and moreover are filled with her amazing lies. Trying to hone an ultrachaste self-portrait for posterity, one of the many falsehoods she puts forward is her assertion that she and Alex had not become lovers until the summer of 1940, *after* my father's death. Notwithstanding the fact that her last will and testament was to leave me all of her "personal possessions," which included a prewar correspondence studded with her passionate exchanges with Alex, she was attempting, with touching naïveté, to remake herself into an impeccably Puritanical heroine.)

Now totally homebound, Mother still spent much time at her multi-mirrored dressing table, every afternoon carefully painting her face, arranging her hair, and getting into a satin pantsuit before emerging from her room. And each time I came into town, the same stylistic critiques took place. "Come close so I can see you better," Mother would say, reaching for her blue-tinted bifocals. "I haven't changed," I'd tease. "All right, you haven't changed," she'd mutter, scrutinizing me with her habitually critical gaze, "someday before I die I'd like to see your eyebrows under those blasted bangs."

In February 1991, Alex was hospitalized again when he had his first massive heart attack, which was aggravated by his severe diabetes and the havoc already wrought on his health by prostate cancer. I rushed back from Florida, where I'd been visiting my ailing mother-in-law. Mother was in and out of hospital because of failing kidneys, and even after Alex had come home there followed a period of weeks when both my parents were hospitalized, sometimes simultaneously, sometimes overlapping by a few days. I felt a sorrowful ache of separation, sensing that I was going to lose one of them soon, dreading to speculate on which of them would be the first to go. ("Be a gentleman—ladies always first," Mother had joked to Alex for many years, dreading the prospect of surviving him.) When Mother was alone at home she grew barely manageable, refusing to get out of bed, refusing to see doctors, refusing to eat Yuri's delicacies. "I can't bear to look at her this way, she looks like something out of Buchenwald, it's all so complicated," Alex complained to me during one of my visits to New York. "I worry so about who's going to take care of all her needs if I'm not there to direct everything. . . . Seventieth Street is becoming a madhouse, it's all very complicated." "Complicated" is a word I'd simply never heard Alex Liberman use. So far everything, for Mother's Superman, had been flexible, doable, manageable. Through the use of that novel word I was beginning to hear him say, "I'm trapped. This is ghastly. She's killing me."

Our worst flaws and our grandest qualities, so I've observed, tend to be intensified by the weight of time. As if it were too fatiguing to carry the burden of all our attributes, with the advance of age we shed most moderation, pare down to essentials, become in every way more extreme. Colette grows both kinder and more voracious, Isak Dinesen more anorexic yet more clement, you, dear reader, may see an increase in both your altruism and your hypochondria. My mother, alas, was an exception to this rule: Shedding all her legendary generosity, her capricious but often extravagant kindness, in her last years she grew only more devious, more intractably selfish, more self-absorbed. There was the inevitable ravage wrought on her psyche by the Demerol addiction. What struck me as most painful in this last phase of my parents' lives was Mother's impulse to totally deny that Alex, too, was ill. Both his prostate cancer and his heart attack had seemed to fill her with jealousy and anger: Through his new illnesses, he was threatening to become a greater center of attention than she was, and this, for her, was beyond the pale. Deprived of her life's central dynamic—to remain the principal focus of Superman's concern—she resorted increasingly to the only weapon she could manipulate him with, food. She turned into the hunger artist and starved herself for everyone to heed; her diet became the central topic at Seventieth Street, her blackmail was now carried out through the primal orality of the infant. In the space of eighteen months, Alex hired and fired thirty-four cooks in a vain attempt to get her to eat. He would send all over for the delicacies she had loved in the past—Menshikoff chocolates, a sweet that could only be found in Chartres, France; *quenelles de brochet* and chocolate mousse from La Grenouille; white truffles and *Calissons d'Aix* from Fauchon in Paris. She would pretend to be pleased by the sight of these old favorites, take one tiny taste of them, and push them away, saying they were not as good as they used to be.

Whereas Alex's first query to me, during the room-to-room shuttling I engaged in when they were both hospitalized, was to ask how Mother was, she never once asked me about Alex's condition. "She was so devoid of any concern for Alex," Dr. Rosenfeld recalls, "that I couldn't detect her love for him." Her principal distraction, in those last months, was to probe the degree of control she still maintained over the family. I particularly remember an episode some five weeks before she died when she was lying in her hospital bed, looking frail, tidy, and conniving. I brought her greetings from

Cleve. "He sends kisses," I said. "He loves you very much." "Everyone loves me, except you," she retorted. Before I could counter with some denial, she sat bolt upright in bed, raised her wasted arm and pointed an accusing finger at me. "*You* don't love me, you're just *afraid* of me," she said loudly. Then she fell back onto her bed, looking very pleased, and added, "I'm just kidding." Oy, I thought to myself; ace, set, match.

Beyond Alex taking center stage as the gravely ill patient, there were several aspects of his behavior that had alarmed and irritated Mother in their last few years together. He was making new friends, engaging in novel ventures, without her advice. Alex's central project in those years was a biography of himself being written by a young author, Dodie Kazanjian, who quickly became his closest friend. Mother was too smart not to realize that the choice of Dodie, a petite, dark-haired, vivacious woman who adulated Alex, signaled his rebellion against the tall, blond, aloof Valkyries (Hilda, Mother, me) who had heretofore dominated his life. "Alex and Dodie had a passionate relationship," says Anna Wintour. "He had a huge impulse to self-promotion, and here was a woman who admired him unreservedly, praised him constantly."

Mother was dismayed by the gentle, docile Dodie and appalled by the prospect of such a book. Did Alex really think any honest, decent biography could be written during one's lifetime? she repeatedly asked him. And was he really important enough to deserve a biography? "*Tu vas te couvrir de ridicule*," "You will be an object of ridicule," she warned him again and again when deriding the project. "Who *is* that woman?" she would ask me about Dodie Kazanjian, miffed because he had never before made a close friend on his own. "That girl is simply not *our* kind, she doesn't even speak a word of French—how can she expect to understand us?" (Indeed, even I, who liked Dodie very much, once asked Alex why he had not chosen a multilingual Condé Nast writer such as Joan Juliet Buck. "She knows too much," Alex quickly replied. "I want a tabula rasa.")

In sum, Mother remained, until her end, a court jester of sorts, pricking at Alex's inflated ego, relentlessly prodding him to remain more modest, curbing both the wild child and the gypsy in him. But what invoked her greatest fury, I suspect, was her sense that in this biographical project, in his friendship with doting Dodie, Alex might be preparing a new, post-Tatiana life for himself. For Mother was far too possessive to wish for Alex's extended survival. Well might she say, "Be a gentleman—ladies first"; but in her mind's eye she saw him walking right behind her in that revolving door to the beyond, and she was furious to see the arch survivor balking at her scheme.

I particularly think back to the time when Mother had returned from a stay at New York Hospital on the same day Alex had been readmitted to it with a new rash of cardiac symptoms. It was shortly after dinnertime, and I found her all dressed up in her satin pantsuit, lavishly made up and manicured, watching television with Melinda. She seemed to have been eagerly waiting for me, for she even rose to greet me, leaning on her cane, and then motioned to me, with her familiar beckoning—"Psst psst!"—to come into the adjoining room. She cornered me in the living room and whispered, with great urgency: "About Alex, those doctors are barking up the wrong tree. He does *not* have any heart problem—that's all foolish gossip! He's just at the hospital for a diabetic checkup!" She straightened herself up with whatever majesty she could summon and added imperiously: "So he's not at all as sick as I. I'm the only one who's really sick."

The oracle had spoken. She returned to the library and resumed watching TV. I went upstairs for a bath and before going to bed dropped into her room to say good-night. Her body, whenever the elaborate finery came off, looked piteous. By this time, she was taking only tiny batches of liquefied foods—spoonfuls of mashed potato and broth, Yuri's *kisel,* and oatmeal if it was made by Alex himself. Her weight was down to ninety pounds and her thin-as-sticks thighs were totally covered with boils and lacerations, caused in some part by protein deprivation, in greater part by the Demerol shots, which had penetrated every available inch of her limbs. There were threats of infection, and the nurses had carefully treated the wounds with antibiotics. She may have noticed me looking at her legs, and to veer my mind away from the injections, said, "You remember Aunt Sandra's legs in her last years. . . . They were always bandaged, it's genetic."

Alex came back from the hospital a few days later, and then family dynamics grew even more complex. The day after he came home, Melinda phoned me to say that Mother had awakened Alex several times during the night, calling out to him or throwing magazines onto his bed. Moreover, at 5:00 A.M. she'd tried to persuade him to go downstairs and make her some oatmeal—his oatmeal, she said, was the only thing she could still eat. "But *Boubous*, I've just had a heart attack," Melinda quoted Alex as saying. "I'm not allowed to go downstairs yet." By this time, Mother's retort could have been expected: "But I'm sicker than you are." The following day, I heard that Mother had asked Alex to find her some oysters and a special kind of mocha ice cream she craved: It was midnight, most stores were closed, and he'd complied by going to the Waldorf-Astoria for these goodies, which after sampling Mother declared worthless. Upon hearing these reports, I left for New York and called Isadore Rosenfeld, asking him to lay down the law and have Alex and Mother sleep in separate rooms: Alex should have my old room across the landing from theirs; I could stay with a friend a few blocks away.

Dr. Rosenfeld grasped the problem immediately and appeared at Seventieth Street, dictating the separation. "I can't assure his survival if he doesn't have a quiet room of his own!" he commanded over Mother's virulent protests. But Mother's ever-powerful instinct told her that it was I who had initiated the new sleeping arrangements, and she was furious at me. As soon as the doctor was out of the house, she shouted down to the library, where I'd been reading: "Francine!" I always knew I was in hot water with my parents when they called me by my French name rather than the russified "Frosinka." I walked up to her room and saw her standing up, which she'd refused to do for weeks, leaning on her chest of drawers. "It's up to us and us only to decide where we're going to sleep in this house!" she tried to shout, emitting a thin, hoarse whimper. "Don't you ever meddle in such things again! I've never done anything to keep him up! He's getting plenty of sleep!" And she slammed the door in my face harder than she'd ever slammed it.

I walked across the landing, shaking, into Alex's new room. He lay on my old bed as he'd lain for fifty years on his own bed at evening rest time, his arms folded behind his head. "Thank you for being here, darling," he said. "I've just called the carpenters and painters to fix up a room for you

Alex and Tatiana at their country house in Connecticut in the late 1980s, during one of their last years together. (Dominique Nabokov)

upstairs, in my old studio." And indeed, two weeks later—this was the old Liberman magic—his fourth-floor studio had been remodeled into a room and bath for Cleve and me. I spent as much time as I could at Seventieth Street, observing the tragic aura that marked this late, demented phase of my parents' mutual lifetime passion. What tolls hadn't drugs and illness taken on this legendary marriage? Alex the tough exile, the self-preserving survivor, had started to withdraw from his great love as soon as he'd sensed that she wished to lure him into her self-destructive path. And when she'd realized that her Superman couldn't dance his subservience to her anymore, that her magic spell on him was waning, Mother had seen no more reason to live.

Yet however ill she was, however discarded she felt, until the very end

Mother never lost her need to study and perfect her looks. "I'm dying, we're all dying, Frosinka," she moaned to me on the phone every few days. "Listen, can you go down to my closet at Hillside and get me my rose satin pajamas and the St. Laurent velvet jacket? Alex is sending a car for them, I need them for tonight." And occasionally I saw her trying to recapture her spell over Alex by the most traditional feminine wiles. On one such occasion, on an afternoon when he lay resting in my old room, she sat at her dressing table for an hour, carefully painting her face, putting electric curlers in her pathetically thin hair, in preparation for making a late-afternoon visit to him. Next came the decision-making process: She sat in a chair in front of her closet, Melinda gently advising her on which pantsuit to put on. Finally, there came the tedious labor of slipping her needle-torn limbs into the vestment. And then, once dressed, leaning on her cane, her aureole of blond hair surmounting her wasted face, she hobbled across the corridor to what had been my old room, knocked timidly on the door, heard her husband's tender words, hobbled to the bed, and lay down next to him. She held his hand, telling him how lonely and wretched it was to sleep alone in their bedroom, grouching about the fact that she had not had anything decent to eat all week, asking him when he could come downstairs and have dinner with her again. And he lay quietly in his place, looking at her with a sorrow and compassion admixed with dread, stroking her arm, happy that she still had the strength to put on her finery for him. "If you knew what pain I'm in," she then moaned. "No one knows what pain I'm in. . . . Is it time for my next *piqûre?*"

Her end came swiftly. By the last week of April 1991, Alex was at home, somewhat stabilized, but Mother was waning fast. "I'm really worried about her this week," Alex called on a Thursday. "You'd better come, she's . . . I can't tell you, she's different." I arrived at about 6:00 P.M. It was the first time I'd sensed that she was in a terminal state. She sat in a chair splunk in the middle of her bedroom in a white terry-cloth bathrobe, without a trace of makeup, her hair very flat and slicked to her scalp—it was the first time she had ever let herself go in this manner, the first time her chair was pulled out this way into the middle of the room, the first time she hadn't had the strength to sit at her dressing table and stare at her image in a mirror, she was dying from a dearth of mirrors. . . .

"What's new?" she whispered weakly as I came in. It was also the first time she had ever addressed me in English. I sat down and quietly told her about the only thing that had always seemed to interest her, whatever her state of health: what the boys were up to. She appeared to listen patiently, with some interest, but her eyes were devoid of any emotion, any desire, and after a minute her head began to nod. I helped Melinda move her to her bed. Her lips moved, her trembling hand confusedly rose toward the blue-tinted spectacles on her night table, then fell again on her bed. She made an effort to open her eyes and looked at me up and down, with all the strength her gaze could muster. "I think," she whispered, "you're wearing pants. You must always wear pants." She closed her eyes. I sat with her another ten minutes and then left the room. Those were the last words I heard her say.

I had the illusion that she would linger some time in this way, so I returned to the country for the night. But the following evening, a Friday, Alex called to say that she'd suffered horrible abdominal pains, and he'd had to take her to the hospital. The diagnosis was ischemic bowel, almost certainly a fatal case. There was a fearful scene at the hospital, he related: As he left her in her room shortly before midnight, she was crying out, "I want to die at home, take me back, don't abandon me. . . ." As she shouted this, she paced dementedly through the room, with a sudden, demonic fund of energy, the nurses had to hold her away from him—the love of his life was clutching at him, howling, begging him to take her with him as he fled her room. "I can't get that terror out of my head," he repeated to me in the next days. She lived on for another day and a half, but he never returned.

On Saturday morning, I rushed in to see her at the ICU. My mother lay in a quiet space filled with the sound of softly whirring machines, looking thirty years younger and both peaceful and angry—looking very pink in the face, as if sunburned—nothing ugly, nothing dreadful here except for the mouth twisted slightly askew by the respirator tube—as I held her wrist, her hand, she felt very hot, I realized it was her high fever—when I pressed my forehead to hers, there was no response, though I'd been expecting one, as I'd been expecting one for most of our years together—I had a sense of recall, I thought back to previous moments of her life when she had looked just this way, fiercely pink, her brows furrowed as in concentration—ah yes, there it was, she'd looked this way when she used to lie in the sun, on rocks and sand dunes and beach chairs and boat decks in Long Island or Europe, fiercely imbibing the sun, her brows deeply furrowed, as they were now, as if concentrating on the beautiful fierceness of the sun—I was so happy to see her die young and beautiful, the way she would have liked to have seen herself, to have others see her, in her last moments—I put my flooded cheek against her burning face, and asked her forgiveness for any pain I'd ever caused her and poured out mine, for whatever that was worth.

I came home to Seventieth Street. I walked into the dining room. It was dinnertime. Cleve had come in from the country also. Alex rose from his chair by the window. "Here," he said rather formally, "you sit here," assigning me to the same place, facing the garden, where my mother had sat for a half century. I was taking over for a brief while, I had a keen sense of taking over.

The doctor's phone call came at 2:00 A.M. Cleve and I went to visit with Alex in my old bedroom for a half hour. He lay in his pajamas, his hands folded behind his head as if it were his evening rest hour, looking blank, resigned, relieved. There were no tears. Man of iron, then or at any other time, few would ever see him cry.

"I worked with her at Saks, she was terrifying!" one woman in the crowd of many visitors said at Frank Campbell's Funeral Home two days later. Numerous colleagues of Alex's from Condé Nast were there—editors from *Vogue, Self, Glamour, Mademoiselle, Gourmet, GQ, Details, Condé Nast Traveler, Vanity Fair, Allure*—as were many luminaries from the Libermans' world: the de la Rentas, the Kissingers, Pat Buckley, Lady Dudley, and the Ehrteguns, and Bill Blass and Kenneth Jay Lane.

The funeral service was at the Russian church on Park Avenue and Ninety-third Street. Alex, Melinda, and I had chosen her garment, a brown satin tunic. The Orthodox ritual requires the coffin to be open for the first part of the service, as three members of the immediate family must file by it to "recognize" the deceased before the coffin can be closed. The Orthodox service also calls for worshipers to stand throughout the service, but by special dispensation Alex sat in a chair, head a little bowed, eyes cast downward, tearless throughout. By then, he had a bad cardiac cough, and Melinda, whom he'd asked to stay on indefinitely to take care of him, was holding his cough syrup. She gave him a spoonful after his first coughing fit, and he took it like a penitent child, head still bowed, eyes still cast downward. His colleagues were terrified by the change that had come over him. "When I saw him at the funeral, so ashen and desperate," the eerily perceptive Anna Wintour recalls, "I knew he was going to put his entire former life behind him."

At the appointed time, Thaddeus and Luke and I went up to pay our last regards to Mother. She looked so peaceful, so fragile, and for the first time so polite. It remains an image I shall treasure all my life, an image dear to me and consoling, an image the serenity of which I would like to share with others. I cherished that particular aspect of her mien that day—so polite, for the first time so polite. I wished I'd known her like that all my life—benevolent, with the good athletic tan, the total serenity, and that politeness, I wished I could have sat with her alone for hours there in that church, weeping and speaking to her.

Then from under my ocean of sorrow, amid that brutal sense of severance which is most deeply suffered by daughters, something akin to a sense of gratitude emerged: Dear God, I've survived her.

After the service, Alex, too tired to offer the hospitality himself, asked Cleve and me to take out to lunch those friends who had traveled to New York for the occasion: the Parisian crowd and a few who had come from other parts of the United States. We sat around the table in a Lexington Avenue restaurant around the corner from Seventieth Street, sharing reminiscences of Tatiana. The time she had greeted our friend Frederic Tuten as he arrived at Hillside by saying, "Take off sweater, ees disgusting." That time in the 1940s when high hairdos were in fashion and the woman sitting behind her at a theater had asked her to remove her hat and Mother had turned around and angrily said, "Tees not my hat, tees my *hair*." The time she'd chewed off Helen Frankenthaler's ear for bringing her fresh

Tatiana Yakovleva du Plessix Liberman, photograph by Irving Penn, c. 1960.

flowers—it was bad manners for guests to bring fresh flowers, Mother said, it forced a busy hostess to take time out and put them in a vase, only *plants* would do for the occasion. The time a team of *Vanity Fair* editors had come to Hillside to see Alex—Mother had appeared in a large straw hat and all her jewels and proceeded to speak exclusively to Genna in Russian over lunch; in midmeal, she had suddenly looked at the lunch guests and announced, in English, "Thees week we go to New York to see S/M at Mineshaft," and then resumed speaking Russian to Genna. The time in the 1970s when Alex had taken the whole family to dinner at the Tour d'Argent in Paris and had ordered a fabulous bottle of wine and the sommelier had begun to go through the whole folderol of smelling the cork, candling, tilting the wine, and Mother had so impatiently asked him to hurry up and cut out the nonsense that the sommelier, grown nervous, spilled the fabulous wine all over the tablecloth and our clothes. And the time she'd sat on a beach in St. Tropez and undressed Lucien Vogel with her toes—she had these miraculously agile toes with which she could undo a man's tie, unfasten his shirt and pants, take off much of his clothing, and as she performed her act (she said that back in the twenties as a poor young Russian exile just arrived in France she'd sat on beaches and done it for money) she ceaselessly emitted a series of low, sadistic chuckles. Over that lunch, we talked about Tatiana's scathing brilliance and her appalling rudeness and her occasional tenderness and her rage to live and her extravagant acts of kindness and her absolute uniqueness.

Alex had gone home to rest immediately after the funeral service. As I came home from lunch, he was waiting for me at his old post in the dining room, in the gray chair by the window that overlooked the garden. There was an attentive, almost excited air about him as I walked in, which let me know he had been waiting eagerly for my report, the way he had when I had come home from my psychoanalytic sessions or from any important occasion which he had not been able to attend.

"How did she look?" he asked.

TWENTY-TWO

After Tatiana

My memories of mourning Mother, in the days that followed her death, remain shrouded in the hundreds of yards of fabric—the fine wools and silks and velvets—that passed through my hands as I cleared out her clothes. They were all hanging in the long series of closets that ran the entire depth of Seventieth Street's cellar, a half century's hoard of them, hung with pitifully little care on the kind of cheap wire hangers on which clothes are returned from the dry cleaner. Many of them were now mildewed, torn, or stained with rust—there was something disturbing about the sight; it spoke of my parents' narcissism, sloth, and self-centeredness. Might it ever have come into her mind to give her discarded apparel to charity or even to institutions such as the Metropolitan Museum? Civic-mindedness was hardly the Libermans' forte. So here was an unfolding panorama of my mother's life as a fashion icon: the genteel tweed dresses she had worn as a hardworking émigré during our first American years; the wide-shouldered black outfits—shades of Joan Crawford's *Mildred Pierce*—she had put on to board the *Queen Mary* when she returned to Europe in the postwar years; the beige silk suit, bearing the Sophie of Saks label, that she wore to my wedding in 1957; the numerous copies, made to order in various hues, of Dior's 1960s A-line dresses, of which she had one original.

Some of Mother's clothes had still been redolent of her perfumes; sorting them, handling these powerful vestiges of her presence, was both boring and extremely painful. The impulse to clear them out instantly was hardly mine: Disposing of the dead's belongings is a risky business, and I would have preferred to keep her personal effects in place for months, letting go of them gradually, piece by piece. The task of discarding, in fact, was imposed on me by Alex, and in a surprisingly brusque manner, a day or so after the funeral. He had been lying on his bed in my old room, and as I was going up the stairs to my new quarters, he'd called out to tell me he was going out to dinner that night. "But is that wise, darling?" I asked. "Are you well enough?" It was in a burst of fury, with a kind of meanness I'd never yet witnessed in him—Dr. Jekyll suddenly turned into Mr. Hyde—that he snapped, "I'm going out tonight, and from now on don't ever delve into my affairs!" He continued to look vexed and barked after me, "And please clear out Mother's closet as fast as possible. I want everything out in the next three days!"

Amid the painful emotions his abrupt, icy rudeness evoked in me, I found myself suddenly murmuring the word "gypsy." The association was not totally unexpected. I'd occasionally given thought, in the past, to the gypsy provenance shared by Alex and his mother, seeing it as a source of their volatility and frequent deviousness. Perhaps this is the way gypsies deal with death, I said to myself on that occasion, with no need to take time out for the work of grief, with an impulse to erase all traces of the dead with utmost speed. (Researching their culture a few years later, I learned that gypsies do indeed deny the very validity of grief or mourning. Under the gypsy ethos, everything connected to the dead must be burned within twenty-four hours of their passing: tent, clothes, pillows, household items, drinking vessels. And under the banner principle that life must be lived exclusively in the moment, whatever personal grief there be, even for a person who had supposedly been deeply loved, must be kept minimal.)

A few weeks after Mother's funeral, I went to France to finish research for my book in progress, a task which I'd postponed for months because of my parents' ill health. By late May, with Alex settled at Seventieth Street in the company of Melinda and Yuri and slowly resuming his schedule at Condé Nast, I felt his condition enough improved to leave the country. One evening, a few days after I'd arrived in Avignon, I got a call from Cleve. "Guess what?" he said. "Alex has sold Seventieth Street." "Sold Seventieth Street?" I cried out. "It's not possible, he never even told me he was putting it up for sale!" "Well, that's the nature of the beast," Cleve commented. We talked for a while, I pouring out my hurt and my disbelief, Cleve, as usual, trying to calm me down. The shock was fierce. Couldn't Alex at least have given me a call? Seventieth Street was a space infused with even more rites of passage than the country house I'd called home for more than three decades, it had been Mother's creation far more than Alex's—every inch of it, every object, every mirror placement were dictated far more by her tastes and predilections than his own, which, as the family joked, would tend to have expressed themselves in an icy cube. Where would Alex be, indeed, without that house of Mother's creation, which played a pivotal role in the Libermans' scramble to success?

So I mulled it over. I recalled a time when, lying in his hospital bed, Alex had expressed the wish to move into a flat in which he could "pick up the phone . . . to get the lightbulb changed." An hour after Cleve's call I collected myself and phoned him back. "Where might Alex be moving to?" "UN Plaza, Forty-ninth Street and the river, a few floors below Si Newhouse," he said. "He's made a point of saying there'd be a room for us there." I couldn't repress a smile. Alex had done all he could, at every moment of his career, to cozy up to power. As Anna Wintour put it, "Alex was very much Si's courtier." His life was falling into place again.

A few weeks after I returned from France, Alex suggested we make a visit together to the apartment he had bought on the East River, which wouldn't be ready to move into for another few months. As soon as I entered the building's lobby, a ponderous Mussolinian space, I knew that Alex's first bachelor dwelling in a half century, as the family had always speculated, would be icily anonymous. His future quarters were perched directly over the East River. There was a large master bedroom for Alex, and two smaller rooms for Melinda and for us. The glaring light pouring through the large, bare windows, the constant screech and roar of sirens and motorcars rising from the FDR Drive below, let me know that these rooms could never be infused with even a flicker of my mother's cushy, serene gemütlichkeit. In fact, not until I walked into the ersatz glamour of that flat and was overtaken by its great chilliness did I totally realize that my mother was dead.

Throughout the summer months the apartment was being repainted, the entire family was trying to resume the semblance of a normal routine. Chauffeured by his favorite Condé Nast driver, a gracious elderly Algerian named Frenchy, Alex traveled to Hillside on Fridays in the company of Yuri and Melinda. He had not been in a restaurant for the past years of Mother's seclusion—"I've forgotten how to read a menu," he said wistfully upon his first outing—and as a distraction we took him and his entourage to sample local Connecticut bistros on Saturdays. On Sundays, I'd often spend a few hours at the Hillside pool to observe his household and make sure that it was running well. I'd see him pacing up and down the cement rim of the pool, up and down, hands behind his back, face bent down and brooding— it was his way of keeping to that walking regimen the doctor had prescribed to maintain his cardiovascular health.

While observing Alex's new life, I often thought back to the after-Tatiana scenario that I had envisioned for Alex ever since I'd realized that Mother would be the first to go. I'd imagined him becoming a near-recluse, making Hillside his primary residence, going to New York two or three times each month to see doctors and a few select friends, finding his principal solace in being able to paint full-time, as he'd always said he'd wanted to do. . . . I would have visited him daily, brought him his meals, or would have prepared delicate French dishes for him at my home, offering all the Cordelia-like solace and dedication I could summon . . . how benign he would have become, how gratefully he would have smiled at us daily across the dining-room table. . . . In retrospect, I find it amazing, grotesque, that an intelligent sixty-year-old woman could harbor fantasies about a parent that turned out to be so far-fetched, so distant from the reality at hand. In point of fact, Alex, now unable to spend a minute alone, was more sur-rounded than ever by a regiment of acolytes and sycophants.

On a mid-August weekend, in that very span of weeks Alex was sup-posed to move to his new flat, he was plagued with a new rash of cardiac problems. Melinda had first taken him to our local Connecticut hospital, had found it inadequate, and within a few hours had him flown by heli-copter to our old family hangout, New York Hospital, where he underwent an angioplasty. Cleve and I were in Cooperstown, New York, for an overnight stay and had left our phone numbers with Alex and Melinda. Having heard the news by phoning Connecticut, I rushed back to New York City to see him at the hospital and found him to be plaintive, accusa-tory. "I couldn't find you. Where were you?" he asked with bitterness in his voice.

"I left our numbers with you and Melinda, hour by hour," I said.

"I guess she must have lost them," he mumbled. He went on to grouch about his Connecticut house. It reminded him too much of Mother, he complained—the evenings were unbearable, everything there carried a mem-ory of her. He couldn't wait to move into the new New York flat, and he went on to talk about its decor. At one point, he said, he'd had fantasies of blowing up an Irving Penn picture of Mother to fit the gigantic wall in the entrance hall, but then he'd decided it should have just one of his paintings on it. It was so hard to sort out which objects of memory to keep and which to cast out—wasn't it a sacrilege to retain her picture everywhere? And yet wasn't it also a sacrilege to cast out too much? (In view of his fu-ture demeanor, I was to particularly remember that comment.) "Well, you should sell Hillside as fast as you can if you feel uncomfortable there," I said, as I left him to go back to Seventieth Street. "It'll be a great relief," he said, having most probably made up his mind on the issue already but look-ing relieved that I agreed.

I came home to Seventieth Street. It was to be my last night at our old home, which over the past weeks had become gradually denuded. Alex had sold almost all of its furniture, including the pieces that had been in my mother and father's prewar Paris apartment. All the beloved art I'd grown up with—the Giacometti, Braque, Picasso, and Chagall drawings, some of which were signed to Mother—had also been taken off the walls. Alex was giving most of it to various museums throughout the country to offset the taxes he would have to pay on the sale of Seventieth Street. To allay my sadness at having to say good-bye to the house, I'd made a date for dinner with my son Thaddeus, who was almost as attached to the site as I was. We hugged and kissed the familiar white door as we parted, crying our hearts out at the memories it summoned. Although there was thrilling family news that week—Thaddeus had announced his engagement to a remarkable young woman—it was an evening on which I was relieved not to be alone.

After my son left, I stayed up late on my makeshift folding bed in the old library, watching the Soviet Union dissolve on television. A special feature came over the air shortly after midnight that particularly caught my attention: there was talk about Leningrad soon being renamed St. Petersburg. I thought back to Mother's refusal to ever say the word "Leningrad." The seventy-year-old Soviet appellation was an anathema to her, and for decades, ever since her arrival in Paris in the 1920s, she had referred to the city of her birth as "Petersburg," had continued to say "Petersburg" to scores of learned gentlemen at dinner parties on both continents who thought she'd gone into early dotage, had adamantly stood her ground—and *voilà!* Just a few months after her death she was again about to be proved right.

A lex's cardiac condition having greatly deteriorated after he moved into his new flat, Dr. Rosenfeld decided to take a gamble and ordered bypass surgery. Given the poor condition of Alex's heart muscles, it was a huge risk—Rosenfeld even had to sign a document stating that he alone was responsible for the decision to do surgery. But the amazing patient came through with flying colors. There was an interesting moment the evening after the operation, when Cleve, Melinda, and I went to see Alex in the intensive-care unit. Cleve and I briefly held his hand, watched his eyes blink in what might have been recognition, and then it was Melinda's turn. She proceeded to throw herself on him with a tenderness that bordered on the hysterical, adjusting the angle of his breathing tube, resetting his pillow, asserting that the hospital nurses had done it all wrong, stroking his face as she repeated the phrase, "This is my baby, this is my very own." Aha, I thought at that moment, but the suspicion flitted away on the wings of what I deemed to be the impossible.

That fall, Cleve and I resumed our one-night-a-week routine at Alex's new apartment, visiting with him for a half hour before we went out to dinner with friends, occasionally staying on to have lunch or dinner. His career at Condé Nast, up to now so obsessively pursued, had vastly receded before the far more urgent goal of preserving his health. "After Tatiana's death," Anna Wintour comments, "he perhaps breezed in for a few hours once or twice a week. He'd become a bit of a hypochondriac, concerned with his health and his new home life."

Yet even though I observed how blissfully Alex was wallowing in Melinda's doting care, there were three principal reasons why I never imagined that a romance between them might be brewing: because I'd always thought of Alex as a deeply asexual man; because of the extent of his ambition and snobbism and because like the rest of the world, I still held to the Pollyanna view of Alex's passionate devotion to Mother. "He'll never recover from the loss of Tatiana" was the commonly held judgment, and notwithstanding my glimpses into the darker aspects of my parents' relationship I'd bought it lock, stock, and barrel. This illusion suffered its first erosion in November, when I received a semihysterical phone call from Lance Houston, the young houseman who had been hired the previous year to replace José and who had followed Alex to UN Plaza. "I'm calling to say that I may have to leave this service," Lance said in an anguished tone. "It's becoming unbearable here, that nurse has alienated us all—she's making believe she's already the new Mrs. Liberman." I thanked him for the call, told him there was little I could do about Alex's household, and asked him to stay in touch. The guy's paranoid, I thought to myself as I hung up. . . . But then I had a flashback to that scene in the recovery room.

And from Lance's call on, evidence accumulated. There were Yuri's reports, offered on the plane ride to Thaddeus's Texas wedding in early 1992. (Alex was increasingly impatient with Yuri, leading us to wonder what led him to keep him in his pay, and had happily gotten rid of him for three days by buying his plane ticket.) Alex was now totally under Melinda's sway, Yuri related, constantly adjusting his opinions to hers, and the two were now holding hands and calling each other "Babycakes."

But nothing was truly clear until the Labor Day weekend of September 1992, which Cleve and I were spending at the beachfront Long Island estate Alex had rented for the summer. The previous day, Melinda had arranged an extravagant party for his eightieth birthday: there were Filipino belly dancers gyrating to live bands, a dozen roast suckling pigs, fountains spouting champagne, planes scribbling "Happy Birthday Alex" in the sky. ("Mother could never have done this," Alex quipped to me during an interlude. "Can't you just hear her saying, '*quelle vulgarité, tout ce que je déteste*'?") The following afternoon, when we were alone on the terrace, he ventured into a soliloquy, which cannily began with a diatribe against Yuri. All Soviets are exploitative hustlers, he said, polluted by the evil regime that ruled them for seventy years—Yuri was no exception, he was talking about having his boyfriend join him in the States, wouldn't that be a nightmare? So he would soon pay Yuri to return to Russia, give him three months' salary to return to his damn Moscow. "I feel I must do everything very fast because I'm not going to live much longer," he continued, changing tack with the agility of

Alex's portrait of his third wife, Melinda Pechangco, 1992.

the nimblest sailor. "I can't stand solitude, I go crazy when I'm alone, I need a female presence, I'm completely alone . . . you live far away, you have your life—what can I do? Melinda is my savior, she's the only thing I've got. I can't stand being alone, I'm afraid, I can't stand being without a female presence," he repeated. "Perhaps in a few years I'll marry her. . . . It's so wonderful to experience skin contact again," he added in a whisper, looking at me meaningfully.

Oh, the poor darling, I said to myself, remembering only too well how cold my mother could be at times. Good-bye, Yuri, I also thought, finally realizing why Alex had shrewdly kept him on all these months—as a chaperone, to maintain appearances and keep his relationship with Melinda more respectable! As we parted to change for dinner, Alex's voice grew harsh again. "I feel that Cleve is hostile to the idea of my marrying Melinda," he added, referring to a mention he had made concerning remarriage some months earlier, less than a year after Mother's death. For the sake of our sons, who had doted on their grandmother, Cleve, whose sense of family was absolute, indeed had then told Alex that it might be "a terrible idea" for Alex to remarry so fast. Alex had never tolerated criticism; since Mother's death, he was increasingly given to nursing grievances; and even though he'd long repeated that his son-in-law was his "best friend in the world," Cleve's forthrightness, to my sorrow, created a barrier between my family and Alex that lasted for the rest of the time he had left to live.

But at least he had given us a little time to adjust to the idea. Two months later, in November 1992, Cleve and I were in Paris, staying with our close friend Ethel de Croisset, who had also been one of my parents' dearest friends in Europe. It was a Sunday night, and we had just started a cold supper upon returning from Chartres. The phone rang—it was Alex; Cleve took the call. Ethel's phone was one of those Parisian gadgets that broadcasts both ends of the conversation, so we were all three privy to the exchange. Alex was calling to say that he and Melinda were getting married three weeks hence, on December 2, but that he was asking only the Newhouses and Dodie Kazanjian and her husband to be present—Si and Dodie were to be his witnesses.

"If you're asking your boss and your biographer to your wedding, it would be nice to have your family there as well," Cleve said.

"I have no family," Alex said. "You're creating difficulties, I can't stand such difficulties."

"You're the one creating difficulties, and since you have no family, good-bye, Alex," Cleve replied. And he hung up, bursting into virulent army-sergeant talk—goddamn son of a bitch, I never want to see him again!

Five minutes later, the phone rang once more. "This new Alex is *too* appalling," said Ethel, still fuming, irate. "This is *not* a man I ever knew."

I still sat in the dining room, weeping my heart out. "Make up with him, please," I sobbed out to Cleve as he went to the phone. "Please, for Tatiana's sake."

"Cleve, dear," we heard Alex saying this time, "of course you and Francine and the boys must be at the wedding. You know I love you very much."

"Alex, dear, we love you, too—that's why these things happen," Cleve replied. By the following morning, I was looking on the incident with cynical bemusement: Alex had only wanted his boss and his biographer. Power and publicity—those were the two motivations that had inspired much of his life.

And so they were married in a chamber of City Hall by Judge Pierre Leval, the son of Beatrice and Fernand Leval—that very couple to whom the Libermans had fled on that summer evening in 1941 when Gitta Sereny broke the news to me about my father's death. I stared at Melinda's canary-yellow suit, her little diamonded hand, and thought wonders would never cease. Since Alex had been denied his original wish of limiting the event to his boss and his biographer, he made a party of it. We were twenty or so—several beautifully dressed women from Condé Nast were in attendance. Immediately after the brief ceremony, a wedding lunch was held at a chic Italian restaurant in the West Village. And a few weeks later, there came a coolly cordial phone call from Alex asking Cleve and me to sign papers that would exempt us from being executors of his will, a duty he had asked us to assume thirty-five years earlier, shortly after our marriage. The phone call came from Miami, where he had just bought a duplex overlooking the Bay of Biscayne. His trustees, he told us in passing, were now to be Paul Scherer, a Condé Nast executive, Melinda and Dodie Kazanjian, who got along famously and had become close friends. In effect, he had fired his original family—an activity he had trained for well at Condé Nast—and hired a new one, including a symbolic daughter whose style was comically opposite to Mother's and mine.

Going into "the Libermans'" living rooms at 870 UN Plaza or at their Miami flat, one entered spaces as starkly white as Seventieth Street but made far more glacial and blinding by the harsh glare that poured in from the huge, uncurtained windows; by the white plastic upholstery that covered all the furniture; by the absence of any paintings on the wall beyond Alex's latest creations—the large, gaudy 1980s canvases that continued, with somewhat diminished energy, the Expressionist style he'd been working in for the past two decades. In both apartments, the rooms' bleak modernist whiteness was curiously at odds with the dainty accoutrements that were the hostess's personal touches: finicky antimacassars and lace doilies placed on the dining-room chairs, fussy pink porcelain vases, and, in

Annie Leibovitz's photo of Alex and Melinda at home in Miami,
published by Alex in the November 1993 issue of Vanity Fair.

New York, a massive crystal chandelier hung over the dining-room table (at the sight of which I heard Mother's voice emit the same kind of censure Alex had conjured at his birthday party, *"Tout ce que je déteste"*).

There was a distinctly Oceanic, faintly corrupt aura about both the Libermans' flats—one could have been in the homes of shady diamond dealers in Singapore or in Jakarta. These new quarters were inevitably accompanied by an abundance of habits very new to Alex's life. In Florida, he spent most of his leisure time accompanying Melinda to shopping malls or lounging in a white plastic recliner as he watched game shows and QVC. "I love Miami. I love shopping malls. We're happy just sitting on the terrace and seeing no one," he'd exult when I'd call him in Florida. "He was watching all that junky television," Charlie Churchward recalls. "When a few of us would fly down to visit him, he'd say, 'There's this marvelous new television show, we should do a piece on it!' We'd look at each other as if he'd lost it."

And although Alex had never much liked children, the couple was now blessed with an abundance of visiting Filipino babies. As one of eight siblings, of whom only she had remained childless, Melinda had several nieces and nephews to whom she was devoted and who had children of their own. Their young offspring were all taught to salute "Uncle Alex" with a salaam, touching their heads to his knees, in Filipino custom. It was indeed an improbable vision: the once-dapper Alex—maestro of decorum, paragon of impeccable British public-school manners—become a T-shirted patriarch, smiling with embarrassment as Filipino toddlers were thrust onto his lap. There might have been dynastic concerns: As my son Thaddeus began to have children of his own, Melinda placed a baby carriage in the entrance hall of her New York apartment, a permanent reminder to Alex that it was all those little nieces and nephews of hers who were now *his* family, *his* babies. (They were to be well remembered in his will.) "Survival was his Jewish mode," Isadore Rosenfeld comments today about the new family life Alex took on with Melinda. "However hard it might have been to adapt to all those barefoot children, he never said a critical word about Melinda, the way he had never said a critical word about Tatiana."

Alex's vastly extended new family was further expanded by those of

Melinda's friends from nursing school who were living in Miami or New York. In New York, there was Jannett, a lusciously beautiful single woman who had been several classes below Melinda. In Miami, there was Joy, married to a German car dealer named Hans, who was inseparable from the Libermans until some falling out estranged her from them. (Elaborating on the details of a visit to Miami, so Oscar de la Renta reported, Anna Wintour delighted many New York friends by reporting that the Libermans saw mostly garage mechanics.) On their days off, these ladies—all as impassively smiling as Melinda—came to the Libermans' to play long games of mah-jongg with their hostess. And on such occasions, the flat's silence was broken only by the sharp clink of the tiles and the cracking of innumerable amounts of pistachio nuts. Meanwhile, Alex, lounging on his terrace, would look at whatever Condé Nast fashion magazines had come in the mail that week or even glance at *The New Yorker* or *The New York Review of Books*. As I watched him loll about the house on my few visits to Miami, he kept reminding me of the Russian fictional character Oblomov, who as he grows older regresses into infancy, becoming increasingly indolent and immobile as he is absorbed into his housekeeper's womblike, all-invasive care. "It's paradise here, paradise, these Filipino ladies are so beautiful!" he exclaimed in the first few years of his Miami life. "I want to learn Filipino, I'm thinking of going to live there. . . . I want to look Filipino. I'm thinking of having my eyes slit so I can look Filipino!"

The dynamics of Alex's new world did not always ease relations with the friends and the family he had shared with Mother. Living in great idleness, often feeling slighted by the world at large, the new ménage tended to harbor petty grievances. With the exception of Leo Lerman and of Marti Stevens, a chanteuse who had been a close friend of Marlene and of Mother's and who lavished affection on Alex, by the third year of his marriage to Melinda most of his "old friends" were denied access to him. The ostracized included such ancient pals and family mainstays as Beatrice Leval, whose Yorkshire terrier, Alex complained, "yapped too loudly"; and, to my great sorrow, Alex's once adored own grandchild, my oldest son

Thaddeus, who was eventually blacklisted for failing to invite the Libermans for Thanksgiving dinner at a time when they had already left New
York to spend the entire season in Miami (and whose own children might
possibly have been seen as competition to Alex's newly adopted brood). Finally, there were also those former acquaintances whose usefulness was not
self-evident anymore, such as Andre Emmerich, who had long considered
himself to be one of Alex's closest friends. "I used to worry that Alex was
harboring grudges against me," says Emmerich, who never heard from Alex
after he'd closed his gallery in 1994. "Then one day I realized that with my
gallery gone, I was of no use to him anymore."

For diverse reasons, the entire slew of Alex's Parisian acquaintances had
equally been dropped. For he had taken his bride abroad in the summer of
1994—it was her first trip ever to Europe—to show her the sights and introduce her to his friends; due, in part, to a few gaffes Alex committed, the
expedition had not quite worked out as he would have wished. One such
faux pas occurred as Alex was introducing his new wife to Pierre Bergé, the
fastidious Parisian who had founded the house of Saint-Laurent in the
1960s and had become, over the ensuing decades, Mother's closest friend
in Paris. "I opened the door," as Bergé tells it, "and there Alex was with his
lady, saying to me in English, 'Pierre, I want you to meet the love of my life.'
I answered him in French, I said, '*Ne te fous pas de moi mon vieux, j'ai bien connu
l'amour de ta vie*'" (roughly translatable as "Don't shit me, man, I knew the
love of your life"). Another close friend, François Catroux, reports that
Alex had phoned everyone days ahead of time to tell them that Melinda
only ate fish. "We all went out of our way to take her to fish restaurants,
but inevitably she sat at her plate, eyes cast down, not making any effort
whatever at communicating with anyone, and not even touching her fish."
So Alex's experiment had not worked: Having tried to draw Melinda into
his old world and finding her not willing to enter it, he had discarded that
world as readily as he'd already discarded much of his old self and dedicated himself exclusively to the goal of making her feel secure.

In this process, the lavish, prodigal Alex of old quite disappeared. His
new household was run on principles of frugality and vigilant suspicion.
The wine closet was kept under lock and key, and every liquor bottle and

box of cookies was carefully observed. "Have you been nipping out of that bottle of brandy in the bar?" Alex once asked me as he and Melinda and I rode uptown in a cab.

"My palpitations, Alex, dear, remember? I haven't had anything stronger than wine for over thirty years," I replied.

"I forgot she has palpitation problems, babycakes," he repeated sheepishly to Melinda. "She hasn't been allowed brandy for decades."

Having grown up in that former household of Alex's in which no locks existed beyond the one on the front door, in which everyone was far too busy to nurse griefs or aggrandize others' failings, I was often astounded. "Alex watching" became a fatiguing new sport among the meager remains of his family and friends: Whom is he going to drop next, and who will be the next flavor of the week?

For there were so many new friends and diversions to amuse our gypsy's chameleonic new persona! Beyond Melinda's relatives and fellow nurses, Alex's new family up north consisted of two couples who got along smashingly with his bride. They were Dodie Kazanjian and her husband, the distinguished *New Yorker* writer Calvin ("Tad") Tomkins, of whom Mother had been unfairly dismissive, perhaps because she'd sensed that they would be central to the post-Tatiana phase of Alex's life; and another couple who had never met Mother but whom, ironically, she might have much liked, Denise Barbut and Murk-Hein Heineman. The latter were both multilingual medical doctors, a profession amid which Alex had long found many friends (he'd always enjoyed having an extra doctor to access around the clock in times of crises). Thirty-foot-long white stretch limousines were a great new delight in his life—the bad-boy side of him had long enjoyed the vulgarity never permitted him by Tatiana—and now he could hire them to take his new friends for a little gambling in Atlantic City or to pseudo-Asian eateries in town. ("*Tout ce que je déteste!*" one might again have heard Mother whispering.)

But why should we allow Mother to be our ventriloquist, and listen to her cackling sarcastically from the beyond at the populist novelties of Alex's surroundings? Melinda's devotion to Alex was heroic, Melinda was Alex's ticket to a few more months, a few more years of life. Grandiose, imperious Mother was a hard act to follow. Melinda did her own act with admirable dig-

*Alex and Melinda at home
in Miami, late 1990s.*

nity and dedication and tenderness, and the toughened old exile, the archsurvivor, hung on with gratitude unbounded to every extra shred of time she offered him. After a half century of playing Superman to whatever female held him in her sway, he was finally enjoying the luxury of being utterly self-centered. It often occurs that when a nurse-and-invalid partnership is dissolved by death, the former nurse swiftly becomes an invalid and finds a partner to be nursed by. Precisely such a reversal of roles had occurred in Alex's life—Melinda was now to him what he had been to Mother. The cherished "baby" she had hovered over in the recovery room was now all her own, to be nurtured and preserved with every ounce of energy in her powerful body. She tied his shoes in the morning, knotted his ties, meticulously directed his extremely complex schedule of medications, cut his meat, put a napkin around his neck when she saw his hand trembling more than usual before meals. "It's so wonderful to have someone tie your *shoes* in the morning," Alex exclaimed. "It's something I've been longing for all my life!" She was leonine, fierce about his not touching any sweets, and when she caught him cheating she growled, "Babycaaaakes" at him so threateningly that he did not dare try again for many days. In fact, the only small flaw I could detect in her nursing is that like many a doting mother she allowed Alex to indulge his love for food and grow rather fat.

What was interesting to witness was the speed with which photographs of the former Mrs. Liberman vanished from view. Upon moving to the UN Plaza flat, Alex had placed, on a bookcase facing his bed, the same family photographs he'd kept on his desk at Seventieth Street: one each of his mother and his father, one of Cleve and me and our kids when they were little, and five or six pictures of Mother at various moments in her life. My family and I were the first to be put away, a process that didn't take more than a few weeks. Then little by little, Mother started to wane. She had first occupied center place on the bookcase, but then the whole collection was gradually moved to the extreme left, and one by one the pictures of her disappeared. In the same manner did Mother eventually fade from conversation. In the first year after her death, Alex had brought her up nearly every time we were together. "When are you going to write about Mother?" he'd ask, trying to look ingenuous. "She always dreamed of your writing a book about her." Aha, I said to myself, he wants me to do it as fast as possible so he can be sure to control it! In fact, I had a totally different agenda: I wished to do this book about Mother *and* Alex, and having recently had a few problems with my own health I was hoping to survive him long enough to write it after he was gone. So I nodded my head mysteriously, saying it was too soon yet, the topic was too emotional, I had to wait.

When two years had passed, however, Tina Brown encouraged me to write an essay for *The New Yorker* on my mother as fashion icon. So I phoned Alex, who by that time had ceased to make any more mention of Mother, to talk it over with him. "I'm going to do a piece about Mother for Tina, as you've been wanting me to," I said. "Oh wonderful, dear, very nice. . . . Babycakes, what's wrong with that coffee?" he replied, absorbed in delicious domesticity. "Do you think I can still find people who knew her at Saks?" I persevered. "Of course, dear, of course you can. . . . Babycakes, why can't I have a good cup of coffee?" So I wrote the piece without his help. And having heard several friends praise it—he remained a publicity hound, still loving to get feedback on anything written about the family—he seemed delighted with the results. "Any more comments about the piece on Mother?" he'd ask when I came into his room in New York as he lay on his bed next to Melinda, looking at magazines. I prattled on about the notes I'd gotten from Si and Victoria Newhouse, Pierre Bergé, Andre Emmerich. "Good, good, anyone else?" he said eagerly. As I began to tell him about a few other notes I'd received, valiant Melinda reached for her eye mask, clamped it over her head, and pretended to go to sleep.

That was one of the last times Alex mentioned Mother. There was another ironic occasion. It occurred after the publication of Dodie Kazanjian and Calvin Tomkins's biography, *Alex*, reviews of which he found insufficiently admiring. This time, I could tell he wanted to talk as soon as I entered his apartment. He came toward me in his slow, now halting step and immediately asked me to sit down—Melinda, that afternoon, was not around. And it was clear that he wanted to speak out his regrets about the book. "We've become the three clowns of the media world," he said bitterly, referring to himself, Mother, and Dodie. "Take my advice, never, never allow a book to be done about you while you're alive. Your mother was always right!" he added with emphasis. "What I can't stand is how those reviews demean your mother," he continued (it was the first time he'd mentioned her that year). "That grand woman, why people came all the way from Norway to see her, from all over the world." For the rest of our talk, he engaged in an effusive rehabilitation of Tatiana.

It is only fair to add that throughout the years following Mother's death, there were a variety of tiny, covert ways in which Alex expressed the remains of an affection for us and of a nostalgia for Mother. Even if he displayed his feelings in ways that evaded Melinda's attention, on such occasions the doting, extravagant Alex of old fleetingly resurfaced. Upon hearing about Thaddeus's engagement, for instance—it was the very day after his angioplasty—he got hold of a phone in the recovery room and called La Grenouille, long our family's favorite restaurant, to order a posh dinner and an extravagant bottle of Bordeaux for his grandson and his fiancée. When my friend Joanna Rose had a book party for Gitta Sereny or me, he would struggle to his feet and attend it, if only for ten minutes. Both he and Melinda maintained excessively close bonds with our younger son Luke, whom he admired beyond measure and who was living that hazardous artist's existence that Alex had never dared to choose. When I had hip-replacement surgery in the mid-1990s, the bouquet of flowers he sent me was accompanied by a note in which the phrase "I love you" was written in Russian, "*Ia tebia liubliu.*" (Once my drillmaster in the Cyrillic alphabet, he now seemed to be forgetting it—he'd gotten two of the letters wrong and had painfully overwritten them.) He occasionally remembered to phone on our birthdays, and upon hearing the greeting accompanied by the word "Frosinka," my heart bled for the love we'd shared in decades past.

Moreover, might the spate of books Alex published in the decade after

Alex on his eighty-fifth birthday, September 1997: at left, Luke Gray with his future wife, Dorke Poelz. At right, Thaddeus Gray with his sons Oliver and Austin.

Mother's death—compendiums of photographs, most of which he'd taken with her at his side—be a way of retaining some form of contact with her memory? The first such publication was *Marlene*, issued in a great rush in December 1992, seven months after the death of Mother's star pal. (As it went into production, Alex's increasing self-absorption came strikingly in evidence—he asked his assistant, Crosby Coughlin, to postpone his honeymoon by six months to help him put *Marlene* together. But the admirable Crosby, whose honeymoon was booked in difficult-to-reach Zimbabwe, stood his ground and refused to alter his dates, forcing Alex to find another assistant for the book.) After *Marlene* came *Campidoglio*, a slender volume of Alex's photos of Michelangelo's superb piazza in Rome, which he'd visited innumerable times with Mother; the text was by Tatiana's close friend Joseph Brodsky.

Alex's most substantial volume of the decade was *Then*, a handsome though occasionally self-serving anthology of photographs he'd taken of just about every friend or art-world figure he and Mother had known since their youth. Among them were Henri Cartier-Bresson, who after viewing the 1959 exhibition of Alex's photographs at MOMA "came in a very formal French way to congratulate me and express his admiration for what he had seen"; Robert Hughes, "a staunch supporter of my art"; Pablo Picasso, who was so charmed by Alex that he asked Alex to "stay and live with [him] for two or three months"; Yves Saint-Laurent, "a man of taste and refinement" who "loved Tatiana and always tried to find clothes that would fit her from his collection"; Tina Brown, "the brilliant editor of *The New Yorker* . . . whose admiration for my work gives me a new courage"; Alex's first wife, Hilda Sturm, "the blond goddess" whom he married "as quickly as possible" because of his parents' opposition to her; Tatiana Yakovleva du Plessix herself, "my great love, . . . descended from minor Russian nobility, . . . who continued to fascinate and astonish for half a century"; our sons, Thaddeus and Luke Gray, "Tatiana's and my great joy"; and Melinda Pechangco Liberman, about whom he wrote: "Her presence, laughter, intelligence and love give me the courage to live. She is beautiful, a sculptured beauty that is softened by her innate tenderness and deep wisdom. . . . She presides over her very large family in the Philippines like a firm and generous aunt. We can talk for hours about a way of life that I will never know."

Then was followed by *Prayers in Stone*, photographs that chronicled various places of worship in Italy, France, and Greece. A sense of rehashing, recycling, often pervades these volumes. But if they helped Alex to maintain the balance he seemed to be seeking in those years—retaining some flimsy contact with his past while making it the goal of his life to offer the gallant Melinda constant reassurance—their purpose was well served.

The communication that started churning through my fax machine on the morning of January 25, 1994, was from Si Newhouse, and its most significant sentences read as follows:

I have asked Alexander Liberman to assume the new title of Deputy Chairman and I have asked James Truman to assume the title of Editorial Director of Condé

Nast. .... Alex joined the company in 1941 and for 31 years has served Condé Nast as Editorial Director with extraordinary distinction. . . . In his new role, Alex will continue to make available to us his vast experience. . . . As the second Editorial Director in Condé Nast history, James Truman succeeds Alex to one of the most significant titles in American magazine journalism.

Si's decision, I realized, had been made inevitable by the increasing indolence with which Alex had attended to his office work since Mother's death—even as the announcement came through, he was whooping it up in the Miami malls and had not been in the office for some months. (As Anna Wintour put it to me later, "Si distinctly felt that Alex was disengaged.") But I feared this might be a depressing event for him, so I immediately phoned him and was surprised to hear him fairly jolly. "It was time, I'm tired," he said matter-of-factly. "And I'm keeping my office and my staff just as it was!" he added with emphasis. I was grateful for Si's legendary generosity to the company's elder statesmen: Alex and Si had been talking about this changing of the guard for the past months; and Alex's devoted and superefficient office team—Crosby Coughlin, Susan Peters, and Lorna Caine—would indeed keep their jobs as his staffers for the remainder of his life.

Alex's successor, James Truman, was a thirty-five-year-old Englishman who had made his name as a writer and editor of the influential British magazine *The Face*, which was heavily geared to underground style and music. The rock scene was one that Alex had particularly detested, and had always resisted chronicling in the Condé Nast magazines. But Si Newhouse had considerable faith in Truman; and in 1990 he had put him in charge of Condé Nast's newest magazine, *Details*, which by 1993 had made a huge success. A self-effacing, vaguely counterculture, beautifully mannered man with gentle eyes and a strikingly sophisticated literary culture, Truman was invited to call on Alex at his UN Plaza flat a few weeks after the changing of the guard was officially announced. He received a two-hour briefing about the various problems he would be facing. It was indeed a strange meeting of minds— the venerable Old World wizard of high-class fashion publishing and the young Brit who describes himself as having come from "a violent, abrasive, confrontational street culture." But the two got along splendidly and had already become good friends. "There were five major principles that guided Alex's remarks that day," Truman related a few years later. "They went something like this: 'Be extremely Machiavellian at all times.' 'Act as if you're the proprietor and your colleagues are the hired help.' 'Flattery is the only way of getting *your* way.' 'Don't worry if people oppose you, sit it out and they'll fall by the wayside.' And 'Don't make this job the center of the world or you'll go mad.' " (Within a few months of succeeding Alex as editorial director, Truman became a very serious practitioner of Zen Buddhism. Eleven years later, he resigned from Condé Nast, citing "boredom.")

Alex may have felt relieved by these changes, but from 1994 on I felt a certain arrogance and smugness about his attitude toward Condé Nast. The perks still offered—the chauffeured limos, the domestic staff—now seemed to be the most treasured aspects of whatever remained of his career: He was using his staff exclusively as a means of booking his flights between Florida and New York, hiring cars, and making restaurant reservations, and he dropped into the office only once or twice a year, when a story of considerable personal interest to him was being published.

Such was the sudden visit *Vanity Fair's* literary editor, Wayne Lawson, remembers Alex making to the magazine when it was preparing a story on a group of Impressionist and modern paintings that had been in vaults since World War II, and were being exhibited for the first time in Moscow's Hermitage Museum. "Alex got very involved in selecting the specific works that were to be shown in the magazine," Lawson says. "He wanted personally to oversee the design of that story, and he did a brilliant job laying it out." But such rare and indolent involvement could not possibly keep him abreast of the times or of the magazines. Anna Wintour particularly felt his growing insularity in the late 1990s, when she published a portrait of Hillary Clinton on the cover of *Vogue*—a historic first for the publication, which had never had a First Lady on its cover before. "He was in Miami when the Hillary cover came out, and he phoned me in great fury," Wintour relates. " 'How could you do this?' he said. 'This is so appalling, this is so tacky, she looks like a housewife, where's the glamour?' I then realized that he'd lost some of his journalistic feel. People had begun wanting contact with that kind of reality, the issue was a greater success than anyone could have dreamt—in fact, when Alex realized how successful it was, he phoned me to apologize, and heaven knows he wasn't big on apologies."

So the same unfortunate tendency that had governed Mother's last decade—an exacerbation of latent faults—seemed to prevail in Alex's own advancing years. His innate egotism now bordered on total self-absorption. His vanity had swelled into smugness and unabashed conceit. Not only had he grown quite fat, but his psyche had begun to match his physique. A few weeks after the Condé Nast announcement was made, when I went to attend yet another exhibition of his paintings at the Emmerich gallery, I recorded the following impression of him in my journal: "A swollen, greying balloon of a man, totally devoid of his former elegance, comes towards us. . . . It is as if he is being constantly refilled with some inflating medium, the hot air of the endless flattery that surrounds him."

A decade later, that is still the way I remember Alex in his last years. I keep being haunted by a phrase of Shakespeare's, "catch the conscience of the King." Mother had constantly pricked at his inflated ego, perpetually reminding him that he was a common mortal, that the world didn't owe him everything. Now, uncurbed by Tatiana, fawned on by a wife whose life revolved around him, surrounded by adulating women who assured him that he was one of the great artists of his time, his entire personality was gradually disintegrating. He had developed a childish way of boasting about the importance he still had at Condé Nast: Upon one of his health emergencies, he broadcast the news that Isadore Rosenfeld had flown to see him in Miami at Si Newhouse's behest in Si's private jet. And just as he took it for granted that he could perennially keep a four-person staff at Condé Nast without ever going to the office, he seemed incapable of making a judgment without referring it to his grandiose self-image. "What do you think of Simon Schama?" he had recently asked me. "I loved *Citizens*," I answered, "one of the best books I've read in years." "I don't *need* to read any Schama," he said with half-mocking grandeur. "I like him because he told Tina [Brown] he loves my new book." But the self-mocking tone didn't work—

it was clear that by now, his power eroded, he was readier than ever to be seduced by anyone who flattered him.

By 1997, I felt wretchedly isolated from Alex. I was briefly visiting with him a half-dozen times a year during the months he spent in New York, sharing no more than two or three meals each year with him and Melinda. I, too, was ready to fawn on him to recapture a bit of his affection. And to regain some contact, during a dinner we shared in the spring I offered to give him a party for his forthcoming book, *Prayers in Stone*. He hugged me more effusively than he had in years. I was his darling Frosinka again! No one I'd ever known so loved being celebrated, no one had a more childish need for any form of attention. However steeped he was in flattery, I began to sense the fundamental melancholia of his old age, its frequent sense of obsoleteness. "I miss my table at the Four Seasons," he said to me wistfully a year or two after James Truman had assumed his job. What I knew he missed were not so much the fine food and service but the elite center-of-the-room table, available to only a handful of the city's press moguls, over which he had reigned several times a week, "receiving homage from passersby" as Andre Emmerich described it, "just like a Mafia don."

In the post-Tatiana years, Alex's tastes and impulses grew even more capricious and volatile than ever. By the spring of 1997, over a dinner at Restaurant Daniel—his new favorite—he told us that Miami was becoming "boring." The weather wasn't what he had hoped it would be; there was so little to do. After four years in Miami, the Libermans were now flirting with the notion of selling their flat there and were looking for a place in the New York suburbs. And sure enough, within a few weeks, before even putting Miami up for sale, they found a house on Long Island—a grand ungainly dwelling in Sands Point—and borrowed a million dollars from Si Newhouse to purchase it. ("Why did you buy this monstrosity?" Rosenfeld asked Alex. "Because Melinda wanted it," Alex replied.) Upon my first visit there, Mother's voice cackled with particular derision as I stared at the entrance door of elaborately carved oak, the kitchen countertops flecked with gold. Alex was fond of justifying the purchase by saying Sands Point was the first vacation site that he, Mother, and I had shared in the United States. And indeed, as I drove there in the following months, I kept looking for some landmark that would point me to the ramshackle house that had so warmly sheltered our first American summer.

T he Libermans had only a year in which to enjoy their new house. In the fall of 1998, Alex became truly, deeply ill. It is possible that his deteriorating health—the return of his prostate cancer, complicated by cardiac problems, diabetes, and chronic anemia—had been further aggravated by a severe psychological shock. In the spring of that year, Condé Nast was preparing to move from 350 Madison Avenue—its headquarters for a quarter of a century—to a new building at 4 Times Square. And Alex had learned that there would be no office space for him in the new Condé Nast building: Along with the office staff still maintained for the estate of Leo Lerman, who had died four years earlier, his assistants were to be moved, instead, to a puny room on East Forty-fourth Street.

Even though he had barely set foot into his office in the past years, the announcement that he had no place in the new building led Alex to a severe depression. He had such vainglory about his status at the company that he'd imagined it to be in every way untouchable. "They might as well drag me out of the stable and shoot me," he told Melinda when he heard the news. Did he really expect that at a time when cost-cutting principles governed all corporate decisions, a semi-invalid retiree would receive a suite of his own alongside the company's hardworking staffers? If so, the delusions of grandeur encouraged by his circle of flatterers had grievously misled him. When we arrived at his New York flat on a fall night that year, he was in a wheelchair, looking furious at the world. As we came toward him, he continued glowering at us, as if our presence, this time, was a dreadful annoyance. Had some new paranoia led him to the illusion that we had recently done wrong by him? Or was it a blow to his great pride that his original "family" was seeing him in this pitiful state? Ten minutes into our visit, Dodie arrived. How he loved his post-Tatiana coterie! As she came into the room, Alex managed a faint smile to greet her.

He was in Miami through most of the late winter and spring, and in the summer of 1999 Melinda brought him back to New York to have his condition—which was now desperate—evaluated by Rosenfeld. By this time, Alex was so medicated that he was sleeping twenty hours out of twenty-four. There were times he was too weak to eat on his own and had to be spoon-fed. Throughout the day, Melinda had to keep slapping his thigh every few minutes, shouting "Hey, Babycakes!" to keep him from sleeping round the clock.

It is upon this trip of Alex's to New York, on an occasion when Melinda had gone around the block to do an errand, that I confronted him one last time on the issue of the famous poet's letters; that I asked him, "Alex, dear, could you tell me where the letters are?"; that he answered "Oh, somewhere here," waving his silvery hand in various directions of the room; that he then fell into another deep sleep. Those were among the last words I'd hear him speak in New York City. On the following afternoon, he flew back to Miami to wait for his death. And a few days hence, I returned to his flat, found my inheritance—Mayakovsky's letters to Mother—in his bedside drawer, and began to plan the writing of this book.

However, in the years that it has taken me to write it, I have toyed with one more hypothesis about Alex's need to retain Mayakovsky's letters: Beyond his desire to remain the one and only love of a legendary woman, he may well have kept them because they had a considerable commercial, as well as a sentimental, value. For after my mother's death, one of the more striking transformations manifested by this once prodigally generous man was frequently to act in a penny-pinching, niggardly manner. His impulse was to retain all those of Mother's possessions that were of material worth, however legally bound he was to deliver them to me and however important they might have been to me emotionally. Thus had he failed to offer me so much as one memento from Seventieth Street. At the time, I was too sorrowful about the house itself to have emotions about its contents; only later did I feel rage at this omission.

The same miserliness guided a far shabbier action: Beyond a portrait of my mother, in his last will and testament Alex did not leave one of the many Iacovleffs he owned to me—all of this revered relative's works passed on to his widow. Yet another sign of crass insensitivity: The day after Mother died, leaving all her personal effects to me in her will, Alex had asked me to bring him her jewelry tray, so that he might choose a gift for Melinda as a token of his gratitude. As I set the tray on his bed, he immediately pointed to a diamond-and-platinum brooch I remembered well from my earliest childhood: Not only was it the most valuable item still in Mother's possession, it had been a gift to her from my father, Bertrand du Plessix, who, moreover, had inherited it from his own mother. On that day of mourning, I was too intent on cheering up Alex, on indulging every one of his whims, to demur. It wasn't until a few months later that I asked myself, How did he dare? How could I have allowed this part of my inheritance—a precious memento of both my blood parents—to slip through my hands? And at such times I also wondered, was there a "true Alex" anywhere to be found? Could it be that at the center of this curious man was an icy, vacuous planet that had revolved around a succession of Women-Suns, reflecting each consecutive one's traits and attributes?

The Libermans returned to Miami in the late summer of 1999, and over the following months Alex's health declined even more rapidly. Melinda reported that she'd had to devise a halter device on which she tugged every few minutes to wake him up. I desperately wanted to see him, but she held me off, fearing, with reason, that the very sight of me would alarm him by letting him know his end was near. How much would I have given to hold his hand for a few minutes, to look into his eyes, even if to receive their blank nothingness in return! But I had to make do with imagining him in his last months in Miami—riding down the stairs of his duplex on his electric chair, falling asleep even as Melinda spoon-fed him, being wheeled to the window for a view of the Bay of Biscayne. . . . I phoned him every day or two, shouted, "How are you?" and listened to him slur out the words "I'm all right" so faintly that they seemed to come through a veil of fog.

Melinda was faithful to her promise to let me know when the end seemed in sight. She called me on a Wednesday in the second week in November. She doubted if he'd ever leave the hospital, she wept, she was counting on me to attend to the obituaries, she didn't know how to handle such things, he had a week or two at the most. I dropped everything and flew to Miami, arriving at the hospital at 8:00 P.M. He lay very still on his bed, as pale and translucent as the plastic mask rising and falling over his face. As I sat down and took his hand, his mustache quavered, he turned his eyes toward me and then away again, with an expression that could as easily have been one of "Oh, God, not she" or "How happy I am that she's here." A half hour later, a doctor, making rounds and testing his cognitive level, asked him, "Who's your visitor tonight?" "My daughter," Alex whispered.

For the following two days, he mostly slept, occasionally communicating through nods of the head or tiny gestures. But then, on the evening before I was scheduled to leave Miami, he suddenly turned his eyes to me and with painful enunciation asked, "Did you go out last night?" It was the question he used to ask me every Sunday morning at Seventieth Street when I was in my teens. "I was here, darling," I said in Russian. "It's the only place I want to be." "*Spokoinoi,*" "calm," he whispered gently as he closed his eyes, perhaps trying to say "*Spokoinoi Noch,*" "good night."

The following day, he seemed stronger, more lucid, and for a fleeting moment the gentle Dr. Jekyll, the ancient nurturing Alex of my childhood, returned. He opened his eyes and stared at me—it was a bit past noon—and asked, as if I were ten years old, "Frosinka, have you had your lunch yet?" Showing him my plate, which I'd just filled, I said, "Oh yes, thank you, look, I've just started." In a barely audible, rasping voice he whispered, "Is it good?"

And upon those phrases I returned to the very first day I had landed in his care, to that morning in the south of France in 1940 when I'd wandered through his house, lonely and hungry, and Alex had come bursting out of the kitchen with a bowl of black-market cornflakes topped with a fried egg, and as he watched me devour my meal had asked me, "Is it good, Frosinka?" How many selves he'd been since we'd shared that moment: the ambitious young refugee, the pushy émigré editor, the dapper, best-dressed-listed man-about-town, the thriving paterfamilias, the venerable elder statesman of magazine publishing, the perplexed widower, and now the dying pensioner being tended by his last powerful woman. And how many selves I, too, had been since that shared moment of sixty years past: the docile, grieving child, the rebellious, wisecracking teenager, the tomboy journalist, the earnest workaholic bride, the striving author, the fragile matriarch. Yet in those phrases, "Did you have your lunch? . . . Was it good?" Time was dissolved in obeisance to a

Portrait by Irving Penn of Alex standing near his sculpture studio in Warren, Connecticut, 1977.

memory that was powerfully, uniquely ours. In that imperishable 1940 of our shared recollection, we became again the nurturing father and the hungry child, thrown together by the forces that had cleft our generations' lives in twain, who were about to escape the greatest destruction of life in human history. And in that everlasting Now, which by dissolving time absolved whatever griefs might ever have stood between us, we offered each other the sweetest gift any parent and child can exchange——that of total conciliation.

He closed his eyes and slept once more. It was 1999 again. I had a half hour before leaving for the airport and sat by his side, waiting to catch his last hint of recognition, feeling certain that it would not come again. When I kissed him one last time before leaving, his forehead was of a *surnaturel* sweetness and freshness, barely human in its purity, as if he were some magical sleeping knight I'd come across in an enchanted forest or a freshly bathed child I was putting to bed.

The call from Melinda came ten days later, in the middle of the night. I flew back to Miami; it was up to me to do the final "recognition" at the funeral parlor. He lay on a stretcher of sorts, a green blanket drawn up to his chin, so silvery, so lyrical, so Greek. The head was thrust back, so delicate and noble and warriorlike, I couldn't get away from that heroic aura of the warrior on the battlefield—in a minor way, he had indeed had a heroic existence, living more lives than most of us would dare to take on in three rounds of reincarnation, fighting for his survival—and Mother's and mine and occasionally that of others—in most every moment of his century. Yes he looked noble, the way he'd wanted all his creations to be. Love of my early youth, mentor and protector, my tears finally came for you. I touched my hand to your marble head—not freezing yet but fairly chill—and remembered that hot, pulsating, oh-so-warm still-tender flesh I'd put my lips to ten days earlier, when I'd kissed you in your sleep and sensed more keenly than ever before the preciousness of breath, the absolute uniqueness of each human person. I made the sign of the cross over you and went my way. I was the little kid to whom you'd given a life to live, and I'd run with it, run as hard as I could.

TWENTY-THREE

Epilogue

I t is June of 2004, and there's so much to do at Mother's grave! I must prune the rhododendrons I planted here more than a decade ago, give them a particularly good feeding after the arduous winter, perhaps put in some new evergreens on either side of the tombstone that surmounts her ashes and bears her name: Tatiana Yacovleff du Plessix Liberman, 1906–1991. She lies half a mile from my house as the bird flies, less than a mile on foot. In the proper weather, I can even walk a few hundred yards down my road and cut across a swath of fields, and there she is under a bed of myrtle, at the northwest end of my village cemetery; and how suited to her Confucian, deeply rooted nature to lie in this engaging site, overlooking a splendid view, close to the country home upon which she lavished such care, readily visitable by those she loved.

We chose this plot for our entire family a few decades ago, ever since my near breakdown at my father's grave I have been easy, familiar with death— during our cemetery visits Cleve and I used to often sit and argue about what kinds of tombstones we wanted over our own remains. Mother had gone in first, waiting for us. Upon finding her a handsome stone, Alex had his name and the year of his birth engraved below hers, followed by a dash, and some years ago we filled that gap with the date of his own passing, 1999. After I've pruned and fed the rhodies, I must weed the myrtle—a hellish task to get at the lawn grass without breaking the plants' delicate roots. I'm possessive, tidy, if not narcissistic, about her resting place, as she was about her own appearance in life: Beyond my frequent horticultural checks and birthdays and Christmases, I visit her upon most every one of my life's important occasions—before taking a trip abroad, for instance, as if to get her blessing, and upon crises, to glean counsel, and when a new grandchild is born, to share the joy.

You may well ask, attentive reader, why I say "Her," not "Them," and refer to the site as "Mother's grave." Let me explain: Though I engraved the date of Alex's death to commemorate his half-century's presence at Mother's side, he is here only symbolically, out of my respect for the sacredness of memory. His ashes are actually in the custody of his third wife, kept within her sight wherever she may be. When in New York, for instance, they repose on a chest of drawers facing her bed, surrounded by a shrine of votive candles and fresh flowers, as is the custom of her country. But she has been restless since his passing, and Alex is often on the road, wandering with her: Sealed up in a neat little traveling case, causing increasing consternation to airport security officials, he travels in and out of hotels and homes, to Miami, to the Philippines, to Atlantic City, to Las Vegas, to wherever her fancy may take her—what destiny could be more perfect for a nomad's remains! Like the gypsy, the perennial exile he was at heart, he is perpetually on the road, rootless, uncommitted, with no fixed base, his whereabouts as fluid and elusive, as continually dictated by a woman's caprices, as they were in real life—"Is he in heaven? Is he in hell? That damned elusive Pimpernel!"

But since graves commemorate the transit of immortal souls in temporal flesh, Alex is here, too, in the Warren, Connecticut, cemetery, for no two spirits so demonically bonded as his was to Mother's could ever be sundered by anything as trivial as death. So I occasionally say "Their" grave; now and again I address the two of Them. What models you have been for me, I tell Them, despite your cowardice, your deceitfulness, your arrogance, what force and shrewdness and power of survival you passed on to me! I suppose that having you near me, visitable upon a moment's notice, is a way of continuing to tame you, of keeping you in my control. Now that you are in my custody, fierce parents, you have become my own docile little children, sandstone soft, every recollection of you to be sculpted and honed according to my whims, I can erase the sites of darkness and retain only the very best of you—your wild largesse, your rage to succeed, your Homeric hospitality. Thank you, my loves, I tell Them, I'll never cease to thank you.

. . .

In December of 2004 my closest friend, my tender comrade, my cherished husband of forty-seven years, Cleve Gray, joined my parents at the Warren, Connecticut, cemetery, in the plot he chose for us a quarter of a century ago. Come spring, when the ground thaws, he too will have his rhododendrons, his myrtle, his tombstone, and my fastidious domestic care in maintaining the beauty of his resting place. Through frequent visits to the graves of these treasured beings I'm gradually learning that healthy mourning has to do with relearning reality; that however immense our grief, we must cease to desire our loved ones' return, must create a new psychic space in which we continue to love them in absence and separation. Above all I've come to know that we can only grasp the meaning of their existence, and therefore the meaning of ours, by some dynamic interaction with the story of their lives; that this information is our most valuable treasure; that we may have to learn their life narratives before we can truly begin to be ourselves. There's nothing like a grave, particularly if one's youth was nearly botched for lack of one. Now my Guardians are all gone, I reflect as I prune back the rhododendrons, they're all gone and I'm the sole custodian of their memory, the weight of remembrance and information is all on me, to share or to withhold. How painful and bittersweet to be finally alone, in charge.

Acknowledgments

My first and foremost debt is to Ann Godoff, my publisher and editor, whose enthusiasm for this work has been a source of inspiration and encouragement, and who has given me precious guidance at every step of its composition. Equal gratitude to Liza Darnton of the Penguin Press, whose patient dedication to the art of fine editing is nothing short of miraculous.

For research assistance I am deeply grateful to my friend Vasili Rudich, whose encyclopedic knowledge of Russian history and culture has been a source of great personal enlightenment, and to my cherished multilingual aide Nadia Michoustina, who has come to my rescue at many critical moments of the past few years. Equally treasurable has been the help of my friend George Lechner of the University of Hartford, whose skills as a cultural historian have been invaluable, and of my neighbor Lillian Lovitt, whose expertise in handling photographs is terrific.

I'm deeply indebted to Dodie Kazanjian and Calvin Tomkins, whose biography of my stepfather, *Alex,* has corroborated many details of oral history and sheer memory that are at the core of this (or any) family memoir. Their careful documentation of pivotal events in Alex's life has been of inestimable help in writing this book. Barbara Rose's earlier study of Alex, *Alexander Liberman,* has also been of great value in my research.

Acknowledgments

Among the persons who have offered the benefit of their own memories of my parents, I'm particularly indebted to my stepmother, Melinda Liberman; to Gitta Sereny and Patricia Greene, cherished friends of my parents' first years in the United States; to S. I. Newhouse Jr., who was a central figure in my stepfather's last forty years; to Crosby Coughlin, Alex's trusted aide-de-camp in his last decade; and to my dear friend Rosamond Bernier, whose memories of my parents go back to 1944, and who gave me precious insights into the dynamics of a shared milieu. For their valuable insights into the dynamic of my parents' lives and career, gratitude also to Dr. Isadore Rosenfeld, Irving Penn, James Truman, Anna Wintour, Tina Brown, Charles Churchward, Daniel Salem, Pierre Bergé, Mary and Bernard d'Anglejan, Susan Train, Claude Nabokov, Edmonde Charles-Roux, Zozo de Ravenel, Lord Snowdon, Liuda Shtern, William Raynor, Linda Price, Anya Kaialoff, Mary Jane Poole, Elizabeth Sverbeyeva, Sarah Slavin, Susan Peters, Gray Foy, Thomas Guinzburg, Jean-Michel Montias, Grace Mirabella, Nadine Bertin Stearns, Bill and Elaine Layman, Betty and François Catroux, Kathleen Blumenfeld, Diane Von Furstenburg, Wayne Lawson, Oscar de la Renta, Alexis Gregory, Andre Emmerich, the late Despina Messinesi, Jean-Pierre Fourneau, who was Alex's closest comrade during his boarding school days seventy-five years ago, and the late Richard Avedon, a treasured friend. Last but hardly least, I thank those of my editors at *The New Yorker* who have published excerpts from this book, Tina Brown and David Remnick, for their generous encouragement and support.

To my beloved chum Gabrielle Van Zuylen, gratitude everlasting for offering me a second home in Paris, for the affectionate concern with which she helps me to keep body and soul together during my working stays abroad, and for the inspiration she has offered me at every stage of my career.

I could not have written this book without the assistance of Moscow's Vladimir Mayakovsky Museum, whose director, Svetlana Strizhneva, had the wits to alert me to the existence of the museum's Tatiana Yakovleva archive. Of the colleagues at that institution, whose thoughtfulness and hospitality were prodigal, I owe particular gratitude to Natasha Andreevna and Adolf Aksionchik, who offered me inestimable aid in helping me to access and translate their archive's precious documents.

Acknowledgments

I could not have illustrated this work without the help of the Getty Research Institute, the Condé Nast Archives, the Irving Penn Studio, the Estate of Erwin Blumenfeld, and the Alexander Liberman Trust. The Getty generously allowed me to access the archives in which some 100,000 photographs of Alex's are stored, and I'm particularly indebted to its curator of Special Collections, Wim de Witt. Anthony Petrillose offered me invaluable help in collecting precious images stored in the Condé Nast Archives. Dee Henle of the Irving Penn Studio cordially processed my requests to reproduce five of this great artist's photographs of my family. Henry Blumenfeld provided the same kind of aid in accessing his father's work. And the trustees of the Liberman Trust, Dodie Kazanjian and Melinda Liberman, were most gracious in granting me copyright permissions to use letters and photographs which are in the keeping of the trust.

Finally, to my first readers: my agents, Georges and Anne Borchardt, who've stood by me steadfastly for three decades; my cherished friend of more than half a century, Joanna Rose; my eagle-eyed pals Jennifer Phillips, Marguerite Whitney, and Karen Marta; and my own beloved male trinity— Thaddeus Gray, Luke Gray, and the late Cleve Gray—whose affection and wisdom have helped me not only to grow as a writer, but to survive every day of my life.

Notes

12   "the milliner's milliner": *New York Times,* July 23, 1963, p. 12.
12   "the feminine elegance": *Saks News,* September 1959, p. 19
12   She was perhaps: Saks press release, spring 1962.
12   bretons of rose-printed silk: Saks press release, spring 1964.
21   The three women: Gennady Smakov interview with Tatiana Yakov-
       leva, unpublished, archive of Francine du Plessix Gray, henceforth
       referred to as "FG Archive, Smakov."
21   And upon the great famine: Ibid., p. 19.
28   His skills were noticed early: cited by Benois in "A.E. Iacovleff
       1887–1938, V.I. Shakhaev 1887–1973, *100 Letiu so Dnya
       Rozhdenie,*" exhibition catalogue, Leningrad, 1988.
29   "We entered a fantastic decor": Grand Central Galleries, memorial
       exhibition catalogue, 1939.
30   "A body, a musculature": *Art et Decoration* 49 (January–June 1926).
34   "Iacovleff, indefatigable": Quoted in Caroline de la Baume, *Le Peintre
       voyageur,* Paris: Flammarion, 2000.
36   "I love traveling": Iacovleff in *L'Art et les Artistes,* March 1926, unpagi-
       nated.
36   They were entranced: Ibid.
38   The very difficulties: Ibid.

505

39   It had to do with the veneration: Quoted in *L'Illustration*, June 3,
         1933, unpaginated photocopy.

39   "[General Tchou] posed for me": Ibid.

39   "Why is the joy?": Ibid.

40   "It's a sinister": Ibid.

41   "To interpret, through successive images": Alexandre Iacovleff,
         Dessins et peintures d'Asie, Paris: J. Meynial, 1934.

41   "Boston's atmosphere": Ibid., p. 154.

43   Upon this visit: Martin Birnbaum, *Iacovleff and Other Artists*, New
         York, Paul A. Struck, 1946, pp. 3–24.

48   "a handsome youth": Boris Pasternak, *I Remember: Sketch for an Auto-
         biography*, trans. David Magarshack, Cambridge, Mass.: Harvard
         University Press, 1983, p. 91.

48   "sat in a chair": Boris Pasternak, *Safe Conduct*, New York: New Direc-
         tions, 1958, p. 102.

48   "young terrorist conspirator": Pasternak, *I Remember*, p. 92.

48   "spit out the past": Wiktor Worozylski, *Life of Mayakovsky*, translated
         from the Polish by Boleslaw Taborski, New York: Orion Press,
         1971, p. 46.

49   "throw Pushkin, Dostoyevsky, Tolstoy": Ibid., p. 47.

49   In "The Cloud in Trousers": Vladimir Mayakovsky, "The Cloud in
         Trousers," in *The Bedbug and Selected Poetry*, ed. and with an introduc-
         tion by Patricia Blake, trans. Max Hayward and George Reavey
         (henceforth "Blake"), New York: Meridian Books, 1960, pp.
         71–108.

49   "The line/Is a fuse": Ibid., pp. 195, 201.

50   His patriotic odes: Pasternak, *I Remember*, p. 93.

50   "I am as lonely": "Man" (1916–1917), cited in Blake, p. 26.

50   "The heart yearns": Ibid.

51   Gorky is said to have been: Edward J. Brown, *Mayakovsky, a Poet in the
         Revolution*, Princeton: Princeton University Press, 1973, p. 112.

51   In fact, upon hearing: Quoted in Gonzague Saint Bris and Vladimir
         Fédorovski, *Les Egéries russes*, Paris: Lattès, 1994, p. 11.

52   "If I'm a complete rag": Bengt Jangfeldt, ed., *Love Is the Heart of
         Everything: Correspondence Between Vladimir Mayakovsky and Lili Brik,
         1915–1930*, Edinburgh: Polygon, 1986, p. 126 (henceforth
         Jangfeldt).

52 For years, with her tacit: "The Backbone Flute," in Blake, pp. 111–29.

52 "It is *my* revolution": *Mayakovsky,* ed. and trans. Herbert Marshall, New York: Hill and Wang, 1965, p. 88.

53 "But now's no time": Vladimir Mayakovsky, "Vladimir Ilyich Lenin," in ibid., p. 266.

54 "Clothe the body": Quoted in Ilya Ehrenburg, *People and Life,* vol. 2: 1918–1921, New York: Knopf, 1962.

54 "The best pacifiers": Brown, *Mayakovsky,* p. 262.

54 "The genuine/wise": Mayakovsky, "Vladimir Ilyich Lenin," in Marshall, pp. 250, 256.

54 Increasingly, he realized: Blake, pp. 225, 221.

54 Jakobson looks on 1928: Cited in Benedikt Sarnov, ed., *Stikhi, poemy, piesy i pisma Mayakovskogo, a takzhe otryvki iz stikhov, statei, pisem, vospominany i otklikov sovremennikov—druzei i vragov poeta,* "Russky Parnas" series, Moscow: Knizhnaia Palata, 1997, p. 491.

56 "Babushka would have had": FG Archive, Smakov.

57 "Picture this": Blake, pp. 209–13. (Translation adjusted by FG.)

58 "Come to the crossroads": Translated from Russian original in Sarnov, *Stikhi,* p. 464, by Nadezhda Michoustina and Francine Gray.

58 "Who is that woman": *Lili Brik–Elsa Triolet: Correspondance, 1921–1970,* ed. Leon Robel, Paris: Gallimard, 2000, pp. 43–44 (henceforth Brik-Triolet Correspondence). Also cited in Sarnov, p. 487.

59 "He's a remarkable man": Yakovleva to Orlova, early December 1928, Yakovleva Archive, Mayakovsky Museum, Moscow, #19594. Photocopy in FG Archive, Mayakovsky Letters.

59 "However spoiled I am": Ibid., December 24, 1928, #19596.

60 "Write more often": Telegrams of V. V. Mayakovsky to Tatiana Yakovleva, 1929, FG Archive, Mayakovsky Letters.

60 "My own beloved Tanik": Mayakovsky to Tatiana Yakovleva, December 24, 1928, FG Archive, Mayakovsky Letters.

61 "You've deceived me": Quoted in Arkady Vaksberg, *Zagadka I Magiia Lile Brik,* Moscow: Ast Olimp Astrel, 2003, p. 212.

62 "Sweet Tanik, my beloved": Mayakovsky to Yakovleva, December 31, 1928, FG Archive, Mayakovsky Letters.

62 "Letter to Comrade Kostrov": See Roman Jakobson, "Unpublished

Majakovskij," in *Harvard Literary Bulletin* 9 (1955): 286. Jakobson
quotes an eloquent but unidentified source that describes the role
this poem played in increasing public hostility toward the poet.

62   "I've not at all decided": Yakovleva to Orlova, January or early Febru-
     ary [before February 10] 1929, Yakovleva Archive, Mayakovsky
     Museum, #19595.

63   "He did not criticize Russia": Quoted in Sarnov, *Stikhi*, p. 481.

63   This impression coincides: Quoted in Jangfeldt, p. 272, footnote to
     letter #378.

64   "My dear, my sweet": Mayakovsky to Yakovleva, May 1929, FG
     Archive, Mayakovsky Letters.

64   "My dear, my own": Mayakovsky to Yakovleva, July 29, 1929, in
     ibid.

65   "Write me and let me know": Alexandra Yakovleva to Lyubov
     Orlova, May 14, 1929, with a postscript from Tatiana. Yakovleva
     Archive, Mayakovsky Museum, #19597.

65   "I was very sad": Yakovleva to Orlova, July 13, 1929, in ibid., #19598.

65   On the rare occasions: FG journals, summer 1990, unpublished, FG
     Archive.

65   His "exquisite manners": FG Archive, Smakov, pp. 16, 4A.

68   "Tanik, I've begun to miss you": Mayakovsky to Yakovleva, July
     1929, FG Archive, Mayakovsky Letters.

69   "My own beloved Tanik": Ibid., summer 1929.

69   "My own beloved [rodnaia]": Ibid., October 1929.

73   Her last October communication: Yakovleva to Orlova, Yakovleva
     Archive, Mayakovsky Museum, #22652 (9).

73   "We were quietly sitting": Brik-Triolet Correspondence, pp. 1415–16.

73   "Do excuse me": Ibid.

75   "We're not French viscounts": Ibid.

75   "I loved [Mayakovsky]": FG Archive, Smakov, transcript in Russian
     version, also cited in Sarnov, pp. 481–82.

75   He was "enormously caring": Yakovleva to Orlova, late December
     1930, Yakovleva Archive, Mayakovsky Museum, #22652 (2).

76   His play *The Bathhouse:* Wiktor Woroszylski, *The Life of Mayakovsky,*
     trans. Boleslaw Taborski, New York: Orion Press, 1970, p. 483.

76   He paced the empty rooms: Polonskaya, in *Imia etoi teme-liubov:
     sovremennitsy o Mayakovskova,* Moscow, 1993, p. 291.

76   He felt increasingly isolated: Ibid., p. 294.

77 Friends noted that: Ann Charters and Samuel Charters, *I Love: The Story of Vladimir Mayakovsky and Lili Brik*, New York: Farrar, Straus and Giroux, 1979, p. 334.

78 "Between eleven o'clock and twelve": Pasternak, *Safe Conduct*, p. 127.

78 "He killed himself": Pasternak, *I Remember*, p. 89.

78 "To All [Vsem]": Vladimir Mayakovsky, suicide note, April 14 [?], 1930, Archives of Mayakovsky Museum (photocopy in FG Archive).

79 "I'm rummaging": Quoted in Charters and Charters, *I Love*, p. 364.

79 "It was outrageous": FG Archive, Smakov, pp. 21–22.

79 "Past one o'clock": Blake, p. 237.

80 "I was destroyed": Yakovleva to Orlova, April 24, 1930, Yakovleva Archive, Mayakovsky Museum.

80 *"Mamulechka moia rodnaia":* Yakovleva to Orlova, May 2, 1930, in ibid., #19600.

80 Lili Brik, having been named: See *Maiakovski, vers et proses*, ed. Elsa Triolet, Paris: Les Éditeurs Français Réunis, 1957. Triolet may well have written this volume at her sister's urging to counter the effect of Roman Jakobson's publication, in 1956, of Mayakovsky's "Letter to Tatiana Yakovleva." Brik obviously had never included this poem in any editions of the poet's oeuvre, and until then it had remained unpublished. There is not one mention of Yakovleva in Triolet's book.

80 Along with her sister: Brik-Triolet Correspondence, pp. 1425–26.

81 "There are many phrases": Polonskaya, p. 298.

81 "It seems to me": Quoted in Sarnov, *Stikhi*, p. 490.

81 "He wrote her some beautiful lines": FG Archive, Smakov.

81 In 1935, with the help: Charters and Charters, *I Love*, p. 365.

81 Stalin replied: Joseph Stalin, reply to Lili Brik, Archives of the Mayakovsky Museum.

81 In Pasternak's scornful phrase: Pasternak, *I Remember*, p. 101.

82 "In December of 1929": David Burliuk, letter to Viktor Pertsov, undated, collection of Alexander Parniss, Moscow, unpublished.

83 "If he had come back": FG Archives, Smakov, Russian transcript, cited in Sarnov, pp. 480, 482.

91 "This early feeling": Simon Liberman, *Building Lenin's Russia*, Chicago: University of Chicago Press, [1945], p. 44.

92 "I had come out of": Ibid.

93   Through this family: Ibid., p. 48.

94   She was immediately taken: Henriette Pascar, *Le Coeur vagabond*, p. 74. This was published by a vanity press in Montreal. The copy of it at the New York Public Library was missing the title page with the name of the publisher.

96   "To me these stopovers": Liberman, *Building Lenin's Russia*, p. 53.

96   He was constantly horrified: Ibid., p. 50.

98   In February 1917, five-year-old Alex: Barbara Rose, *Alexander Liberman*, New York: Abbeville Press, 1981, p. 19.

98   "Like any child of five": Ibid.

98   "As a child brought up": Ibid., p. 21.

100   "Our conversations were so pleasant": Liberman, *Building Lenin's Russia*, p. 12.

100   "Vladimir Ilyich," Semyon replied: Ibid., p. 41.

100   Dodie Kazanjian and Calvin Tomkins, *Alex: The Life of Alexander Liberman*, New York: Knopf, 1993, p. 28.

109   "I went anyhow": Ibid., p. 186.

118   The exhibition was: Rose, *Alexander Liberman*, p. 25.

119   She admits that: Pascar, *Coeur vagabond*, p. 200.

119   "what I feel for him": Ibid., p. 218.

119   "Do you feel better?": Kazanjian and Tomkins, *Alex*, p. 46.

138   "A peppy, high-spirited young woman": Ibid., p. 72.

140   "Just leave, Shurik": Quoted in ibid., p. 75.

141   "I was both afraid": Quoted in ibid., p. 77.

145   "The feeling was indescribably strong": Quoted in ibid., p. 90.

162   *Lieutenant du Plessix: Le Lieutenant du Plessix, fin, distingué, cultivé, était avant la guerre attaché a l'Ambassade de France a Varsovie. Mobilisé, il avait fait toute la campagne de Pologne comme officier de liaison auprés de l'Armée Polonaise. Aujourd'hui, il n'hésite pas a suivre la voix de sa conscience.*

173   "Neither 18 Brumaire": Maurice Sachs, *Le Sabbat: Souvenirs d'une jeunesse orageuse*, Paris: Gallimard, 1960, pp. 68–69.

203   "Is your husband": Cardinal de Richelieu's full name was Armand-Jean du Plessis, duc de Richelieu. The courtesan who is the heroine of Dumas's novel, on which Verdi's opera *La Traviata* is based, is named Marie Duplessis.

255   "Cordially yours, Lucien Vogel": interoffice memo, courtesy of Condé Nast Archives.

256   "or occupying the elevator shafts": Kazanjian and Tompkins, *Alex*, p. 107.

256   Condé Nast, who was then: Helen Lawrenson, *Stranger at the Party*, New York: Random House, 1972, p. 59.

257   "Dr. Agha never said a word": Caroline Seebohm, *The Man Who Was Vogue*, New York: Viking Press, 1982, p. 235.

269   "Numbers of families": E. B. Lanin, *Russian Characteristics*, London: Chapman and Hall, 1892.

277   And both she and Alex: Kazanjian and Tompkins, *Alex*, p. 124.

297   Tatiana's spry creations: *The New York Times*, September 11, 1951.

308   "When he said 'Dear friend' ": Helmut Newton, *Autobiography*, New York: Nan A. Talese/Doubleday, 2003, p. 192–93.

371   "The attachment to the mother": Sigmund Freud, *Female Sexuality*, quoted in Anni Bergman, "Considerations about the Development of the Girl During the Separation-Individuation Process," in *Early Female Development*, New York: Spectrum, 1982, p. 61.

375   *The New York Times*'s Virginia Pope: *The New York Times*, September 11, 1951.

381   "Tatiana specializes in the Bow Geste": *The New Yorker*, September 14, 1959.

398   "the intangible, the visionary": Rose, *Alexander Liberman*, p. 76.

398   "men in religions orders": Ibid., p. 78.

405   He loved the company and the magazines: Kazanjian and Tompkins, *Alex*, p. 219.

412   "a call to spiritual arms": Rose, *Alexander Liberman*, p. 158.

Index

dread of being alone of, 266
drinking of, 420–21, 424
drug use of, 240–42, 367, 424, 436–39,
    440–42, 449, 454, 456
earliest memory of, 19
effect of Genna's death on, 450–51
elitism of, 14
as émigré icon, 421
encounters with Nazis of, 202–3
English as spoken by, 13–14, 452–53
evacuation to Tours of, 194–96
exhibitionism of, 58
family of, 16–26, 151–52
final decline in health of, 461–62
first marriage of, 35–36, 71, 73, 74,
    75–76, 146–51
flamboyance of, 12–13, 14
Francine's first evening gown selected by,
    366–68
Francine's idolization of, 162–63, 369,
    370
and Francine's writing success, 376–77,
    380
friendship with Marlene of, 361–62
friends' reminiscences of, 464–66
funeral of, 463–64
generosity of, 58
Genna's audio tapes of, 454
gravesite of, 497–98
grooming rituals of, 162–63, 339–40,
    454–55, 461
growing fame in fashion circles of, 375, 381
guilt over Bertrand's death of, 219
as hat designer, 46, 153, 154, 156,
    163–64, 186, 189, 252, 296–301
homesickness of, 47
hospitality and entertaining style of, 266,
    268, 321, 330, 332, 335
immigration to U.S. of, 221–26, 226
inability to share Bertrand's death with
    Francine of, 273–78
increased fussiness in old age of, 440
invalid self-image adopted by, 430
Jewish friends of, 159–60, 167
at La Croze, 177–80
letters to mother of, 59–60, 62, 63, 80,
    152–55, 157, 186
loyalty to friends of, 165–66
marital aspirations for Francine of, 377

Mayakovsky affair kept quiet by, 158, 218,
    421
Mayakovsky's relationship with, 54, 55–66,
    71–72, 80, 81, 151
and Mayakovsky's suicide, 80, 83, 147,
    148, 157
meetings with Kommandant Herbert of,
    203–4, 207–8
meeting with Alex of, 117–18, 139
memorizing poetry talent of, 21
as model, 44
myths about, 82–83
narcissism of, 12, 58, 338–39
need for control of, 14
opinion of Alex's paintings, 392
opposition to détente of, 385
Paris arrival of, 23–24, 25, 26, 31
personality of, 13, 58
physical description of, 352
preference for Russian culture in old age by,
    427
pregnancy of, 146, 148
professionalism of, 352
profession of, 12, 46
proposed biographies of, 432, 454
puritanism of, 55
reactions to Alex's illnesses of, 410
refuge from past sought by, 148, 149
restrictions imposed on, 44–45
reunion with father of, 234–37
revision of personal history by, 454
rumors of Alex's affairs and, 308
rumors of Bertrand's affairs and, 156–57,
    158
at Saks Fifth Avenue, 296–301, *300*, 375,
    381–82
seasickness of, 224–25
secretiveness of, 85
self-involvement in old age of, 456
snobbery of, 150
soirees held by, 266–70, 271–73, 371
spending habits of, 155–56
split with Mayakovsky of, 71–72
superstitions of, 46
timidity concerning money of, 382
travel disliked by, 352
truce with Lili of, 84
tuberculosis of, 21–22, 44
U.S. visa obtained by, 216, 221